Ninth Edition

CURRICULUM DEVELOPMENT

A GUIDE TO PRACTICE

Jon W. Wiles

Joseph C. Bondi

PEARSON

Boston   Columbus   Indianapolis   New York   San Francisco   Upper Saddle River
Amsterdam   Cape Town   Dubai   London   Madrid   Milan   Munich   Paris   Montreal   Toronto
Delhi   Mexico City   São Paulo   Sydney   Hong Kong   Seoul   Singapore   Taipei   Tokyo

Vice President and Editorial Director: Jeffery W. Johnston
Senior Acquisitions Editor: Meredith Fossel
Editorial Assistant: Janelle Criner
Vice President, Director of Marketing: Margaret Waples
Senior Marketing Manager: Darcy Betts Prybella
Production Project Manager: Jennifer Gessner
Procurement Specialist: Pat Tonneman
Senior Art Director: Jayne Conte
Cover Designer: Karen Noferi
Cover Photo: © Kokhanchikov, Fotolia
Media Project Manager: Noelle Chun
Full-Service Project Management: Niraj Bhatt/Aptara®, Inc.
Composition: Aptara®, Inc.
Printer/Binder: Courier/Westford
Cover Printer: Courier/Westford
Text Font: Palatino LT Std 10/12

Credits and acknowledgments for material borrowed from other sources and reproduced, with permission, in this textbook appear on the appropriate page within the text.

Every effort has been made to provide accurate and current Internet information in this book. However, the Internet and information posted on it are constantly changing, so it is inevitable that some of the Internet addresses listed in this textbook will change.

Library of Congress Cataloging-in-Publication Data

Wiles, Jon.
  Curriculum development/Jon W. Wiles, Joseph C. Bondi.—Ninth edition.
  pages cm
  ISBN-13: 978-0-13-357232-2
  ISBN 10: 0-13-357232-3
  1. Curriculum planning—United States.   2. Education—Curricula—United States.   I. Bondi, Joseph.
II. Title.
  LB2806.15.W55 2015
  375'.001—dc23

2013041302

10 9 8 7 6 5 4 3 2 1

ISBN 13: 978-0-13-357232-2
ISBN 10:   0-13-357232-3

This edition of Curriculum Development: A Guide to Practice *is dedicated to Dr. Joseph Bondi (1936–2013), who died after a brief illness. Our 40-year partnership as authors and consultants was ever stimulating, and he will be missed.*

I also dedicate this edition to his wife, Patsy Bondi, to his children Pam, Beth, and Brad, and to his grandchildren Jake, Emma, Evan, Rex, Brad, Rhea and Patton.

Finally, this edition is dedicated to my wife, Michele, our children Aimee, Michael, Cochran, and Amy, and to our grandchildren Casey, Paige, Max, Santiago, and Ava.

Jon Wiles

ABOUT THE AUTHOR

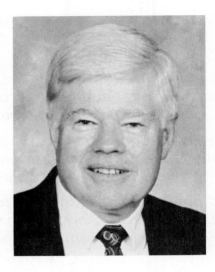

Dr. Jon Wiles is an educator who has served in many roles over a 40-year career: teacher, researcher, professor, administrator, author, and consultant. He hails from a family of educators and has worked as a consultant with schools and teachers in 44 states and 14 foreign nations. Jon Wiles is the author of over a dozen books, used worldwide, to train teachers, curriculum specialists, and school administrators.

Dr. Wiles received his doctoral degree from the University of Florida. Jon and his wife Michele, who is a superior teacher by any measure, reside in the historic city of St. Augustine on the northeast coast of Florida in the United States.

PREFACE

For over 40 years this text has served to guide education leaders in translating curriculum theory into practice. With each new edition, there are major changes in professional education, and these changes influence how the practice of curriculum development is conducted. In previous editions, topics such as diversity, standards, technology, and international influences have been featured. In this 9th edition, the Common Core State Standards and curriculum assessment are two dominant themes. Standards and assessment reflect our nation's effort to keep our schools relevant in a new age of a global economy.

NEW TO THIS EDITION

- In-depth analysis of the role of curriculum work in the new global era.
- Detailed treatment of the Common Core movement and its meaning.
- Greater exploration of curriculum assessment.
- Updates on the emerging role of technology in learning.
- Discussion of how the school curriculum is responding to immigrant populations.
- Reviews of changes in language, multicultural, and special education instruction.
- New programs and issues for the various levels of schooling.
- New bibliographies and resources in each chapter.

This edition of *Curriculum Development: A Guide to Practice* differs from previous editions in several significant ways. There is, in this edition, an attempt to help the reader understand school curriculum as a very critical function in both our formal education system and in the development of our nation. As we develop curriculum programs for students in our schools, we also program our country's readiness for the future. All nations, regardless of their stage of development, are busy modifying their school curriculum in order to adjust to a new and interdependent world economy. Those nations most effective in accurately anticipating the future, and designing school programs that will serve their students well in that future, will prosper. Those nations unable to re-design their curriculums for this new age will flounder or fail. Curriculum is that important!

The Common Core State Standards initiative in the United States is this nation's response to these world-wide-changes. This major activity in 46 states, and thousands of communities, represents the single most ambitious change in the history of American education. If successful, the curriculum derived from the Common Core Standards will prepare American students for both future work and further schooling. If the Common Core stalls, or does not meet the expectations of the participating states, the education being planned for our students may well be irrelevant and maybe even dysfunctional. Curriculum leaders, at all levels, will play an important role in the eventual outcome of this effort and these challenging steps.

The author hopes that this edition provides the reader with new knowledge about our society, the students who attend our schools, our new learning approaches, and the impact of new communication technologies on the delivery of the curriculum. Using this knowledge and these tools, our future curriculum workers can begin to prepare to assume the responsibility of curriculum leadership.

ACKNOWLEDGMENTS

I wish to thank the following reviewers of the Ninth Edition: Dennis Attick, Clayton State University; Maliika Chambers, California State University, East Bay; Kristal Curry, Coastal Carolina University; Paul Hanna, Columbia College; and Angela Wells, Calumet College of Saint Joseph.

Jon Wiles

BRIEF CONTENTS

Resources

CONTENTS

The philosophy of the school room in one generation will be the philosophy of government in the next.

—Abraham Lincoln

1

Curriculum Development in a Global Age

Learning Outcome

■ To gain a social and historical perspective of the curriculum development role.

C urriculum is a century-old area of professional study within the field of education. For those persons not in professional education, the term *curriculum* is usually associated with a physical document such as a textbook, syllabus, teacher's
guide, or learning package. For professional educators, however, the word is usually
more broadly defined. The term may refer to a set of plans, intentions, activities, or outcomes that are delivered in a variety of ways and in different settings. Above all else,
curriculum leaders are always concerned with the value or purpose of the curriculum,
with the philosophy of the effort. A clarification of the purpose of a curriculum is prerequisite to every sound curriculum development effort. The element of choice is found
in every curriculum decision, anywhere in the world, and these choices reflect both
national and local priorities and values.

Most curriculum work in school settings is mechanical, concerning itself with
updating and renewal of existing material. For instance, throughout much of the 20th
century, curriculum work addressed the formatting of subject matter and the method-
ologies of delivering that content.

Through a sort of layering process, new knowledge was added to old knowledge,
and new programs were appended to older programs. Many methods and media have
come and gone during that period. Such an orderly and predictable process depended
on a general agreement about the purpose of education. In the 21st century, such an
agreement is no longer fully present. Throughout the world, education is being redefined by many forces, but especially by globalization, interdependence, and the new
technologies that can deliver learning directly to the individual.

At the beginning of the 20th century, the general conception of education was
uniformly a process of becoming knowledgeable. Less than two decades into that century, however, there were conflicting views of what constituted a formal education and
what role schools might play in the process. There were also early differences of opinion about how the act of learning occurred. The field of curriculum was born in the

United States with Franklin Bobbitt's small book simply entitled *Curriculum* (1918), and the field quickly became an area of professional study that assessed and sorted out educational choices and procedures. As the options for defining what might constitute an education multiplied, the field of curriculum EXPANDED to address the development of entire educational programs, their processes, and their meaning to societies.

Curriculum development is a process whereby the choices of designing a learning experience for clients (students) are made and then activated through a series of coordinated activities. For a curriculum specialist, development is a logical process that begins with a clear set of goals and proceeds in an if-then manner until finished. In other words, the process of curriculum development is deductive in nature, resulting in finer and finer actions to accomplish the intended purpose of that curriculum. The development process usually begins with a set of questions that initially reveals value preferences and later supports planning efforts, program development, and evaluation. When these value preferences are formalized, we refer to them as *philosophies* or *learning theories.* These preliminary statements can establish boundaries of concern, screen subobjectives, and assist in assessing the efficacy of the programs when they are developed. Through a process of deduction, broad statements become goals, objectives, standards, learning outcomes, and eventually classroom-level lesson plans.

A useful way to think about curriculum and the development process is to use the model of architecture. An architect cannot design a home until some information is provided about style preferences. This style is analogous to a philosophy in education. Once the architect knows the style, be it ranch, colonial, or modern, he or she can then proceed to the more detailed functions (rooms, layout, decor, and so forth). Without clarification, the possibilities for error in design are great. Likewise, the curriculum developer cannot easily develop a program of study without knowing why the program exists. The historical practice of layering on new curricula on top of existing or old curricula has resulted in conceptual confusion in many educational institutions. The absence of such preliminary clarification also explains why so much change in education is not lasting.

The field of curriculum, then, is a subset of professional education that asks questions, provides information, and steers the process of design and development. Curriculum is also the foundation for any subsequent evaluation. Over the years, five uncomplicated elements have become accepted as a regular part of the structure of curriculum work:

1. *Seeing curriculum development as a cycle or a system*   Ralph Tyler, a powerful U.S. curriculum leader in the first half of the 20th century, is credited with framing questions that led to a cyclical model of development that begins with an analysis, proceeds to a design stage, undergoes implementation, and then is evaluated for effectiveness. This evaluation leads to new analysis. In more recent times, this logical progression has been presented as a self-refining system.
2. *Regular foundational areas of concern*   Curriculum workers generally look to four key areas in developing programs, known as the bases or foundations of curriculum. These foundational areas are social forces (the society), knowledge, human development, and learning. Each of these will be addressed in some detail in this chapter. To these four traditional areas of concern, the author nominates a fifth area—technology—for reasons to be discussed.

3. *Use of data in decision making*   Research has become a major part of curriculum work. Curriculum developers have increasingly relied on needs assessments and evaluative data in planning programs. This emphasis reflects the growing awareness that any curriculum should produce some kind of measurable result. Curriculum assessment is vital.
4. *Involving others in the planning process*   In the latter half of the 20th century, curriculum leaders relied on change theory to guide the implementation of new programs. Such theory suggested that involving those affected by curriculum change in the planning process increased the odds of successful development.
5. *Assessing results*   Particularly in the 21st century, educators have incorporated assessment into the planning process to ensure a degree of standardization in outcomes.

DEFINING CURRICULUM

We can understand a lot about what curriculum is, and what it is not, by its semantics. People in the field of curriculum spend a lot of energy arguing about the definition of this term. The word *curriculum* has been in existence since about 1820, and it comes from the Latin word *currere*, which means "to run" or "to run the course." With time, the traditional definition of school curriculum came to mean traversing the course of study.

While most noneducators think of curriculum and curriculum development in terms of this traditional definition, equating the word *curriculum* with a course of study or a text to be completed, most curriculum leaders have a more expansive definition. There are, however, some highly traditional educators who continue to define curriculum this way even today. To do so requires a very narrow definition of education:

> The curriculum should consist of permanent studies—the rules of grammar, reading, rhetoric and logic, and mathematics (for the elementary and secondary school), and the greatest books of the western world (beginning at the secondary level of schooling). (Hutchins, 1936, p. 82)
>
> The curriculum must consist essentially of disciplined study in five great areas: (1) command of mother tongue and the systematic study of grammar, literature, and writing, (2) mathematics, (3) sciences, (4) history, (5) foreign languages. (Bestor, 1956, pp. 48–49)
>
> The curriculum should consist entirely of knowledge that comes from the disciplines. Education should be conceived as a guided recapitulation of the process of inquiry that gave rise to the fruitful bodies of organized knowledge comprising the established disciplines. (Phenix, 1962, p. 64)
>
> The curriculum is such permanent subjects as grammar, reading, logic, rhetoric, mathematics, and the greatest books of the western world that embody essential knowledge. (Marsh & Willis, 1995, p. 13)
>
> The curriculum is a systematic group of courses or sequence of subjects required for graduation or certification in a major field of study. (Oliva, 2012, p. 18)

The definition of "curriculum" as a product, or as a completely contained experience, has proved highly unsatisfactory to most educators involved in the development of learning programs. Very early in the 20th century, for example, the enormous growth in accessible knowledge meant that "knowing" could no longer be contained in books or in document form only. With the dissemination of knowledge through new technical media such as the radio, identifying what constituted essential knowledge became more difficult.

In addition, the composition of the school population in the United States changed considerably in this same period. The population of the secondary school in the United States grew from only 200,000 students in the 1890s to nearly 5 million students by 1924. Schooling was no longer the preserve of a small elite who would attend college; it was now a universal experience. In some cases, acquiring citizenship skills and language took precedence over acquiring classical knowledge, and new courses (social studies, language arts, vocational education, physical education) had to be devised for learners.

As new courses were added to the curriculum and the differences among individual learners became more obvious to teachers and administrators, the definition of the curriculum began to stretch. Specialists in the field began to differentiate among various kinds of curricula: planned and unplanned (the hidden curriculum), technical learning, and practical learning. Bobbitt (1924), for example, observed:

> The curriculum may be defined in two ways: (1) it is the range of experiences, both indirect and direct, concerned in unfolding the abilities of the individual, or (2) it is a series of consciously directed training experiences that the schools use for completing and perfecting the individual. (p. 10)

Expanding on this theme, Hollis Caswell and Doak Campbell (1935) wrote of the socializing function of the schooling experience. The curriculum, they said, "is composed of all of the experiences children have under the guidance of the school" (p. 66). Other writers continued this theme of seeing curriculum as an experience (process) rather than as a product, for example:

> A sequence of potential experiences is developed by the school for the purpose of disciplining children and youth in-group ways of thinking and acting. This set of experiences is referred to as the curriculum. (Smith, Stanley, & Shores, 1957, p. 3)
>
> The curriculum is now generally considered to be all of the experiences that learners have under the auspices of the school. (R. Doll, 1970, p. 9)
>
> Curriculum is all of the experiences that individual learners have in a program of education whose purpose is to achieve broad goals and related specific objectives, which is planned in terms of a framework of theory and research or past or present professional practices. (Tyler, 1957, p. 79)

By the mid-1950s, it had become increasingly evident that schools had a tremendous influence on students' lives. Some of those influences were structured; others were due to the congregation of youth. It was recognized that students also had experiences at school (the hidden curriculum) not planned by the school. During this period, definitions of curriculum were dominated by those aspects of the curriculum that were planned, rather than simply the content or general experiences of students:

> The curriculum is all of the learning of students, which is planned by and directed by the school to attain its educational goals. (Taba, 1962, p. 11)

> A curriculum is a plan for learning. (Saylor & Alexander, 1974, p. 6)
>
> We define curriculum as a plan for providing sets of learning opportunities to achieve broad goals and related specific objectives for an identifiable population served by a single school center. (Johnson, 1970/1971, p. 25)
>
> A curriculum [is] usually thought of as a course of study or plan for what is to be taught in an educational institution. (McNeil, 2008, p. 12)

For nearly 50 years there has been concern about the performance of educational programs. This focus, often referred to as *accountability, outcome-based education,* or *standards-based learning,* has pushed the definition of the curriculum toward an emphasis on ends or results:

> Curriculum is concerned not with what students will do in the learning situation, but with what they will learn as a consequence of what they do. Curriculum is concerned with results. (D. Tanner & L. Tanner, 1995, p. 67)
>
> [Curriculum is] the planned and guided learning experiences and intended outcomes, formulated through systematic reconstruction of knowledge and experience, under the auspices of the school, for the learners' continuous and willful growth in personal-social competence. (D. Tanner & L. Tanner, 1995, preface)

In the mid-1990s, the concept of an evolving and unplanned set of experiences for children emerged under the label *postmodern*:

> A new sense of educational order will emerge, as well as new relations between teachers and students, culminating in a new concept of curriculum. The linear, sequential, easily quantifiable ordering system dominating education today could give way to a more complex, pluralistic, unpredictable system or network. Such a complex network will, like life itself, always be in transition, in process. (W. Doll, 1993, p. 3)
>
> In closed societies, the elite's values are superimposed on the people. Education, as a practice of freedom, rejects the notion that knowledge is extended or transferred to students as if they were objects. (Freire, 1973, p. 96)
>
> As we move into the 21st Century, we find ourselves no longer constrained by modernist images of purpose and history. Elements of discontinuity, rapture, and difference (chaos) provide alternative sets of referents by which to understand modernity as well as to challenge and modify it. The term *post-modern* is a rejection of grand narratives and any form of totalizing thought. It embraces diversity and locality. It creates a world where individuals must make their way, where knowledge is consistently changing, and where meaning is no longer anchored in history. (Aronowitz & Giroux, 1991, p. ii)

Your author sees the curriculum as a *desired goal or set of values that can be activated through a development process, culminating in experiences for learners.* The degree to which those experiences represent the envisioned goal or goals is a direct function of the effectiveness of the curriculum development efforts. The purpose of any such design is, necessarily, the prerogative of the group engaged in such development.

The importance of these various definitions of the term *curriculum* is that they structure the boundaries of responsibility used by school planners. Narrow definitions, such as subject-matter mastery, are quite different from broad definitions, such as all of the experiences at school, and would project very different schooling designs.

Although the definition of curriculum has changed in response to social forces and expectations for the school, the *process* of curriculum development has remained fairly constant over time. Through analysis, design, implementation, and evaluation, curriculum developers set goals, plan experiences, select content, and assess outcomes of school programs. These constant processes have contributed to the emergence of a predictable structure in curriculum planning.

STRUCTURE AND PRINCIPLES IN CURRICULUM DEVELOPMENT

Although definitions of curriculum and visions for the purpose of education were expansive during the entire 20th century, the structure of curriculum development remained primarily a filling-in activity. Major principles in the field of curriculum evolved more from practice than from any logic or enlightenment. As a result, the theory of curriculum has remained narrow and has followed practices found in all school environments. There are few global principles to guide leaders. As Daniel Tanner and Laurel Tanner (1995) noted:

> In the absence of a holistic conception of curriculum, the focus is on piecemeal and mechanical functions. The main thrust in curriculum development and reform over the years has been directed at microcurricular problems to the neglect of macrocurricular problems. (p. 68)

Principles of curriculum have evolved as core procedures (rather than as theoretical guidelines) as a result of the absence of systematic thinking about curriculum planning; the vulnerability of curriculum planning to social, political, technical, and economic forces; and the constantly changing priorities of education in the United States and abroad. Thus, identification of curricular principles is difficult. Hilda Taba (1962) described the almost unmanageable condition of curriculum approaches in this way:

> Decisions leading to change in curriculum organization have been made largely by pressure, by hunches, or in terms of expediency instead of being based on clear-cut theoretical considerations or tested knowledge. The scope of curriculum has been extended vastly without an adequate consideration of the consequence of this extension on sequence or cumulative learning. . . . The fact that these perplexities underlying curriculum change have not been studied adequately may account for the proliferation of approaches to curriculum making. (p. 9)

Prior to the major curriculum reforms in the late 1950s and early 1960s, most curriculum development in school settings was oriented toward producing content packages. In developing courses of study, curriculum specialists sought to refine school programs by redesigning essential topic areas and updating older programs on a scheduled basis. This rather static role for curriculum practitioners in the field resulted in the evolution of both theoretical constructs for developing curriculum and operational procedures that have changed little over time.

An early observation by John Dewey (1902) that "the fundamental factors in the educational process are (1) the learner, (2) the society, and (3) organized subject matter" (p. 4) set the stage for defining curriculum parameters. These themes were echoed by Dewey's former student, Harold Rugg, who wrote: "There are, indeed, three critical factors in the educational process: the child, contemporary American society, and standing between them, the school" (Rugg, 1926). Another student of Dewey's, Boyd Bode, renewed this theme of three parts in 1931 when he observed: "The difference in curriculum stems from three points of view: (1) the standpoint of the subject matter specialists, (2) the standpoint of the practical man, and (3) the interests of the learner" (pp. 543–544).

By 1945, these three general concerns were finding acceptance in most curriculum literature. Taba, for instance, discussed the three sources of data in curriculum planning as (1) the study of society, (2) studies of learners, and (3) studies of subject matter content (p. 58). By the early 1960s, Taba had further refined the study of society to mean "cultural demands—a reflection of the changing social milieu of the school" (1962). Gaining acceptance as a fourth important planning base for curriculum in the mid-1950s and early 1960s was the study of *learning* itself. Studies from various schools of psychology and the advent of sophisticated technology in school settings raised new possibilities and choices for educators who were planning programs. These four major areas of concern for curriculum planners, known as the foundations, or bases, of planning, remain the subject of most analysis, design, implementation, and evaluation in school programs today. These vital areas of concern are addressed later in this chapter.

The importance of these planning bases as organizers for thinking about the development of educational programs is best summarized by Taba (1962), a curriculum specialist concerned with the development aspects of curriculum:

> Semantics aside, these variations in the conception of the function of education are not idle or theoretical arguments. They have definite concrete implications for the shape of educational programs, especially the curriculum. . . . If one believes that the chief function of education is to transmit the perennial truths, one cannot but strive toward a uniform curriculum and teaching. Efforts to develop thinking take a different shape depending on whether the major function of education is seen as fostering creative thinking and problem solving or as following the rational forms of thinking established in our classical tradition. As such, differences in these concepts naturally determine what are considered the "essentials" and what are the "dispensable frills" in education. (p. 30)

Paralleling this conceptual mapping of curriculum concerns was the evolution of some early operational procedures. Early curriculum development focused on *subject content* that was mechanical and that contained rather simple operational techniques developed in the 1920s. These procedures continued as the dominant operational concern until the early 1960s. Writing in the 1926 yearbook of the National Society for the Study of Education, Harold Rugg outlined the operational tasks of curriculum development as a three-step process: (1) determine the fundamental objectives, (2) select activities and other materials of instruction, and (3) discover the most effective organization and placement of this instruction (p. 22).

By 1950, the technique of "inventory, organize, and present" had reached refinement in Ralph Tyler's widely read four-step analysis:

1. What educational purposes shall the school seek to attain?
2. What educational experiences can be provided that are likely to attain those purposes?
3. How can these educational experiences be effectively organized?
4. How can we determine whether these purposes are being attained? (p. 7)

By addressing the assessment of curriculum development, Tyler introduced the concept of the curriculum development cycle whereby evaluation led to a reconsideration of purpose. Such a cycle in schools illuminated the comprehensiveness of the planning activity and later gave birth to refinements such as systems analysis and taxonomies of learning. Tyler's four-step model also rekindled a 50-year-old effort to develop manageable behavioral objectives in education (Mager, 1972; Covey, 1989; Wiggins & McTighe, 2005). The ordering of the development procedure also encouraged a more mechanistic approach to curriculum development. Such approaches, long practiced in schools, are thoroughly represented in curriculum literature through various and common definitions:

> Curriculum development . . . is basically a plan of structuring the environment to coordinate in an orderly manner the elements of time, space, materials, equipment and personnel. (Feyereisen, Fiorino, & Nowak, 1970, p. 204)
>
> The function of curriculum development is to research, design, and engineer the working relationships of the curricular elements that will be employed during the instructional phase in order to achieve desired outcomes. (Hauenstein, 1975, p. 6)

One of the most highly refined versions of Tyler's procedure for developing school curriculum was outlined in 1962 by his former student Hilda Taba. Seven major steps of curriculum development were identified:

1. Diagnosis of needs
2. Formulation of objectives
3. Selection of content
4. Organization of content
5. Selection of learning experiences
6. Organization of learning experiences
7. Determination of what to evaluate and means of doing it (p. 12)

Within each step, Taba provided substeps that identified criteria for action. For example, in the selection of learning experiences, it is important that the curriculum developer consider the following:

1. Validity and significance of content
2. Consistency with social reality
3. Balance of breadth and depth of experiences

4. Provision for a wide range of objectives
5. Learnability–adaptability of the experience to the life of the student
6. Appropriateness to needs and interests of learners

More modern lists of these steps differ from Taba's because they present curriculum as a more comprehensive process, which may or may not be tied to only a content product. In the following example, for instance, Feyereisen et al. (1970) present curriculum development as a problem-solving action chain:

1. Identification of the problem
2. Diagnosis of the problem
3. Search for alternative solutions
4. Selection of the best solution
5. Ratification of the solution by the organization
6. Authorization of the solution
7. Use of the solution on a trial basis
8. Preparation for adoption of the solution
9. Adoption of the solution
10. Direction and guidance of staff
11. Evaluation of effectiveness (p. 61)

The broader focus of the Feyereisen description reflects a growing interest in curriculum development with planning for change in school environments from a macro-perspective. Curriculum development is increasingly a process with systemic concerns.

Other examples of the basic structure of the curriculum cycle could be provided at this point, but it should be clear to the reader that a regular planning and review process developed and was widely practiced in U.S. schools between 1920 and 1960. This process reflected the historical dominance of subject matter content as the focus of curriculum and any subsequent renewal:

> Certainly, a review of the plans made and implemented today and yesterday leaves no doubt that the dominant assumption of past curriculum planning has been the goal of subject matter mastery through a subject curriculum, almost inextricably tied to a closed school and graded school ladder, to a marking system that rewards successful achievement of fixed content and penalizes unsuccessful achievement, to an instructional organization based on fixed classes in the subjects and a timetable for them. (Alexander, 1974, p. 10)

Progress in the so-called substantive dimension of curriculum development continues today. Since the early 1980s, curriculum specialists have employed systems thinking in school planning and in developing standardized learning materials. Such comprehensive planning efforts have allowed curriculum leaders to engineer program improvement in new and efficient ways. Curricula for specific skill development, such as reading and math, have been much improved under approaches such as Common Core, a national curriculum development effort. The process of curriculum development, from the inception of an idea to the final assessment of the reconstruction effort, has become a highly skilled and detailed area of curriculum leadership in the 21st century.

In sharp contrast, the visionary or theoretical dimension of curriculum work has progressed little in the past century. Despite an increased knowledge base, growing understanding of human development, sophistication in the use of technology, and an emerging focus on teaching and learning, curriculum models remain primitive and highly unimaginative. If Rip Van Winkle were to wake up after a long sleep, he would at least recognize schools anywhere in the world. Theoretical dimensions of curriculum development remain suppressed by a dependence on economic sponsorship, political conservatism, and the failure of educators to gain consensus for any significant change in the schooling process. There are signs, however, that many groups wish to challenge school leaders on the subject of purpose.

The introduction of the new interactive technologies in schools, using the Internet and other wireless technologies, are making much of the existing condition irrelevant. Curriculum developers will be hard pressed to even catalog, let alone control, select, and order, all of the new information available to learners. Real-time delivery, any-where delivery, and nonlinear delivery of information to the learner via the Internet does not fit easily into the historical curriculum construct of knowledge mastery. New paradigms and new models will be needed if the process of curriculum development in schools is to survive the rush of the technological age.

HISTORY AND CURRICULUM: THREE ERAS

A sense of history is very important for anyone working in curriculum. Without an understanding of history, many contemporary curriculum practices would seem odd or even illogical. A historical perspective also helps curriculum leaders focus on the long-term goals of education rather than on the events and programs of the moment. In the United States, for example, the development of education can be viewed in terms of three distinct eras: the evolutionary era, the modern era, and the postmodern era. The first era describes U.S. education as it evolved into a unique form. The second era reflects a more scientific period of the 20th century, fitting education to the populace. The third era, beginning in the last years of the 20th century and continuing today, concerns learning in a new information age.

The Evolutionary Era

This history begins only 27 years after the landing of the first English-speaking pilgrims at Plymouth Rock, when they established a regulatory act to govern their first "grammar" school (1635). Early European settlers came to America to escape religious persecution, and they pursued their personal religious beliefs with vigor. Martin Luther had taught that the Bible must be read to ward off the work of the Devil, and so the first known education regulation, the Old Deluder Satan Act (1647), established schools for that purpose.

A second purpose for education in America, established quite early, was to develop a "literate citizen" capable of participating in acts of governance for the common good. Benjamin Franklin, for instance, spoke often of the "rise of the common man" and the need for strong citizen participation. The concept of a "participatory democracy" rationalized many early schools in America.

Finally, a third idea about schools in the colonies was that they were useful for promoting the common good and for bringing about desired changes in society.

Following the War of 1812, for instance, schools were expected to teach about national identity and emerging beliefs.

As settlement spread in the colonial areas and beyond, establishment of schools went hand-in-hand with the development of communities. Usually, such schools were of minimal duration (several years at most), were taught in a one-room schoolhouse erected by the community, and focused on basic literacy skills. Quite early, these "American" schools took on characteristics that were unlike European schools of that era.

Horace Mann (1796–1859), forever linked to early education efforts in this nation, is often called the father of the American public school. Mann, a legislator and U.S. congressional representative from Massachusetts, was instrumental in passing early laws governing education in his home state. He helped establish the first teacher-training institution in 1839 and later served as the first commissioner of education in Massachusetts. He advocated schooling that was universal, free, and nonsectarian. After a visit to Prussia in 1843, Mann returned to the United States to establish a "graded school ladder" concept and helped gain support for the first tax-supported elementary schools in 1850.

As early as 1779, Thomas Jefferson was advocating free schools for the children of colonists. This proposal was in stark contrast to the prevailing European practice in which "dual tracks" of free and private education were maintained. A Free Public School Society was formed around 1800 in New York City and educated more than 600,000 pupils in its 50-year history. Indicative of the early social functions of education in the United States was the provision of the Northwest Ordinance (1787), which mandated that all townships in new states set aside land for schools as a precondition for becoming recognized communities.

Paralleling the establishment of this popular education system in the elementary grades was an unrelated system of higher education dating from the establishment of Harvard College in 1636. The higher education system, unlike the public elementary system, was private and exclusive, and was focused solely on producing learned men and leaders for the emerging nation. It is very important to understand the distinction between the two systems because even in the 21st century, various philosophies compete to define education in our society. The roots of these differences were present from the beginning of our nation.

Private education in the early colonies produced judges, legislators, governors, and persons in other leadership roles. On finishing the elementary years, these students would secure a tutor or attend an academy to prepare for college. This private bridge to leadership roles in American society existed for most of the 18th and 19th centuries. Eventually, laws to support secondary schools with taxes (1821) and the establishment of public land-grant colleges and universities (1862) began to break this private schooling domination. Public taxation for secondary schools became universal in the United States following the historic *Kalamazoo* case, an 1872 Michigan Supreme Court case.

Thus, after two centuries, a solid educational system consisting of both public and private elements had been established in the United States and was being supported by citizens. With the exception of the turmoil surrounding the Civil War, the development of schools was an ever-expanding process leading to the establishment of this nation's largest and strongest institution. The purpose of the American school was clearly the promotion of literacy and knowledge acquisition, but with signs of some social utility mixed in.

The final stage for completing the universal school ladder in the United States came during the 1890s, when a number of national committees met to organize and

```
Free to Attend
Tax-Supported Through Secondary Level
Separation of Church and State
Purposes: Literacy, Knowledge Acquisition, Citizenship
A State's Right
```

FIGURE 1.1   The Uniqueness of the United States Education System, 1900.

coordinate both the subjects taught and the levels of schooling. By far, the best known of these committees was the prestigious Committee of Ten, headed by President Charles Eliot of Harvard University. Working in 1892 and 1893, this committee sought to coordinate the secondary education programs of the states by establishing college entrance requirements. The committee recommended a standard set of high school courses, and a parallel committee established a "unit" measure for each course taken. Thereafter, students were awarded unit credits (Carnegie units) for each course, with a set number required for graduation and college entrance.

Thus, by the end of the 19th century, students could attend tax-supported free public schools for up to 12 years and study a highly standardized curriculum at the secondary level despite the fact that education is uniquely decentralized in America and a "state right" according to the U.S. Constitution (a residual right by omission). As the 20th century began, a traditional and standard form of education was in place (see Figure 1.1).

The Modern Era

In the late 18th and early 19th centuries, new ideas about children and learning were emerging in Europe. The traditional wisdom of that era viewed children as incomplete adults who needed to be shaped into preferred forms. Several European educators challenged those traditional views and became early advocates for working with the young in different ways.

Jean-Jacques Rousseau (1712–1778) was one of the earliest writers to see children as unfolding and malleable. Writing in his book *Émile* (1762), Rousseau argued that children were innately good (not evil) and called for a controlled environment in which positive growth could occur naturally. Rousseau believed that learning was most successful when education began with the student's interests.

Another early child advocate was Johann Pestalozzi (1746–1827), who advocated a learning-by-doing approach to education. In his book *Leonard and Gertrude* (1781), Pestalozzi described the behavior of children at his school in Yverdon, Switzerland, an early laboratory school. This educator is known for addressing the growth of the whole child in learning: the head, the heart, and the hands.

A third widely read European of this era, Friedrich Froebel (1782–1852), has been credited with establishing the early kindergarten (*Kleinkinderschaftig*) and having an important impact on later American education. Froebel, who had studied with Pestalozzi, spoke of the natural development in children and developed readiness materials to help each child move along in his or her early growth.

Finally, the German educator Johann Herbart (1776–1841) influenced the thoughts of U.S. educators, but with a different philosophical orientation. Unlike Rousseau,

Pestalozzi, and Froebel, Herbart believed that schools should be highly structured and should prepare future citizens of the sociopolitical community by shaping their minds. He felt that teachers could "build" the minds of children from the outside using subject matter as building blocks and delivering information through systematic lesson plans. Education for Herbart was a social mission rather than a matter of individual growth in pupils, and his methodology stressed concentration and mental immersion to accomplish the mission.

The effect of these European ideas was to suggest that education might be more than recitation and the "pounding in" of predetermined subject matter. Instead of focusing on what the teacher taught, each of these Europeans looked at the child and the methodology as critical. In doing so, they introduced the concept of choice in educational decision making and launched some of the earliest debates about the what, who, and how of planning for learning.

Also affecting the first curriculum debates in this nation was the work of Charles Darwin (1809–1882) and his theory of natural evolution in living things. As the official naturalist on the ship *Beagle* during its scientific expedition (1831–1836), Darwin documented that different surroundings tend to produce different outcomes in the growth of plants and animals (*On the Origin of Species*, 1859). Although educators did not directly apply Darwin's theory to education, his ideas were certainly in the minds of many educators who first began to explore the possibility that environment influenced learning.

At a centennial celebration in Philadelphia in 1876, many of the ideas just mentioned were showcased for American educators and soon took root in their writings. From that time on, more than one conception of education existed in the United States, and modern educational theory competed with traditional beliefs about education. During this period of early diversity, knowledge became the focus of traditional educators. Francis Parker, for example, began a unification process in 1883 to define subject areas. An early survey of teaching practices by Joseph Mayer Rice (1892) found the public school curriculum to be "meandering" and disorganized. In that same year, Eliot's Committee of Ten began advocating five common content areas (his "windows on the soul") to serve as college entrance prerequisites for all students, regardless of their home state. These notions of a general education quickly shaped all public school thinking and were based on a "like students and single purpose" rationale. Traditionalists saw all children progressing through a fixed, sequential curriculum with progress marked by a ladder of grade levels.

In sharp contrast to these traditionalists, new or progressive educators at the turn of the century were building on the European ideas of the late 19th century. These educators saw each child as unique and sought to broaden the purpose of education to include both social and personal development. John Dewey (1859–1952) is usually credited with bridging this gap from an older and more traditional definition of education to the newer and distinctly American definition of *progressive education*. Dewey built on those earlier European thoughts to advocate a new and very active definition of education for children. Seeing the mind as something to be developed (not filled or shaped), Dewey suggested taking old principles of learning and demonstrating practical applications as defined by the experiences of the learner. The goal of education, according to Dewey, was to both organize and activate knowledge. But, said Dewey, the learner rather than the teacher is the source of such organization. Each individual, he proposed, must find ideas that work in practical experience and see these ideas as truth.

Dewey gained credibility as a writer and theorist as he applied his theories at the University of Chicago Laboratory School (1896–1904). Here, children learned by doing through something called project work. Dewey later advocated the need for citizens in a democracy to find the truths of participation during the school years by living in a democratic institution. His book *Democracy and Education* (1916) is a classic statement of this belief.

Dewey's influence around the beginning of the 20th century is hard to overstate. Many of his students at the University of Chicago, such as Harold Rugg (*The Child-Centered School,* 1928) and George Counts (*Dare the School Create a New Social Order,* 1932), became major advocates of progressive ideas. The formation of the Progressive Education Association (PEA) in 1919 led to many publications and applications of Dewey's theory.

If a single year could be selected for a time when the true differences in approaches to education in the United States became evident, it would probably be 1918. In that year, a new perspective of secondary education, the Seven Cardinal Principles of Secondary Education, was proposed by the Commission on the Reorganization of Secondary Education. The first text on curriculum was written and published (Bobbitt, *The Curriculum,* 1918). Dramatically, the American way of educating was unfolding, and the field of curriculum was emerging as a subspecialty of professional education.

Curriculum emerged as a specialized area of study from the growing need to study, order, arrange, and otherwise rationalize the changing forms of American education. Gathering the many visions, clarifying the intentions, organizing schooling structures, implementing programs, and assessing the success of curricula in meeting goals required a new subspecialty in education. Decisions about whether the school should teach a body of knowledge, help develop the individual student, or promote social programs and priorities could not be effectively made in a decentralized education system. In reality, United States education programs simply evolved during these formative years. The new pattern of schooling that emerged from a traditional model of scholarship was superimposed on a coarse and dynamic culture.

The Commission on the Reorganization of Secondary Education was formed in 1913 and met for 5 years to resolve some of the emerging issues. The committee debated the three conceptions (academic, personal, and social) and studied the many new philosophies and learning theories. In 1918, this committee produced the Seven Cardinal Principles of Secondary Education, which stands today as the definitive statement on the purpose of American education. These purposes (listed below) for United States educational planning are still referred to regularly by educational curriculum workers:

1. Health
2. Command of fundamental processes
3. Home membership
4. Vocation
5. Citizenship
6. Use of leisure time
7. Ethical character

As the 20th century began, American education was in transition from a classical system practiced for centuries throughout the world to a more expedient form of schooling that served broader purposes. Among the accomplishments of the new system by 1900 were the following:

- Schooling was a state responsibility rather than a church role.
- Public education was seen as a social need, not a charity.
- Education was a right of citizens, not a privilege.
- Taxes could be used to support education through secondary levels.
- Education was compulsory for all children in all states.
- Control of education was established at the state level.
- Subjects were a constant in educational planning for learning.
- Human development was perceived as evolutionary.
- Schools could be used to promote social unity.
- Education could be used for social regeneration.

Among the newer realities for curriculum theorists by the time of Bobbitt's first text was an awareness of humanistic thought, an emerging awareness of human development, and the beginning of mechanistic (behavioral) processes used to engineer curriculum development. These forces and others both broadened the horizons for early planners and presented them with a large number of choices in defining education.

The growth of the modern education system in the United States, from the beginning of the 20th century until the early 21st century, reflected all of these early trends. Schools grew in number, curricula diversified, and social forces such as wars, depressions, and the racial integration of the society modified the basic form of the American school. A timeline of many of these important events is shown in Figure 1.2.

The Postmodern Era

Schools during the modern era of education in the United States, like most educational agencies worldwide, operated under some unspoken assumptions that characterized the society. It was assumed, for example, that all Americans held the same values—those of white, Anglo-Saxon Protestants. It was accepted that schools were the place of learning and that only schools could "certify" an education. It was acknowledged that the purpose of becoming educated was "to know" and that the process of education required a knowledgeable teacher to be successful. In sporadic fashion, all these assumptions undergirding a modern and traditional education system began to break down in the United States and throughout the world during the 40-year period from 1960 to 2000.

The signs of change in the United States appeared during the civil rights period in the late 1960s and early 1970s. The concept of *e pluribus unum* ("from many, one") was deemed inapplicable to some populations. Blacks, Hispanics, women, lesbians, gay males, handicapped persons, and other populations were forced to use law and demonstration to establish their place in U.S. society. This discovery of many publics (i.e., various groups advocating for their interests) and multiculturalism was accelerated during the protests following the Vietnam War era. The war in Indochina raised serious questions about race and ethnicity back home in the American society.

By the end of the 1980s, in many communities, schools became the battleground for the promotion of cultural values. In the 1990s, this competition for control of schools would lead a few curriculum theorists to a postmodern stance. The idea that schools were "the learning place" soon came under attack as their biases toward certain populations were

400 B.C.	Height of Greek influence when ideas of tutorial learning and elite leadership training were first formalized`
400 A.D.	Height of the Roman Empire that modeled a far more popular "citizenship model" education system
800	Beginning of Dark Ages, during which civilization declined and knowledge was preserved by individual scholarship and early monastic libraries
1200	Beginning of the Enlightenment, during which civilization reemerged; early universities founded in France, Italy, Spain, and England
1456	First books printed by printing presses—dispersion of knowledge to masses begins
1492	Columbus finds the Americas
1500	First Latin grammar schools in England
1536	First classical secondary school (Gymnasium) established in Germany
1620	Plymouth Colony, Massachusetts, established
1635	Boston Latin grammar schools founded
1636	Harvard University founded
1647	In Massachusetts the Old Deluder Satan Act compels establishment of schools when 50 households are present in a community
1650	First tax support for schools in Massachusetts
1751	Benjamin Franklin establishes the first academy (secondary school)
1779	Thomas Jefferson proposes a "free school" for Virginian men and women for up to 3 years
1787	Northwest Ordinance passed, which established provisions for territories to becomes states, including mandatory school sites in townships
1789	Constitution of the United States adopted
1805	New York Free School society established to educate 500,000 pupils without expense
1821	Boston English Classical School established; first tax-supported secondary school
1852	First compulsory school laws passed in Massachusetts by Horace Mann
1862	Morrill Land Grant Act establishes land for public universities in all states (engineering, military science, and agriculture)
1872	Michigan Supreme Court upholds tax support for secondary schools
1883	Francis Parker establishes the first subject matter groupings as an early form of curriculum
1892	First comprehensive study of American education by Joseph M. Rice
1892	Charles Eliot, president of Harvard University, forms the Committee of Ten
1896	John Dewey opens the University of Chicago Laboratory School to demonstrate alternative teaching methods
1904	First comprehensive physiological studies of school children in New York by G. Stanley Hall

FIGURE 1.2   Timeline of Events in the Growth of the Modern Education System.

Source: Wiles, Jon. *Curriculum Essentials: A Resource for Educators.* Published by Allyn & Bacon, Boston, MA. Copyright © 1999 by Pearson Education. Adapted by permission of the publisher.

1905	First mental measurement scales on intelligence published by Alfred Binet
1909	First junior high school established
1918	Franklin Bobbitt publishes the first text on curriculum
1918	Commission on the Reorganization of Secondary Education publishes the Seven Cardinal Principles
1919	Progressive Education Association founded
1932	The Eight-Year Study begins (1932–1940)
1938	The Educational Policies Commission publishes its four-point objectives for education—The Purposes of Education in American Democracy
1946	Congress passes the G.I. Bill to further the education of veterans
1954	U.S. Supreme Court rules in *Brown v. Topeka* that public schools must racially integrate previously "separate but equal" schools
1957	Russia launches *Sputnik* satellite, beginning both a space and an education race
1958	U.S. Congress passes the National Defense Education Act (NDEA), initiating serious federal funding of public education
1964	Congress passes the Civil Rights Act
1965	The Elementary and Secondary Education Act (ESEA) passes, bringing "titled" programs to public schools
1972	Title IX amendment to the ESEA outlaws discrimination on the basis of sex
1975	Public Law 94-142 provides federally guaranteed rights for all children with handicaps in public schools
1979	U.S. Department of Education established
1985	Personal computers become commercially available in United States
1995	Internet made public May 1995
2001	No Child Left Behind
2010	Race to the Top
2011	Common Core State Standards

FIGURE 1.2 (*Continued*)

revealed. In particular, Ivan Illich's 1971 book *Deschooling Society* and the book by Bowles and Gintis, *Schooling in Capitalist America,* portrayed American schools as simple extensions of an economic system needing to control and select its agents. Popular books by Jonathan Kohl, Jack Heardon, and others painted less than flattering portraits of the American schoolroom. Charles Silberman's *Crisis in the Classroom* gave the condition a name.

Coupled with this unveiling of the "real school" was an accountability movement born out of sheer financial need. As the inflation of the 1970s and 1980s ate into school budgets, the cry for outcome-based education and results eroded general support for schools. Alternative forms of school were invented and even legislated.

Finally, the notion that a knowledgeable teacher was required for the schooling process to be successful fell away with the advent of the personal computer; a drill master far superior to an individual classroom teacher when it comes to mastery instruction. The richness and variety of the Internet completely discounted student dependence on a teacher or any other single source of learning for information.

And so, as the 20th century drew to a close, the purpose and rationale of education, and even the method of becoming educated, was in disarray. Postmodern theorists urged the oppressed and enlightened to throw off the shackles of the public school and create their own curriculum with personal relevance based on their own values. Aronowitz and Giroux, in their text *Postmodern Education*, advised that "curriculum's historic function was to name and privilege particular histories and experiences. In its current and dominant form, the curriculum does so in such a way as to marginalize or silence the voices of subordinate groups" (p. 13).

In the first 15 years of the 21st century the options for learning have continued to expand. The new interactive technologies provide personal avenues to learning for everyone; learning that is distinctively nonlinear and interactive. Schooling choices for students in the form of charter schools are expanding and found in most school districts. Control issues continue to chip away at any uniform school design. With these conditions pressing schools, American education continues to move forward.

GLOBAL REFLECTIONS

The way in which the field of curriculum has developed in the United States, outlined in this chapter, is not unique. Throughout the world, other nations have struggled with similar problems relating to rapid changes in their societies and in their definition of education and schooling. In South Africa, for example, a century-old practice of apartheid ended suddenly, and educational leaders were forced to redesign a public education for all students in that country. Many of the young black students (ages 6 to 12) had never been to school at all when the change occurred in February 1990. The new socialization roles called for in these schools, to overcome the enormous gulf between the races and socioeconomic stations, were monumental. Your author was privileged to participate in planning sessions in the early 1990s to re-create education in that nation and saw firsthand the miracle of such nation building through school planning. The work to create a modern and responsive education system in South Africa continues today.

In Scotland, your author observed a very different example of redesigning a curriculum. While already housing a fine and classical European education system, Scotland desired to align itself with a new world economy in which the nation of China will obviously be a major player. Various language programs and student exchange programs were instituted so that Scotland might serve as a primary "trade door to Europe" for Chinese commerce in the future. Scotland also recognized quite early the influence of new information technologies in world communications and rushed to construct a high-tech 21st-century education system in all of its schools. These activities have dominated national planning for education in Scotland for a decade or more.

In Vietnam, following a period of wars lasting almost three decades, the nation reviewed its educational system's connection to the national economy and found it wanting. While a fine traditional system existed to train a minimal number of leaders and scholars, the popular system was not serving the nation as well as in other Asian countries of similar size. The cost of replicating the 20th-century public systems found in other countries was beyond the means of the Vietnamese government, and educational leaders in that nation began to ponder the possibility of "jumping to the 21st century" using new wireless technologies. In a matter of only a few years, Vietnam has developed a strong technological substructure to aid this goal (see Figure 1.3).

The challenge for Vietnam and other developing nations with similar concerns is how to leave the older system and embrace new educational delivery systems without interruption. A prerequisite to such a transfer is an analysis of the current curriculum,

	Country	Penetration (%)	Users in Millions
1	United Kingdom	83.6	53
2	Germany	83.0	67
3	Korea	82.5	40
4	France	79.6	52
5	Japan	79.5	101
6	United States	78.1	245
7	Spain	67.2	32
8	Italy	58.4	36
9	Iran	53.3	42
10	Russia	48.0	68
11	Brazil	45.7	89
12	Turkey	45.7	36
13	China	40.1	538
14	Mexico	36.5	42
15	Egypt	35.6	30
16	Vietnam	35.6	30
17	Philippines	32.4	33
18	Nigeria	28.4	48
19	Indonesia	22.1	55
20	India	11.4	137

Adapted from Internet World Stats. Updated June 30, 2012.

FIGURE 1.3   Top 20 Countries With the Highest Number of Internet Users.

beginning with a clear definition of purpose. Your author is proud to have contributed to this assessment.

In China, the complete disruption of traditional education under the Cultural Revolution has forced today's leaders to reconstruct the general education system from scratch. A substantial program of education for all citizens has been built in a short period, and China has focused on higher education during the past decade. The work to use education as a vehicle for nation-building continues with a new 10-year plan adopted in 2010.

China is unique in its value system undergirding schooling. In a belief system dating from the time of Confucius (551–479 B.C.), Chinese education seeks to produce productive citizens who can serve society; the child excels for the nation and not for self. In conflict with this goal, however, has been an exam-focused meritocracy that sorts and orders the social roles of students. Focusing the newer system on a program of general education, while maintaining quality control, has proven challenging for curriculum leaders of that nation.

The Cayman Islands, an existing British colony, are in the process of creating a world-class education system through comprehensive curriculum planning. Already a major center for world banking, the Cayman Islands hope to develop a new high-tech education system to serve students living on the three small islands that make up this nation.

Technology will be the centerpiece of a system designed to overcome the nation's small size and isolation. Your author helped to guide that national conception of curriculum.

These five examples of nations that are redesigning education are representative, to some degree, of all nations on Earth. Each nation has its own aspirations, history, resources, and limitations, and each has its own definition of what education should be. In every nation, education is tied directly to that national development and future planning. Curriculum is the critical function in the education of all countries and an important instrument for addressing all nationality issues. More will be said about these common global efforts to reform curriculum in the final chapter.

Summary

Curriculum is a century-old area of study in education, and it is experiencing massive change. Technology, with its new ways of treating information, requires a different paradigm for curriculum leaders. This change presents new challenges and new opportunities.

Definitions of curriculum reflect the scope of school programs. The author has presented three eras in which the definition of curriculum has grown as our society has changed. Multiple philosophies and learning theories present planners with a rich foundation for study and many possible educational choices. A new era of curriculum is unfolding that is witnessing massive changes in how we educate our young in the United States.

Activities

ACTIVITY 1.1

This chapter presents the evolution of curriculum in terms of three phases: evolutionary, modern, and postmodern. What evidence has been presented that such an evolution has occurred?

ACTIVITY 1.2

Consider adding a fifth planning foundation—technology—for curriculum work in the 21st century. How would this newest "basis of planning" affect the other four foundations? For example, how would technology affect knowledge acquisition or learning?

 Click here to take an automatically-graded self-check quiz.

Additional Reading

Gladwell, M. (2008). *Outliers: Story of success*. London: Back Bay Books.

Hattie, J. (2012). *Usable learning for teachers*. London: Routledge.

Jacobs, H. (2010). *Curriculum 21: Essential education for a changing world*. Alexandria, VA: ASCD.

McNeil, J. D. (2008). *Contemporary curriculum: In thought and action* (7th ed.). New York, NY: Wiley.

Oliva, P. (2012). *Developing the curriculum* (8th ed.). Boston, MA: Allyn & Bacon.

Ornstein, A. C., et al. (2011). *Contemporary issues in curriculum* (5th ed.). Upper Saddle River, NJ: Pearson.

Solomon, P. (2009). *The curriculum bridge: From standards to classroom practice*. Thousand Oaks, CA: Corwin.

Wiles, J. (2008). *Leading curriculum development*. Thousand Oaks, CA: Corwin.

2

Philosophy and Curriculum Design

Learning Outcome

■ To understand value dimensions that undergird all curriculum development activities.

A t the heart of all purposeful activity in curriculum development is an educational philosophy that assists leaders in answering value-laden questions, making decisions from among the many choices, and designing quality programs. For John Dewey, America's most famous educator, a philosophy was a general theory of educating. One of Dewey's students, Boyd Bode, saw a philosophy as "a source of reflective consideration." Ralph Tyler, a leader in curriculum throughout much of the 20th century, likened philosophy to "a screen for selecting educational objectives." Your author sees philosophy as the general framework for all curriculum design work.

Philosophies can therefore serve curriculum leaders in many ways. They can help to:

- Suggest purpose in education.
- Clarify objectives and learning activities in school.
- Suggest the format for instructional delivery.
- Guide the selection of learning strategies and tactics in the classroom.
- Organize evaluation activities.

The need for curriculum workers to hold a philosophy of education became increasingly obvious in the second half of the 20th century as the rate of change in education accelerated. Public education witnessed wave after wave of innovation, reform, themes, and other general signals of dissatisfaction with the status quo. Indicative of the seriousness of calls for reform of public schools was the following statement issued by the President's Advisory Commission on Science (1973):

> When school was short, and merely a supplement to the main activities of growing up, the form mattered little. But school has expanded to fill time that other activities once occupied, without substituting for them . . . Every society must somehow solve the problem of transforming children into adults, for its very survival depends on that solution. In every society there is established

some kind of institutional setting within which the transformation is to occur, in directions predicated by societal goals and values . . . In our view, the institutional framework for maturation in the United States is in need of serious examination. The school system, as it now exists, offers an incomplete context for the accomplishment of many important facets of maturation.

A New York state Teacher of the Year, John Gatto, observed that the school was teaching a kind of covert curriculum consisting of confusion, class position, indifference, emotional dependency, intellectual dependency, and provisional self-esteem. Creating such a docile and obedient population, perfect for the factory or the army, said Gatto, was exactly what the Prussians had in mind when America adopted their educational system 200 years ago (Gatto, 2003).

Bill Gates, founder of Microsoft and one of America's leaders in technology, as well as chief financier of the new Common Core State Standards, is even more critical of the status quo. In addressing the nation's governors in 2005, Gates observed that the only word for today's high schools in America was "obsolete" (Gates, 2005).

Most recently, various components of corporate America have called for either the privatization of American public schools through charter schools, virtual schools, and other alternatives, or nationalization of the U.S. curriculum through such instruments as the Common Core State Standards. These latest suggestions for change are treated thoroughly in subsequent chapters.

Although many different kinds of people are calling for substantial change in public education today, there is no absolute consensus for the direction of such change in the United States. The United States is unique in its decentralized control of schools. In the absence of centralized public planning and policy formation from the national government, local school boards rely on input from state departments of education (SDOE), pressure groups, expert opinion, and various forces in the societal flow. Often, decisions about school programs are made in an isolated, piecemeal fashion without serious consideration of the "pattern" of decision making. When goals are unclear, when there is no public consensus about what schools should accomplish, when value-laden decisions must be made, or when curriculum specialists are unable to articulate positions clearly on controversial issues, schools slip into the all-too-common pattern of reactive thinking and action.

The absence of clear direction often results in a curriculum that includes nearly everything but accomplishes little. Given the public nature of United States education, the dynamic nature of public school decision-making forums, and the dependence of school boards and superintendents on curriculum specialists for direction, the beliefs and values of the curriculum leader must be crystal clear. Curriculum is the critical role in establishing a philosophy for operating school programs.

THE SEARCH FOR A PHILOSOPHICAL ATTITUDE

Although there has been a steady interest in educational philosophies for over a century in the United States, the use of such an orientation in program planning has been severely limited in most public education systems. With the exception of the progressive schools of the 1930s, the alternative schools of the early 1970s, and the magnet, charter schools and homeschooling of the early 21st century, few American education programs have emerged that reflect a strong philosophical understanding, consistency, or commitment. As Robert M. McClure (1971) noted:

> With depressing few exceptions, curriculum design has been a process of layering society's new knowledge on top of a hodgepodge accumulation of old knowledge and arranging for feeding it, in prescribed time units, to students who may or may not have found it relevant to their own lives. (p. 51)

The dependence of school leaders on public acquiescence for the development of school programs explains, in large part, the absence of philosophical consistency and the general standardization of all school programs over time. Without public demand for or approval of change, often interpreted in the public forum as no opposition, elected school leaders have failed to press for more distinct school programs. Administrative "safety" is found in taking the middle of the road and the resulting curriculum blandness.

Equally, the mandate of public education to serve all learners under all conditions has acted to restrict the specification of educational ends and the development of tailored programs. The concept of school as the assimilator of diverse cultures, from the turn of the century until the present, has contributed to the "general" nature of public school curriculum.

Another factor resulting from the absence of educational specificity in school programs has been the lack of strong curriculum leadership at the state and local levels. With the exception of some university-based theorists, few curriculum specialists have had the understanding of philosophy, the clarity of vision, the focused activity, and the technical skills to direct school programs toward consistently meaningful ends. Although this condition is rapidly improving due to the greater number of persons trained in curriculum development, the presence of a highly skilled curriculum leader often separates the successful school district from the mediocre one (Wiles, 2008).

The development of a clear and consistent set of beliefs about the purpose of education requires considerable thought because there is much information to consider and strong arguments for the many and different philosophical positions that have developed. Perhaps the most important consideration is the observation by William M. Alexander (1974) that schooling is always a "moral venture":

> A society establishes and supports schools for certain purposes; it seeks to achieve certain ends or attain desired outcomes. Efforts of adults to direct the experiences of young people in a formal institution such as the school constitute preferences for certain human ends and values. Schooling is a moral venture, one that necessitates choosing values among innumerable possibilities. These choices constitute the starting point in curriculum planning. (pp. 144–145)

To illustrate the diversity of beliefs about the purpose of formal education and approaches to educating, consider the two contrasting statements by Robert Hutchins (1963) and A. S. Neill (1960). These statements are representative of two established educational philosophies: *perennialism* and *existentialism*. First, Hutchins:

> The ideal education is not an ad hoc education, not an education directed to immediate needs; it is not a specialized education, or a preprofessional

> education; it is not a utilitarian education. It is an education calculated to develop the mind. I have old-fashioned prejudices in favor of the three R's and the liberal arts, in favor of trying to understand the greatest works that the human race has produced. I believe that these are permanent necessities, the intellectual tools that are needed to understand the ideas and ideals of our world. (p. 18)

Now, Neill:

> Well, we set out to make a school in which we should allow children to be themselves. In order to do this, we had to renounce all discipline, all direction, all suggestion, all moral training . . . All it required was what we had—a complete belief in the child as a good, not evil being. For almost forty years, this belief in the goodness of the child has never wavered; it rather has become a final faith. My view is that a child is innately wise and realistic. If left to himself without adult suggestions of any kind, he will develop as far as he is capable of developing. (p. 4)

Such differences of opinion about the purpose and means of educating are extreme, but they illustrate the range of choices to be made by curriculum planners. These statements also indicate the trends in education that various philosophies favor. Perennialists, for example, favor a highly controlled and standardized curriculum, considerable structure, strict discipline, and uniform treatment for all students. They advocate trends such as back to basics, accountability, curricular standardization, and high-stakes testing. The existentialists, by contrast, favor a school featuring personal growth, an environment with highly individualized activities, low degrees of formal structure, and can identify with movements such as alternative education, student rights movements, homeschooling, and learning via the new technologies.

CRITICAL QUESTIONS TO BE ANSWERED

Each curriculum planner must confront and answer some difficult questions about the purpose and organization of schooling. The answers to such questions are critical to all subsequent curriculum work and establish the criteria for any future decision making and action. According to Alexander (1974), the condition is one of defining responsibility:

> In selecting the basic goals which the school should seek to serve, from among the sum total of ends for which people strive, the curriculum planner faces the major issue: In the total process of human development what parts or aspects should the school accept responsibility for guiding? (p. 146)

Daniel Tanner and Laurel Tanner (2006) observe that three major ends for schooling have been suggested repeatedly in the past:

> Throughout the twentieth century educational opinion and practice have been sharply divided as to whether the dominant source and influence for curriculum development should be the body of organized scholarship (the

specialties and divisions of academic knowledge), the learner (the immature developing being), or society (contemporary adult life). (p. 82)

The decision of the curriculum leader to relate to the knowledge bases of the past, to the social concerns of the present, or to the future needs of society is critical. Among other things, this decision will determine whether the role of the curriculum specialist is to restructure the programs or only to refine the existing system of education.

Most often, curriculum development in schools is a mechanical, static function because the content (subject matter) base is accepted as the main criterion for curriculum work:

> In the absence of reflective consideration of what constitutes the good man leading the good life in the good society, the curriculum tends to be regarded as a mechanical means of developing the necessary skills of young people in conformance with the pervading demands of the larger social scene. Under such circumstances, the school does not need to bring into question the existing social situation, nor does it need to enable pupils to examine through reflective thinking possible alternative solutions to social problems. Instead, the school is merely expected to do the bidding of whatever powers and forces are most dominant in the larger society at any given time. (Tanner & Tanner, 2006 p. 64)

If, however, the curriculum planner accepts the needs of learners as the most important criterion for planning school programs, as was done in the early childhood and middle school programs of the 1970s, the gifted programs of the 1980s, the special education inclusion of the 1990s, or the assimilation of new populations during 2000–2015, the purpose of the formal education program is dramatically altered. The same is true if the purpose of schools is seen as purely social reform or improvement of society, as it was during the integration of schools in the 1960s. In accepting an alteration of the traditional criteria for developing school programs, curriculum developers cross over into an "advocacy role" for change as they attempt to restructure the existing curriculum. The effectiveness of such a position in curriculum work is often determined by the clarity of any new objectives to be achieved. In the first two decades of the 21st century, for example, the Internet has offered options never before imagined, including online learning and the virtual school. Curriculum leaders have been slow to embrace such possibilities.

A number of primary questions override the value choices of all major educational philosophies: What is the purpose of education? What kind of citizens and what kind of society do we want? What methods of instruction or classroom organization must we provide to produce these desired ends? These questions are universal or global, and they are the basis of structuring education in all nations of the world. In our examples in Chapter 1—South Africa, Scotland, Vietnam, China, and the Cayman Islands—all are asking these same questions as they conduct curriculum renewal.

McNeil (2005) poses eight defining questions that are useful in developing the philosophical assumptions needed to screen educational objectives:

1. Is the purpose of school to change, adapt to, or accept the social order?
2. What can a school do better than any other agency or institution?
3. What objectives should be common to all?

4. Should objectives stress cooperation or competition?
5. Should objectives deal with controversial issues, or only those things for which there is established knowledge?
6. Should attitudes be taught? Fundamental skills? Problem-solving strategies?
7. Should teachers emphasize subject matter or try to create behavior outside of school?
8. Should objectives be based on the needs of the local community, the society in general, or the expressed needs of students? (pp. 91–92)

THE STRUGGLE TO BE A DECISIVE LEADER

Few educators would deny the importance of a philosophy in directing curriculum activity, but few school leaders or teachers seem to relish discussions of the topic. Even well-known educators have confessed a dislike for such discourse. James Conant, former president of Harvard University, once observed: "A sense of distasteful weariness overtakes me whenever I hear someone discussing educational goals and philosophy" (Conant, as cited in Silberman, 1970).

In the past, part of the problem with discussing educational philosophies in earnest has been the pervasiveness of the subject-dominated curriculum in schools. This problem has been further compounded by "expert opinion" on the topic in the form of college professors who are products of that system, therefore possessing a monumental conflict of interest in rendering their opinion. When inquiry into educational purpose is honest and open, without preconditions, and can lead to relevant change, philosophical discussions can be among the most exciting endeavors.

Charles Silberman (1970), in his classic book *Crisis in the Classroom,* expressed the importance of the philosophy underlying the learning programs of the school:

> What educators must realize, moreover, is that how they teach and how they act may be more important than what they teach. The way we do things, that is to say, shapes values more directly and more effectively than the way we talk about them. Certainly administrative procedures like automatic promotion, homogeneous grouping, racial segregation, or selective admission to higher education affect "citizenship education" more profoundly than does the social studies curriculum. And children are taught a host of lessons about values, ethics, morality, character, and conduct every day of the week, less by the conduct of the curriculum than by the way schools are organized, the ways teachers and parents behave, the way they talk to children and each other, the kinds of behavior they approve or reward and the kinds they disapprove and punish. These lessons are far more powerful than verbalizations that accompany them and that they frequently controvert. (p. 9)

Before curriculum specialists can work with parents, teachers, administrators, and other educators to explore educational values, they must first examine their own attitudes. During this process, curriculum developers seek to identify a value structure that can organize and relate the many aspects of curriculum planning.

To clarify the values and beliefs that will tie together curriculum organization, instructional procedures, learning roles, materials selection, and other components of school planning, curriculum leaders must identify themes that seem true to them. Although this process may be time consuming, the investment is necessary. To be both decisive and effective in their roles, curriculum leaders must combat the urge to ignore the value implications of the job or to reduce all arguments to "thoughtful uncertainty."

DETERMINANTS OF AN EDUCATIONAL PHILOSOPHY

Major philosophies of life and education have traditionally been defined by criteria in the form of three questions: What is good? What is true? What is real? Individual perceptions of goodness, truth, and reality differ considerably, and an analysis of these questions reveals unique patterns of response. When such responses are categorized and labeled, they become formal philosophies.

In the language of philosophy, the study of goodness or values is referred to as *axiology,* knowledge or truth as *epistemology,* and reality as *ontology.* Axiological questions deal primarily with values; in a school context, philosophical arguments are concerned with the ultimate source of values to be taught. Questions of an epistemological nature in a school context are directed toward the media of learning or the best means of seeking truth. Ontological questions, in search of reality, are most often concerned with the substance of learning, or application of the content of study. Thus, the standard philosophical inquiries concerning goodness, truth, and reality are translated into questions concerning the source, medium, and substance of learning in a school environment.

These queries are not simple because there are many ways to select ideas, translate them into instructional patterns, and package them into curriculum programs. Those possibilities are constantly increasing as our knowledge of the world becomes more sophisticated and technology opens new options.

FIVE EDUCATIONAL PHILOSOPHIES

There are many educational philosophies, but for the sake of simplicity, it is possible to extract five distinct ones: (1) perennialism, (2) idealism, (3) realism, (4) experimentalism, and (5) existentialism. Collectively, these philosophies represent a broad spectrum of thought about what schools should be and do. Educators holding these philosophies would create very different schools. In the following sections, each of these standard philosophies is discussed in terms of its posture on axiological, epistemological, and ontological questions. The five standard philosophies are compared in Table 2.1 in terms of attitudes on significant questions.

Perennialism

The most conservative, traditional, and structured of the five philosophies is *perennialism,* a philosophy drawing heavily from classical definitions of education. Perennialists believe that education, like human nature, is a constant. Because the distinguishing characteristic of humans is the ability to reason, education should focus on developing rationality. For the perennialist, education is a preparation for life, and students should be taught the world's permanencies through structured study.

For the perennialist, reality is a world of reason. Such truths are revealed through study and some through divine acts. Goodness is to be found in rationality

TABLE 2.1 Five Major Educational Philosophies

	Perennialism	Idealism	Realism	Experimentalism	Existentialism
Reality Ontology	A world of reason and God	A world of the mind	A world of things	A world of experience	A world of existing
Truth (Knowledge) Epistemology	Reason and revelation	Consistency of ideas	Correspondence and sensation (as we see it)	What works	Personal, subjective choice
Goodness Axiology	Rationality	Imitation of ideal self, person to be emulated	Laws of nature	What is	Freedom
Teaching Reality	Disciplinary subjects and doctrine	Subjects of the mind—literary, philosophical, religious	Subjects of physical world—math, science	The public test	Subject matter of choice—art, ethics, philosophy
Teaching Truth	Discipline of the mind via drill	Teaching ideas via lecture, discussion	Teaching for mastery of information—demonstrating, reciting	Subject matter of social experiences—social studies	Arousing personal responses—questioning
Teaching Goodness (Values)	Disciplining behavior (to reason)	Imitating heroes and other exemplars	Training in rules of conduct	Problem solving, project method	Awakening self to responsibility
Why Schools Exist	To reveal reason and God's will	To sharpen the mind and intellectual processes	To reveal the order of the world and the universe	Making group decisions in light of consequences	To aid children in knowing themselves and their place in society
What Should Be Taught	External truths	Wisdom of the ages	Laws of physical reality	To discover and expand the society we live in to share experiences	Unregimented topic areas
Role of the Teacher	Interprets, tells	Reports, is a person to be emulated	Displays, imparts knowledge	Group inquiry into social problems and social sciences, method and subject together	Questions, assists student in personal journey
Role of the Student	Passively receives	Receives, memorizes	Manipulates, passively participates	Aids, is a consultant	Determines own rules
School's Attitude Toward Change	Truth is eternal, no real change	Truth is to be preserved, antichange	Always moving toward perfection, orderly change	Actively participates, contributes	Change is necessary at all times

itself. Perennialists favor a curriculum of subjects and doctrine taught through highly disciplined drill and behaviorial control. Schools, for the perennialist, exist primarily to reveal reason by teaching eternal truths. The teacher interprets and tells. The student is a passive recipient. Because truth is eternal, all change in the immediate school environment is largely superficial. Perennialist thought is sometimes found in extreme forms in religious or highly politicized schools, which can be characterized by high degrees of inflexibility and certainty of purpose.

Idealism

Idealism is a philosophy that espouses the refined wisdom of men and women. Reality is seen as a world within a person's mind, and truth is to be found in the consistency of ideas. Goodness is an ideal state, something to strive to attain.

Idealists favor schools that teach subjects of the mind, such as are found in most public school classrooms. Teachers, for the idealist, would be exemplars—models of ideal behavior.

For idealists, the schools' function is to sharpen intellectual processes, to present the wisdom of the ages, and to present models of behavior that are desirable. Students in such schools would have a somewhat passive role, receiving and memorizing the reporting of the teacher. Change in the school program would generally be considered an intrusion on the orderly process of educating. Idealists are confident in their sources of learning.

Realism

For the *realist,* the world is as it is, and the job of schools is to teach students about that world. Goodness, for the realist, is found in the laws of nature and the order of the physical world. Truth is the simple correspondences of observation.

The realist favors a school dominated by subjects of the here-and-now world, such as disciplines of knowledge. Students would be taught factual information for mastery. The teacher would impart knowledge of this reality to students or display such reality for observation and study. Classrooms would be highly ordered and disciplined, like nature, and the students would be somewhat passive participants in the study of things. Changes in school would be perceived as a natural evolution toward a perfection of order. Although a teacher in a school dominated by realism would be open to discussion, the curriculum itself would be largely predetermined.

Experimentalism

For the *experimentalist,* the world is an ever-changing place. Reality is what is actually experienced. Truth is what presently functions. Goodness is what is accepted by public test. Unlike the perennialist, the idealist, and the realist, the experimentalist openly accepts change and continually seeks to discover new ways to expand and improve society.

The experimentalist favors a school with a heavy emphasis on social subjects and experiences. Learning would occur through a problem-solving or inquiry format. Teachers would aid learners or consult with learners, who would be actively involved in discovering and experiencing the world in which they live. Such an educational program, which focuses on value development, would factor in group consequences.

Distinguishing experimentalism from the previous three philosophies is a belief that the student is the focus of the teaching–learning act. Experimentalism, sometimes called *progressivism*, arrived in the United States early in the 20th century and has been reinforced by human development studies.

Existentialism

The *existentialist*, a proponent of the newest philosophy, sees the world in terms of personal subjectivity. Goodness, truth, and reality are individually defined. Reality is a world of existing, truth is subjectively chosen, and goodness is a matter of freedom.

For existentialists, schools, if they exist at all, are places that assist students in knowing themselves and learning their place in society. If subject matter existed in a curriculum, it would be largely a matter of interpretation in subjects such as the arts, ethics, or philosophy. Teacher–student interaction would revolve around assisting students in their personal learning journeys. Change in school environments would be embraced as both a natural and necessary phenomenon. Nonschooling or homeschooling, and an individually determined curriculum, would be a possibility.

Because schools are complex places with many forces vying for prominence, few educators hold a pure version of any of these philosophies. These various schools of thought have evolved as distinctive forms of philosophy following the examination of beliefs on pertinent issues (e.g., grading, grouping, discipline, or the role of the Internet). When an educator chooses not to adopt a single philosophy, or blends several philosophies, or selectively applies educational philosophies in practice, he or she is said to hold an *eclectic* position. Most classrooms and public schools come closest to an eclectic stance, applying philosophical preferences as conditions demand.

PHILOSOPHIES AS FOUND IN SCHOOLS

During the 20th century, U.S. public schools evolved from highly standardized content-focused institutions (Idealism-Realism) to more flexible and diverse institutions (Realism-Experimentalism). Our understandings of human development and the learning process, and the pressures on our rapidly changing society, account for these alterations of philosophy and the form of schooling. In the early 21st century, under the implementation of the Common Core, schools are pursuing more of a structured approach (Perennialism-Idealism).

All formal schools are designed to promote an education, but the curriculum designs of school differ just as educational philosophies differ. Schools represent a kind of blueprint, or plan, to promote a type of learning; because the ends sought by planners differ, all schools are not alike. This section introduces the 15 dimensions of any school design—dimensions by which schools can be compared and contrasted. Each dimension has been prepared to illuminate the various philosophical ranges within schools. Although these continua do not match the five philosophies precisely, you can begin to see a rough parallel between these philosophies and the various observable dimensions of the school setting. Questions for curriculum planners are highlighted for your consideration.

The intentions of schooling might be thought of as a continuum of choices. On one end of such a continuum is the belief that education is the process of shaping raw human talent into something definitive and useful to society. This classic view of education sees schools as shaping and refining human thought, behavior, and feelings through an increasingly controlled program of study. Such control, in the legitimate sense of the word, is accomplished by structuring the learning environment to facilitate (force) highly predictable ends.

On the other end of that same choice continuum is the belief that human talents are best managed by allowing the natural capacities of individuals to develop through the removal of growth barriers. This definition of education would have schools acting to release the student from behaviors and perceptions that limit personal development. Thus, the institution of the school would formally seek the expansion of human potential and differences in the process of learning by promoting "flexibility" in the learning environment.

Strong arguments can be made for either of these positions, as well as for the many intermediate stances on such a continuum. The crucial concept to be understood is that schools are institutions created by any society to accomplish certain ends. Because there are many possible goals for the institution of the school, there are many different and legitimate forms of schooling. To the degree that the organization of the school corresponds to the objectives of the school, the school can effectively educate students; it is consistent in its mission.

The range of possible intentions for a school program, bordered on one end by a school seeking maximum control and on the other by a school promoting maximum freedom, can be translated into the universal variables of structure versus flexibility. These two variables are used to facilitate the analysis of 15 major dimensions of schooling, all of which can readily be observed by a visit to any school:

1. Community involvement
2. School buildings and grounds
3. Classroom spaces
4. Organization of knowledge
5. Uses of learning materials
6. Philosophy of education
7. Teaching strategies
8. Staffing patterns
9. Organization of students
10. Rules and regulations
11. Disciplinary measures
12. Reporting of student progress
13. Administrative attitudes
14. Teacher roles
15. Student roles

Systematically examining the school by these criteria will help you see a school philosophy in its totality. The underlying beliefs about educating will become more obvious, and the program congruence or inconsistencies will be more visible. In short, you will be able to analyze the dimensions of a school setting in a selective and regular way and to understand the philosophical intent of the curriculum. The reader will also begin to know his or her own philosophy. The numbered rating scales in the following sections refer to the list above.

THE LEARNING ENVIRONMENT

Environments, both real and perceived, set a tone for learning. What people feel about the spaces that they occupy or in which they interact causes them to behave in certain ways. For instance, churches call for discreet behavior, whereas stadiums elicit a different behavior altogether. Traditionally, schools have been solitary, sedate, and ordered environments. This atmosphere was the product of many forces: a narrow definition of formal education, a limited public access to knowledge, and a didactic (telling-listening) format for learning.

In contrast, many innovative schools seem to be the organizational opposite of the traditional, structured school. They are often open, noisy, and sometimes seemingly chaotic activity centers. Such schools are the result of both a changing definition of education and a new understanding of the environmental conditions that enhance learning.

Three measures of the learning environments of schools are the relationship of the school and the surrounding community, the construction and use of buildings and grounds, and the organization of learning spaces within buildings. Within each of these three areas, selected dimensions have been identified that may help you understand the learning environment of the school.

Community Involvement

Individual schools differ according to the degree and type of interaction that they enjoy with the immediate community. Schools that perceive their role as shaping the behavior and thoughts of students into acceptable patterns normally seek to limit community access and involvement in the school program. By limiting community access, the school also limits community influence on the school program and thus ensures more predictable student outcomes.

Conversely, schools intent on expanding student responses to the educational process generally encourage community access and involvement in school activities. By encouraging community access, the school encourages community influence, thus ensuring the divergent input characteristic of most communities.

Measures of community access to and involvement with a school are plentiful. A simple measure readily available to the observer is to note how many and what kinds of nonschool personnel are in a school building on a given day. Perhaps a more analytical approach to the assessment of involvement, however, is to observe the school operation in terms of physical, legal, participatory, and intellectual access. The descriptive continua in Figure 2.1 suggest the potential range of alternatives present in schools.

PHYSICAL ACCESS.   In a physical sense, community involvement can be measured by the amount of quasi-school-related activity occurring in the school building. Activities such as school-sponsored visits to the building, community-sponsored functions in the building, parental participation in school-sponsored activities, and school programs conducted in the community are indicative of interchange and involvement (F). On the other hand, schools in which the public is never invited to visit; in which classes never leave the building; and in which the public is fenced out or locked out, held at the office when visiting, not welcome after school hours, or discouraged from moving within the spaces of the school have limited access and involvement (S).

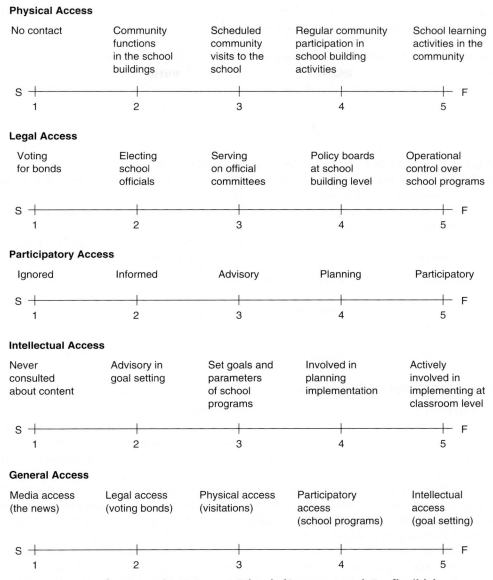

FIGURE 2.1 Types of Community Access to Schools (S = structured; F = flexible).

LEGAL ACCESS.   Legally, the community is allowed to become involved with the school at varying levels. In a tightly structured or closed school, legal access is normally restricted to setting limits and voting on school bonds (S). Increasing participation can be measured by community election of school officials and the administrative officer of the school district. Additional legal access to the school is indicated by school-building-level committees (such as a textbook selection committee) that allow community members to play an active role in policy formation. Not surprisingly, so-called community schools allow the ultimate access; parents and the community at large serve in govern-ance roles over school operation and activity (F).

PARTICIPATORY ACCESS.   In terms of participation in the daily operation of the school program, the community can be ignored (S), informed, included at an advisory level, or asked to participate wholly (F). Whether a school chooses to include the community in the type of school program that is being experienced by the students depends on whether such participation is seen as contributing to or detracting from the mission of the school.

INTELLECTUAL ACCESS.   Finally, there is an intellectual dimension to community involvement with the school that is indicated by access to goal setting, resource alloca-tion, and program development. To the degree that the community is excluded from thinking about the substance of what is taught and the method of instruction, the school is characterized by limited intellectual access and is highly structured (S). If the school encourages programmatic and instructional participation from parents and members of the community, it shows evidence of access or high flexibility (F).

Questions.   What is the relationship of the school to the community? What rights do the tax-paying public have in school governance? How much autonomy should professionals have in operating public schools?

There are great differences in the degree of access and community involvement with individual school buildings. Community involvement represents one salient dimension of the learning environment.

School Buildings and Grounds

The physical nature of school buildings and school grounds may be subtle indica-tors of the school's perceived mission and may therefore be useful measures for a visitor or interested observer. Features such as access points, building warmth, traf-fic control inside the building, and space priorities may reflect the intended pro-gram of the school.

Architects have observed that buildings are a physical expression of content. A dull, drab, unexciting building may reflect a dull, drab, unexciting educational process. An exciting, stimulating, dynamic building may reflect an active, creative learning center. A building not only expresses its interior activity but may also reflect, and even control, the success of these functions. If school corridors, for example, are colorful, well lit, and visually expansive, excitement and stimulation direct the individual in such a space. This is why most new airports have extremely wide and brightly colored corri-dors. The environment sets the tone for participants' dispositions.

School buildings changed a great deal during the 20th century, and those changes in architecture and construction reflect more subtle changes in school programs. A ster-eotypical drawing of the evolution of school buildings in the United States would show a progression from a cellular lecture hall (many one-room schoolhouses together) to an open and largely unstructured space, as illustrated in Figure 2.2.

Although many of these changes might be explained by evolutions in architecture and cost-effectiveness demands, a primary force behind the diminishing structure in school buildings has been the dissemination of knowledge through other media. As the

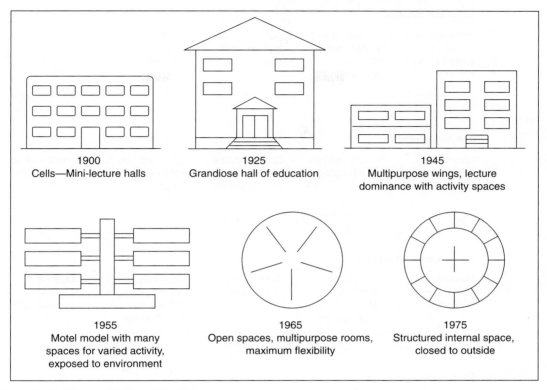

1900
Cells—Mini-lecture halls

1925
Grandiose hall of education

1945
Multipurpose wings, lecture
dominance with activity spaces

1955
Motel model with many
spaces for varied activity,
exposed to environment

1965
Open spaces, multipurpose rooms,
maximum flexibility

1975
Structured internal space,
closed to outside

FIGURE 2.2   Evolution of School Buildings.

essential curriculum of the turn of the century gave way to a more broadly focused academic preparation, buildings were designed to incorporate diversity. Because spaces had multiple uses, the construction was necessarily flexible in design. With the advent of interactive computers and a universe of possible knowledge, the role of buildings is becoming less clear. Storefronts could serve learning as well as traditional schools if homeschooling and learning networks structure the curriculum.

However, the design of a school building does not always reflect the current philosophy of the school. Many flexible programs are found in old egg-crate buildings, and highly structured programs are sometimes found in modern open-space schools. Returning to our analytical tools, though—the degree of access, the warmth of the building, traffic control patterns inside the building, and space priorities—we can begin to guess the educational philosophy of the school. The descriptive continua in Figure 2.3 suggest the potential range of alternatives present in schools.

DEGREE OF ACCESS.   Many schools, because of genuine danger in the immediate neighborhood, limit the number of access points to the school building. Other schools deliberately limit public access as a means of controlling the environment and personnel in the building. Signs of extreme control in school buildings are a single entrance for all entering the building; constantly locked spaces such as bathrooms and auxiliary spaces;

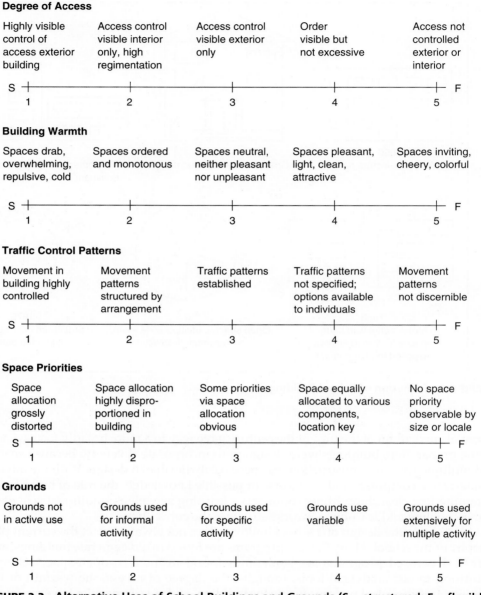

FIGURE 2.3 Alternative Uses of School Buildings and Grounds (S = structured; F = flexible).

and purposeful physical barriers to movement, such as long unbroken counters in school offices.

Cues such as these tell visitors, students, and even teachers in the building that there are acceptable and unacceptable ways to enter the building and to move in it. Highly controlled access and mobility in school buildings indicate a belief that only certain types of movement in a building are conducive to successful education.

BUILDING WARMTH.   Related to physical access is the concept of building warmth. The size of spaces, the shape of spaces, the scale of the environment (relationship between the size of the people and objects in the environment), coloration, and use of lighting all affect the warmth of a school building. Generally speaking, a combination of extreme space (large or small), extreme light (bright or dim), extreme coloration (too drab or too bright), repelling shapes (not geometric or too geometric), or disproportionate scale (too large or too small) can make occupants feel uncomfortable.

In the past, small classrooms with oversized furniture, drab coloration, and square walls were used purposefully to control environment stimulation and direct attention to the teacher. Such a discomforting setting presupposed that teacher behavior was the significant action in the learning environment.

More recently, schools have used bright colors, curved walls, large expansive spaces, and acoustical treatments to encourage student mobility and mental freedom. Such an environment presupposes that education is an act that is highly individual and conducted through exploration. Control under such environmental conditions can be difficult.

Although a few school buildings are constructed to promote an identifiable pattern of instruction, environmental warmth greatly affects instructional procedure. Failure to consider this factor has led to many unsuccessful and inefficient teaching episodes.

TRAFFIC CONTROL PATTERNS.   Traffic control within a school building, made famous by Bel Kaufman's 1965 book *Up the Down Staircase,* is also a reflection of the school's belief about the nature of education. Many schools go to great lengths to communicate order to inhabitants of the building. Adhesive strips dividing hallways into acceptable paths, turnstiles, fences, and children marching single file along walls are indicative of such structure in a building. Buildings in which flexibility is encouraged will have curved sidewalks, doorless entrances to learning spaces, seating spaces where occupants can stop and rest en route to their destinations, and multiple patterns of individual progression from point to point in the building.

SPACE PRIORITIES.   Finally, space usage and priorities reflect the learning environment in school buildings. Priorities are indicated by both the size and location of spaces in the building. In some schools, old and new, a significant portion of total available space is dominated by single-event spaces such as auditoriums, gymnasiums, swimming pools, and central office suites. In terms of construction costs and use, these spaces speak subtly of the priorities of the resident educators. The number, kind, and quality of spaces can be a measure of the definition of educational priority in a school building.

A second and perhaps more accurate measure of space priority in a school building is the location of various areas. Studies of school buildings have indicated that teachers who have more seniority in a building have better resource bases than do the other teachers. How much space, for instance, does the English department have? Where is the fine arts complex located? What new additions have been made to the building, and which program do they serve?

GROUNDS.   Beyond the structural walls of the school building lie the school grounds. Sometimes, these spaces reveal the attitude of the school toward learning. One interesting measure of the schoolyard is whether it is being used at all. Some schools located on

10-acre sites never plant a bush or add a piece of equipment to make the grounds useful to the school. Other schools, by contrast, use the grounds extensively and perceive them as an extension of the formal learning spaces.

Another question to be asked about the school grounds is whether they are generally used for student loitering, casual recreation, physical education, or comprehensive educational purposes. Equipment and student behavior indicate which, if any, uses are made of this valuable resource.

Questions.   In continuing to build traditional school buildings, do we force function to follow form? In this age of technology, could significant cost savings be realized by providing an alternative to school buildings?

There are great differences in how individual schools use their buildings and grounds. Thus, the use of these resources represents another dimension of the school philosophy.

Classroom Spaces

Just as the school learning environment may be revealed in school dimensions such as community involvement and building use, the organization, movement, and ownership of physical space in the classroom often indicate the intentions of the school. Viewing these characteristics of the classroom makes it again obvious that not all schools are alike.

CLASSROOM ORGANIZATION.   One way to view classroom spaces is in terms of organization for instructional effectiveness. In a traditional pattern, the room is arranged so that all vision and attention are on the teacher. Figure 2.4 shows that there is little opportunity for lateral communication. Activity is fixed by the arrangement of furniture. The conditions are perfect for teacher lecture but little else.

Another way to organize classroom spaces is to create multipurpose spaces with the focus of attention generally in the center of the classroom (as shown in Figure 2.5). This style permits increased student involvement, mobility, and varied learning activities simultaneously. It does not focus attention solely on the teacher and cannot easily be controlled in terms of noise or lateral communication among students.

The extreme degree of flexibility in organizing classroom spaces means that the classroom is not simply a place where learners meet to prepare for educational experiences both in the school building and in the community.

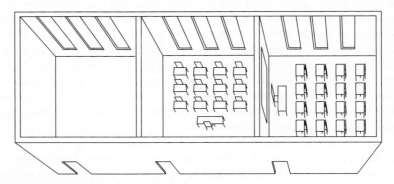

FIGURE 2.4   Traditional Classroom Arrangement.

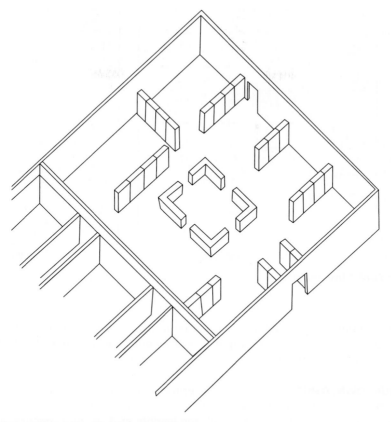

FIGURE 2.5   Classroom with Multipurpose Spaces.

CLASSROOM MOVEMENT.   Pupil movement within the classroom may be another subtle indicator of the structure or flexibility present in the learning environment (see Figure 2.6). Movement in some classrooms is totally dependent on the teacher. Students in such classrooms must request permission to talk, go to the washroom, or approach the teacher. Such structure usually minimizes noise and confusion but restricts activity to only verbal exchange. When movement occurs in structured classrooms, it is generally to and from the teacher's desk.

In a less stationary classroom, movement is possible within controlled patterns monitored by the teacher. Movement is usually contextual, depending on the activity. During teacher talk, for instance, movement may not be allowed; at other times, students may be able to sharpen pencils, get supplies, or leave the room for water without complete dependence on teacher approval.

Pupil movement is sometimes left to the complete discretion of the student. Even during a lesson or a teacher explanation, a student may leave to use the washroom. In open-space buildings with high degrees of program flexibility, students are often seen moving unsupervised from one learning area to the next. Parents who have attended more structured, traditional programs often view such movement as questionable

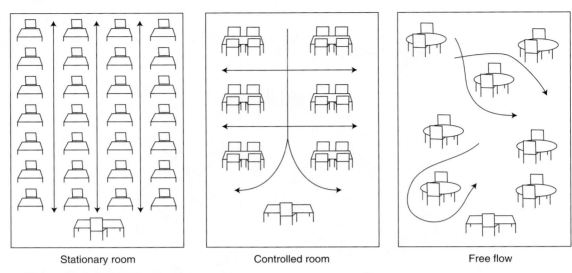

Stationary room   Controlled room   Free flow

FIGURE 2.6 Patterns of Pupil Movement.

because they believe that the teacher must be in direct contact with students for learning to occur. Yet self-directed, unsupervised movement is an integral part of any open, activity-centered curriculum.

CLASSROOM OWNERSHIP. A third consideration in viewing classroom spaces is what might be considered ownership, or territoriality, of the area. In most classrooms, this dimension is revealed by the spaces both the teacher and students occupy and by items that belong to those persons inhabiting the classroom.

At the most structured end of an ownership continuum in a classroom, the teacher has total access to any area or space in the room, and the students "own" no space. In some classrooms, particularly in elementary schools, teacher ownership of space can extend even into the desks, pockets, and thoughts of students.

In somewhat less structured environments, students have zones where they can locate without being inspected or violating the teacher's territoriality. In the average classroom, about two thirds of the space is allocated for students and one third for the teacher (as illustrated in Figure 2.7).

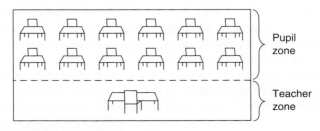

FIGURE 2.7 Division of the Average Classroom.

The most flexible pattern of ownership is seen in the classroom with no overt symbols of territoriality. Either the teacher's desk is accessible for all purposes, or the teacher has a private place somewhere else in the building, which is often the case in newer schools. Furniture in such classrooms is uniform for students and teachers alike.

Another measure of ownership visible to the observer is the number and type of personal items on display in the room. In particular, the display of student work or student art is a useful indicator. When student work is displayed, for example, are samples drawn from the work of all students or simply a few? Are the samples on display uniform (everyone colors the same picture the same color) or diverse?

Ownership is also revealed by the kind of teaching visuals on display (standard or tailored), the presence or absence of living objects, and any signs of reward for creative or divergent thinking. A highly structured classroom will generally be bland and uniform; a highly flexible room will be nearly chaotic in appearance.

Questions.   How might teaching staffs use their limited spaces to better serve all learners? What does emerging research tell us about the organization of learning spaces?

There are great differences in school classrooms, and these differences reflect the intentions of the school in educating students. Classroom spaces thus represent another important dimension of the learning philosophy. The descriptive continua in Figure 2.8 suggest the potential range of alternatives present in schools.

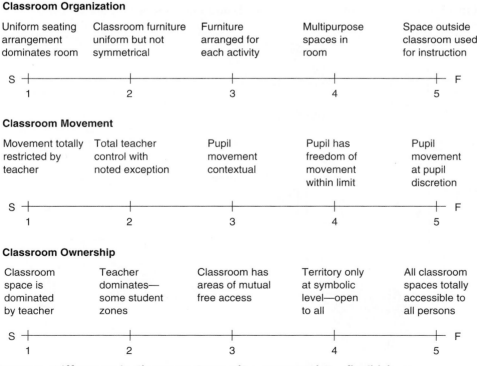

FIGURE 2.8   Differences in Classroom Spaces (S = structured; F = flexible).

Programs of Study

Schools differ to a great extent in how they organize and use knowledge and materials in their programs of study. The Internet is also radically changing this conception. In highly structured schools, knowledge is, for all practical purposes, the curriculum, and ordering knowledge represents the major activity of curriculum development. In highly flexible schools, by contrast, knowledge can be a simple medium through which processes are taught.

ORGANIZATION OF KNOWLEDGE. Organization of knowledge can best be understood by viewing it in several dimensions: the pattern of its presentation, the way in which it is constructed or ordered, its cognitive focus, and the time orientation of the context.

PRESENTATION OF KNOWLEDGE. In most schools, knowledge is presented as an essential body or set of interrelated data, as shown in Figure 2.9(a). In some schools, however, this essential knowledge is supplemented by other useful learning, which may appear as unequal satellites around the main body of information, as shown in Figure 2.9(b).

To the degree that student needs and interests are considered in planning the program of study, the satellites, or electives, are expanded and become more important parts of the program. In some schools, electives are equal in importance to essential knowledge areas and consume up to half of school time. See Figure 2.9(c). Once the school acknowledges the value of student-related content, it may find that it can teach the essential content in a form that accounts for student needs and interests. See Figure 2.9(d).

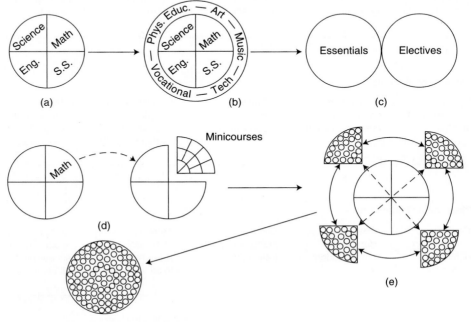

FIGURE 2.9 Patterns of Knowledge Presentation.

As the interrelatedness of essential courses is verified, coursework may be cross-referenced (interdisciplinary instruction). There may be a maximum of flexibility in the ordering and use of knowledge when a problem-oriented activity is the common denominator for organizing knowledge. See Figure 2.9(e).

CONSTRUCTION OR ORDERING OF KNOWLEDGE.   Another distinguishing dimension of the organization of knowledge is how it is constructed or ordered. Most programs of study employ one of three standard curriculum designs: (1) the building blocks design, (2) the branching design, or (3) the spiral design. It is also possible, however, to order knowledge in school programs in terms of (4) task accomplishment or (5) simple learning processes. These five patterns of knowledge construction are shown in Figure 2.10.

The building blocks design orders a clearly defined body of knowledge or skills into a pyramid-like arrangement. Students are taught foundational material that leads to more complex and specialized knowledge. Deviations from the prescribed order are not allowed because the end product of the learning design (mastery) is known in advance. Also, activities that do not contribute to this directed path are not allowed because of the efficiency of this model. Building blocks designs are the most structured of curriculum organizations.

Another common learning design found in schools is the branching design. Branching is a variation of the building blocks design that incorporates limited choice in the knowledge to be mastered. Branching designs recognize the value of foundational knowledge in learning but allow choice within prescribed areas beyond the common experience. Like the building blocks design, branching prescribes the eventual outcomes of the learning program, although the prescription is multiple rather than uniform. The branching design allows for some variability in learning but only within tightly defined boundaries of acceptance.

A third organization of knowledge in programs of study is the spiral curriculum. In this design, knowledge areas are continually visited and revisited at higher levels of complexity. This design does have some flexibility, but it still controls what is taught and learned and even predetermines when it is to be received by the student.

A fourth possible organization of knowledge has a goal accomplishment of specified tasks. In specific tasks or skills designs, the purpose of the learning experience is predetermined, but the student interaction with data in terms of both content and order of content is flexible. Competency-based skill continua are an example of this design.

A fifth organization of knowledge in a school program of studies might use knowledge simply as a medium for teaching processes. Thus, reading could be taught regardless of the particular material used by the student. Such a process pattern features great flexibility in terms of the knowledge used, its order in learning experiences, and the expected outcomes for its selection and use.

COGNITIVE FOCUS.   Still another dimension of the treatment of knowledge is the cognitive focus of instruction. In addition to focusing on factual material, such as learning important dates in history, knowledge can also be organized for teaching generalizations. Sometimes, conceptual treatments of information are related to the lives of students. Maximum flexibility in the treatment of knowledge is gained by focusing on the personal world of the students, drawing concepts and facts from their experiences.

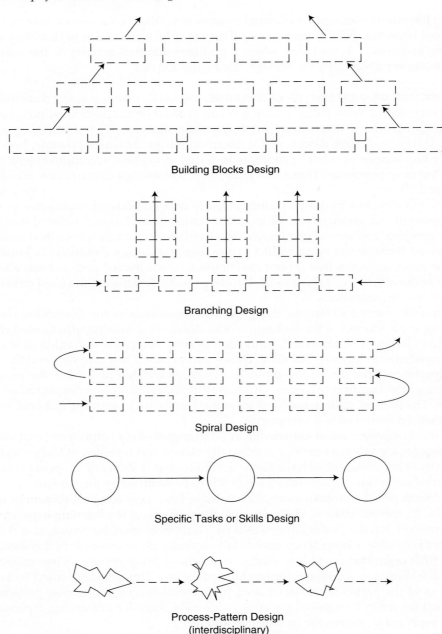

Building Blocks Design

Branching Design

Spiral Design

Specific Tasks or Skills Design

Process-Pattern Design
(interdisciplinary)

FIGURE 2.10   Patterns of Knowledge Construction.

TIME ORIENTATION.   A final area related to knowledge in school settings is the time orientation of the instructional material. In some classrooms, all information is drawn from past experiences of humankind. In other rooms, information from the past is mixed with that from the present. Some classrooms are strictly contemporary and deal

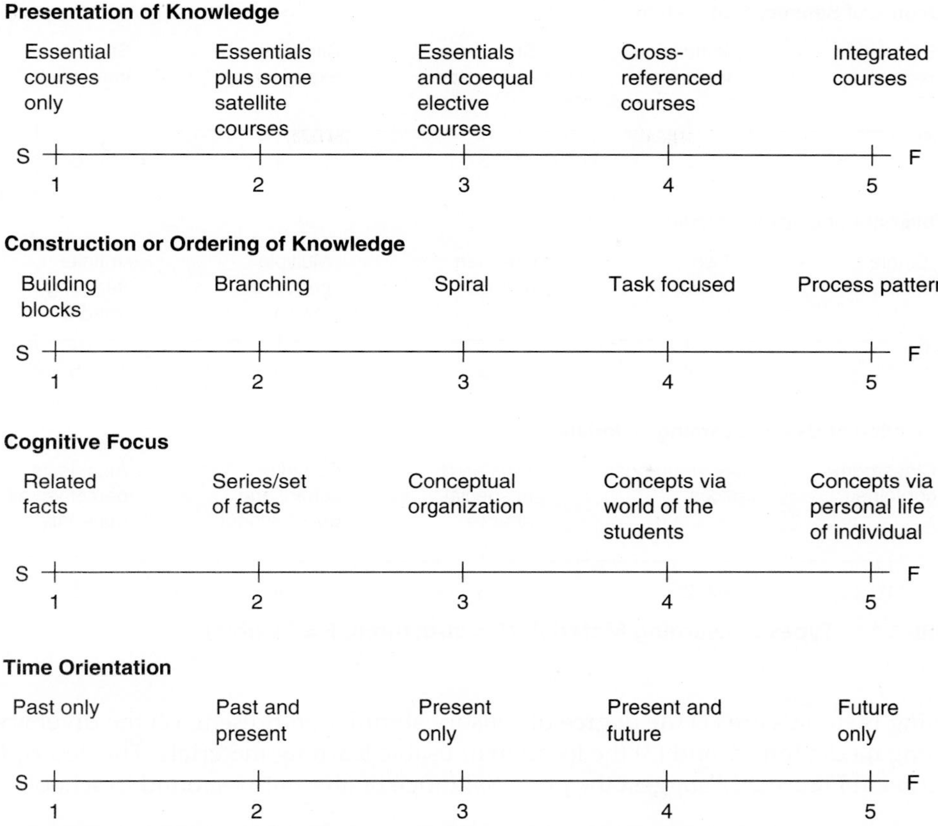

Presentation of Knowledge

Essential courses only	Essentials plus some satellite courses	Essentials and coequal elective courses	Cross-referenced courses	Integrated courses

S ├───────────┼───────────┼───────────┼───────────┤ F
 1   2   3   4   5

Construction or Ordering of Knowledge

Building blocks	Branching	Spiral	Task focused	Process pattern

S ├───────────┼───────────┼───────────┼───────────┤ F
 1   2   3   4   5

Cognitive Focus

Related facts	Series/set of facts	Conceptual organization	Concepts via world of the students	Concepts via personal life of individual

S ├───────────┼───────────┼───────────┼───────────┤ F
 1   2   3   4   5

Time Orientation

Past only	Past and present	Present only	Present and future	Future only

S ├───────────┼───────────┼───────────┼───────────┤ F
 1   2   3   4   5

FIGURE 2.11   Types of Knowledge Presentation (S = structured; F = flexible).

only with the here and now. Beyond the present-oriented instructional method are those that mix current knowledge with projected knowledge and some that deal only in probabilities. With each step from the known (past) to the speculative (future) content, flexibility increases.

The descriptive continua in Figure 2.11 suggest the potential range of alternatives for constructing or ordering knowledge in schools.

Questions.   Why are schools unable to break away from the traditional content curriculum? Which format for organizing knowledge seems most applicable to life in the 21st century? How has new technology-assisted learning using the Internet altered our conception of "knowing"?

Use of Learning Materials

The ways in which learning materials are used or not used in classroom spaces vary tremendously from room to room. In some settings, no materials are visible to the observer except perhaps a single textbook. In other classroom spaces, the volume and variety of learning materials give the impression of clutter. Three measures of the use of

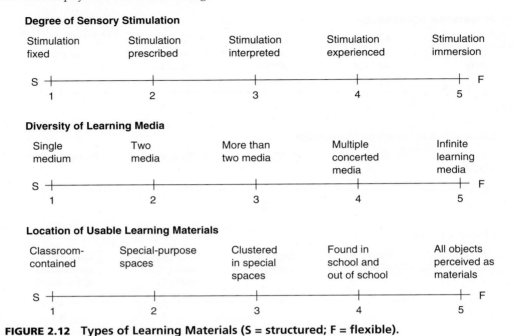

FIGURE 2.12   Types of Learning Materials (S = structured; F = flexible).

learning materials are (1) the degree of sensory stimulation present, (2) the diversity of learning media found, and (3) the location of usable learning materials. The descriptive continua in Figure 2.12 suggest the potential range of alternatives found in schools.

SENSORY STIMULATION.   At the most structured end of a continuum, the stimulation from learning materials can be fixed and absolute, as when all material is written or programmed. Sometimes, stimulation from learning materials is prescribed or controlled, as it is during lectures. Slightly more stimulation is available when the materials are interpreted, such as during an animated film or game playing. Still greater stimulation occurs when the learner is in physical proximity to the materials and has a tactile experience. Immersion of the learner in multisensory experiences represents the greatest degree of stimulation.

DIVERSITY.   Another measure of the effect of learning materials is found in the diversity of media present. Although some classrooms have only textbooks, others have printed matter, audiovisual aids, games, displays, and interactive materials. An important question is, How many types of learning media are interacting with the learner at any moment?

LOCATION.   The location of usable learning materials is a variable in classroom settings. In some schools, all learning materials are contained in standard classrooms. Still others have special-purpose spaces in which students may interact with materials. In a third, more flexible arrangement, the school has areas (instructional materials centers) where learning materials are clustered. An even more flexible pattern allows learning materials to be identified and selected both inside and outside the school. Maximum flexibility, of course, would perceive all objects as possible learning materials for instruction.

Questions.   How might teachers be provided with a greater variety of learning resources? How might technology be used to enhance the learner–materials interface? How could these new media be directed to support the existing school curriculum? Should they be?

Instructional Orientation

Three measures of instructional orientation are (1) philosophy of education, (2) teaching strategies, and (3) staffing patterns.

PHILOSOPHY OF EDUCATION.   The descriptive continua in Figure 2.13 suggest the potential range of alternatives for instructional orientation found in schools.

   Instructional Format.   In some classes, learning is absolutely structured. The teacher controls the flow of data, communication, and assessment. Such a condition is characterized by drill. Slightly more flexible is a pattern of didactic teaching whereby the teacher delivers information, controls the exchange of ideas, and enforces the correct conclusions through a question-and-answer session. In a balance between complete structure and flexibility in the learning process, the teacher allows the free exchange of ideas in the classroom but enforces a standardized summation of the process. In an even more flexible pattern, students are allowed to experience a learning process and then draw their own conclusions about meaning. Most flexible is an instructional process that is not uniformly structured for all students, allows an exchange of ideas, and leaves the process open-ended.

   Acceptance of Diversity.   Yet another measure of philosophy in the classroom is the acceptance of diversity among students. Sometimes this is observable in norms relating to dress or speech enforced by the teacher. Sometimes such a measure can be assessed by the appearance of the learning space. The key to this variable is whether students are made to act in standardized ways or whether differences are allowed. On the most

Instructional Format

Teacher drills	Didactic format with closure	Free exchange with summation	Experience learning with individual summation	Nonstructured learning with no summation

S ⊢———————⊢———————⊢———————⊢———————⊢ F
   1   2   3   4   5

Acceptance of Diversity Among Students

Teacher enforces conformity	Teacher communicates expectations for conformity	Teacher tolerates limited diversity	Teacher accepts student diversity	Teacher encourages student diversity

S ⊢———————⊢———————⊢———————⊢———————⊢ F
   1   2   3   4   5

FIGURE 2.13   Types of Educational Philosophies (S = structured; F = flexible).

extreme end of structure would be a classroom in which no individuality was allowed. In a classroom with maximum flexibility, diversity among students in appearance and behavior would be significant.

Questions.   What evidence exists to show that learners are diverse or unique? What is the essential difference between education and training?

TEACHING STRATEGIES.   Like the actions that suggest educational philosophies, the teaching strategies found in classrooms often give clues regarding the degree of structure in the learning program. Such strategies can often be inferred from teacher behaviors and organizational patterns. For instance, some teachers behave in ways that allow only a single learning interface with students, as in the case of the didactic method. Other teachers provide multiple ways for students to interact and communicate during instruction.

Two behaviors that reveal the learning strategy employed in the classroom are the motivational techniques being used and the interactive distances between the teacher and student. By watching these phenomena, the observer can anticipate a pattern of structure or flexibility in other instructional areas.

The descriptive continua in Figure 2.14 suggest the potential range of alternatives for teaching strategies in schools.

Motivational Techniques.   A range of motivational techniques is available to classroom teachers, and all are legitimate in certain situations. Some techniques seek to control and structure learning, however; others encourage flexibility. Teachers using threats or fear as a motivator generally seek maximum structure in the classroom. Coercion, as a rule, arrests behavior and encourages conformity to previous patterns of behavior. Extrinsic rewards, immediate or deferred, also encourage structure by linking desired behaviors with rewards. Intrinsic rewards, whether immediate or deferred, have an opposite effect. Intrinsic rewards encourage student participation in the reward system and thereby encourage a wider range of acceptable behaviors. If the

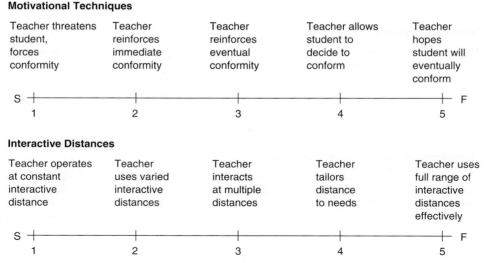

FIGURE 2.14 Types of Teaching Strategies (S = structured; F = flexible).

motivational technique is observable, the overall learning strategy (to constrict or expand student behavior) becomes evident.

Interactive Distances. Another dimension of the learning strategy in a classroom setting is the interactive distance between the teacher and students. To the degree that it is important to have two-way communication in the classroom, and to the degree that the instructional strategy values multiple learning styles among students, the teacher will make adjustments for differences.

In his book *The Silent Language,* Edward Hall (1959) made observations about the appropriateness of certain distances between persons for certain activities. Some distances (15 feet and beyond) are appropriate for broadcasting; other distances (6 inches or less) are reserved for intimate moments. In a classroom setting, it is possible to observe whether the teacher makes adjustments in interactive distances during instruction or chooses to treat all situations alike.

Questions. What are some combinations of teaching behavior that reflect motivational theory? What advantage can be gained by designing a classroom that allows for teacher mobility?

STAFFING PATTERNS. Another indicator of structure versus flexibility in schools, in terms of instruction, is found in the staffing patterns observed. Two staffing indicators are the role of teachers in staffing and the organization of teachers in the school building. The descriptive continua in Figure 2.15 suggest the potential range of alternatives for staffing patterns in schools.

Role of the Teacher. In some schools, all teachers are hired and assigned on the basis of subject-matter preparation. Such teachers are perceived as solitary artisans with the highly structured task of teaching a subject to students. In other schools, a teacher may be hired as a subject specialist but assigned to an interdisciplinary team. A more flexible pattern would be to staff a school with teachers having two or more subject specialties. It might even be possible to have one teacher (as in the elementary grades)

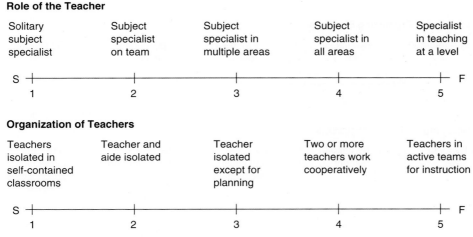

FIGURE 2.15 Types of Staffing Patterns (S = structured; F = flexible).

responsible for all subjects, or to hire a teacher to teach students at a certain level, rather than specific subjects.

Organization of Teachers.   Another staffing pattern is the organization of teachers in the building. Teachers may be isolated in *self-contained classrooms*, and they may or may not have instructional aides? Some classroom teachers meet in teams to plan activities. Sometimes teaching units are combined into new curriculum forms.

Administrative Conditions

ORGANIZATION OF STUDENTS.   The way in which a school organizes students can give an observer some measure of the degree of structure in the school. Two different measures of student organization are the criteria for organization and the grouping patterns found in the school. The descriptive continua in Figure 2.16 suggest the potential range of alternatives found in schools.

Criteria for Organization.   Because most schools in the United States admit children according to age, students are grouped by age. Schools use a more flexible criterion when students are organized by subject taught. Still greater flexibility is evidenced in schools that group students within grades and subjects according to capacity. Even greater organizational flexibility is found in schools that group students by needs and by student interests.

Grouping Patterns.   Besides criteria for grouping, the actual organization patterns of students can indicate the degree of structure or flexibility in the school. Perhaps the most structured situation exists when the size of the room determines the number of students present. A uniform number of students for all activities is also a highly structured condition. When a school begins to recognize that some activities should have large or small classes, a degree of flexibility exists. The greatest flexibility in the organization of students is represented by the assignment of students on the basis of tasks to be accomplished and the individualization of instruction, whenever possible.

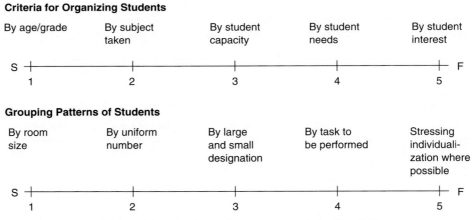

FIGURE 2.16   Ways of Organizing Students (S = structured; F = flexible).

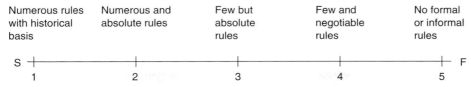

FIGURE 2.17 Types of Rules and Regulations (S = structured; F = flexible).

Rules and Regulations

Within schools and within individual classrooms, rules and regulations vary. Perhaps the most structured situations are those in which an excessive number of regulations exist based on historical precedent. Slightly less structured is the school with numerous and absolute regulations. A more flexible condition exists when there are a few rules that are formal and enforced. When there are few rules and the rules are negotiable, or when no formal or informal regulations are stated, maximum flexibility is indicated. The descriptive continuum in Figure 2.17 suggests the potential range of alternatives in schools.

Disciplinary Measures

Discipline techniques used in schools to influence student behavior cover a wide range of actions. In some schools, all infractions are given the same treatment regardless of severity. More flexible schools use a hierarchy of discipline measures for dealing with differing discipline problems. Sometimes, the pattern found in schools is to deal only with the severe or recurrent discipline problems. In schools where great flexibility is found, the pattern for discipline is sometimes unclear because of the uneven application of discipline measures. In some schools, no discipline measures are observable. The descriptive continuum in Figure 2.18 suggests the potential range of alternatives for discipline in schools.

Reporting of Student Progress

The reporting of student progress in the most structured schools and classrooms is a mechanical process whereby students are assessed in mathematical symbols such as 83 or upper quartile. A generalization of such preciseness is a system whereby student progress in learning is summarized by a letter such as a B or U. Increased flexibility in reporting student progress is evidenced by narrative descriptions that describe student work and by supplemental reporting by other interested parties, such as the student or the parent. Maximum flexibility in reporting student progress is found when such reporting is

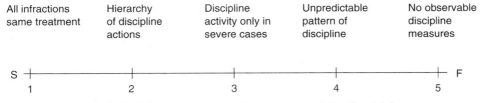

FIGURE 2.18 Types of Disciplinary Measures (S = structured; F = flexible).

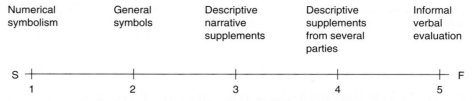

FIGURE 2.19 Ways of Reporting Student Progress (S = structured; F = flexible).

informal, verbal, and continuous. The descriptive continuum in Figure 2.19 suggests the potential range of alternatives for reporting student progress found in schools.

Questions.   What is the purpose of any student control system? What adult behaviors are learned in school settings?

Roles of Participants

ADMINISTRATIVE ATTITUDES.   Administrative style, more than any other single factor, determines the atmosphere of a school building. How those in the school building perceive the administrator affects both teacher and student behavior. For this reason, clues about the structure or flexibility of a school or classroom can be found by observing the administrator. The descriptive continua in Figure 2.20 suggest the potential range of alternatives for administrative behavior found in schools.

Decision-Making Role.   Administrators often assume one of five attitudes that characterize their pattern of interaction with others. At the most structured end is a warden who rules by intimidation. Closely allied to this model is the benevolent dictator who maintains absolute control while giving the impression of involvement. A more flexible posture for the administrator is to act as the program manager, reserving key decisions for the only person with the comprehensive viewpoint. Still more flexible is the collegial

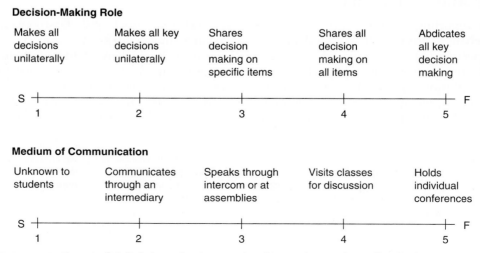

FIGURE 2.20 Types of Administrative Interaction (S = structured; F = flexible).

leader who shares all decision making with the teaching faculty. Finally, there is a leadership style that is nondirective or laissez-faire.

Mediums of Communication. A second interesting variable for studying administrative attitudes is the medium used to communicate with students. In some schools, the lead administrator is a phantom, known only by the presence of his or her portrait in the foyer. Such an administrator generally leaves communication with parents or students to an intermediary such as a vice principal. Another impersonal medium is the intercom, which is often used to communicate to students. Slightly more personal is a live address at assemblies. Finally, some administrators communicate with students by coming into the classrooms and sometimes even by holding individual conferences.

Teacher Roles

The role of a classroom teacher in a school can vary from being an instructor who teaches a prescribed set of facts to being a multidimensional adult who interacts with students and others in the building. For the most part, such perceptions are self-imposed. A key observation can be made from teacher responses to the question, What do you teach? The descriptive continuum in Figure 2.21 suggests the potential range of responses to that question.

Student Roles

Like teachers, students in schools hold a role perception of what they are and what they can do in a classroom setting. Sometimes such perceptions are self-imposed, but more often they are an accurate reflection of expected behavior for students. A question that usually receives a telling response is, How do students learn in this classroom? The descriptive continuum in Figure 2.22 suggests the potential range of responses to such a question.

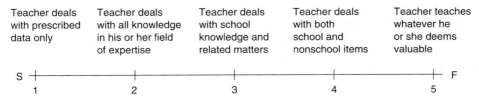

FIGURE 2.21 Teachers' Perceptions of Their Roles (S = structured; F = flexible).

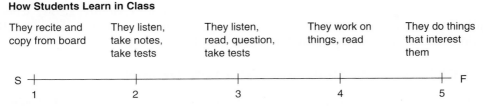

FIGURE 2.22 Students' Perceptions of Their Roles (S = structured; F = flexible).

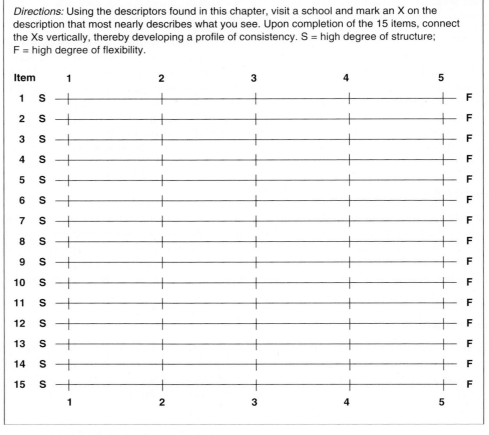

Directions: Using the descriptors found in this chapter, visit a school and mark an X on the description that most nearly describes what you see. Upon completion of the 15 items, connect the Xs vertically, thereby developing a profile of consistency. S = high degree of structure; F = high degree of flexibility.

FIGURE 2.23   School Assessment Worksheet.

Questions.   How might roles and relationships in school be altered to restructure education? What teacher and student roles seem appropriate for the 21st century?

School Assessment

The value of viewing school components on a continuum, such as the degree of structure versus flexibility, is that program congruence or inconsistencies can be identified (see Figure 2.23). In schools in which the program intent (philosophy) is clear, the degree of structure or flexibility should be relatively constant; that is, if the 15 dimensions were plotted across the five degrees of structure and flexibility, strong schools would have reasonably vertical columns. A zigzag pattern in such a school profile would indicate an inconsistency in the learning design.

SCHOOL PHILOSOPHIES AND CURRICULUM DESIGN

From the preceding discussion, it should be clear that schools represent a design for learning. Certain ends or values drive decision making to establish patterns and

TABLE 2.2 Eight Common Curriculum Designs Found in Schools		
Type	**Purpose**	**Activity**
Content-based instruction	Knowledge acquisition	Facts, data, representative forms
Skills- or standards-based instruction	Processing and manipulation	Practice, ordering, applications
Inquiry approach	Awareness, interest	Unknowns, sampling
Conceptual learning	Understanding	Big ideas, familiarity
Interdisciplinary learning	Making connections	Applications
Cooperative learning	Coordinating social skills	Group work
Problem solving	Applying skills	Current events
Critical and creative thinking	Construction of new forms	Model building, imagination

practices and design experiences for students. Consistency in such decision making is critical if the curriculum is to have the desired outcome in the form of student knowledge, behavior, and attitudes.

Although there are a great number of curriculum designs, consider eight common patterns, found in the literature of education and in practicing schools, for consideration (see Table 2.2). The designs range from "most structured" to "most flexible" in their intent and form.

Summary

Curriculum development is a value-laden process in which leaders choose from many possibilities. A prerequisite to leadership in curriculum is identification and development of a philosophy of education; a clear set of assumptions that will guide decision making. Also important for the effectiveness of any curriculum is consistency among the variables found in all classrooms.

The ability to compare and contrast individual schools and their beliefs is a necessary skill. Use a continuum ranging from highly structured to highly flexible. In this chapter, observation points are identified and discussed.

Activities

ACTIVITY 2.1

What Is Your Philosophy?

Respond to the 40 questions in Figure 2A.1 as directed.

The survey question numbers from Figure A.1 that relate to the five standard philosophies of education are as follows:

1. Perennialist: 6, 8, 10, 13, 15, 31, 34, 37
2. Idealist: 9, 11, 19, 21, 24, 27, 29, 33
3. Realist: 4, 7, 12, 20, 22, 23, 26, 28
4. Experimentalist: 2, 3, 14, 17, 25, 35, 39, 40
5. Existentialist: 1, 5, 16, 18, 30, 32, 36, 38

Scoring Steps

1. For each set of numbers (e.g., the eight perennialist questions), add the value of the answers given. In a single set of numbers, the total should fall between 8 (all ones) and 40 (all fives).

Directions: Respond to each of the following items according to the strength of your belief, scoring the item on a scale of 1 through 5. A one (1) indicates strong disagreement, a five (5) strong agreement. Use a separate sheet of paper.

1. Ideal teachers are constant questioners.
2. Schools exist for societal improvement.
3. Teaching should center around the inquiry technique.
4. Demonstration and recitation are essential components for learning.
5. Students should always be permitted to determine their own rules in the educational process.
6. Reality is spiritual and rational.
7. Curriculum should be based on the laws of natural science.
8. The teacher should be a strong authority figure in the classroom.
9. The student is a receiver of knowledge.
10. Ideal teachers interpret knowledge.
11. Lecture–discussion is the most effective teaching technique.
12. Institutions should seek avenues toward self-improvement through an orderly process.
13. Schools are obligated to teach moral truths.
14. School programs should focus on social problems and issues.
15. Institutions exist to preserve and strengthen spiritual and social values.
16. Subjective opinion reveals truth.
17. Teachers are seen as facilitators of learning.
18. Schools should be educational "smorgasbords."
19. Memorization is the key to process skills.
20. Reality consists of objects.
21. Schools exist to foster the intellectual process.
22. Schools foster an orderly means for change.
23. There are essential skills everyone must learn.
24. Teaching by subject area is the most effective approach.
25. Students should play an active part in program design and evaluation.
26. A functioning member of society follows rules of conduct.
27. Reality is rational.
28. Schools should reflect the society they serve.
29. The teacher should set an example for the students.
30. The most effective learning does not take place in a highly structured, strictly disciplined environment.
31. The curriculum should be based on unchanging spiritual truths.
32. The most effective learning is nonstructured.
33. Truth is a constant expressed through ideas.
34. Drill and factual knowledge are important components of any learning environment.
35. Societal consensus determines morality.
36. Knowledge is gained primarily through the senses.
37. There are essential pieces of knowledge that everyone should know.
38. The school exists to facilitate self-awareness.
39. Change is an ever-present process.
40. Truths are best taught through the inquiry process.

FIGURE 2A.1   Philosophy Preference Assessment

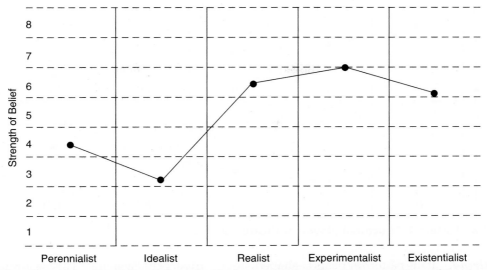

FIGURE 2A.2   Composite Graph for Philosophy Preference Assessment Interpretation of Scoring.

2. Divide the total score for each set by 5 (4, 4, 5, 5, 8 were obtained for our fictional example).

3. Plot the scores on the graph shown in Figure 2A.2. We used the scores listed in number 2 for the graph in the figure.

Having scored and plotted your responses on the grid provided, you now have a profile of your own beliefs about schools. Note that some patterns are common and therefore easily subject to interpretation. The pattern already on the grid in Figure 2A.2, for instance, is a composite response by over 5,000 students, both graduate and undergraduate, at five universities.

Pattern 1. If your profile on the response grid is basically flat, reflecting approxi-mately the same score for each set of questions, an inability to discriminate in terms of preference is indicated (see Figure 2A.3).

Pattern 2. If your pattern is generally a diagonal/slanting line across the grid, you show a strong structured (slanting down) preference or nonstructured (slanting up) orientation in your reported beliefs about schools (see Figure 2A.4).

Pattern 3. If your pattern appears as a bimodal or trimodal distribution (two or three peaks), it indicates indecisiveness on crucial issues and suggests the need for further clarification. The closer the peaks (adjacent sets) are, the less the contradiction is in the responses (see Figure 2A.5).

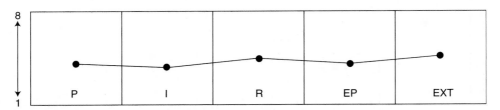

FIGURE 2A.3   Pattern 1: Little Discrimination in Terms of Preference.

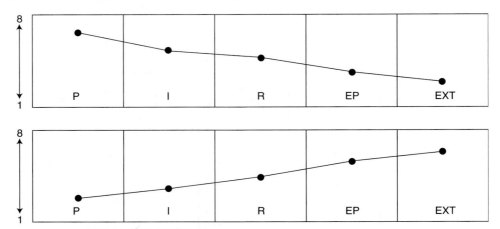

FIGURE 2A.4 Pattern 2: Structured (down) or Unstructured (up).

Pattern 4. If the pattern appears U-shaped, as in either of the graphs in Figure 2A.6, a significant amount of value inconsistency is indicated. Such a response would suggest strong beliefs in very different and divergent systems. This is unusual and somewhat confusing.

Pattern 5. Finally, a pattern that is simply a flowing curve without sharp peaks and valleys may suggest either an eclectic

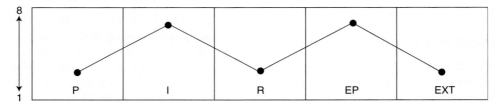

FIGURE 2A.5 Pattern 3: Need for Clarification.

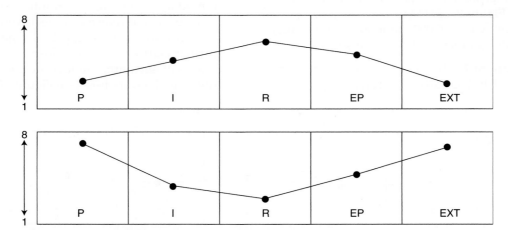

FIGURE 2A.6 Pattern 4: Strong Beliefs in Divergent Systems.

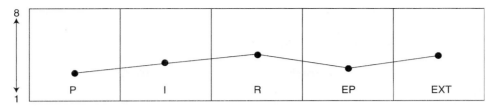

FIGURE 2A.7   Pattern 5: Eclectic or Beginner.

philosophy or a person only beginning to study his or her own philosophy (see Figure 2A.7).

The plotted score for a perennialist might be 8, 5, 4, 3, 1. An existentialist might score 2, 2, 4, 5, 7. A realist would have a plotted score something like 3, 4, 7, 4, 2. Regardless of your score, return to the question items, and see if they describe what you believe about the purpose of education.

 Click here to take an automatically-graded self-check quiz.

Additional Reading

Cahn, S. (2011). *Classic and contemporary readings in the philosophy of education.* England: Oxford University Press.

Common Core. (2011). *Curriculum maps.* Hoboken, NJ: Jossey-Bass of Wiley and Sons.

Feinberg, J. (2013). *Reason and responsibility-Readings in some basic problems of philosophy.* Columbus, OH: Wadsworth.

Gutek, G. (2008). *New perspectives on philosophy and education.* Upper Saddle River, NJ: Prentice Hall.

Johnson, T. (2011). *Philosophical documents in education.* Upper Saddle River, NJ: Pearson.

Kliebard, H. (2004). *The struggle for the American curriculum 1893–1958* (3rd ed.). New York: Routledge.

Noddings, N. (2011). *Philosophy of education* (3rd ed.). Boulder, CO: Westview Press.

Ornstein, A. (2011). *Contemporary issues in curriculum.* Upper Saddle River, NJ: Pearson Education.

Tozer, S., Senese, G., & Violas, P. (2008). *School and society: Historical and contemporary perspectives.* New York: McGraw-Hill.

Wiles, J. (2008). *Leading curriculum development,* Thousand Oaks, CA: Corwin Press.

Foundations of Curriculum Planning

Learning Outcome

■ To assess the five foundational planning areas of Curriculum Development.

In the evolution of curriculum as a professional focus in education, four major planning areas have dominated thinking about schools. To these four areas, your author advocates adding a fifth, technology:

1. Social forces in society
2. Treatment of knowledge
3. Human growth and development
4. Learning as a process
5. Technology

Collectively, these areas (called the *foundations of curriculum,* or *bases of curriculum*) organize information for planners and help them see critical patterns in the "who, what, when, and why" of education planning.

SOCIAL FORCES

The United States and most other developed nations are entering into a major period of transformation in the years 2010–2030. Changes in the composition of populations, dramatic changes in economies, new and powerful global technologies, and a different kind of world order all portend changes for these nations and for their systems of education. Lesser-developed nations will also have to react to these structural changes in our global institutions.

In the lifetime of our grandparents, the United States transitioned from an agrarian society to an industrial society. Work became mechanized, the population became urban and mobile, and the role of an individual in society was redefined. Today, with the transformation to a new postindustrial society dominated by technology and global interdependence, our nation is once again redefining itself, and schools must follow or disappear (Wiles and Lundt, 2004).

In advanced countries, the relationship between education and such change is dynamic and interdependent. To the degree that a nation's education system "programs" its children for a society that no longer exists, such education is dysfunctional for that society. By the same token, if a changing society insists that schooling retain traditional forms in the face of massive changes, it may well doom itself to obsolescence and cultural decline. Curriculum planners must seek to understand this complex relationship between education and national destiny so that they can build required changes into the schooling process. Communication is one example of many such social forces.

At the beginning of the 20th century, communication was primitive by 21st-century standards. There was a great dependence, of course, on the printed page. The telegraph existed, the telephone was in the infant stages of development, and motion pictures were a promising medium. Mass communication, however, was both scarce and inefficient. Any communication, such as the result of a presidential election, took weeks to disseminate. Within a short 50-year period, three mass communication devices appeared that altered this pattern: (1) radio, (2) television, and (3) computers.

Radio was the first communication medium to broaden the scope of the organized knowledge that had previously been the domain of schools and print documents. Large amounts of information could now be distributed quickly and, by early in the century, could even be broadcast to other countries.

> The effect of radio on the expansion of non-related and non-applied knowledge is analogous to the distribution of seed by a grass spreader, creating in effect a "carpet of knowledge" by cultivating a lawn so thick that single blades became indistinguishable. Said simply, knowledge on the radio was both equal and without value. Perspectives of knowledge under such conditions can be clouded; conjecture can be misinterpreted as fact. (Wiles & Reed, 1975, p. 58)

In the second half of the 20th century, television was even more influential than the radio. Broadcast into 96% of all homes an average of 6 and 1/2 hours daily by 1970, this medium influenced the values and standards of U.S. society. By the late 1970s, concern for controlling the impact of television, particularly as a medium affecting the thoughts and perceptions of children, was intense. Congressional hearings, campaigns by parent–teacher organizations, and criticism by members of the television industry were common.[1]

This theme has been presented by James P. Steyer in his book *The Other Parent: The Inside Story of the Media's Effect on Our Chidren* (Steyer, 2003). Citing thousands of studies, Steyer documents the effects of television, videogames, and the Internet on children. Of particular interest to educators is the detail provided, which describes how

---

[1] Paddy Chayefsky, "Network," United Artists, 1977

media companies expose children to sex, coarseness, violence, and commercialism before they are ready to understand such complexities.

A third communication innovation of the 20th century that has had a major effect on both society and schools is the computer. The initial impact of the computer has been more subtle than that of radio or television because of its mystique and inaccessibility, but the computer was destined to become much more powerful than either radio or television because of the far-reaching implications of the Internet and advanced search engines.

> While the computer habituates the pinnacle of man's intellectual genius, it is likewise the jailer who holds the key to our intellectual freedom. With his piece-by-piece orientation to information and knowledge application, man is, quite simply, presented with an unchallengeable opponent in the computer. The variance in speed in processing knowledge posits man in the impossible position of receiving computation as *fait accompli* from the computerized savant. In creating the computer, man has performed the heretofore-thought-impossible task of devising a being superior to himself in intellectual capacity, a being who can theoretically "out think" all men combined. (Wiles & Reed, 1975, pp. 61–62)

In terms of data processing and the generation of cross-referenced knowledge systems delivered at lightning speed and in multiple media, the computer age has presented a momentous challenge to school planners. In one decade, we have grown accustomed to satellite-transmitted instantaneous relays, home video cameras, direct-dial networked wireless telecommunication (cell phones), handheld wireless receivers, text messages, and facsimile capacities. We are no longer surprised by wearable technology and tens of millions of unique websites. The advanced world and even segments of the Developing World are awash in technology that is significantly altering our conceptions of school.

Social changes and technological access during the past 25 years have called the knowledge-based curriculum into question. Steven Wozniak, co-founder of Apple Computer, stated the case almost 30 years ago:

> It's healthy to learn basic concepts such as arithmetic and logic, but there is just no point in having to solve the problems over and over again every day. It's a waste of time . . . machines can do that stuff and leave us to think about more important things . . . personal computers are going to free people from the mundane things . . . they will allow people's minds to work at a higher level.

Because of radical advances in communication capability, some fundamental issues about schooling have been revived:

- If knowledge is being generated, disseminated, and delivered at a pace beyond our capacity to absorb it, what is the point in organizing schools around the mastery of essential data?

- If there is too much to be known today, what essential knowledge should all our citizens possess?
- If radio, television, and personal computers can disseminate fundamental information about the society in which we live, at a fraction of the cost of the schooling process, what, if any, should be the role of the formal educating system?

As of 2012, the Internet had penetrated 78.6% of all American homes and a significant percentage of many nations on Earth. School planners throughout the world can only guess at what additional changes will occur in social institutions and structures. The first quarter of the 21st century calls for us to focus our full attention on many of the following:

- The power of new technologies for learning
- The need to reallocate educational resources
- Understanding the difference between education and training
- The connectivity of information between schools and the society

TREATMENT OF KNOWLEDGE

The kinds of social changes outlined in the previous section have had a major effect on the treatment of knowledge in curriculum planning. Not only has knowledge become more plentiful and more widely disseminated because of technological advances, but the shifting social currents in the United States and throughout the world have also acted to redefine the utility of knowledge in everyday life. Because all knowledge contains value when applied, knowledge can no longer be treated as a value-free commodity or good in and of itself. The public is increasingly interested in what is being taught in school and how that information is valuable to students. Curriculum leaders of the 21st century are having a difficult task in sorting out and explaining the many new forms of knowledge.

Arno Bellack (1966), writing over 50 years ago during the early curriculum reforms, outlined the planner's dilemma in this manner:

> In current debates about what should be taught in schools, the "conventional wisdom" long honored in pedagogical circles about the nature of knowledge and the role of knowledge in the curriculum is being called into question. The enemy of conventional wisdom is the march of events. The fatal blow comes when conventional ideas fail to deal with new conditions and problems to which obsolescence has made them inapplicable. The march of events in the world at large that is placing new demands on the schools, and in the world of scholarship that is making new knowledge in great quantities, is forcing us to reexamine our ideas about the nature of knowledge and its place in the instructional program. (p. 42)

The scope of information available to scholars, and to schoolchildren, has been overwhelming for longer than 50 years. Estimates of the rate at which organized knowledge doubled its volume ranged from every 7 years in the mid-1960s to every 2 years by the mid-1970s. In the first decades of the 21st century, such estimates seem laughable. The millions of new websites each month worldwide tell us that knowledge is no longer controlled or even quantifiable. Traditional curriculum tasks such as reviewing and updating subject content are simply no longer manageable.

Related to the problems of scope and volume of organized knowledge is that of organization. Cases of knowledge overload are plentiful, conjuring up visions of a nation choking on the proliferation of its own wisdom:

> The American crisis, and particularly in terms of its schools, seems clearly to be related to an inability to act. It is not that we do not will action but that we are unable to act, unable to organize our knowledge or put existing knowledge to use. The intellectual machinery of our society no longer works or we no longer know how to make it work. (Reich, 1970, 43–44)

Educational planners, in general, have ignored the glut of data that relates to traditional school subjects or have dealt with it as minutiae in testing programs. There have been some serious efforts to confront the problem of knowledge overload by focusing on the structure of information rather than on information itself. One of the best-known leaders of this reorganization movement was Jerome Bruner. Bruner (1963) rationalized the shift away from the mastery of essential data to the study of representative data structures in this way:

> Teachers ask me about the "new curricula" as though they were some special magic potion. They are nothing of the sort. The new curricula are based on the fact that knowledge has an internal connectedness, a meaningfulness, and that for facts to be appreciated and understood and remembered, they must be fitted into that internal meaningful context. (p. 26)

Another response in the 20th century, related to the reorganization of knowledge sources for the school curriculum, was the advent of "new" fields of knowledge created from crossing standard disciplines of study. Knowledge in the sciences, such as biochemistry, and in the social sciences, such as demography, gave rise to new structures of organization. The incorporation and management of such new areas posed difficult problems for school planners because of the compactness of traditional knowledge organizations, the assessment procedures, and the scarcity of time in teaching.

With the dramatic increase in both the volume of knowledge and the number of corresponding questions about how to organize it meaningfully, came even more pressing inquiries about the purpose of knowledge in organized learning. Although challenges to the knowledge-based curriculum were not novel, the frequency with which educators questioned the traditional motif of educating in public schools during the 1980s and 1990s was surprising. Defining education in a new way called for a different definition of *learning*. As early as 1947, Earl Kelley observed:

> The only man who is educated is the man who has learned how to learn; the man who has learned how to adapt and change; the man who has realized that no knowledge is secure, that only the process of seeking knowledge gives the basis for security. (p. 12)

Futurist Alvin Toffler (1970), in assessing the onrush of the knowledge explosion as it related to the role of schooling, observed:

> Instead of assuming that every subject taught today is taught for a reason, we should begin from the reverse premise: nothing should be included in the required curriculum unless it can be strongly justified in terms of the future. If this means scrapping a substantial part of the formal curriculum, so be it. (p. 130)

By the year 2005, the delivery of knowledge direct to the learner was increasing dramatically. Bypassing the traditional schooling format were new interactive video networks and a host of personal computers with sophisticated software capability. Many students were learning music, art, languages, geography, and other topics at home, thus breaking the monopoly of schools over knowledge and its delivery. The competition for students from home schools, virtual schools, charter schools, and other proprietary schools increased dramatically. Homeschooling paralleled the increased usage of the Internet in the United States. The traditional educational system was beginning to dissolve.

The reaction of educational planners to the problem of knowledge organization was to emphasize the identification of goals and objectives for education, to serve as guidelines for content selection. Intensive testing for information acquisition in select areas such as basic skills followed quickly. The new buzzword for accountability was *standards*, and this orientation placed knowledge in a new and different role in educational planning, organization, scope, and sequence variables (Feyereisen et al., 1970, p. 138). By 2012, educators could only speak of Common Core and its focus on reading and mathematics.

A final area that affected the planning of knowledge use in schools was the advent of serious forecasting of the future. As educators reviewed past use of knowledge and studied the present knowledge explosion, they questioned the wisdom of continuing with a content-dominated curriculum. After all, facts, by definition, are phenomena of the past and present rather than of the future. In some respects, traditional knowledge placed blinders on our ability to escape the pull of the present and open our minds to the possibilities of the future. The call for creative, nonlinear thinking presented an interesting challenge.

The Internet and the development of search engines and browsers accelerated this concern to unimagined levels in the early years of the 21st century. If creativity amounts to making unusual associations, then any student in the Internet age can be considered creative given the many possible combinations of knowledge. Nonlinear learning is an area that all curriculum developers will have to confront in the first quarter of this new century.

In summary, the questions raised in assessing organized knowledge as a planning foundation are significant: What is to be taught? What should be the role of organized knowledge? What is the relative importance of knowledge bodies? What is the correct organization of information? What is the best form for bringing knowledge to students? How are all these factors affected by the instantaneous and global access of information by any learner without teacher assistance? Curriculum planners must address such questions.

HUMAN GROWTH AND DEVELOPMENT

A third foundational area considered important to educational planners has been the growing body of information related to human development. These data have been critical in regular school activities such as placement and retention, counseling, and planning curricular content and activities. Knowledge about human development has also provided the impetus for the development of a host of new school programs: early childhood education, special education, compensatory education, and middle school education. Perhaps most important, understandings about patterns of growth and development have caused educators to consider formal educational planning from the perspective of the individual student.

Contributions to our understanding of human development were gradual throughout the 20th century. As information about human development accumulated, various schools of thought emerged in an effort to organize the data. These interpretations of knowledge about human growth are the basis for the differences in educators' philosophies and learning theories. Such differences can be understood most clearly in relation to several basic issues related to human development.

One issue revolves around the question of what constitutes normal development. Because of records kept over an extended time on the physical maturation of schoolchildren, educators are now able to predict fairly accurately the ranges of growth for chronological age. It appears, in general, that children in the United States are achieving physical maturation at an earlier age. Such findings are attributed to better health and nutritional care during childhood. Our knowledge of intellectual, social, and emotional development during the school-age years is considerably less precise. However, organized inquiry has developed significant studies that guide our present decision making about development-related factors in these areas.

In the area of cognitive and emotional intelligence, considerable documentation exists regarding student performance on intelligence-measuring devices such as the Stanford-Binet scale. Little concrete evidence exists, however, to support hypotheses about intellect or intellectual capacity. Current operational models reflect how people are believed to develop and the normal ranges of development in the capacity to think.

Without question, the dominant model in this area is one developed by Swiss educator Jean Piaget nearly 75 years ago. Piaget hypothesized four distinct but chronologically successive models of intelligence: (1) sensorimotor, (2) preoperational, (3) concrete operational, and (4) formal operational. Piaget's model of continual and progressive change in the structure of behavior and thought in children has assisted educators in preparing intellectual experiences in schools (Piaget, 1959).

In the areas of social and emotional growth of students, even less precise data about human development exist. Classic studies such as Project Talent (Flanagan, 1964), *Growing Up in River City* (Havighurst, Bowman, Liddle, Mattens, & Perce, 1962), and the Coleman Report (Mosteller & Moynihan, 1972) provided long-term studies of particular populations. Data related to emotional development have been compiled by the National Institutes of Mental Health but are focused on abnormal populations. For educational planners, the question of what constitutes "normal" growth is largely unresolved, particularly in areas such as creativity (Wiles & Bondi, 1981).

Cultural dimensions of human development are becoming more important in an age of a new global economy. Some nations appear superior to others in certain types of learning and tasks (see *Outliers: The Story of Success* by Malcom Gladwell, 2008). The assumptions made for education and learning, in various nations, present curriculum developers with different values and priorities for planning school programs. Why do children in China, for example, score better in mathematics aptitude than students in the United States, *even before* starting school?

Another issue relating to human development is whether such growth can be or should be controlled or accelerated. Primary research with infants and children by White and associates (1973) suggests that development can indeed be accelerated through both experience and environment (1987, pp. 46–48). The work of behaviorist B. F. Skinner (1972), on the other hand, is conclusive in its demonstration that behavior can be shaped. These two options leave the curriculum developer with significant value decisions about both the anticipated outcome of an education and the more mechanical aspects of planning learning experiences.

Two final human development issues are indicative of the many planning considerations facing curriculum developers. First, because human development is somewhat malleable, we have the mind-boggling question of the ultimate human being that we might create. For instance, medical research in the 1980s and 1990s demonstrated an amazing capacity to change gene pools, transplant organs, re-generate body parts (stem cells), and apply chemistry to alter behavior. Diet and direct stimulation seem capable of emphasizing one human behavior over another. Studies in mind control and extra-sensory perception promise that directing human intelligence is within the domain of formal schooling. The notion that a computer could program the human brain for learning is not far-fetched; television has been doing that for decades.

Even more curious is our growing understanding of emotion and affective growth. Work with individuals of different personality styles and preferences may offer schools the possibility of selecting instructional strategies to match the emotions and perceptions of the learner (Kohlberg & Mayer, 1972, pp. 452–453).

Issues such as defining normal growth, promoting preferred kinds of growth, and emphasizing certain types of cognitive and affective growth make the study of human development, or human engineering, a necessary foundation for curriculum planning in the 21st century.

LEARNING AS A PROCESS

The result of new understandings of human development, new perspectives of the role of knowledge in learning, and new technologies useful to the schooling process has led to a variety of learning approaches that have become fashionable and acceptable in schools. These "new realities" suggest that schools can promote multiple types of learning in the classroom and therefore facilitate different types of learning environments in schools. Learning theory will continue to become a more important part of curriculum work in the near future.

At the level of philosophy, educators differ considerably regarding the type of learning that schools should promote. Three major approaches to learning have evolved: (1) a behavioral approach, (2) an approach incorporating drive theories, and (3) an environmental approach. These basic approaches to learning have numerous identifiable sub-theories; an abbreviated discussion is presented here to indicate the range of learning theory that exists among school planners.

The *behavioral approach* is characterized by an external perspective of the learning process, viewing learning as a product of teacher behavior. Under this approach to learning, educational planners and teachers who deliver such plans study the student to ascertain existing patterns of behavior and then structure specific learning experiences to encourage desired patterns of behavior. Armed with terms such as *conditioning* (repetitive response), *reinforcement* (strengthening behavior through supportive action), *extinction* (withdrawing reinforcement), and *transfer* (connecting behavior with response), the behavioral learning theorist seeks to shape the student to a predetermined form. Common school practices under this learning approach are fixed curricula, didactic (question-and-answer) formats, and programmed progression through materials. Perhaps the most interesting and controversial use of this learning approach in schools today is the practice of behavior modification.

Behavior modification is a simple cause-and-effect programming of observable behavior. The procedure uses a four-step technique: (1) identifying the problem, (2) recording baseline data, (3) installing a system to alter behavior, and (4) evaluating the new condition. As an external system of behavior control, behavior modification is not concerned with the attitudes or motivations of students but rather with the results of the modification system. According to this learning approach, behavior that is rewarded will continue; behavior that goes unrewarded will be extinguished.

A second learning theory is the *need-structured approach,* which is concerned with the needs and drives of students and seeks to use such natural motivational energy to promote learning. Teachers often analyze and use the interests and needs of students as instructional vehicles when following this approach. Key terms used with the need-structured approach are *readiness, identification, imitation,* and *modeling.* Taking a cue from Freudian psychology, this theory orders the curriculum to coordinate with developmental readiness. Students learn through the pursuit of unfulfilled needs, often modeling the behaviors of others or developing predictable identification patterns. Drive theories rely heavily on findings of human growth and development in planning curricular activities. This set of theories depends on student growth in planning school experiences.

The *environmental approach* to learning is concerned with the restructuring of the learning environment or of students' perceptions so that they may be free to develop. Unlike the static definition of growth presented by the behavioral approach or the dependent theories of need-structured approaches, the environmental approach is dynamic in nature. It acknowledges human diversity, believes in human potential, and promotes both uniqueness and creativity in individuals. The basis of the environmental approach is the belief that behavior is a function of perception and that human perceptions are the result of both experiences and understandings. When students have positive experiences that are self-enhancing, their perception and understanding of themselves and the world around them are altered. These new perceptions, in turn, allow for additional growth experiences. Student potential for development under this learning approach is limitless.

These three primary approaches to the structuring of learning in schools are very different in their assumptions about people and possibilities for human development. They differ, for instance, in their beliefs about human potential, in their vantage points in describing learning (external versus internal), and in their beliefs about the source of academic motivation. Selection of any one of these approaches to learning means that basic classroom considerations such as the design of learning spaces, the choice of materials, and the roles of participants will have a distinct form. The learning theory of the planner is crucial to decision making and projection. As such, learning as a process represents a strong fourth planning foundation.

TECHNOLOGY

Technology is a fifth possible foundational area for curriculum planning in the 21st century. The pervasiveness of its influence, which is far more than just a social force unfolding, is changing each of the other four foundations for planning. Our society is literally being transformed by computers. Knowledge bases are exploding and have become totally unmanageable in schools. Students are developing intellectually along new and nonlinear lines. Learning theory has entered new territory, and students and machines combine to use all the senses in learning. (See Chapter 5 for more on this topic.)

Technology as a planning variable is difficult to grasp because of the focus on the products of technology rather than the uses of technology. Each year, schools buy new and exotic applications of technology. Because such technologies have a short commercial life, school leaders find such expenditures unsatisfying and even frustrating. A better criterion for selecting such technology would be to ask, "How can this device improve our school program?" It is interesting to contemplate that the telephone, a century-old technology, is scarcely used in schools even though it is found in 96% of all homes in the United States and can be used to connect to persons throughout the world with only 15 to 17 numbers.

Likewise, decisions about technology usage are often made without understanding the future of such technologies. In today's world there are now more cell-phones-only residences than landline-phone-only residences (by 2008 in the United States), reflecting the advantages of mobility to the user. Still, schools continue to purchase stand-alone computers when handheld minicomputers have obvious advantages for many kinds of school learning. Even texting as a learning tool is virtually unexplored in many school districts.

Much has happened since the Internet became available in the United States in May 1995. For one thing, the sheer volume of information has become overwhelming. Organized knowledge is now doubling approximately every 100 days. Millions and millions of new webpages, as opposed to 120,000+ new book titles, appear each year. The average person in the United States is receiving almost 3,600 hours of data per year via television, radio, and computer. Eighty percent of information traveling over telephone lines is now data; 80% of telephone communication in 1990 was voice. In a nutshell, chasing information has become impossible (Thornburg, 2005).

The delivery of information into our schools, offices, and homes has become complex. Wider bandwidth digital subscriber lines (DSL) mean more data capacity and technological fusion of words, sounds, and pictures. Each day, 8 billion emails zip around the nation bringing pictures and voices from other computers, cell phones, and a host of wireless devices. Bandwidth is tripling every year, connectivity is increasing 10% a month, digital cameras are outselling conventional cameras, and there are 6 billion mobile phone users in the world (UN Telecom Report 2012). In 2012, over 2.3 billion persons (37% of world population) used the Internet worldwide. Each application of the new technologies is increasing the power to inform, influence, communicate, and educate.

We are leaving the silicon chip and approaching a future of magnetic memory, atomic memory, holographic memory, and then quantum computing (by 2025), which will be a billion times faster than the silicon chip. Experts say that we will be able to put the entire contents of the Library of Congress on a single 1-gram wafer and send it (bits, gigabits, multigigabits) anywhere in about a second. The capacity to make things small and fast is astounding (Thornburg, 2005).

An entire subculture of techies has sprung up in the United States, India, China, Russia, and around the world. These so-called neomillennials (children of the Internet age) are particularly adaptive to the change around us. For a few hundred dollars, any 10 year old can command technologies that cost billions to develop (Dede, 2005). They are wired, they are active, and they are frightening to those of us over 10! The Sun never sets on their new cyberspatial empire. Our children are out there on the new electronic frontier, especially after school is out.

In the short 20 years since the Internet appeared in the United States, our way of living has experienced significant change in the areas of acquiring information, buying and selling, work habits, basic communication, and mobility, to name a few. A systems break has occurred, and our ability to predict the future has become less reliable. Change seems to be the only constant in our lives. Worse, the experts tell us that there is more, much more, to come. Bill Gates (2005), whose name is synonymous with all that is the world of computers, predicts more change in the next 10 years than in the last 25 years.

Futurists and technologists are unified in describing the need for educating young people who will live and work 25 years from now. They use words like *impermanent, unlearning,* and *extrapolation* when speaking of knowledge. They project that a person's career will encompass 10 to 14 occupations in a lifetime, observing that the jobs that will be listed as the top 10 seven years from now do not yet exist. There will be workers who identify, solve, and broker problems by manipulating images; a project that sounds unsettling to those of us who still live in a physical world of freeways, workplaces, and biweekly paychecks.

The experts are in agreement that workers of the future will need new skills. They speak of systems thinking, collaboration, technical reading and writing, creating, being an entrepreneur, and contracting (electronically, of course) for jobs. Workers will need to be retrained in the latest technology throughout their lives. Technology will be a tool for using and integrating information. Education, as it exists, will be completely contextual rather than generic or holistic. It is, as they say, a whole new ballgame.

We could continue further on this theme, but the reader has probably concluded that defining education in terms of fixed knowledge delivered at a site called a school by a person called a teacher will be insufficient. Education throughout the world, a monopoly with an eroding base, will have to change and adapt if schools are to survive the next two decades (J. B. Williams & J. C. Williams, 2004). These conditions, problems, and needs will form the basis for future curriculum work in education. Although the past and the present are valuable guides to understanding the existing situation, they have seriously limited value in preparing for the future that is rushing toward us. A paradigm shift in education must occur if schools are to survive, and curriculum leadership must lead education to these new understandings. We are just now becoming aware of the connectedness of these new technologies to learning and, as such, they represent a fifth basis for curriculum planning in the 21st century.

A NEW GLOBAL AGE FOR CURRICULUM

The professional field of study known as *"Curriculum"* is nearly 100 years old, and for nearly a century curriculum development has been perceived as a kind of historical unfolding. Students of curriculum review ideas, writings, concepts, theories, model programs, research, and social events of the past in order to understand the present. Such references have also been used as a lens to project the future of education. The assumption has been (and still is) that the past and the present are the key to the future. Remarkably, all of that has seemed to change in only a decade.

As we settle comfortably into the 21st century, it is becoming obvious that what has transpired in education in the past century is no longer a certain or reliable guide to what is occurring in the present or what will happen in even the coming decade. As students and developers of curriculum, and as educators in general, we shall need some new frameworks to understand the changes around us; our old views are handicapping us in adjusting to the new age of interactive technologies.

In the final decade of the 20th century, the developed nations of the world experienced what 1960s futurist Kenneth Boulding called a "systems break." Boulding (1964) defined such breaks as the "dissolution of patterns of linear thinking or statistical series related to the activities of humankind" (p. 46). Such breaks, he observed, would divide human history into separate parts and introduce new eras for humankind. The break, an onset of many new interactive technologies, was most often described by the word *Internet*. Thomas Kuhn (1962) is credited with coining the word *paradigm* to explain the phenomenon. A paradigm, according to futurist Joel Barker (1993), is "a basic way of perceiving, thinking, valuing, and doing associated with a particular vision of reality" (pp. 16–19). Paradigms often exist unquestioned, and they define boundaries in fields of scholarship. In the field of curriculum, the old paradigm, which had been working just fine, saw education and schooling as synonymous. Education was going to school and learning predetermined and organized knowledge.

When the new information technology began to arrive in the mid-1990s, it was not generally perceived as a systems break or paradigm shift. Futurist Alvin Toffler, writing in his 1990 book *The Third Wave*, clearly recognized the onset of a new pattern:

> This wave is by far the most extreme and is very difficult to grasp at a comprehensible level. The one way to think about it is to imagine change in every aspect of your life . . . . This wave is marked by the benefit of massive gains in technology. These gains include things such as the unlimited availability of information, the creation of a new economic system, and changed social systems. The concept of work will change; workers can stay at home and work . . . large factories will succumb to technological advances . . . . The wave is marked by the emergence of new disciplines (of study) that were nonexistent twenty-five years ago; quantum electronics, molecular biology, nucleonics and others. (Toffler, 1970/1990, p. 15)

Another futurist, Kenneth Clark, once made the chilling observation that "under extreme conditions, prediction would become the most accurate indicator of future events" (as cited in Boulding, 1964, p. 30). Clark noted that "when a distinguished elder stated that something was possible he would be almost certainly right. When the same elder stated that something was impossible, he would very probably be wrong" (p. 30).

In the first dozen years of the 21st century, many educators continue to operate out of a 19th-century paradigm that holds that education is a process of becoming knowledgeable. By focusing on knowledge acquisition, in the form of courses and testing and credits, these educators completely missed what was transpiring in the world beyond schools. Knowledge, because it is fluid and overly plentiful, can no longer serve as the criterion for becoming educated. Everyone has knowledge, and more than they can use! Knowledge utilization or application, however, could easily become one of the major organizers of formal education. A review of what has happened with information technology in the last decade in the United States will sharpen our understanding of the changes we have experienced.

SCHOOLS RESPONDING

Given the knowledge presented in this chapter, it is clear that not all schools are reduced to thoughtful uncertainty. Over time, American schools have altered their curriculum in numerous ways to accommodate the changing social milieu, rush of knowledge, increased human capacities, understanding of learning, and the potential of communication technologies. In the following section, your author highlights 10 areas in which specific school programs have been developed to meet the changes in the school environment.

Nurturing Intellectual Competence

Modern constructivist views of the teaching–learning act hold that the child is an active participant in making sense of the world. From this vantage point, the world is a laboratory for all of us, and we bring to learning what we already know about life. Students are not empty minds to be filled; they are participants with background and prior knowledge. Possessing intellectual competence, from this perspective, is far more than just "knowing." Competence is defined by the utilization of what is known. Specific teaching strategies can help activate knowledge that the learner already possesses or is presently acquiring. Among the generic skills that assist a learner in becoming more intellectually competent are learning how to acquire new knowledge, consolidating what is already known, gaining deep or conceptual understandings, and seeing connectivity in information.

Learning to acquire new information is generally a process of taking what is known or is being learned and placing it in a context or construct that orders it. Inquiry-based approaches using questions or proofs generally force the student to fit information into preconceived theories or preconceptions. Although these fits may not be precise, they promote connecting knowledge.

Consolidating or placing knowledge is important for overcoming randomness in learning. Learning skills (such as diagramming sentences or doing math problems) and practice can routinize the act of consolidation. Learning to summarize or conceptualize knowledge is a type of shorthand for learning and is reinforced with practice, just as frequent reading makes one more proficient in reading.

Deep understanding is a conceptual level at which much information can be summarized by a thought or symbol that shapes the learning episode. Active learning (authentic) and problem-based learning both contribute to this deeper understanding. Such learning can especially help nonmainstream children whose view of life may already be heavily influenced by their parents' perceptions or previous experience.

Transfer or connectivity of information is the final subskill contributing to intellectual competence. This skill involves applying learning in one context to another context. Teacher modeling or suggestion plays a big role in this kind of learning. Teacher questions and activities structure such transfer of learning.

Transfer of Knowledge

Students are sent to school to learn ideas, to acquire skills, and to develop abilities that will serve them in life, not to pass a standardized test! During the past 100 years, numerous pedagogic approaches have been developed that reflect our best understanding about how to use knowledge. These practices must be applied in the classroom to make the standardized curriculum of value.

Among the best-known ideas in this regard are that knowledge cannot be too contextualized if transfer is to occur, that knowledge transfer is an active not a passive process, and that the design of instruction must reflect the notion that the child possesses previous knowledge. These three ideas can be illustrated in basic learning approaches that promote transfer of learning.

To help students overcome what is too often a totally contextualized environment in standards-based learning, teachers should allow them to practice retrieving information and forming that knowledge in their own words. Teachers should also encourage representing knowledge in alternative forms. To encourage students to participate actively, teachers should build on students' prior knowledge and background, infuse lessons with strategies for learning, and vary the conditions of learning. Because students are associative learners, teachers should use alternative assessments and emphasize skill development as well as knowledge acquisition.

Curriculum workers use these guidelines for modifying the standardized learning process to help teachers acquire the skills necessary to act differently in the standards-based classroom. Specific learning strategies for such a classroom would include the following areas:

Acceptance of Multiple Intelligences

Studies of effective leadership in industry suggest that future leaders will need to possess not only well-developed intellectual abilities but also equally impressive social and emotional skills to guide their organizations. Until recently, educators focused primarily on two types of intelligence, logical and linguistic, with almost no attention to other kinds of performance. In the standards-based era, this focus has been even tighter. Accepting the fact that there is more to education than "school smarts" is a first step in modifying the standards-based classroom.

The development of practical intelligence is highly relevant to adaptation, shaping, and selection in everyday life. Traditional theories of intelligence hold that "intelligence is a goal-directed mental activity marked by efficient problem solving, critical thinking, and effective abstract reasoning" (Thorndike, 1920). Sternberg (1997), speaking of emotional intelligence, defines human intelligence as the mental abilities necessary to adapt to, as well as to shape and select, any environment. Such noncognitive intelligence, including intrapersonal and interpersonal skills, may be more important for the future lives of students than traditional skills and knowledge taught in schools. Some research studies (Pool, 1997) suggest that up to 80% of a person's success in life is determined by emotional intelligence.

An example of such substantial research can be drawn from the Somerville Study, a 40-year longitudinal study of 450 boys who grew up in Somerville, Massachusetts. According to this study, conventional IQ had little to do with the success they experienced in life. What made the biggest difference were childhood abilities such as being able to handle frustration, control emotions, and get along with other people (Cherniss, 2000).

Another study of 300 top-level executives from 15 global companies found that six emotional competencies distinguished the stars from the average executive: influence, team leadership, organizational awareness, self-confidence, achievement drive, and leadership (Tucker, 2000). Other studies have shown that failure in leadership (attainment below expectation) is frequently attributed to the interpersonal and intrapersonal skills of the leader (Spencer, 1997).

Curriculum personnel in schools should become familiar with these and other studies that suggest that "knowing" is no longer the critical element. They must intercede to help teachers set up the correct environment, which consists of adult nurturing, healthy peer relationships, and sensitive and responsive support services. These climate factors mediate between the academic requirements and the motivation of students to use knowledge and apply skills after schooling. Students need opportunities to problem-solve with others and to examine what worked and what did not in such actions and collaborations. They need such introspection more than they need to master predetermined outcomes that are tested in schools.

Accepting multiple intelligences is the keystone to accepting diversity in our world. It is not difficult to argue that the increasingly global nature of business, the growing reliance on technology, and the cooperation needed to complete global projects call for future citizens who are capable of interacting and relearning. Figure 4.7 displays the nine intelligences proposed by Howard Gardner.

Understanding Learning Styles

Knowing about learning styles can help teachers become more sensitive to the differences students bring to the classroom. Such knowledge can also contribute to the design of meaningful learning experiences that meet student learning preferences. Knowing about learning styles can help teachers help poorly prepared students, those who most often drop out of school, and those who perform poorly on standardized tests.

Three types of style dominance found in the literature include visual dominance, auditory dominance, and spatial dominance. Visual learners acquire knowledge through a broad visual screen that can include teacher body language and facial expression. They prefer displays and illustrations, handouts, and multimedia sources such as the computer. Auditory learners do best in verbal lectures and discussions, by hearing what others say. The tone, pitch, and speed of the input are important to understanding. Tactile learners learn best by doing, by completing hands-on activities, and by interacting with the world around them. Such learners crave activity and movement.

Futurists tell us that new information in our lives today doubles about every 5 years. Teachers cannot base their practice on imparting information alone but must help students learn how to learn. Making learning natural by building on learners' strengths will help students become lifelong students of the changing world. Some students, for instance, like their learning concrete, or directed to their senses. Other students, who favor abstraction, like to conceive ideas and use intuition, looking beyond the present. Information may best be received as linear and piece-by-piece, or in chunks, according to the learning style of the student (Claxton & Murrell, 1988). A simple model would place all students in one of four patterns: concrete sequential, abstract and random, abstract sequential, or concrete random.

The bottom line on learning styles is that, when there is a mismatch between student learning style and teacher methods, students may become bored and listless, perform poorly on tests, get discouraged about the curriculum and their own capability, become hostile or unresponsive, and even drop out. A curriculum, even one teaching to a standards-based format, can be varied in its presentation format.

Curriculum Differentiation

Curriculum differentiation is a broad idea that addresses the need to tailor the classroom environment and instructional practices to create a unique learning experience for each child. This adaptation might include deleting material that is already mastered from the curriculum, adding content or skill practice to the existing curriculum, extending enrichment activities, allowing early entry into study areas, or writing units for groups of students with similar needs. Altering the environment or the process of learning, modifying the content, and tailoring evaluation products all would be considered differentiation.

The logic of differentiation can best be understood in terms of the range of learning in a single classroom. According to the rule of thumb, there is 1 year of range for each year in school (i.e., a 6-year range by sixth grade.) A typical seventh grade could have near nonreaders and college-level readers. A differentiated classroom seeks to tap into the readiness level, interests, and learning profile of each student with the goal of maximizing achievement. This strategy is quite different from insisting that all students master minimal-level skills and demonstrate them on a standardized test.

Tomlinson (1999) lists four characteristics of a differentiated classroom: Instruction is introduced at the conceptual level, with several avenues to mastery; assessment is flexible and found within the curriculum; grouping is flexible and changes as tasks change; and students are active participants. Instruction is characterized by abstraction, complexity, variety, and flexibility. In the classroom, one may see multilevel texts, learning contracts, group investigation, Internet use, and interest centers.

Is there a conflict between this type of teaching and standards? Most standards are not finite points to be memorized but consist of skills such as problem solving or using information. These skills can be demonstrated at many levels of competence and therefore can be learned at many levels of abstraction. There is simply no evidence that treating all students alike promotes achievement or standards mastery.

Cooperative Learning

Interacting with others cooperatively is an obviously needed skill in the present century. Work, communication, travel, and education all demand various forms of cooperation. The cooperative learning methodology found in schools since the 1980s is an invaluable tool in the age of standards-based education. As a method, cooperative learning is a carefully structured procedure in which students are held accountable for individual contribution to a group project. Various designs teach that the group as a whole is stronger than the sum of its individual members. Positive interdependence is structured by having mutual goals, shared resources, and assigned roles.

Examples of skills taught through cooperative projects are joint planning, decision making, deferring judgment, consensus building, listening, formulating good questions, learning to ask for help or give assistance, giving and receiving directions, and sharing materials. All these skills are needed in the everyday work world.

Supplementing intellectual growth with both social and personal development pays long-term dividends in knowledge utilization. Group assignments, for instance, help students combine prior knowledge with new knowledge, and re-form knowledge based on new input.

The various common models of cooperative learning such as jigsaw, group investigation, think-pair-share, or teams-and-games allow individual student learning styles to be integrated into the classroom. Research by Slavin indicates that simply grouping the middle and the upper classes of students will produce achievement as high as that achieved by the upper-level students alone (Slavin 1991).

Interdisciplinary Learning

The explosion of knowledge, increased state mandates for specific information to be taught, concerns about curriculum relevancy, and the lack of meaningful connections among school subjects have produced an artificial curriculum in schools. Interdisciplinary learning can provide a context for standards-based instruction. Global interdependence and the interconnectedness of complex systems compel curriculum leaders to find some way to pull these disparate elements together.

Interdisciplinary learning, sometimes called *integrated study*, occurs when students explore knowledge as related to certain aspects of their environment. Cutting across traditional subject areas and organized around real-life themes, the curriculum is meaningfully associated with the broad goals of education. Such content-rich and skill-rich curricula develop a learner's power to create new models, systems, and structures. Interdisciplinary instruction prepares students for lifelong learning.

Problem-Based Learning

Schools are moving the curriculum toward the application of knowledge using problem-based learning (PBL). These curricula purposefully create scenarios and ill-structured problems based on desired curriculum outcomes (skills, knowledge). The student is led to actively define the problem and construct potential solutions.

Effective problem solving is a goal of almost every standards-based document (SCANS, for example), and most district goal statements allude to the need for critical-thinking and problem-solving skills (California Frameworks in Math and Science).

Producing effective problem solvers in the new information age is a primary goal of education.

Students working in PBL environments learn to define problems clearly, develop alternative hypotheses, access and evaluate data, alter hypotheses to accommodate new data, develop solutions that specifically fit problems, and so forth. The Internet is a perfect connector of the problem and the information that can serve as a solution. The imperfect problems, and the imperfect solutions developed by students using PBL, mirror the real world in which we live.

Mentoring

Mentoring programs come in all shapes and sizes, with the most common being a way of assisting poor learners in elementary and middle schools. Another is to have adults as work partners in a problem-based curriculum. Adult mentors can provide a time perspective to tasks as well as involve the community with the school and its students.

The world outside school operates much differently than that inside a school. Real-world problems and solutions are often moral dilemmas calling for choices and compromise. The real world is more technological than the school world and a lot more interdependent. Values often define choices in the real world, and such values are often the result of long-term experience.

Mentors who have undergone training are usually good listeners. They can dedicate time to helping students see relationships, and they serve as extensions of the student into the outside adult population. They are usually willing to share their life experiences and are sometimes open to learning new things themselves. Most mentors like young persons, and they are volunteering their most valuable commodity—time.

Service Learning

New on the scene is something called *service learning,* which in another time might have been called *community work.* Service work connects classroom learning to real-world experiences and makes students more aware of their surroundings. Research suggests that service learning can make a student more altruistic and caring. The development of interpersonal skills through service-learning projects cannot be overstated. Research suggests fewer disciplinary referrals, higher trust of adults, and a greater acceptance of cultural diversity (Billing, 2000).

There is significant evidence to suggest that students who participate in service-learning activities show gains on achievement tests in reading and basic skills and earn higher grade point averages. Schools using service learning on a regular basis report higher attendance and stronger student motivation. The impact on communities where service learning has become part of the curriculum is positive. In these environments, students are perceived as valued resources and contributing members of the community.

In summary, curriculum work in a standards-based era is not just about high-stakes testing. Knowledge acquisition or skill development alone is not adequate preparation for the rapidly changing world of the 21st century. Your author believes that the role of curriculum workers is to enliven state-mandated or national standards curriculum by working directly with teachers in the classroom. Accepting the notion of multiple intelligences; understanding learning styles; differentiating curriculum delivery; employing cooperative learning in classrooms; using interdisciplinary teaching, problem-based learning, and mentoring; and using the community for service learning can all direct standards toward utilization.

Curriculum Assessment

Given these many new approaches to "teaching and reaching" students, the concept of curriculum assessment has become important for the sake of accountability. Curriculum assessment, or curriculum-based assessment (CBA), means "measurement (observing and recording) of student performance as a basis for making instructional decisions." Undergirding the concept of curriculum assessment is the idea that what is being taught should be what is tested—direct and repeated assessment of academic target behaviors.

In curriculum assessment, student responses are measured for speed and proficiency. From these data, proficiency or performance criteria are established to determine acceptable levels of student mastery. A checklist, or rubric, is developed by the teacher and is used to assess student work. Finally, these student results are used by the teacher to plan further instruction.

In the word of Grant Wiggins (*Understanding by Design*), "Teachers adopt a practice of beginning with what they want a student to do and then create assessments, lessons, units, and the curriculum accordingly." Using such assessment, regardless of the instructional design, allows both teacher and student to communicate clearly on what is to be learned.

The most common type of student assessments are performance, projects, and portfolios. Performance assessments tend to be dominated by real tasks conducted by students or short-answer or extended answer exams based on that student work. Projects are designed to measure skills learned by the student. Portfolios are collections of student work, often selected by the student. The state of Vermont has adopted the portfolio approach statewide.

OLD ISSUES, NEW IMPEDIMENTS

Obviously, many choices face those who plan educational programs, wherever they might be, and these choices address major issues reflecting bedrock values. The scope of school programs, their purpose and organization, the focus of their delivery, and many other issues remain largely unanswered. Contrast the following list of questions compiled by Thomas Briggs in 1926 with those being asked today:

1. What are the desired ends of education?
2. What is the good life?
3. To what extent shall education modify the character and actions of future citizens?
4. For what ends are the schools responsible?
5. What subject areas are most vital in attaining these ends? (p. 20)

Questions such as these encourage, as they always have, debate, inquiry, and experimentation in education. Curriculum has developed as a field of inquiry to study such issues and to translate what is learned into viable educational programs. In the new age of technology, it is vital that curriculum personnel continue in this role of questioner.

Specifically, 21st-century curriculum developers must begin thinking of a curriculum beyond knowledge acquisition and beyond school buildings. We must begin considering a global or international curriculum that does not recognize nation-state boundaries. We must think of a curriculum tied to work and living applicable to all persons and all ages. What is keeping us from this most important task? Here are some answers to that question:

- The absence of clear goals
- The unpredictable entry of power sources from outside
- The consistent dependence on money as the moving force
- The absence of systems thinking in problem solving
- The operational orientation to the present rather than the future
- The incomplete linkage to vital information and research
- The inadequate training of curriculum leaders

Your author believes that curriculum developers should provide active leadership by being both dynamic and intellectual and by achieving a global orientation to education. Bruce Joyce (1990) provides the strongest argument against the all-too-familiar traditional posture of maintenance in curriculum work:

> In the past, educational planners have been technically weak (unable often to clarify ends or engineer means) and morally or technically unable to bring about a humanistic revolution in education . . . curriculum workers have defined themselves as helpers, not leaders, letting the community and teachers make decisions and then assisting in the implementation of those decisions.
>
> By focusing on only schools and teachers in schools, curriculum is currently being forced to operate within the parameters of the institution . . . By far the most paralyzing effect of the assumptive world in which the curriculum specialist lives is that it tends to filter out all ideas which might improve education but which fit awkwardly into the school pattern. (p. 7)

The perception of a curriculum specialist as a thinker, designer, leader, and projectionist goes back to the writings of John Dewey, George Counts, and other progressives of the early 20th century. Counts, for instance, observed that "the goals of education must be determined by philosophical and analytical concepts of the good life" (as cited in Schaefer, 1972). Among those persons perceiving curriculum development as a dynamic operation, there is a great fear that the gravitational pull of bureaucracy in education has won out. With each consolidation of schools, with each new piece of legislation, with each new regulation, with each standard and test, the school becomes more closed to change, more self-perpetuating, and more product-oriented.

Ultimately, the choices and decisions related to the selection, activation, and evaluation of educational designs are normative matters. Before educational planners can be effective and consistent in their work, they must understand their own personal belief systems and formulate a philosophy of education that complements that system. The following chapter introduces some established philosophies of education and assists you in determining your priorities for education.

Summary

Curriculum planning rests on assumptions about people, learning, and other realities. Workers in curriculum rely on data from five key areas in planning school programs: our society, the world of knowledge, human development research, learning theory, and communication technology. These data support certain beliefs and approaches regarding planning curriculum experiences.

Changes in our world during the past quarter century are disrupting old ways of thinking about schools and planning curriculum. These "paradigm shifts" are forcing changes on schools and new programs are being developed worldwide to accommodate these events.

Activities

ACTIVITY 3.1

React to the following statement regarding the use of knowledge as the basis of curriculum.

> There is no way that the instantaneous retrieval of all information can be filtered or controlled. The boundaries of our understanding, in all fields, have been overrun; there is neither scope nor sequence to the new information age. In addition, the multimedia integration of concepts, facts, images, data, and sound create meanings in ways that even Marshall McLuhan and Quentin Fiore (1967) could not have envisioned. We are awash in knowledge, and there is no end in sight to the avalanche of new information.

ACTIVITY 3.2

Your author has suggested adding a fifth planning foundation, technology, for curriculum work in the 21st century. How would this latest "basis of planning" affect the other four traditional foundations? For example, how would technology affect learning?

 Click here to take an automatically-graded self-check quiz.

Additional Reading

Drake, S. (2012). Creating *standards-based integrated curriculum*. Thousand Oaks, CA: Corwin Press.

Gladwell, M. (2008). *Outliers: Story of success*. London: Little, Brown and Company.

Jacobs, H. (2010). *Curriculum 21: Essential education for a changing world*. Alexandria, VA: ASCD.

Mcmillan, J. (2010). *Classroom assessments*. Upper Saddle River, NJ: Pearson Education.

Oliva, P. (2013). *Developing the curriculum* (8th ed.). Boston, MA: Allyn and Bacon.

Ornstein, A. (2012). *Curriculum foundations, principles and issues* (6th ed.). Upper Saddle River, NJ: Pearson Education.

Steyer, J. (2003). *The other parent: The inside story of the media's effect on our children*. New York, NY: Atria Publishing.

4

Large Scale Curriculum Development

Learning Outcome

- To understand the scale dimensions of curriculum planning

Curriculum development is, at its best, a comprehensive process that (1) facilitates an analysis of purpose, (2) designs a program or event, (3) implements a series of related activities, and (4) aids in the evaluation of this process. At its worst, curriculum development accomplishes none of these four activities. Clearly, there are basic tasks that distinguish quality curriculum work from accidental instructional change. It is also evident that modern curriculum development involves much more than implementing a new course of study or simply adding a set of new standards. Curriculum planning is complex.

Curriculum development at the national, state, or district level should proceed in a deductive manner using an if-then logic (see Figure 4.1). The initial step in large-scale curriculum work is to clarify the purpose of the planned change which involves, first, identifying a philosophy (see Chapter 2) and then deducing appropriate goals and objectives for any project (see Chapter 3). Once this framework for program development is established, an assessment of need is conducted to sharpen the focus in terms of the target of any change. Finally, the intended curriculum should be analyzed through a mapping-out process, and the instructional activities ordered and aligned with major learning standards for maximum effect. The curriculum development process strives to attain a near perfect correspondence between the intention and the outcome of instruction.

As we will see in this chapter, curriculum development may proceed without some of these time-tested structures. The United States is currently pursuing massive

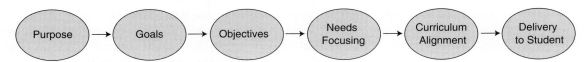

FIGURE 4.1 **Tasks for Curriculum Development.**

changes to its overall school curriculum without a thorough analysis, a comprehensive needs assessment, an overall design, or any kind of objective progress assessment for the effort. For the past 50 years, America has been pursuing a standardized curriculum for all students using political persuasion, law, and money to promote desired changes.

FIFTY YEARS OF LEGISLATED CURRICULUM CHANGE

Significant standards-based curriculum reform has been ongoing in the United States for half a century (1965–2015). While a large number of other change efforts have addressed innovation to meet the challenges of our changing society, the constant theme from 1965–2015 has been the standardization of the school curriculum. New teachers and curriculum leaders will find that this perspective explains much of what is currently in progress in our schools.

A logical point of origin for general understanding of the present is the Elementary and Secondary Education Act of 1965. ESEA (Public Law 89-10) that was enacted by Congress as part of President Lyndon Johnson's "Great Society Initiative." This act required the first learning standards in all schools receiving federal funds, and it set the tone for all subsequent state reforms. Reauthorized by Congress on several occasions, ESEA is the most far-reaching federal legislation affecting education, and has served as the primary source of funding for recent reform initiatives such as "No Child Left Behind" (2002) and, tangentially, the "Common Core State Standards" (2009).

In 1983 the federal government published a report of the National Commission on Excellence in Education entitled *A Nation at Risk: The Imperative for Educational Reform.* An 18-member blue-ribbon panel of educators and elected officials examined the quality of elementary and secondary public education in the United States and found a "rising tide of mediocrity" that threatened the nation's future.

In support of their conclusions, the commissioners presented numerous indicators of risk, including Americans' poor academic performance relative to students in other nations, high levels of "functional" illiteracy among U.S. adults and 17 year olds, and declining achievement-test scores on national and international "normed" tests. The commissioners also cited increasing enrollments in college remedial courses, increasing business and military expenditures on remedial education, and a diluted curriculum in the schools. They detailed low expectations for student performance and college admissions, less time devoted to instruction and homework, and poor-quality teaching and teacher preparation.

The national commission called for a renewed public commitment to excellence and education reform anchored in higher expectations for all students. Specifically, the commission recommended tougher high school graduation requirements, rigorous and measurable standards of student performance and conduct, more time devoted to learning, better classroom teaching and teacher preparation, more effective leadership at the school level and, where appropriate, greater fiscal support. The report A Nation at Risk initiated several dozen follow-up reports from various commissions, business groups, and philanthropic organizations criticizing the current education system. This public dialogue about school quality stimulated state action and legislation for education reform.

During the mid-1980s, the National Council of Teachers of Mathematics (NCTM) produced the first educational standards by content specialists. These math standards were soon followed by standards in other subject areas by professional organizations. A framework of recommended content was established.

A Governor's Education Summit in 1989, headed by future President Bill Clinton of Arkansas produced the first set of national Educational Goals (Goals 2000) and these were quickly re-enacted in many states. In Florida, for example, the Goals 2000 document became the Florida Sunshine State Standards. Other states also created a similar set of state-level goals.

In 1990, the United States Secretary of Labor appointed a blue-ribbon commission, the Secretary's Commission on Achieving Necessary Skills (SCANS), to gather proposals from the business sector for schools. The Commission suggested five areas of competency found that might serve as a framework for a new curriculum in our United States' schools. Goals 3 and 5 were given particular emphasis by the SCANS commission (see Figure 4.2):

> American students will leave grades four, eight, and twelve having demonstrated competency in challenging subject matter including English, mathematics, and science . . . and every school in America will ensure that all students use their minds well, so they may be prepared for responsible citizenship . . . and employment in our Nation's modern economy. Every adult American will be literate and will possess the knowledge and skills necessary to compete in a global economy.

By the early 1990s, leading states began legislating powerful levers to encourage school reform. Public reporting requirements of school performance, grade level performance tests, fiscal rewards for exemplary performance, and even sanctions and state interventions for failing schools. This sort of carrot-and-stick method of encouraging change worked quite well in promoting state-level development.

During the period 1995–2010, major change occurred in what was studied and tested in schools. As early as 1998, the District of Columbia and 48 states had instituted some type of testing program for schoolchildren, and many of those states had also adopted a standards-based curriculum. By 2000, more than 20 states had developed progression testing around grades 4, 8, and 10 and an assessment of competency to graduate from high school. New institutions, such as school site councils, charter schools, and school vouchers appeared as a reflection of the changing educational landscape. The driving force for such change was politics, law, and money.

What started as a simple demand for performance and cost accountability soon became an avalanche of curriculum reform in every state of our nation. During the 1990s, the standards movement stimulated change in the very infrastructure of our schools. Rigorous academic course standards were developed, new performance testing programs were instituted, and an extensive engineering of the new curriculum was demanded by state legislatures. In a nutshell, the curriculum of public school education in the United States was substantially redesigned by non-educators, politicians and businessmen, and often without significant input from any curriculum personnel or school leaders. Jumping over any analysis or design stages, the new programs went straight to the full implementation stage; a classic error in any curriculum work.

Resources: Identifies, organizes, plans, and allocates resources
    A. *Time*—Selects goal-relevant activities, ranks them, allocates time, and prepares and follows schedules
    B. *Money*—Uses or prepares budgets, makes forecasts, keeps records, and makes adjustments to meet objectives
    C. *Material and facilities*—Acquires, stores, allocates, and uses materials or space efficiently
    D. *Human resources*—Assesses skills and distributes work accordingly, evaluates performance and provides feedback

Interpersonal: Works with others
    A. *Participates as member of a team*—Contributes to group effort
    B. *Teaches others new skills*
    C. *Serves clients/customers*—Works to satisfy customers' expectations
    D. *Exercises leadership*—Communicates ideas to justify position, persuades and convinces others, responsibly challenges existing procedures and policies
    E. *Negotiates*—Works toward agreements involving exchange of resources, resolves divergent interests
    F. *Works with diversity*—Works well with men and women from diverse backgrounds

Information: Acquires and uses information
    A. *Acquires and evaluates information*
    B. *Organizes and maintains information*
    C. *Interprets and communicates information*
    D. *Uses computers to process information*

Systems: Understands complex interrelationships
    A. *Understands systems*—Knows how social, organizational, and technological systems work and operates effectively with them
    B. *Monitors and corrects performance*—Distinguishes trends, predicts impacts on system operations, diagnoses deviations in system's performance, and corrects malfunctions
    C. *Improves or designs systems*—Suggests modifications to existing systems and develops new or alternative systems to improve performance

Technology: Works with a variety of technologies
    A. *Selects technology*—Chooses procedures, tools, or equipment including computers and related technologies
    B. *Applies technology to task*—Understands overall intent and proper procedures for setup and operation of equipment
    C. *Maintains and troubleshoots equipment*—Prevents, identifies, or solves problems with equipment, including computers and other technologies

FIGURE 4.2 Five Competencies of SCANS.

Source: "What Work Require of Schools." SCANS Report for America 2000. U.S. Department of Labor, June 1991.

For the first time in our nation's history, the curriculum content that all children would master in school was explicitly spelled out in detail by state-level legislation. The energy and enthusiasm behind these changes is evident in the words of then–California state superintendent Delaine Eastin (1998):

> We intend to completely align state efforts to these standards, including statewide testing programs, curriculum frameworks, instructional materials, professional development, pre-service education, and compliance reviews. We will see a generation of educators who think of standards not as a new layer but as the foundation itself.

In a flurry of political activity, state legislatures mandated learning standards, and state departments of education (SDOE) sponsored the creation of new curriculum and standardized tests. In the national press there were continuous efforts to use international testing results to compare and contrast American students with other students worldwide. The largest single study of this type was the Third International Mathematics and Science Study (TIMSS 1995), which looked at academic performance of some 40 countries. Other studies, conducted by the International Association for the Evaluation of Educational Achievement (IEA), found the United States lacking compared with other industrialized nations such as Japan or Germany.

> Curriculum experts and researchers like Berliner and Biddle (*The Manufactured Crisis*, 1996) protested the gross manipulation of such data. How could the efforts in such unlike cultures be compared; it was a matter of apples and oranges. The public, unclear of the issues being debated, opted for the easy path of reduced costs and a simplification of the curriculum issues.

In 1994, the U.S. Congress re-authorized the Elementary and Secondary Education Act with a special provision that required all states to have a triad of standards for school subjects including:

1. Content standards
2. Performance standards
3. Content aligned assessments for all students

In 2001 the 107th Congress of the United States once again re-authorized ESEA, this time renaming the general legislation "No Child Left Behind." This Act purported to finally "close the achievement gap in America with accountability, flexibility, and choice, so that no child is left behind." In the many provisions, NCLB set strict expectations for achievement for all students. The premise for this standards-based reform legislation was that "setting high standards and establishing measurable goals can improve individual student outcomes in education." The NCLB Act, which became law in 2002, mandated immediate testing in math and reading and required all states to finally close the achievement gap for all students by 2014.

A controversial part of NCLB was that of required reporting of Adequate Yearly Progress (AYP). Schools that did not show regular projected growth by its students on performance tests could be penalized. After five years of low performance, schools could even be closed, turned into charter schools, or taken over and run by the state. All students were expected to achieve legislated learning standards.

NCLB, the educational centerpiece of the George W. Bush presidency, concluded in late 2007 and was renewed and supplemented by a new kind of incentive program under newly elected President Barack Obama called "Race to the Top" (RTTT). This 4.35 billion dollar program, using economic Recovery Funds, was announced in the summer of 2009, and like earlier legislation it vigorously promoted educational standards. The program rewarded states and school districts for encouraging certain targeted goals such as better teacher training (teaching standards), developing curriculum standards and assessments (the Common Core), and encouraging charter schools (school choice). Of particular importance to today's curriculum development efforts, RTTT made it mandatory that for any state to apply for a grant, it had to first adopt the Common Core State Standards that were still under development. Adjusting to the August 2010 deadline, 46 states initially signed on to adopt CCSS.

THE COMMON CORE STATE STANDARDS

Extending the RTTT is a new curriculum development initiative proposed by the National Governors Association (NGA) and the Council of Chief State School Officer's (CCSSO). Citing a report entitled "Ready or Not: Creating a High School Diploma That Counts" (2004), these two political leadership groups advocated an educational experience designed for both college and job readiness. Guiding standards, they stated, should be "robust and relevant to the real world, reflecting the knowledge and skills that our young people need for success in college and careers." As noted, states and the District of Columbia signed on to this initiative, pledging to use the adopted "common standards" as the basis for the development of their state curricula standards, thereby having the effect of nationalizing the curriculum. These standards, released in 2012, are currently available in mathematics and English-language arts only; the two most commonly tested areas of the curriculum.

Also noted above, states were required to adopt these internationally benchmarked standards that prepare students for success in order to be eligible for Race to the Top grants. The initial round of applications and awards for RTTT grants saw only 11 states receive grants, and it was unsatisfying to some states who held that first-round grants were distributed politically rather than on merit. The State of Texas withdrew from participation citing a growing federal control of education. Virginia withdrew citing a lack of quality in the Common Core Standards. Alaska and Nebraska failed to sign on to the Common Core, and Minnesota joined only for the English/language arts standards. Recently (2013), state legislatures in Georgia and Kansas were considering legislation to force withdrawal from the Common Core requirements.

Also unusual, and highly controversial, was a significant amount of additional funding available to some organizations, states, and districts by the Gates Foundation, Charles Stewart Mott Foundation, Pearson Education Foundation, and the federal government contributions for partial implementation of the Common Core Standards and various pilot curriculum and assessments. Business, as well as politics, law, and money, was now driving large-scale curriculum development in the United States.

THE COMMON CORE

The transition from No Child Left Behind (NCLB) to Race to the Top (RTTT) and then to the new Common Core State Standards has been gradual (2002–2012) and often times confusing. Standards developed under NCLB (the old ESEA 1965) became the benchmarks for funding under RTTT. The Race to the Top legislation forced states to endorse a Common Core of standards in order to apply for funding. While an optimist might describe this as a "seamless" transition (ESEA >NCLB >RTTT > CCSS), the steps have been calculated by power groups in the United States and have been extremely stressful for districts and schools that were forced by state Departments of Education to implement a flurry of mandates (see Figure 4.3).

In theory, the Common Core K-12 standards are needed in order to insure that all students, no matter where they live, are prepared for success in post-secondary education and/or in the workforce. The standards will provide greater clarity in what is expected of all students, and establish a kind of staircase to college and career readiness. The standards will also help insure a smooth transition when students change schools in our highly mobile society. CCSS should allow states, districts, and individual schools to experience a more simple process in developing curriculum (materials and assessments). Finally, the CCSS will demand a more complex level of reading, thinking, speaking, and writing of all students.

It is important to note that the Common Core is not a curriculum, per se, but rather a brand new "bottom up" design to boost achievement in our schools. It builds on the best of existing state standards and lessons from other nations with high performance in test taking (Norway, Singapore, Korea). In its development, the Common Core has drawn on the expertise of teachers, researchers, and subject-matter professional associations to create the best possible roadmap to success. Most development of the Common Core occurred from 2009–2011, and the official Common Core Standards were unveiled in 2012. The summary standards (final version) will be available to students "on line" by the 2014–2015 school year.

Following widespread observations in the media that the old curriculum (pre-1990s) in the United States was both shallow and superficial, these new standards recommend less topical coverage and more time to master the content. "Teaching less and learning more" is the new political slogan and the suggested path. Students will gain conceptual understanding, perceptual skill and fluency, and make personal applications of subject content. It is recommended, in CCSS documents, that students spend at least three fourths of their time experiencing a focused, coherent, and rigorous procedure of learning. Exactly what that new procedure will be is not described.

High yield	ESEA	Meaningful discourse	Rich conversations
Value added	Rollout	Capacity building	Scalable
Ramp-up	Frameworks	Unpacking	RTTT
EOY	Best practice	Strategic approach	Authentic understanding
Big Tent emphasis	CCSSI	NGA	PARCC
NCLB	Rigor	District infrastructure	Transparent

FIGURE 4.3   Common Core Bingo – The New Language of Reform

The differences between this latest large-scale curriculum effort and other previous large-scale attempts in the United States to upgrade the curriculum are:

1. This effort is state led and implemented locally. It is not a national mandate (although the federal government is a major funding source).
2. This effort has the support of a wide range of organizations: the PTA, National School Boards Association, American Association of School Administrators, National Governors Association, NEA, and American Federation of Teachers.
3. This effort to develop the common standards has been endorsed by 46 states and will be a consistent platform across all states.
4. In this effort, the Common Core addresses only two subjects, English/language arts (ELA), and math.

It is important for the reader to understand that these standards cannot, by themselves, raise student achievement. Likewise, the standards can't make all students learn. The impact of these common standards will be only as good as the states and school districts defining the new curriculum and the classroom teachers who implement the new standards in their classroom. The implementation of the CCSS will be, necessarily, uneven across the 46 states.

Widespread concern about the low quality of standards and performance in some states led to the call for adopting Common Core State Standards (CCSS). The development of these standards began in earnest in 2009 with a federal grant to the National Governor's Association Center for Best Practices (NGA Center) and the Council of Chief State School Officers (CCSSO) made up of Commissioners of Education in each state. The new common standards were developed in mathematics and English language arts and provided a clear and consistent understanding of what was expected of students. Six criteria define the standards in all states:

- Aligned with college and work experience
- Clear, understandable, and consistent
- Based on rigorous content and knowledge applied through higher-order skills
- Built on the strengths and lesson of current state standards
- Informed by other top performing countries
- Evidence based.

The Common Core Standards are not magical but rather outline a "new way" of mastering a subject. For instance, only eight areas comprise the math standards for mathematical practice:

1. Make sense of problems and persevere in solving them.
2. Reason abstractly and quantitatively.
3. Construct visible arguments and critique the reasoning of others.
4. Model with mathematics.
5. Use appropriate tools strategically.
6. Attend to precision.
7. Look for and make use of structure.
8. Look for and express regularity in repeated reasoning.

CCSS is something of a "work in progress" in most states. There are also two multi-state consortia that are engaged in developing computer-based assessments for the CCSS and these are projected to be ready by 2014–2015. Best known of these consortia is the PARCC group (partnership for assessment of readiness for college and career) that includes states in the eastern half of the continental United States In the western United States, the consortia is called the Smarter Balanced Assessment Consortia (SBAC).

The PARCC role "is to develop model content frameworks to "bridge" the gap between the CCSS and the assessments of progress." The PARCC assessment systems will be developed to measure knowledge, skills, and understanding essential to achieving college and career success. SBAC differs from PARCC only in a more flexible definition of test performance.

Finally, and unusual in the United States, there is private funding from the Bill and Melinda Gates Foundation (76 million dollars from 2009–2011) and from the Pearson Education Foundation that is currently providing momentum to what constitutes the most massive effort ever to change America's school curriculum. These contributions from industry, mentioned previously, are highly controversial in ways to be discussed below.

Also unique is the fact that the Common Core addresses high-level skills and standards whereas the No Child Left Behind addressed minimal learning standards for all students. The Common Core is a product of the individual states and not a direct federal education mandate, and implementation of the Common Core will be the responsibility of each individual state. The federal government is contributing financially to the Common Core development. The completed assessment system for evaluating student progress, in place by the 2014–2015 school year, will feature both Performance-Based Student Assessment (PBA) and End of the Year (EOY) student assessments.

DISCUSSION

Not everyone is equally excited about the new Common Core; only 45 states, 3 territories, and the District of Columbia have fully adopted all of them. Texas, Alaska, Virginia, and Nebraska have rejected participation and Minnesota has adopted only the English standards of the Common Core. In spite of the possibility of losing significant RTTT grant funding, several other states have voiced concern about participating in the CCSS due to the high cost of abandoning their current learning standards and adopting the CCSS. California, for example, will pay nearly 1.6 billion dollars of their public tax dollars to drop their existing standards and adopt the Common Core. Texas, a state that did not join other states in adopting the CCSS, estimated a three billion dollar price tag "to go digital" (buy equipment needed to participate) using CCSS. A 2012 study by the Pioneer Institute estimates that the total cost for implementation of the Common Core in all participating states would be 15.9 billion over the next seven years including a whopping 5.3 billion for the re-training of classroom teachers. Currently, the federal government contributes about 1 billion a year to local districts for teacher training.

Since only 11 states were given grants in the first round of RTTT funding, other states unsupported by RTTT funding may also find the price simply too high to continue to implement the standards. States, and local districts, must individually consider the ultimate cost of developing new curricula, developing new learning materials, purchasing technology, conducting additional professional development and developing new teacher evaluation systems.

In reality, there is not even a clear philosophical consensus behind the multi-state efforts to make the Common Core a reality. Splinter groups in various states, and within the two multi-state consortia, do not agree in the "focus of the curriculum standards." The reader will also note that the Common Core, by using a "consistent progression of learning" approach, requires both schools and teachers to practice a highly traditional learning approach (see description of Structured Learning in Chapter 2). The many creative ways of teaching mathematics, and learning to read, are challenged by the format of the CC standards and their assessment. And, ultimately, it is the classroom teacher who will make the decisions about what the Common Core will actually be. Teachers are always the final filters in curriculum work.

Finally, in the case of Virginia, there is simple professional doubt that these new standards are as useful as their own state learning standards that have been in place since 1995. Virginia standards, dating to their Standards of Quality (1972), have long been a model in the United States and the legislature of that state has chosen to keep their tried and true approach rather than gamble on a new one. In other states, there have been observations that the common set of standards could possibly drive out other curriculum innovation and even curtail regular curriculum development in areas not tested. This "skewing" or unbalancing of the curriculum has been a recurring problem in states with strong assessment/testing schedules.

There are some educators who feel that the Bill and Melinda Gates Foundation has been given far too much power and influence in the implementation of the CCSS because of their generous donations to the development of various parts of the CCSS conversion. One Georgia educator described the Gates monies as "turning our schools into kill-and-drill testing factories." The Bill and Melinda Gates Foundation, officially, is dedicated to "creating a full service digital instructional resource network for America," including four free prototype courses and teacher training for schools.

Like the Gates monies, the Pearson Education Foundation funds are being used to develop 24 model courses, covering math in grades K–10 and English in grades 3–12. Some educators have observed that Pearson Education will be the first resource districts will reach for when they begin to redesign their local curriculum to comply with the Common Core. Panic-purchasing of the available Pearson materials by school districts under deadlines in 2014–15 is a real probability in some states.

It is noteworthy that in 2001, Gates, Pearson, and several proprietary schools including the University of Phoenix, combined forces to capture much of the huge online college market in America and abroad. With each U.S. public school pupil valued at $10,615 (2013), it is no wonder the motives of these corporations are being questioned. To have the largest software corporation in the world and the largest publisher and distributor of learning materials in the world combining to lead America to the CCSS and a new age of online curriculum and assessment should be an area of concern for every education leader.

Some educators believe that not enough research has been conducted to attempt a project of this scale. Critics have even suggested that the business interests have featured research in their studies that only define learning effectiveness as only the ability to increase test scores. Tom Loveless, of the prestigious Brookings Institute, has questioned whether there is any connection whatsoever between learning standards and test achievement, noting that the states with the most highly developed learning standards in the United States have some of the lowest achievement in our nation. Also, says

Loveless, schools and districts in some states have been operating under common standards for years without result.

For your author, the real concern with CCSS is the lack of regular curriculum planning that has characterized the large-scale projects like NCLB, RTTT, and Common Core. Political slogans and ideas are being implemented at full speed through state laws drafted without adequate planning data. For example, do we know that all schools and district have the hardware to go "digital" in 2014–2015? No individual, or agency, or foundation has the entire picture in mind regarding the CCSS, or even a clear idea of how and in what order the parts of the puzzle fit (called *staging* in the curriculum literature). Schools and districts are currently following the money in order to comply with the new laws.

Ultimately, after the enabling funds run out, local districts, schools, and classroom teachers will be responsible for finishing a job that will be perceived by many as "just one more thing to do." The real educators will be asked to repair the new and unfinished curriculum while they are still flying the old school curriculum. And, if these educators fail to implement the Common Core Standards, without adequate time and budgets, they will be once again perceived as incompetent by the organizations that have launched these mandates. In some states, failure to succeed will lead to charter school initiatives.

It is, as always, vitally important to engage classroom teachers in the planning and implementation of the Common Core. According to one survey of some 12,000 math teachers, (Schmidt and Burroughs, 2012) 80% of the teachers think that the new CCSS standards are "pretty much the same" as previous standards. In a survey of just elementary teachers, the same researchers found less than one-half felt well prepared to teach Common Core Standards at their grade level. Obviously, a great deal of work must be done, and quickly.

Particularly disturbing to your author, from a curriculum planning perspective, is the action in his home state of Florida, where the legislature mandated by statute that the 2015 deadline for all schools to implement the CCSS will coincide with a date (2015) when no additional state funding will be available for textbooks. Classroom learning, says the Florida legislature, will be completely digital by 2015, "and failure is not an option." Other state legislatures are passing equally risky education laws.

The general English/language arts standards of the CCSS rest on a basic assumption that the subject skills will also be taught and reinforced in history, social studies, sciences and technical subjects. How this will be done is unknown at the time of this writing; there is no planning for this assumed responsibility of having high school teachers reinforce the teaching of English. There are five key components in English/language arts: reading, writing, speaking and listening, language, and media/technology. All components are lightly defined for implementation, and there is progressive development in each of the areas.

In the mathematics standards, there is also light definition. For instance, the eight principles of mathematical practice include:

1. Make sense of problems and persevere in solving them.
2. Reason abstractly and quantitatively.
3. Construct viable arguments and critique the reasoning of others.
4. Model with mathematics.
5. Use appropriate tools strategically.
6. Attend to precision.

7. Look for and make use of structure.

8. Look for and express regularity in repeated reasoning.

School districts and schools are expected to use outlined "bullets" such as these from the Common Core to develop their own curricula in math and English/language arts. The emphasis on coherence seeks to overcome the traditional "mile wide and an inch deep" coverage of math found in many schools. For math teachers, there will be an entirely new emphasis on student learning; the math structure seeks in-depth understanding of math and its applications. More information about the Common Core will be featured in the Elementary Programs and Issues chapter of this book.

Three things have happened as a result of these latest standards-based curriculum reforms in the United States. First, in a very short period of time, the curriculum has been narrowed and simplified. In many cases, the definition of the curriculum reflects an absence of professional input when standards legislation is simply enacted and handed to state departments of education for implementation. Second, the content to be taught at all levels of schooling is being skewed by high-stakes testing. The curriculum is unbalanced. Because of the pressure to perform, teachers and entire schools have simply taught what is tested or redefined the school day to be overbalanced in reading and math. Third, after years of such activity, about half the teachers in today's schools think that a standards-based curriculum is completely normal or they are unfamiliar with other options. Teachers turn over in public school by approximate 10% per year.

Until around 1990, schools taught all subjects in a holistic manner. Teachers would convey their subjects in numerous forms and at various levels of complexity in an attempt to meet the differences known to be present among students. After the new standards-based legislation mandated the form of the curriculum to be taught, all students were required to master an identified subject content or set of skills at a level of performance that was being tested, including students with learning disabilities. This highly specific outcome-based approach did not attempt to account for the differences in students' backgrounds, aptitude, or intelligence. Nor did the new curriculum format recognize that content can be taught for a variety of reasons, in varying levels of detail, for different purposes. The new "business-like engineered approach" to teaching also did not acknowledge the so-called art of classroom teaching or 100 years of research on the topic.[1]

Standards-based documents in most states are consistent in identifying the curriculum as a uniform list of things the student must master. Whether these lists are drawn from books like Mortimer Adler's *The Paideia Proposal* (1982), E. D. Hirsch's *Cultural Literacy: What Every American Needs to Know* (1986), or government documents such as the SCANS (1990) report, they are absolute in identifying both the content or skills and the desired form of performance.

Read, for example, the statement on this matter from the Tennessee State Board of Education (2001):

> Achieving proficiency in a discipline is based on a continuum of knowledge and skills development. Such learning begins with awareness, passes through a level of literacy, and culminates in mastery.

---

[1] See Raymond Callahan, *Education and the Cult of Efficiency* (1962) for a recounting of a similar period in 1920–1930.

The reader will recognize from Chapter 2 that such a definition of curriculum is highly structured (Perennial) and fails to consider student background, the level of student capacity, or the new tools of the information age that preclude most need for "storing" or mastering information. Nonetheless, such an approach is easily understood and currently serves as a rationale for the many highly structured curriculums of the new standards-based education.

Another curiosity about the new standards-based curriculum, from a development perspective, is that not all subject areas are seen as important—a long-running curriculum issue. In almost all states, reading and mathematics are tested regularly. Sometimes, areas like social studies and science are also considered critical, but in most states areas such as physical education, music, art, health, and foreign languages are not tested. In many standards-based states, what is not tested is not taught, resulting in a highly "unbalanced" curriculum for students.

STATE LEVEL PLANNING—EXAMPLE: STATE OF FLORIDA

In addition to national initiatives, such as the ESEA programs, individual states also develop curriculum on a large scale. The Constitution of the United States does not mention education, and therefore states have the final responsibility (residual rights) for schooling. Much of the work that takes place in SDOE is routinely "pass-through" work coming from federal programs such as Title I or Special Education mandates. Continuing our review of large-scale planning in schools, this section follows work in the state of Florida.

Like many states, Florida has been heavily involved in the standards/testing movement since the late 1980s. The national governors' conference headed by Bill Clinton (cited earlier) produced a set of goals that became known as Goals 2000. Florida, and most states, followed that action by duplicating in law a set of state-level standards, the Florida Sunshine Standards. Among many other things, these standards called for defining all subject areas experienced by students in Florida, and tying student performance in the mastery of some subjects to assessment testing.

Over a number of years, the Florida Legislature has written laws governing all aspects of public education and these various laws are defined and implemented by the Florida Department of Education. The many parts of the Florida Education Act include things such as subject matter standards, course directories, graduation and student progression requirements, the Florida Comprehensive Assessment Test (FCAT), teacher and administrator training requirements, library-media services, and a funding formula for many new items. As in most states today, the construction of learning standards and corresponding student assessments are the dominant activities in Florida.

Florida began using its Florida Comprehensive Assessment Test (FCAT) in 1998, as a part of a larger plan to increase overall student achievement. This "criterion-referenced" test was administered to students in grades 3, 5, 8, and 11 in the areas of math, reading, science, and writing (Florida Writes) to measure their progress toward meeting the new Sunshine State Standards. FCAT replaced a nationally "normed" test, the Scholastic Aptitude Test. The reader will note that Florida was a bottom quartile state in the national normed test (SAT), but could immediately show a much more positive pattern of achievement to the public using a criterion-referenced test like FCAT. Many other states followed Governor Jeb Bush's new political path to achievement.

True measurement of student progress in Florida proved problematic for educators due to the various new editions of the FCAT test and the ever-evolving Sunshine State Standards. Final versions of the subject standards were achieved in different periods:

Science adopted 2008

Social Studies adopted 2008

Physical Education adopted 2008

Health Education adopted 2008

World Languages adopted 2010

Fine Arts adopted 2010

Career and Adult Education–pending

Voluntary Pre-Kindergarten–pending

As noted previously, all states were required to commit to the Common Core State Standards in order to be eligible for Race to the Top Funds by August of 2010. Florida made such a commitment despite strenuous efforts to define the Sunshine Standards over the previous 5 years. In 2011, the Florida Department of Education convened a committee that decided "no changes were needed" for the English/language arts and math standards of the CCSS. The new standards were to be fully implemented with the beginning of the 2013–14 school year.

In 2010 FCAT transitioned to FCAT 2.0 and featured new end of course (EOC) exams in major subject areas. Beginning in 2012–13 school year, incoming 9th graders were required to pass (70% proficiency) Algebra I, Biology, and Geometry end of course exams in order to earn a Florida high school diploma. Students with specific learning disabilities were no longer required to take these mastery tests. In the spring of 2013, the Florida legislature scrapped these new graduation requirements.

In Florida, as in so many other states, politics influenced these curriculum development activities. Charter schools, teacher merit pay, and cultural issues with testing have become news items that detract from the large-scale development process. Change is everywhere, and the legislated mandates seem unending. All of the tasks undertaken by states, such as Florida, to meet federal mandates and state laws ultimately are applied in practice by districts and school faculties. These activities will be addressed more fully in later chapters.

HOW DISTRICTS IMPROVE PROGRAMS

The methodology of school district curriculum work depends on both an understanding of the curriculum development process and the sophistication of the district in carrying out a review procedure. Sometimes, districts review themselves in terms of external criteria, such as when they seek professional accreditation or rely on the expert opinion of consultants who survey the district. Other districts choose to conduct an internal needs assessment, for instance, after a change of leadership when new leaders wish to have a status report. Three common approaches are compared and contrasted in (Table 4.1).

School districts can be differentiated by the degree to which they are successful in assessing themselves and improving programs. This behavior is more rare in schools than you might imagine. Some districts, of course, never enter into such a cycle; for

TABLE 4.1 Three Methods of Assessing School Conditions: Characteristics and Data

Characteristics		
(1) Accreditation	**(2) Survey**	**(3) Needs Assessment**
Organization orientation	Administrative orientation	Programmatic orientation
Concern with structure, organization	Concern with structure and management	Concern with clients and corresponding programs
Analysis of what actually exists (descriptive)	Analysis of what actually exists (descriptive)	Assessment of what should be in existence (prescriptive)
Scheduled	Self-contained	Ties to remediation
Comprehensive	Quasi-comprehensive	Focused on client needs
Validation emphasis	Judgmental	Objective with design
Data		
(1) Accreditation	**(2) Survey**	**(3) Needs Assessment**
Pupil-teacher ratio	Community background	School-community history
Number of library books	Administration and organization	Achievement patterns
Statement of purpose	Instructional patterns	Attitudes toward school
Quality of buildings	Finance	Motivation, self-concepts
Financial patterns	Extracurricular	Student interests
Pupil-personnel services		Teacher perception
Standards	Standards	Problems
External	External	Internal
Post evaluation	Post evaluation	Pre-evaluation

them, school programs are simply a historical accident or something mandated from above. Others go through the motions year to year but do not seem to gain traction or momentum for all their efforts. These districts may have beautiful documents, but programs rarely change. Still a third pattern is seen in districts that plan well but are continually interrupted by external social forces such as legislation, lack of finances, or local pressure groups. These districts have numerous false starts and experience serious frustration with the lost investment in curriculum development. Your author can also report that some school districts do it right and see the satisfying results of an ever-improving program. The next section focuses on what these more fortunate districts seem to do to ensure success.

COMPREHENSIVE PLANNING

As early as 1970, Kathryn Feyereisen and others called for the application of a "systems" concept of curriculum work. These early systems analysts realized that, despite a rigorous process of curriculum review and honorable intentions by school leaders in assessing their programs, sometimes nothing happened. All the regular methods of upgrading school programs could not guarantee results because they could not control

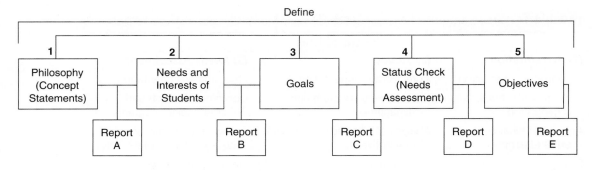

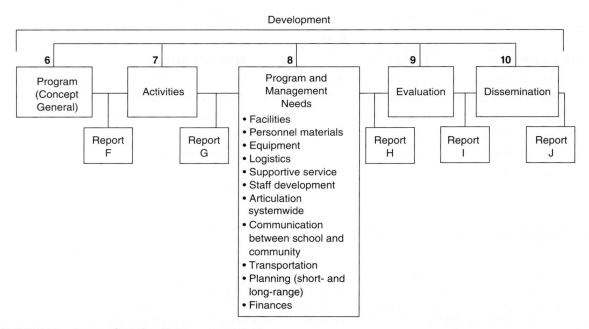

FIGURE 4.4   Comprehensive Management System.

or manage the many variables of curriculum change. These early advocates of a systems approach to curriculum development called for more comprehensive planning and an integration of the many functions involved in school improvement. The outline of a comprehensive planning process is shown in Figure 4.4. Note that actions to implement the desired change occur after the direction has been set, not vice versa.

In working with some of the better school districts in the United States, your author has identified four premises that seem critical to successful and lasting curriculum improvement:

1. For lasting change to occur, the persons to be affected must be involved in planning the change.
2. In a bureaucratic environment (schools), change must be directed from the top level of school leadership.

3. Good decisions are best made on the basis of data, and such data should be shared with all those involved in planning.
4. Evaluation and expectations can drive change efforts forward.

The traditional failure patterns in curriculum development disappear in schools or school districts that develop a management plan for curriculum development that ensures these four conditions. A review of the traditional cycle of development reveals some of the most common problems in districts and schools.

In the analysis stage, many districts fail to engage fully in dissecting the current program. Reasons for this vary, but they include the following:

- The existing program has no design and therefore cannot be analyzed.
- Leaders fear that analysis will reveal weaknesses or problems that will reflect on them in their leadership role.
- The analysis never gets beyond words (jargon), and true assessments of local conditions are not made.
- Leaders enhance the assessment because they feel it is expected.

If any of these conditions occurs in the analysis stage, subsequent curriculum development will fail because a deductive logic rests on its original premise. If goals are not clear, the project will fail.

In the design stage, numerous possible failures can sabotage the process, including the following:

- The design is blue sky (unreal) or is part of a bandwagon (everyone else has it).
- The design is unachievable because of existing conditions (financial, logistical, academic).
- The design challenges bedrock values of those who must implement it.
- The design is couched in terms that are vague or wordy.

In the implementation stage, regular conditions that undermine successful efforts include the following:

- The primary supporter of the design (such as the legislature, school board or superintendent) changes or leaves.
- The change is too complex, or too demanding, and the purpose is obscured.
- Timeframes for changing are unrealistic, and the design is abandoned.
- Training to implement the design is not sufficient to carry out the change.

In the traditional cycle, an evaluation step assesses the completion of the effort. This evaluation step can break down if any of the following occurs:

- No baseline data were obtained for a comparison with the desired condition.
- Evaluation is not in a form useful for redirecting efforts.
- Those involved in the process do not trust those evaluating the process, or they do not believe the reported outcomes.

These common failure conditions are not meant to be all-inclusive, but they do illustrate some of the things that can go wrong in school improvement at the district level. If such errors are common, curriculum development can be overwhelming, frustrating, and even counterproductive. If these conditions are controlled through management actions, the cycle of curriculum development becomes the most important function of school leadership.

In the following section, your author introduces his own model of a curriculum management planning, developed over the years with Dr. Joseph Bondi in some 400 school districts large and small.

CURRICULUM MANAGEMENT PLANS

A *curriculum management plan (CMP)* increases the odds that the curriculum cycle will be completed successfully by providing structure for (1) how changes are to be made and (2) the order of those changes and (3) control of interference. Such a plan also seeks to provide continuity across a district or school effort. When implemented, the CMP minimizes political interference and single-issue crises. Most important, the CMP provides a means for the philosophy of education desired by planners to intersect the development process over a long period.

A curriculum management plan begins with an acknowledgment of power, that is, an understanding that certain persons in each state, district, or school have the power to make decisions, to set or alter policy, to allocate resources, and to use procedures and regulations to emphasize activities. It is this allocation of scarce resources to meet certain goals and purposes that makes curriculum work a political process. Curriculum leaders must realize that without such top-down support, instructional improvement efforts will not usually succeed.

In the CMP model, curriculum leaders form a management team that initiates action, communicates upward and downward for logistical purposes, and helps define political reality in districts or schools. This group "allows" a process to be initiated, pursued, and completed. Figure 4.5 shows the relationship of this group to other groups in the CMP.

FIGURE 4.5 Committee Structure for Curriculum Management Plan (CMP).

Source: J. Wiles and J. Bondi, copyright © 1988. *Planning for Middle School Programs,* Wiles, Bondi & Associates (Tampa, FL: 1988). p. 12.

Analysis Stage

In the CMP, the management team plays a crucial role in the analysis stage of development. Many of the proposed changes in U.S. education during the past 30 years have come from external sources such as the federal government or the state legislature, or have bypassed this influential analysis group. In practice, as opposed to theory, this management team can facilitate or sabotage any change effort from above or within the district. Securing this team's endorsement, as a formal step in the development process, will eliminate problems of ownership down the road. Such an endorsement is best if it is in written form (see Figure 4.6).

The management team's endorsement is also a necessity for conducting a true assessment, for coordinating efforts across the district, and for gaining true and accurate

DADE COUNTY PUBLIC SCHOOLS

SCHOOL BOARD ADMINISTRATION BUILDING • 1450 NORTHEAST SECOND AVENUE • MIAMI, FLORIDA 33132

DR. JOSEPH A. FERNANDEZ
SUPERINTENDENT OF SCHOOLS

DADE COUNTY SCHOOL BOARD
DR. MICHAEL KROP, CHAIRMAN
MR. G. HOLMES BRADDOCK, VICE-CHAIRMAN
DR. ROSA CASTRO FEINBERG
MS. BETSY KAPLAN
MS. JANET R. McALILEY
MR. ROBERT RENICK
MR. WILLIAM H. TURNER

The Middle School Design Report was developed through a collaborative effort between staff of the Dade County Public Schools and members of the United Teachers of Dade (U.T.D.). This collaboration represents the continued effort of the district and union to work together for the betterment of education in Dade County's public schools.

The Design Report is to be considered a working blueprint that allows individual school communities maximum flexibility in developing programs and implementing the philosophies of the middle school.

The document is the result of the work of an ad hoc committee formed to provide a model for education to all middle schools in the district. The model recommends a shared philosophy; identified programs and components; and objectives, standards, and evaluative criteria for all middle schools.

The Dade County School Board has adopted a four-year plan to convert all its intermediate level schools to fully functioning middle schools by 1991-92. This four-year conversion process utilizes a Curriculum Management Plan (CMP) as a guide. The CMP focuses on using needs assessment, developing a clear set of goals, tying school needs to program needs, involving teachers, administrators, union, parents, and community, and providing an analysis of progress to the general public.

It is the hope of Dade County Public Schools that this type of long range planning and collaborative working arrangement will allow us to accomplish our goal of "National Excellence in Middle Grades Education."

Joseph A. Fernandez
Superintendent of Schools

FIGURE 4.6 Official Endorsement.

	Low	High
Enrollment range	670	1389
Average daily attendance	83%	95%
Absences per teacher per month	.36	1.27
Number of students of low socioeconomic status (percentage)	11%	56%
Ratio of gifted students to other exceptional education students	1/104	179/63
Number of students moving in or out during year	33%	70%
Number of students experiencing corporal punishment	44	619
Number of students experiencing suspension	37	240
Number of students dropping out in academic year	0	22
Average score of students on CTBS total battery	36	80

Findings: These data confirm that a wide range of conditions and performance exists in the junior high schools of Orange County. The single greatest variable reflected in these data is variance in student population.

Implications: These statistics suggest that the quality of intermediate programs experienced in Orange County may depend on the individual school. Efforts should be made to equalize programs and performance of the individual schools during the transition to middle schools.

FIGURE 4.7 Sample Baseline Summary of Existing Conditions in the Junior High Schools in District.

Source: From *Making Middle Schools Work*, Fig. 5, p. 18, by J. Wiles and J. Bondi. Copyright © 1986, by the Association for Supervision and Curriculum Development, Alexandria, VA.

evaluation data. Without the management team, the effort to improve curriculum will be external, will lack coordination, and will be destined to failure from an absence of internal support.

Of course, other groups, such as the teacher's union, parents, and political action groups, must be consulted if the change process is to succeed. These groups are combined in the Wiles–Bondi CMP model into a *coordinating committee*—a group of all-powerful individuals and organizations apart from the management team. This standing committee (as opposed to a temporary, or ad hoc, committee) is a vehicle for involvement and dissemination. Involving the teacher's union, for example, may help planners gain access to classrooms. Such access to classrooms reveals the pattern of instruction found in Figure 4.7.

Placing a member of a powerful political action committee, such as the Christian Coalition, on a "team" can lessen his or her ability to influence decision makers. By contrast, permitting such an advocate to rally citizens from outside the decision-making circle and giving him or her access to board members in open meetings is a formula for chaos.

In this stage, the primary task is to clarify purpose and goals. The following criteria can be applied to any set of goals as a measure of their usefulness to the organization:

- *Are the goals realistic?* If goals are attainable, they possess a quality that allows members of the organization to relate to them in daily work.
- *Are the goals specific?* Specific goals imply behaviors that need to be changed.

- *Are the goals related to performance?*   Goals that are developed in an organizational context suggest patterns of interaction.
- *Are the goals suggestive of involvement?*   To be effective, goals must be stated in a way that allows individuals in the organization to see themselves as being able to achieve the objective.
- *Are the goals observable?*   Can people in the organization see the results of their efforts and monitor progress toward the desired condition?

After goal statements are identified, stated, and reviewed, the next major step is to determine whether these goals are realistic. A preliminary needs assessment, which views both hard data and perceptions of key groups, tells planners what actually exists and what aspirations are present.

Although many districts conduct this assessment informally using internal staff, your author believes that such a step must be formal and open to the public. Failure to reveal true conditions at this point will deter the setting of attainable goals and will prevent a consensus of shared goals and beliefs.

In the example of the Common Core State Standards found earlier in this chapter, gaining consensus for implementation at the district level might be difficult for financial reasons and possibly for philosophical reasons dealing with the instructional process. If teachers at the local level believe that this is just the "same ol' same ol'," as they indicated in the 2012 survey cited earlier, organizing professional development to accomplish the many curriculum tasks will likely be resisted.

Using data (numbers) in decision making, as opposed to philosophical statements, promotes meaningful curriculum change. Use of the coordinating committee to monitor an assessment and interpret the reality provides assurances to the public that there are no hidden agendas. For example, does the district have enough computers for online assessments under the CCSS and, if not, can the district afford such tools? Your author also recommends a standing evaluation committee, comprising at least some lay citizens, to provide continuous access to information from the coordinating committee.

Because most schools and districts do have access to computers, the process of assessing data is easier than it was in the past. Whether there are 500 pupils in a school or 50,000 pupils in a school district, the task is to gather data and look for patterns. Figure 4.8 shows a typical questionnaire that asks for teacher positions on various statements and the summarized responses of those teachers, respectively.

In question 10, 94% of the teachers felt that the school should have a child-centered focus—certainly a strong enough consensus for planners to proceed, but not good news for a progression-driven standards system. Computers are excellent tools for sharing such data with those beyond the schools.

When a philosophy has been established (by consensus) and documented (by numbers), when recommendations for change have been presented to the board by a representative body of citizens and groups, and when the superintendent and his or her staff have been responsible for coordinating all such activities, then planners can advance to the design stage.

One of the key points of such a process is to keep political interference in schools to a minimum, thus overcoming one of the largest problems school planners have faced in the last 25 years. If someone at a parent-teacher association or school

EAST BATON ROUGE PARISH SCHOOL BOARD

SURVEY OF: MIDDLE SCHOOL TEACHERS
GROUPING: OVERALL TOTALS

Each item lists response categories A, B, C, D, E with counts and percentages (%), and M (mean).

1. A 497 71.10% · B 152 21.70% · C 42 6.00% · D 7 1.00% · E 1 .10% · M 1.37
2. A 309 44.20% · B 280 40.00% · C 87 12.40% · D 19 2.70% · E 4 .50% · M 1.75
3. A 77 11.00% · B 235 33.60% · C 283 40.50% · D 91 13.00% · E 12 1.70% · M 2.61
4. A 292 41.80% · B 267 38.30% · C 119 17.00% · D 16 2.50% · E .10% · M 1.81
5. A 374 53.50% · B 178 25.50% · C 106 15.10% · D 26 3.70% · E 14 2.00% · M 1.75
6. A 189 27.00% · B 239 34.20% · C 184 26.30% · D 72 10.30% · E 14 2.00% · M 2.26

7. A 264 37.80% · B 264 37.80% · C 113 16.10% · D 42 6.00% · E 15 2.10% · M 1.97
8. A 243 34.80% · B 272 38.90% · C 146 20.90% · D 26 3.70% · E 11 1.50% · M 1.98
9. A 341 48.90% · B 245 35.10% · C 98 14.00% · D 9 1.20% · E 4 .50% · M 1.69
10. A 136 19.50% · B 216 30.90% · C 240 34.40% · D 71 10.10% · E 34 4.80% · M 2.50
11. A 403 57.60% · B 201 28.70% · C 85 12.10% · D 7 1.00% · E 3 .40% · M 1.58
12. A 290 41.50% · B 254 36.30% · C 112 16.00% · D 27 3.80% · E 15 2.10% · M 1.89

13. A 192 27.50% · B 275 39.50% · C 164 23.50% · D 43 6.10% · E 22 3.10% · M 2.18
14. A 166 23.30% · B 225 32.30% · C 158 22.70% · D 82 11.70% · E 65 9.30% · M 2.50
15. A 292 41.80% · B 189 27.10% · C 112 16.10% · D 49 7.00% · E 55 7.80% · M 2.12
16. A 559 79.90% · B 108 15.40% · C 24 3.40% · D 1 .10% · E 7 1.00% · M 1.27
17. A 284 40.60% · B 212 30.30% · C 113 16.10% · D 60 8.50% · E 30 4.20% · M 2.06
18. A 292 41.80% · B 281 40.20% · C 109 15.60% · D 9 1.20% · E 7 1.00% · M 1.79

19. A 369 52.80% · B 236 33.80% · C 74 10.50% · D 13 1.80% · E 6 .80% · M 1.64
20. A 197 28.30% · B 239 34.40% · C 196 28.20% · D 45 6.40% · E 17 · M 2.20
21. A 288 41.20% · B 296 42.30% · C 101 14.40% · D 12 1.70% · E 2 .20% · M 1.78
22. A 150 22.80% · B 249 35.60% · C 204 29.10% · D 57 8.10% · E 29 4.10% · M 2.35
23. A 494 70.60% · B 161 23.00% · C 35 5.00% · D 6 .80% · E 3 .40% · M 1.37
24. A 306 43.80% · B 267 38.20% · C 106 15.10% · D 15 2.10% · E 4 .50% · M 1.77

25. A 267 38.10% · B 263 37.60% · C 133 19.00% · D 29 4.10% · E 7 1.00% · M 1.92
26. A 353 50.50% · B 189 27.00% · C 101 14.40% · D 34 4.80% · E 22 3.10% · M 1.83
27. A 353 50.50% · B 189 27.00% · C 101 14.40% · D 34 4.80% · E 22 3.10% · M 1.83
28. A 486 69.60% · B 163 23.30% · C 37 5.30% · D 9 1.20% · E 3 .40% · M 1.40
29. A 474 68.30% · B 171 24.60% · C 43 6.20% · D 2 .20% · E 3 .40% · M 1.40
30. A 303 43.40% · B 195 27.90% · C 123 17.60% · D 53 7.60% · E 23 3.20% · M 1.99

31. A 221 31.70% · B 192 27.50% · C 141 20.20% · D 82 11.70% · E 60 8.60% · M 2.38
32. A 151 21.70% · B 237 34.10% · C 181 26.00% · D 80 11.50% · E 45 6.40% · M 2.47
33. A 196 28.00% · B 212 30.30% · C 165 23.60% · D 76 10.80% · E 50 7.10% · M 2.39
34. A 267 38.40% · B 185 26.50% · C 134 19.30% · D 65 9.30% · E 43 6.10% · M 2.18
35. A 264 37.90% · B 271 38.90% · C 128 18.40% · D 16 2.30% · E 16 2.30% · M 1.92
36. A 363 52.20% · B 226 32.50% · C 84 12.00% · D 13 1.80% · E 9 1.20% · M 1.67

FIGURE 4.8 Sample Printout of Teacher Responses.

Source: Reprinted courtesy of East Baton Rouge School District.

board meeting objects to a book, a program, or a practice, and if the planners have done their homework, the intrusion can be countered if compelling data and facts are on hand.

In the CMP model, the school board receives information from the coordinating committee in small segments rather than as a grand plan. Using semester or quarterly reports, the committee walks the board into change, much like a novice swimmer walks into the water. First, a philosophy is determined; then general goals and objectives are set, a preliminary plan is endorsed by the public (evidenced by numbers), and critical decisions are made. A track record of progress is established with time, making it increasingly difficult for a new player to change the game. This gradual unfolding process is crucial because school board composition can change in any year, and the superintendent's tenure may last less than 4 years. Establishing this track record prevents a common worst-case scenario in which massive planning is undone by a change of players.

Because it is internal and seeks only instructional direction, the needs assessment provides both macro and micro vantage points. This process is in contrast with accreditation, which seeks endorsement, or surveys, which are often for public consumption. Figure 4.9 outlines some of the problem areas that may be revealed by a comprehensive needs assessment. Figure 4.10, by contrast, reveals a larger pattern for planners. These graphs show that the district is doing quite well until students reach the intermediate years, when achievement drops off sharply.

In the Wiles-Bondi model for curriculum management, a series of temporary (ad hoc) committees are used to process this information into school programs. A design committee, a program development committee, and a staff development committee are used to involve people in the process of curriculum work and to eliminate distortion of the process.

Design Stage

The design stage of the CMP is carried out by a new, temporary committee whose job is to define the goals for the school or district in broad strokes that establish a framework for subsequent curriculum work. This critical committee needs to be visionary, but it must work within the parameters of both the endorsed philosophy of the board and the realities of the data gathered. Below, examples of this process for a Florida school district are provided.

CURRICULUM MANAGEMENT PLAN—DISTRICT EXAMPLE The district example comes from Dade County in Miami, Florida, a district that undertook the largest curriculum change effort ever in American education. Using the Wiles-Bondi CMP, 52 schools housing nearly 60,000 intermediate pupils were converted to a middle school design over a 5-year period. The effort began with a broad view of what students may need for life in the 21st century (see Figure 4.11) and the role of the middle grades in meeting those needs.

Once these broad strokes were passed to the design committee, their task was to define them further. Figure 4.12 provides an overview of the desired program, followed by a definitional statement concerning the critical elements of the desired program in Figure 4.13. Figure 4.14 illustrates the type of thinking skills that will be taught to students across all subject areas.

As the program design is given form by the design committee, certain tasks begin to emerge. These identified tasks will be handled by the new and separate program

1. **Improvement of basic academic achievement**
   - Pupils perform below real ability.
   - Students are not prepared for grade level.
   - Students consider the curriculum irrelevant.
   - Instructional materials are too difficult.
   - Advanced course offerings are not available in some subjects.
   - Standardized test scores are low.
   - Students do poorly on daily work.
   - Graduates seem unprepared for the job market or for higher education.
   - There is a high rate of student failure.
   - Students cannot apply basic skills.

2. **Continued commitment to reduction of racial isolation**
   - Students are polarized along racial lines.
   - Faculty are divided along racial lines.
   - There is student–teacher antagonism along racial lines.
   - Hostility in the community is racially motivated.
   - Curriculum materials contain unequal status roles for minorities.
   - Transported students feel unwelcome.
   - Racial groups establish certain areas of the school as their territory.
   - School lacks a unified approach to reducing racial isolation.
   - Parents of transported students are not involved in the school.
   - School personnel avoid problem situations.

3. **Improvement in staff attendance and continued upgrading of staff performance**
   A. Attendance
      - Frequent staff absences
      - Habitual staff tardiness
      - Patterns of staff absences and tardiness

   B. Performance
      - Expectations for student achievement and behavior are low.
      - There is an apparent lack of productive teaching techniques and methods.
      - Instruction is not geared to student needs.
      - There is resistance to progressive change and professional growth.
      - Learning experiences seem passive.
      - A positive learning environment is lacking.
      - Classroom management is poor.
      - Staff cooperative effort is lacking.

FIGURE 4.9 Some Symptoms of School Problems.

development or the staff development committees. A critical part of the CMP model is that the function of the general program design (design committee) is separated from the specific development of programs (done by the program development committees). This "fading away" of one committee and the assumption of more detailed work by another committee prevents "special pleading" by members of the design group for their respective subject area. The program development committees must stay within

4. Improvement in school morale and community relations

   A. School morale
- School administration is viewed as cold and detached from student concerns.
- Administrator and staff feel isolated; mutual support is lacking.
- Teachers view some subject areas as having low status.
- There is extensive vandalism.
- Student attitude toward learning is negative.
- Students are uninvolved, unmotivated.
- There is a lack of harmonious staff relationships.

   B. Community relations
- Efforts to involve students in the community are inadequate.
- Parent interest is lacking.
- Teacher involvement in the community served by the school is lacking.
- Principals and teachers do not try to involve parents and community in the school program.
- Communication between school and community is lacking.

5. Student attendance, behavior, and discipline

   A. Attendance
- Frequent truancy
- Frequent tardiness
- Frequent class cutting
- High absentee rate
- High dropout rate
- High rate of student mobility

   B. Behavior and discipline
- Vandalism
- Violence
- Disruptive classroom behavior
- Use of illegal drugs
- Disruptive behavior on campus or playground
- Frequent referrals to office for disciplinary action
- Disruption caused by outsiders
- Excessive noise level and confusion throughout the school
- Disrespect for authority

FIGURE 4.9 *(Continued)*

the design parameters; its work is reviewed by the coordinating committee for compliance with the criteria that the board adopted.

Implementation Stage

After the goals and objectives are clarified and the parameters of programs are established within an overarching structure, the next curriculum task is to coordinate the

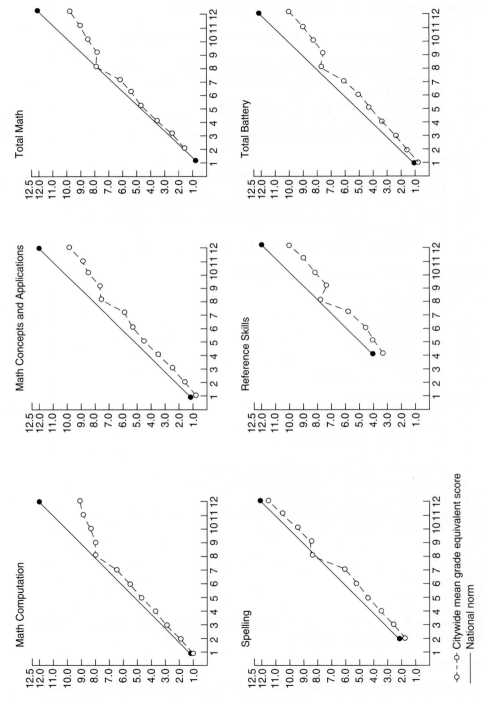

FIGURE 4.10 Graphs Showing the Relationship of Local District Achievement to National Norms by Grade Levels.

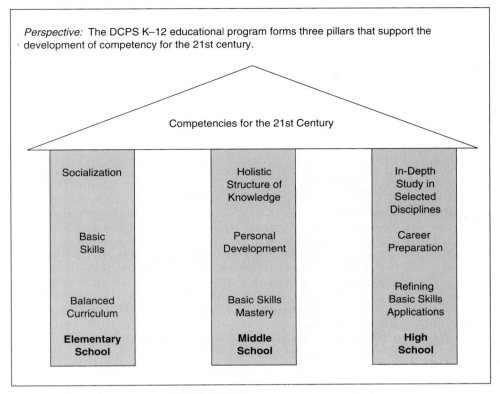

FIGURE 4.11   Generic Competencies Outlined.

many efforts needed to implement such programs. In your author's opinion, this is where 90% of all curriculum work fails and, incidentally, where concern for the Common Core resides. In the future, all curriculum specialists will also need managerial skills to succeed in curriculum development.

One of the first tasks for the planner is get the big picture in order. This requires establishing a timeframe and deciding on a natural order of development. All work from here on is a refinement of basic concepts and programs into instructional prescriptions; the project can be envisioned as a basic distance–rate–time problem, with resources determining the rate. If resources are interrupted, for example, the project will simply take longer. Figure 4.15 shows the outline of the steps in one such project in Denver, Colorado.

The process of developing the curriculum falls to subject-area subcommittees and special groups who are assigned to develop their areas. Math and science groups, for example, would define their areas anew in terms of the parameters of the design report to the board. They would formulate standards to further define the subject area (see Figure 4.16.) These standards would establish purpose and guarantee that groups in other areas could see the contribution of each part to the whole. Subsequent action plans in each area would help planners understand the logistical needs of the area to meet its goals. The collection of all action plans would form the bulk of the implementation plan.

I. **Philosophy**
    A. Child centered
    B. Holistic knowledge structure is developed
    C. Thinking skills are priority goals
    D. Safety is essential
    E. Students' developmental needs are important

II. **Curriculum**
    A. Academic excellence/social competence
        1. Academic core
        2. Exploration and developmental programs
    B. Personal development
    C. Mastery of continuous learning skills

III. **Organization**
    A. Interdisciplinary teams
    B. Advisement program
    C. Block scheduling and flexible scheduling within blocks
    D. Team planning and shared decision making
    E. Exploratory and developmental experiences
        1. Elective classes
        2. Wheels and exploration credits
        3. Minicourses
        4. Clubs, activities, interest groups, intramurals
    F. Integrated curriculum
    G. In-service education and professional development

IV. **Implementing strategies** (delivery systems)
    A. Cooperative learning
    B. Interdisciplinary teaching
    C. Learning styles
    D. Student services and career planning systems
    E. Home–school partnerships and communications

FIGURE 4.12   Overview of Middle School Parameters.

General administrative standards would also be established to encompass the program areas and service them. Areas of concern would include grouping and use of time and staff development (Figure 4.17). When these concerns are wedded to the program standards and identified needs of specific areas, an overall calendar of activity and budget can be developed.

Assessment Stage

The CMP emphasizes assessment from the beginning to support the curriculum development cycle. This assessment is used in at least five ways:

1. To make explicit the rationale of the instructional program as a basis for deciding which aspects of the program should be evaluated for effectiveness and what types of data should be gathered

The Critical Elements Summarized

The middle grades education program has important functions different from the elementary and high school programs. Middle school students (transescents) have special needs that identify them as a unique group in the K–12 learning continuum. There are specific philosophical approaches, educational strategies, and school organizations that are effective during this period. Twelve critical elements are needed in the DCPS middle school.

1. The core of the middle school education program is based on the following beliefs:
   - Every child can learn.
   - Middle school is a key time during which students learn that the various disciplines and subjects are all related to humanity's search for understanding.
   - Learners must feel physically and psychologically safe.
   - Thinking-skills instruction is a middle school responsibility.
   - Every child's individual differences must be respected.

2. To accomplish its mission, the middle school curriculum has three interwoven and connected threads, namely, the pursuit of
   - academic excellence as a way to achieve social competence in a complex, technological society;
   - self-understanding and personal development; and
   - continuous-learning skills.

3. The traditional academic core must be taught in a way that ensures that our students recognize
   - the relationships between such disciplines as math, language arts, science, and social studies and can transfer learning from one discipline to another; and
   - that their exploratory and developmental experiences are related to the academic core and are a way to broaden each individual's insights and potential for personal growth.

4. The middle school curriculum contains a variety of exploratory experiences (into disciplines beyond the academic core), which will enable students to
   - recognize, through exploratory experiences, that there are a multitude of routes to take to understanding and successful independence;
   - sample fields they may wish to pursue in greater depth in high school or beyond;
   - develop a realistic overview of talents, aptitudes, and interests; and
   - begin to develop talents and special interests in a manner that provides balance and perspective.

5. Thinking skills expand in scope and nature during the middle grade years. While problem-solving strategies need to be part of the K–12 learning continuum, formal instruction in critical and creative thinking skills is essential in the middle grades program.

6. Middle school students need someone to whom they can relate as an advisor and guide during the transescent period. Middle schools provide such advisors and ensure that advisors and advisees have time to work on the developmental issues of early adolescence.

7. Middle schools integrate academic knowledge and skills by using interdisciplinary teaching teams. The structure of such teams may vary widely, but the essential elements are common planning time and teaching the same group of students.

8. The teachers of the academic core and the exploratory/developmental programs work together to foster transfer of learning from one discipline to another, to enhance application of basic skills, and to help students develop a "big picture" on the scope and nature of our efforts to understand ourselves and the environment.

FIGURE 4.13 Definitional Statement About Critical Elements of the Middle School Program.

9. The exploratory program is provided in a variety of ways in addition to formal classes. These may include minicourses, clubs, special activities, and interest group meetings built into the school day at regular intervals.

10. In-service education and methods for teachers to share insights and information are an important part of the middle school conversion.

11. Instructional delivery strategies used at the middle grades allow for the developmental traits of the students. Cooperative learning strategies, accommodation of different learning styles, recognition of attention span limitations, and understanding the transescents' preoccupation with personal development issues are all needed in the middle grade program.

12. The middle school must develop a closer relationship with the parents and community and serve as a guide to the student's departure from childhood and embarkation on the route to adulthood and citizenship.

FIGURE 4.13 (*Continued*)

Teaching skills needed for continuous learning in school and in life are the joint responsibility of the entire educational staff.

The middle school seeks to instill mastery of the basic communication and mathematical skills taught in elementary school.

Owing to the emergence of abstract thinking abilities during the transescence period, critical and creative thinking skills are infused through the curriculum and taught as specific skills.

Social cooperation skills and their application to problem solving are infused throughout the curriculum.

Perspective: Middle school students develop a unified set of skills that promote continuous learning, as the diagram illustrates.

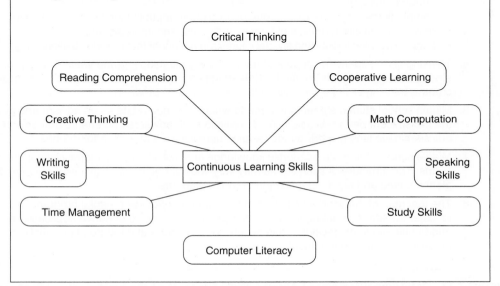

FIGURE 4.14 Thinking Skills Emphasized in the Middle School Program.

Analysis Stage
1. Identify Denver public schools' philosophy.
2. Identify board policy relative to middle schools.
3. Obtain superintendent (public) statement on middle schools.
4. Outline time frame for implementation.
5. Form a centralized coordinating group.
6. Delineate tasks and appoint subcommittees.
7. Develop "definition" of Denver middle schools.
8. Structure an awareness/orientation campaign for
    a. administrators,
    b. teacher groups.

Design Stage
9. Translate philosophy into goal statements.
10. Project preliminary budget/resource base.
11. Prioritize goal statements.
12. Translate goal statements into objectives format.
13. Block out 3–5-year plan for implementation.
14. Establish management/information system to monitor progress of implementation (external audit).
15. Establish evaluation targets, time, responsibilities, resources; identify baseline data needed.
16. Conduct needs assessment.
17. Develop a final management system (PERT).

Implementation or Management Stage
18. Provide advanced organizers (simple plan) to all interested persons.
19. Provide each school with resource kits, glossaries, data bank from needs assessment (local planning/decision-making data).
20. Form teams in each school to serve as
    a. study group for mapping curriculum/skills,
    b. planning group/house plan,
    c. team/cooperative teaching unit.
21. Provide preliminary staff development (demonstration teaching) in all schools on
    a. advisor/advisee program,
    b. continuous progress curriculums,
    c. team planning and teaching.
22. Require school-by-school development plan including curriculum, staff development, evaluation, community involvement.
23. Provide local budget supplement based on plan.

Evaluation Stage
24. Conduct formative evaluation (external audit) every 6 weeks to monitor management outline.
25. Conduct major review after 6 months—revise timeline, goals, needs, and so on.
26. Develop master evaluation plan (sum of all schools) for 3-year period.

FIGURE 4.15   Comprehensive Plan of the Denver Public Schools.

Source: Author's notes, Denver, Colorado.

PERT: Program Evaluation and Review Technique. A management system to develop Polaris submarines.

Curriculum Area: Computer Education

Purpose: The overall goal in the educational use of computers is to integrate computer literacy into all content areas of the middle school curriculum, thus providing an additional tool for interdisciplinary curriculum development. In addition, elective computer courses in application and programming provide for personal development and the reinforcement of essential skills.

Program Descriptors

	Status		
	Yes	No	Action Plan to Achieve
1. Microcomputers, either permanently located in all classrooms or on mobile carts, will be available for classroom use.			
2. Additional mobile computers will be available to move into classrooms when necessary or to develop a minilab when desired.			
3. Each school will have at least two qualified full-time computer education teachers.			
4. Each school will have at least two complete computer labs containing a minimum of 16 microcomputers and have a ratio of two students per computer. Each lab will include necessary computer-system hardware, software, and peripheral equipment to meet current and future trends and developments. The complete computer lab will consist of necessary space, lighting, seating, air-cooling system, electrical system, and security, plus access to telecommunications.			
5. Daily lab schedules will include time set aside for independent student use.			
6. All students in Grades 6 and 7 will be scheduled into one of the computer labs for a minimum of 3 hours a week to meet the state requirements for computer literacy.			
7. A minimum of two computers with needed peripherals will be located in the teachers' work area for teacher use (for grade recording, software review, word processing, and so on).			

Note: The Computer Literacy Program for the sixth and seventh grades should be interdisciplinary and taught through the team concept.

Both the media center and administrative offices need computerization. These noninstructional needs should be addressed by the appropriate middle school ad hoc committee.

Essential Skills: (skills reinforced regardless of discipline or program spiral)

Reading	Writing	Problem solving	Thinking	Computation or calculation
Listening	Vocabulary	Decision making	Computer literacy	Motor

FIGURE 4.16   Mapping Worksheet with Standards in Skill Areas.

	August			September								October							November							December				
	22	26	27	5	6	12	13	19	20	26	27	10	11	17	18	24	25	31	1	7	8	14	15	21	22	5	6	10	12	13
Teachers																														
Leadership group						1		2		3	1	4	2				3	7	4	8	5	9	6	10	7	8				
Principals										1							2							3				1		
Assistant principals				1								2						3												
Management team	1									2			2												3					
School visits (as needed)						1														3						5	6	7	8	
School board																												1		
Coordinating committee																1										2				
Staff development														1																
Grant																1						2					3			
Evaluation committee											1										2					5				
Program consultants				1								2						3				4								
Public relations committee						1																	2							

FIGURE 4.17 Middle School Staff Development and Meetings Schedule.

Source: From *Making Middle Schools Work*, Fig. 21, p. 36, by J. Wiles and J. Bondi. Copyright © 1986 by the Association for Supervision and Curriculum Development, Alexandria, VA.

2. To collect data on which judgments about effectiveness can be formulated
3. To analyze data and draw conclusions
4. To make decisions based on the data
5. To implement the decisions to improve the instructional program

In professional education at this time, demand for accountability, for student achievement, for global testing competition, and for public satisfaction with education all contribute to the need for assessments. The CMP, now in its 20th year of use, emphasizes this modern expectation.

Summary

Large-scale curriculum planning is complex and requires a way of working. Your author has developed and practiced techniques that have proven useful in overcoming distortions of the planning process. The absence of detailed curriculum planning can insure failure in any national, state, district, or school curriculum projects.

Comprehensive school planning means that all areas of school operations are seen as a system. All planning in a system must begin with a clear conception of purpose. The formalization of that purpose is important for continuity in program development. Assessing present conditions, usually through a needs assessment, provides planning data to support philosophical goals.

A curriculum management plan (CMP) can be used to tie together the many activities needed to accomplish the planned change. Activation of this system depends on identifying responsible agents to carry out tasks and setting a timeframe for the planned change. Various technical aids can assist the curriculum leader in managing the many variables.

The design phase of curriculum development proceeds deductively from goals previously identified and endorsed. Broad conceptualizations of the programs desired are projected, and plans for specific components of the program are developed. Placing these plans into a holistic understanding of the desired change leads to the management or implementation stage of the cycle.

Assessment, the fourth step of the curriculum development cycle, is the critical stage. Accountability by school leaders for their performance should encourage them to be both effective and efficient in developing quality school programs. Historical criteria for curriculum quality, plus sound educational research, will guide curriculum leaders in evaluating school programming.

Activities

ACTIVITY 4.1

Means and *ends* are often confused in education. If a school were implementing the following means, what ends must be driving the curriculum design?

Means

Teams

Block schedules/common planning

Multiage grouping

Cooperative learning

Transitional sixth and eighth grades

Mentoring

Continuous-progress curriculum

Individualized instruction

Looping

Electronic learning

Differentiated instruction

Service learning

Multiple intelligences/learning styles

Problem-based learning

ACTIVITY 4.2

Develop an outline of events that would lead a school or district from having no clear philosophy to a state of logical internal consistency in program development.

 Click here to take an automatically-graded self-check quiz.

Additional Reading

DeVos, B. "Meet the Billionaires Who Are Trying to Privatize Our Schools and Kill Public Education," ThinkProgress.org 5-21-11

Feng, L. How Online Companies Bought America's Schools, The Nation, 12-05-11.

Loveless, T. (2013, December/January). The Common Core initiative-What are the chances of success? *Educational Leadership* 70(4) 60–65.

Marzano, R. (2013). *Using Common Core Standards to enhance classroom instruction*. Bloomington, IN: Perfect Paperback.

Oliva, P. (2013). *Developing the curriculum* (8th ed.). Boston, MA: Allyn and Bacon.

Ornstein, A. (2012). *Curriculum: Foundations, principles and issues*. (6th ed.). Upper Saddle River, NJ: Pearson Education.

Parka, (2013). *Curriculum leadership: Readings* (10th ed.). Upper Saddle River, NJ: Pearson Education.

Wiles, J. (2009). *Developing successful K–8 schools*. Thousand Oaks, CA: Corwin Press.

Curriculum Development in Schools

Learning Outcome

▪ To understand the connectedness of large- and small-scale planning efforts.

Schools and classrooms are the terminal point for all curriculum planning. National standards and state-controlled curricula are only as effective as the implementation in individual schools and classrooms. A teacher, delivering an instructional lesson, is always the final filter on curriculum design and development.

Schools in most states are reviewed periodically to see how effectively they are delivering instruction. Whether through state or regional accreditations, district surveys, or school-level assessments, individual school faculties periodically compare the curriculum planned to the curriculum experienced by students. Just as regularly, often on 5-year cycles, schools work to upgrade subject areas and to retrain teachers. All teachers are regularly involved in curriculum development activities.

Curriculum development at the school level (instructional level) proceeds in a deductive manner using an if-then logic. The initial step in curriculum work is to clarify purpose, which involves first identifying a philosophy (Chapter 2) and then deducing appropriate goals and objectives. Once this framework for program development is established, an assessment of need is conducted to sharpen the focus in terms of the target—the learner. Finally, the curriculum itself is analyzed through a mapping-out process, and the instructional activities are ordered and aligned with learning standards for maximum effect. The curriculum worker strives to attain a nearly perfect correspondence between the curriculum planned and the curriculum experienced by students. (Figure 5.1)

In the real world of schools, success at curriculum development often means being good at managing the curriculum development process. In this chapter, your author shares his experience in accomplishing such management in the real world of schools.

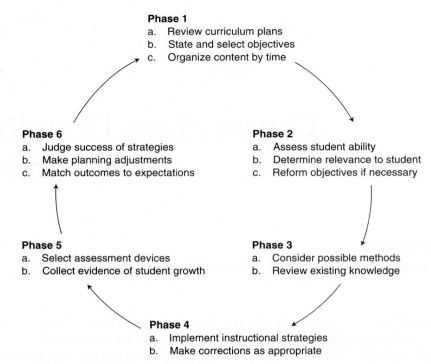

Phase 1
a. Review curriculum plans
b. State and select objectives
c. Organize content by time

Phase 6
a. Judge success of strategies
b. Make planning adjustments
c. Match outcomes to expectations

Phase 2
a. Assess student ability
b. Determine relevance to student
c. Reform objectives if necessary

Phase 5
a. Select assessment devices
b. Collect evidence of student growth

Phase 3
a. Consider possible methods
b. Review existing knowledge

Phase 4
a. Implement instructional strategies
b. Make corrections as appropriate

FIGURE 5.1   The Instructional Planning Cycle.

ESTABLISHING THE PHILOSOPHY

A *philosophy*—the clarification of beliefs about the purpose, goals, and objectives of instruction—is the foundation for all curriculum development efforts. School programs without this essential foundation are often disjointed, and can be either targets for social pressure or operate in a state of programmatic contradiction. The development of a working philosophy of education is prerequisite to all other leadership efforts in school improvement.

The task of goal setting is a national function in almost all countries of the world. (Figure 5.2)

In the United States, goal setting is a continuous process led by curriculum workers at various operational levels (national, state, district, school, and classroom). Such goal-setting is generally done in one of three ways:

1. Others can be asked to review existing statements of philosophy or related documents and restate them in terms of desired changes.
2. Others can be asked to transfer their own personal philosophy of living into a school context, setting goals for school from general life goals.
3. Others can be asked to look for patterns in current behavior in society that might suggest goals for schools.

Methods that can be used to help others achieve goal clarity and consistency include writing personal goal statements, assigning priorities to various items, surveying existing

Australia	1. Fulfilling lives and active citizenship 2. Joining the workforce 3. Overcoming disadvantage and achieving fairness in society
Taiwan (ROC)	The three principles: geography, history, and economy (the meaning of nation) Utilization of group life (operation of democracy) Productive labor (livelihood) Eight moral virtues: loyalty, kindness, love, faith, righteousness, harmony, peace, fidelity
People's Republic of China	1. Develop good moral character 2. Develop love of motherland 3. Literacy and intellect 4. Healthy bodies 5. Interest in aesthetics

FIGURE 5.2   Sample Statements of Purpose for National Education Systems.

Source: National documents from respective state education departments. See also C. Postlethwaite, *Encyclopedia of Comparative Education and National Systems of Education,* Oxford, Pergamon Press, 1988.

documents, and analyzing school programs. One widely practiced method of clarifying philosophical positions is to have persons develop belief statements. These statements rest on a simple premise: Each time a person acts, there is a rationale for action. Without a formalization of such rationales, it is impossible to coordinate or manage individual activities.

Belief statements can be organized in numerous ways, and the correct way for any individual district depends on the planning format. Figure 5.3 lists examples of belief statements organized around students, learning, teaching roles, grouping of students, and educational programs in general. The generic philosophy from which these are drawn is that the school exists to meet the needs and interests of students.

After identifying a philosophy and stating it in easy-to-understand belief statements, the school district or school is ready to develop goals that serve to guide development. Such goals are drawn from the philosophical orientation of the district, the needs of the school population, and the unique characteristics of the community.

As curriculum specialists clarify their own beliefs about the purpose of education and assist others in finding their value systems, the odds for meaningful curriculum development increase. Shared values can form the bond of commitment to change. The time spent in assessing group philosophies pays off significantly in areas such as continuity in school programs and articulation among school levels, development of relationships and roles among school faculties, selection of learning activities and materials, evaluation of school programs, and redesign of basic curriculum offerings.

Most important, however, is the connection of philosophy to leadership and decision making in education. To be decisive leaders and consistent decision makers, curriculum specialists must know their values and those of the persons around them.

Students
1. WE BELIEVE that students are individuals with unique characteristics and interests.
2. WE BELIEVE that students should have an equal opportunity to learn, based on their needs, interests, and abilities.

Learning
1. WE BELIEVE that students learn best when content is relevant to their own lives.
2. WE BELIEVE that students learn best in an environment that is pleasant and in which the democratic process is modeled.

Teaching
1. WE BELIEVE that the role of the teacher in the classroom is primarily that of a facilitator of learning.
2. WE BELIEVE that student learning may be affected more by what teachers do than by what they say.

Grouping
1. WE BELIEVE that a more effective program of instruction can be provided for students if they are grouped according to maturation level and similar interest.
2. WE BELIEVE that a high school should include those students who are mature enough to participate in a program that is more specialized than the middle school and those students beyond the age of 18 who have a need to complete the requirements for a high school diploma.

The Educational Program
1. WE BELIEVE that all special programs should incorporate specific educational objectives that complement the total school program.
2. WE BELIEVE that evaluating and changing programs to more effectively meet the needs and interests of students should be a continuous process.

FIGURE 5.3   Example of Belief Statements.

FORMULATING GOALS

Educational goals are statements of the intended outcomes of education. The scope of the entire educational program can be found in the goals espoused by a school. Goals are also the basic building blocks of educational planning and curricular programs.

Goals may be stated at various levels of specificity. Many school goals are purposefully broad so that a majority of the public can support the intentions of the school. Sometimes, there is an attempt to state the goals in terms of student behaviors that the school seeks to promote. Over the years, commissions have attempted to define U.S. education by developing formal goals. These statements, while often impressive, are not tied to any endorsing or regulating body and rarely have a long-term impact.

Perhaps the most familiar goals in the United States are those defined by the Commission on Reorganization of Secondary Education in 1918. Those goals were (1) health, (2) command of fundamental processes, (3) worthy home membership, (4) vocation, (5) citizenship, (6) worthy use of leisure time, and (7) ethical character. These became widely known as the Seven Cardinal Principles of Secondary Education. A second attempt at defining the purposes of secondary education by the Educational Policies Commission of the National Education Association and the American Association of School Administrators in 1938 resulted in the development of a number of goals under the headings (1) self-realization, (2) human relationships, (3) economic efficiency, and (4) civic responsibility.

The Association for Supervision and Curriculum Development (1982), a national organization of curriculum specialists, identified a set of valued learning outcomes "that reflected the 'holistic' nature of individuals." Hundreds of organizations, including state departments of education and regional research and development centers, were requested to share their goals with the group. The group identified 10 major goals for youth:

1. Self-conceptualizing (self-esteem)
2. Understanding others
3. Basic skills
4. Interest and capability for continuous learning
5. Responsible member of society
6. Mental and physical health
7. Creativity
8. Informed participation in the economic world of production and consumption
9. Use of accumulated knowledge to understand the world
10. Coping with change

CLASSIFYING GOALS AND OBJECTIVES

Educational goals inherently reflect the philosophical preferences of the writer of the goals. Objectives also have a philosophical underpinning and form the fabric of instructional development at the school and classroom levels.

Goals for educational planning generally occur at three levels (see Table 5.1). Level I goals are broad and philosophical in nature; for example, "The environment of the school must be conducive to teaching and learning—safety for all is a primary concern."

TABLE 5.1 The Relationships Among Levels I, II, and III Learning Objectives

Level of Objectives	Type	Origin	Features
Level I	Broad goals or purposes	Formulated at district level by councils or school board	Seldom revised
Level II	General but more specific than Level I	Formulated at school or department level	Contain an outline of process to accomplish Level I objectives
Level III	Behaviorally stated	Formulated by teams of teachers or single teacher	Describe expected outcome, evidence of assessment of outcome, and level of performance

Level II goals are more specific than Level I goals and are often used to define or give form to such aspirations. For example, the following indicators might be used to define an orderly and safe environment:

Indicators

1. The school climate reflects an atmosphere of respect, trust, high morale, cohesiveness, and caring.
2. Expectations for student behavior are clearly stated in a student handbook.
3. A variety of classroom management skills are used to create a businesslike, orderly, and comfortable classroom environment, conducive to learning.
4. Discipline within the school is enforced in a fair and consistent manner.
5. Parents are informed of disciplinary action as it relates to their child.
6. Positive reinforcement of expected behavior is observable throughout the school.
7. Student work is attractively displayed throughout the school.
8. The physical plant is clean, aesthetically pleasing, safe, and well maintained.
9. School improvement needs are assessed annually, the needs are prioritized, and the principal is resourceful in getting the tasks accomplished.
10. The principal is involved in prioritizing countywide maintenance requests.

Level III objectives are specific to the classroom level and are stated in terms of student behavioral outcomes. These objectives structure learning activities and tell the teacher if the intention of the curriculum has been met.

Behavioral objectives are statements describing what learners are doing when they are learning. Teachers need to describe the desired behaviors well enough to preclude misinterpretation. An acceptable objective lets students know what is expected of them. It also enables teachers to measure the effectiveness of their own work. Behaviorally stated objectives contain three essential elements:

1. The terminal behavior must be identified by name. An observable action must be named indicating that learning has taken place.
2. The important conditions under which the behavior is expected to occur should be described.
3. The criteria of acceptable performance should be specified.

A simple method of developing a complete behavioral objective is to apply the *A, B, C, D rule,* where *A* stands for the "audience," *B* for the "behavior," *C* for the "condition," and *D* for the "degree of completion." A behavioral objective containing all these elements is a complete objective. For example:

A. The student will (audience)
B. successfully complete the multiplication problems (behavior)
C. during the class period (condition)
D. getting 80% correct (degree).

The advocacy of behavioral objectives by those seeking to clarify educational purpose has met resistance from those who believe describing learner outcomes in this fashion is simplistic and reduces the act of education to a state of mere training.

In the rush to write clear precise statements, teachers sometimes choose simple objectives that require little thinking on the part of their students. These teachers are writing objectives at the lowest levels of cognitive behavior. Through in-service training, teachers can master the skill of writing objectives requiring higher forms of thinking on the part of their students. In addition, teachers should write objectives leading to affective and psychomotor behaviors, which are discussed next.

USING OBJECTIVES TO ORDER LEARNING

Anyone familiar with program development in schools knows that there is regularly a discrepancy between the intentions of the curriculum and what the teacher actually delivers to students. This "disorder" is a result of not refining goals and objectives, not specifying what the teacher is to do with the student, or not defining what the student is to do after having been taught. Simple tools for "ordering" the curriculum are the three taxonomies of learning: (1) the *cognitive domain,* (2) the *affective domain,* and (3) the psychomotor domain (see Figures 5.4, 5.5, and 5.6).

Each of these hierarchies of learning was developed to assist planners in targeting the level of learning desired and to direct the complexity of the teaching act and the materials encountered by the student. *Cognition,* the mental processing of information, is conceived by Bloom as a six-tier model arranged from the simplest processing (knowledge) to the most complex (evaluation). Krathwohl's affective domain, a five-level model, addresses the degree of "feeling" experienced by the student about the material encountered. Harrow's psychomotor behaviors suggest an order of physical response to learning situations.

When planning learning, the curriculum developer should ask, "What is specifically intended for the learner?" and then write an appropriate objective to guide the teacher in the classroom. For instance, if we are teaching the student about the Civil War, what is our intention? Do we want them to know about it (Bloom's first tier) or to be able to analyze the activities (Bloom's fourth tier)? A corresponding degree of feeling would accompany the learning experience. Seen in this way, planning a curriculum at the instructional level might be thought of as a matrix, as shown in Figure 5.7. At Point A, the junction of cognitive level 2 and affective level 2, the student should comprehend the material and respond to it.

SPECIFYING BEHAVIORAL OBJECTIVES

After goals and general descriptors of direction have been developed, long-range planning requires the specification of objectives that will guide the creation of school programs. *Objectives* are written operational statements that describe the desired outcome of an educational program. Without such objectives, the translation of general goals into programs is likely to be haphazard. With such objectives, the outcomes can be assessed and validated.

The objectives developed by a school or district should be derived from existing goal statements. If objectives are developed that do not directly relate to a goal area, they may suggest goals that need to be addressed by the district. From a planning perspective, the major purpose of identifying objectives is to manage and evaluate the population to be served, the timing of instructional delivery, and the expected outcomes.

Many school districts become bogged down in an attempt to translate goals into objectives because of the behavioral aspect of the task. In general, objectives attempt to

Knowledge	Comprehension	Application	Analysis	Synthesis	Evaluation
(ability to recall; to bring to mind the appropriate material)	(ability to comprehend what is being communicated and make use of the idea without relating it to other ideas or material or seeing fullest meaning)	(ability to use ideas, principles, theories in new particular and concentrated situations)	(ability to break down a communication into constituent parts to make organization of the whole clear)	(ability to put together parts and elements into a unified organization or whole)	(ability to judge the value of ideas, procedures, and methods using appropriate criteria)
					Requires synthesis
				Requires analysis	Requires analysis
			Requires application	Requires application	Requires application
		Requires comprehension	Requires comprehension	Requires comprehension	Requires comprehension
	Requires knowledge	Requires knowledge	Requires knowledge	Requires knowledge	Requires knowledge

FIGURE 5.4 The Taxonomy of Educational Objectives: Cognitive Domain.

Source: From Benjamin S. Bloom et al. *Taxonomy of Educational Objectives.* Published by Allyn and Bacon, Boston, MA. Copyright © 1984 by Pearson Education. Adapted by permission of the publisher.

Receiving	Responding	Valuing	Organization	Characterization
Receiving	**Responding**	**Valuing**	**Organization**	**Characterization**
(attending; becomes aware of an idea, process, or thing; is willing to notice a particular phenomenon)	(makes response at first with compliance, later willingly and with satisfaction)	(accepts worth of a thing, idea or a behavior; prefers it; consistent in responding; develops a commitment to it)	(organizes values; determines interrelationships; adapts behavior to value system)	(generalizes certain values into controlling tendencies; emphasizes internal consistency; later integrates these into a total philosophy of life or world view)
				Requires organization of values
			Requires development of values	Requires development of values
		Requires a response	Requires a response	Requires a response
	Begins with attending	Begins with attending	Begins with attending	Begins with attending

FIGURE 5.5 The Taxonomy of Educational Objectives: Affective Domain.

Source: From David R. Krathwohl, Benjamin S. Bloom, and Bertram B. Masia. *Taxonomy of Essential Objectives, Book 2: Affective Domain.* Published by Allyn and Bacon, Boston, MA. Copyright © 1964 by Pearson Education. Adapted by permission of the publisher.

					Expressive Movements (communicates through body movement, e.g., facial expression)
				Skilled Movements (is efficient in performing complex movements, e.g., dancing)	
			Physical Abilities (uses organic vigor, e.g., lifts weights)		
		Perceptual Abilities (interprets the environment and makes adjustments, e.g., dodges ball)			
	Fundamental Movements (forms by combining reflex movements, e.g., walking)				
Reflex Movements (reacts without conscious volition in response to stimuli)	Begin with movement	Begin with movement	Begin with movement	Begin with movement	Begin with movement

FIGURE 5.6 Levels of Psychomotor Behavior.

Source: Adapted from Table 5, pp. 104–106, in *A Taxonomy of the Psychomotor Domain: A Guide for Developing Behavior Objectives*, Anita J. Harrow (New York: Longman Publishing Group), Copyright © 1972 by Anita J. Harrow. Reprinted by permission of the author.

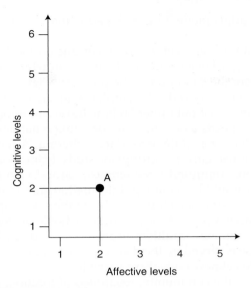

FIGURE 5.7   Curriculum Planning Matrix.

communicate to a specific group the expected outcomes of some unit of instruction. They identify both the capability learned and the performance that the capability makes possible. The process can become mechanical and can sometimes threaten individualized programs when the objectives are stated in behavioral terms. If the emphasis of the school program is on experiencing rather than on being able to exhibit behaviors, such specificity may be altogether inappropriate for curriculum planning.

The following are advantages of using behavioral objectives in planning curricula:

- They help identify the specific behaviors to be changed.
- They increase interschool and intra-school communication.
- They direct instructional activities in the classroom.
- They provide a meaningful basis for evaluation.

The following are potential disadvantages of using behavioral objectives to plan curricula:

- They are sometimes simplistic; human behavior is more than the sum of its parts.
- They disregard the interrelatedness of human activity.
- They frequently limit choice by removing or prohibiting alternatives.
- They limit concomitant learning in the classroom.

ASSESSING NEEDS: FOCUSING FOR RESULTS

Once the basic framework of the curriculum plan is in place, a substantial amount of focusing is necessary to increase efficiency and meet intentions. In many school districts, a failure to assess the true needs of the learners results in a dysfunctional curriculum. The needs assessment technique represents a comprehensive inquiry into the educational status of a district or school. The major goal of the process is to determine whether the intentions are being met through the existing instructional form. Such inquiry often leads to adjustments in goals, instructional technique, and expectations for students.

Needs assessments are characteristically conducted locally by school or district staffs, and differ from *accreditation* visits and surveys in which outside experts usually make observations about the condition of the program. Figure 5.8 shows a typical outline of areas that may be reviewed. The emphasis in the needs assessment is not so much on what conditions exist but rather on how those conditions affect the program.

The first steps of a needs assessment are deciding what data are needed for decision making and developing a strategy for data gathering. A typical needs assessment in a school district will use citizens' groups or study teams comprising a mixture of persons from the school community. Sometimes, natural resources that might affect local school operation should be included. Information should also be included about local commerce and industry, which may indicate the tax support for schools in the area as well as the relative wealth of the parents of schoolchildren.

Special social or economic conditions in an area should also be noted. For instance, if a nearby military base is served by the district, or if there is a seasonal migrant population, it is important to acknowledge these variables.

General data about the community, regardless of location, are available in public libraries in standard census reports. Current information dating from the last census can generally be obtained from the local chamber of commerce or from various Internet sources.

General Information

It is important in any needs assessment to put in perspective the meaning of educating in a public school. Each of the approximately 14,000 U.S. school districts has unique variables that are reflected in its schools. Failure to know and understand such variables often leads to school plans that are inappropriate for community standards or are impossible to implement given community resources. Any needs assessment should begin with an accurate but brief description of the school setting. The size of the district, its population, the governance pattern (elected or appointed officials), and its resource capacity are information items critical to school planning.

General Population Characteristics

When information is gathered about the people who live in the area served by the school district, an attempt should be made to understand the community's educational and cultural levels, general attitudes about schools, and expectations for education in the area. Some of the most important information to be learned about the people who are served by the school district is their cultural heritage and set of traditions. In areas where populations are stable, both in terms of turnover and composition, there is usually minimal social or cultural change. Because schools tend to reflect the communities they serve, a comparable stability should be present in school data. In communities that have experienced considerable growth or turnover of population, however, school planning data tend to be more varied, and corresponding changes in the schools can be expected.

Along with information about population changes, data about economic development in the community often indicate anticipated population changes that will affect schools. The closing of key industries or military bases, declining farm populations, or seasonal industries can signal new patterns for school districts. Out-migration of urban

I. General information
   a.   Location of school district
   b.   Demographic characteristics of immediate area
   c.   Natural resources of region
   d.   Commercial–industrial data
   e.   Income levels of area residents
   f.   Special socioeconomic considerations
II. General population characteristics
   a.   Population growth patterns
   b.   Age, race of population
   c.   Educational levels of population
   d.   Projected population
III. School population characteristics (ages 3–19)
   a.   School enrollment by grade level
   b.   Birthrate trends in school district
   c.   In-migration, out-migration patterns
   d.   Race/sex/religious composition of school district
   e.   Years of school completed by persons over 25 years of age
   f.   Studies of school dropouts
IV. Programs and course offerings in district
   a.   Organization of school programs
   b.   Programs' concept and rationale
   c.   Course offerings
   d.   Special program needs
V. Professional staff
   a.   Training and experience
   b.   Awareness of trends and developments
   c.   Attitudes toward change
VI. Instructional patterns and strategies
   a.   Philosophical focus of instructional program
   b.   Observational and perceptual instructional data
   c.   Assessment of instructional strategies in use
   d.   Instructional materials in use
   e.   Decision-making and planning processes
   f.   Grouping for instruction
   g.   Classroom management techniques
   h.   Grading and placement of pupils
   i.   Student independence
   j.   Evaluation of instructional effectiveness
VII. Student data
   a.   Student experiences
   b.   Student self-esteem
   c.   Student achievement
VIII. Facilities
   a.   Assessment of existing facilities and sites
   b.   Special facilities
   c.   Utilization of facilities
   d.   Projected facility needs
IX. Summary of data

FIGURE 5.8   Basic Needs Assessment Framework.

populations, regional economic prosperity, or the development of new industries based on natural resources can also affect school planning.

A number of population composition variables are important indicators for school planners. Birthrate projections, population stability patterns, racial and economic composition, and special social and cultural characteristics such as languages spoken or national origin of parents all have planning implications for school leaders.

Another influential variable to include in a formal needs assessment is the educational level of parents and persons in the community over 25 years of age. Data about the educational achievement in the community often indicate the amount of belief in, and support for, education.

School Population Characteristics

Among the most stable and useful data available to school planners are the birthrate trends in the district and the school enrollment patterns by grade level. Because of the rise in births in the late 1980s, school populations increased at the elementary levels in the early 1990s, in the intermediate grades in the late 1990s, and in the high schools starting in 2002. All school populations increased after 2000 due to immigration patterns. Using such data, planners can determine how many classrooms and teachers will be needed, as well as how many programs will be required for special students (one in seven students in 2013 was categorized as special). Birthrate information is available through county health department records.

The racial, ethnic, religious, and sexual composition of a school district is also important to school planners. In the United States, the population is becoming increasingly mobile because of changes in family structure and the economy. As a result, primary characteristics of communities can change rapidly, and the educational organization may need to adjust accordingly. When such change goes unnoticed, obsolescence is often a major problem.

Perhaps the most important data about school population come from studies of dropouts. Most school districts in the United States have an alarming number of students who terminate their formal education prematurely. The school and the communities should be particularly concerned about any student who chooses to walk out the door, never to return. Such an exodus can indicate a deficiency in school programming and can have severe implications for the community, which must absorb the dropouts. In Florida, for example, 80% of all persons incarcerated in state prisons (100,000) are school dropouts, and the cost of maintaining each prisoner is seven times the cost of educating each student attending a public school.

Students who quit school prior to graduation usually face employment difficulties, limited job opportunities, low earning power, fewer opportunities for promotions, and emotional stress from related cultural and social pressures. To accept a high dropout rate as a normal event in the schooling process is a shortsighted position for an agency charged with the task of preparing the young to become citizens. Table 5.2 illustrates how one school monitored dropout numbers.

Programs and Course Offerings in the District

The general scope and depth of an educational program can best be identified by reviewing the numbers and types of courses and special activities offered by individual

TABLE 5.2   Sample Dropout Grid for the Class of 2012

Year	Number of Students in Class	Number of Dropouts per Year	Dropout %
2008–2009	258	52	20
2009–2010	206	25	12
2010–2011	181	20	11
2011–2012	161	10	6
Class of 2012 (summary)	151	107	41

Note: These figures are representative of schools in states using standards and high-stakes testing, and with high mobility and large minority populations. The average on-time graduation rate for all states is 68%. (2012)

schools. Of importance in understanding the programs of a school district are the organization of school programs, the rationale for such organization, the breadth and scope of course offerings, and the degree to which special education needs are met.

Many school districts conceptualize schooling according to levels of state standard attainment and refer to programs such as primary school, elementary school, middle school, and high school. In such an organization, students advance through the program by grades rather than by age, maturation, achievement, readiness, or interest.

In such programs, content and skill development are dominant organizers; there is little consideration for individual differences, and curriculum planning focuses on the sequencing of experiences. Such programs are usually organized in quantitative units, with teachers, students, classrooms, and textbooks assigned by a predetermined formula. Supplemental activities, enrichment experiences, and student services are added to the core program as resources allow.

Regardless of the avowed purpose of schooling and the primary organization of the educational program, the heart of the assessment process should address the course offerings and student experiences. Most school districts in the United States, because of history and state and local requirements, arrange programs into subject areas. Nearly all schools provide a core of activities that includes mathematics, science, English, and social studies. Most districts also provide supplemental programs in physical education, art, music, and vocational arts. Beyond such basic programs, courses and experiences reflect the capacity of the district to address individual differences. Often, the degree to which a school district tailors such offerings indicates how aware school leaders are of the needs of students.

In recent years, because of research and legislation, school districts in the United States have become sensitive to the needs of special groups of students in school. A list of all such special students would be lengthy, but addressing programs to serve special education, career education, and adult education can illuminate course offerings outside the general curriculum.

Every community has children and youth with special educational needs that cannot be met within the operation of the general program of instruction. Many definitions of students with special needs exist; most include those children with emotional, physical, communicative, or intellectual deviations that interfere with school adjustment or prevent full attainment of academic achievement. Included in such a broad classification are children who are intellectually gifted, as well as those who have mental, physical, or speech disabilities; behavioral disorders; visual or hearing impairments; autism; or multiple disabilities; and those who are homebound or hospitalized. School districts vary in how they serve these special learners. Legislation at the national level (Public Law 94-142 and the Individuals with Disabilities Education Act [IDEA]) has set firm guidelines for special education programs, which affect about one child in seven.

Career and vocational education is fast becoming a major curriculum component of many school districts in the nation. The impetus for this trend comes from many sources, but career and vocational education still represents the major alternative for secondary school students who choose a noncollege-preparatory program. Student interest in vocational programs is generally high among all types of students. The mandate for school districts to provide quality vocational experiences is heightened given that the majority of all students graduating from secondary schools do not go on as full-time students in postsecondary institutions.

A valuable resource for those assessing student vocational interests is the *Directory of Occupational Titles,* produced by the U.S. Department of Labor. This directory identifies more than 21,000 job titles that may be of interest to students. Using instruments such as the Ohio Vocational Interest Survey, students can identify areas in which vocational experiences might be developed. Questionnaires that seek to pinpoint students' plans following graduation can also provide school leaders with rough indicators of need.

A third type of special education program provided by some school districts is adult education. A program for adults depends on their level of educational attainment, the skills and knowledge they need in the community, and whether their interests are in occupational or personal development. School districts can effectively use adult education programs to increase community involvement as well as to build bridges to parents of schoolchildren.

Adults in the community who have less than a high school education may be interested in programs geared to meeting basic education needs. Such programs often lead to completion of a high school equivalency test. Other adults may be interested in education for job opportunities. Still other adults in the community may participate in education for personal improvement. Popular courses include family-oriented courses, household mechanics, child development, computers, and record keeping.

Professional Staff

A thorough needs assessment also reviews the professional staff in the school district. Among primary concerns are the training and experience of teachers, supervisors, and administrators; the balance among the various teaching positions; and anticipated staff needs. Also subject to analysis is the staff's awareness of recent trends and developments in the field, as well as their attitudes toward change.

A review of staff often indicates a dominance of age, race, or sex among school faculties. These patterns are important in terms of the goals of the district and the specific programs being promoted in the buildings. Such an assessment sometimes reveals an excessive number of graduates from a single university or a pattern of regional dominance among teachers. The latter situation is sometimes unavoidable in remote regions; however, diversity among teaching backgrounds is desirable in terms of the experiences that teachers bring to the classroom.

A district-wide assessment of allocated teaching positions often reveals overstaffing in particular subject areas at the expense of other equally important areas. Such a district-wide review also indicates trends in staffing that can assist planners in projecting future staffing needs.

An analysis of faculty familiarity with new trends and developments in subject areas and new innovative concepts is important if the district anticipates new programs. Such a review can often pinpoint staff development needs that can be addressed during in-service sessions.

School districts can find extremely useful the analysis of professional staff attitudes toward change in general and toward specific curriculum alterations in particular. Such attitudes are the result of many factors, and experience has shown that the age and experience of teachers are poor predictors of readiness to change.

DATA FOR INSTRUCTIONAL PLANNING: INSTRUCTIONAL PATTERNS AND STRATEGIES

By far the most important segment of a needs assessment in schools is the part that focuses on instructional patterns and strategies. Such teacher behaviors should uniformly reflect the intentions of the district to deliver quality programs to students. The types of instruction found in classrooms should result from an understanding of the goals of the district; strategies and techniques can be assessed only after the district philosophy has been clarified.

In some districts, the predominant goal of instruction is that all students master the essential data that will distinguish them as educated persons. In other school districts, the greatest emphasis is placed on the needs, interests, and abilities of students. A key distinction between these two extreme positions is the role of the student in the learning process. Because needs assessments tend to use subjective perceptual data about schools, they are most useful in districts favoring a student-centered curriculum.

Two major techniques can be used to assess instructional patterns and strategies: (1) the observation technique and (2) the administration of projective instruments. The projective approach is by far the more common method of reviewing instruction in needs assessments.

The projective data technique, commonly referred to as the *opinionnaire,* requires the administration of instruments to teachers and, in some cases, students and parents. This perceptual survey is based on findings of phenomenological psychology, which holds that people behave in terms of personal meanings that exist for them at a given moment. In short, behavior is based on perception because we behave and react to what we believe to be real. A personal perception may or may not be supported by facts, but such perceptions serve as facts to each of us.

Projective instruments possess several distinct advantages. First, they are quick to administer and tally. Second, they are easily managed and are less time consuming than interviews or quantitative measures. Most important, however, is that such perceptual techniques allow all teachers in the district to participate in the data-gathering stage. Such involvement is critical if programmatic responses to such findings are to be credible and supported.

DATA FOR INSTRUCTIONAL PLANNING: STUDENT DATA

School districts that attempt to serve the individual needs of learners, as opposed to giving all students the same academic treatment, must gather student data. Data relating to student experiences are valuable as preplanning input, and information about student feelings and achievement can assist school planners in making adjustments to the existing curriculum. Most school districts focusing the curriculum on the student believe that student learning is based on what the student knows coming into the classroom.

Regarding student experiences, a number of variables are useful indicators of both the breadth and depth of the student's world. Most curriculum planners use student data in the belief that a student learns new things based on what that student already knows. A questionnaire that assesses student travel and recreational, aesthetic, and cultural backgrounds can provide teachers with invaluable points of reference for instruction. Examples of such questions at the lower elementary level might be the following:

- Have you ever seen an ocean?
- Have you ever flown on an airplane?
- Have you ever been to a band concert?
- Have you ever been in a public library?
- Have you ever visited a foreign country?

Questionnaires that deal with assessments of experiences, at the secondary as well as at the elementary level, give teachers insights into students' backgrounds and levels of sophistication. When tallied as a percentage, the general level of experience for entire schools can be developed. Another equally valuable assessment device that may provide the same type of information is a projection technique that asks students how to spend extra money or to plan trips.

Information about student attitudes, particularly those relating to self-esteem, can assist school planners in personalizing the instructional program. Beyond learning of student interest, motivation, and attitudes toward learning itself, such assessments often give clear portraits of student confidence in the instructional setting. Research over the past 20 years has shown consistently that individuals who feel capable, significant, successful, and worthy tend to have positive school experiences. In contrast, students who have low self-esteem rarely experience success in school settings (Brookover, 1981, pp. 13–14).

Measures of self-esteem, an individual's personal judgment of his or her worthiness, are plentiful. The *Coopersmith Self-Esteem Inventory,* a 50-item instrument, assesses students' attitudes about themselves, their lives at home, and school life. Students respond to statements such as "I can make up my mind without too much trouble" or "I'm pretty happy" and choose either a "like me" or "unlike me" response. Such instruments can tell school planners a great deal about student confidence, support from home, and attitudes toward the existing curriculum.

Assessments of student achievement can be either broad or narrow in focus. The measure of this essential category is really a reflection of the school district's definition of education. When an educational program is perceived as primarily the mastery of skills and cognitive data, standardized *achievement tests* can be used exclusively to determine progress. When education is defined more broadly, measures of achievement become personal and more affective in nature.

☐ Indicates below-grade placement

Grade level	Number of students by grade							
	2	3	4	5	6	8	11	Total
14.0–14.9								
13.0–13.9							6	6
12.0–12.9							6	6
11.0–11.9						1	8	9
10.0–10.9						5	16	21
9.0–9.9						6	21	27
8.0–8.9					1	14	16	31
7.0–7.9				1	7	9	9	26
6.0–6.9				2	16	29	7	54
5.0–5.9		3	7	9	29	27		75
4.0–4.9		5	27	25	43	13		113
3.0–3.9	3	14	28	55	26	2		128
2.0–2.9	16	40	30	21	9			116
1.0–1.9	75	41	3	11	0			130
0.0–0.9								
Total	94	103	95	124	131	106	89	742

FIGURE 5.9   Summary of Reading Achievement in One School District.

It is useful for school planners to know whether students in a district or particular school are achieving above or below grade level because such information might suggest the retention or elimination of a specific curriculum program. More important, however, are general trends revealed by such tests. A continuing decline in reading scores, for instance, may indicate that a curriculum review is needed. In Figure 5.9, data for students in a district indicate whether they are achieving above or below grade level in reading according to three commonly used standardized tests: (1) *Gates McGinitie* (lower elementary), (2) *Iowa Test of Basic Skills* (middle grades), and (3) *Test of Academic Progress* (secondary grades).

In school districts in which education is defined in terms of comprehensive criteria, there are generally multiple assessments of student achievement. Sometimes such assessments have multiple dimensions, such as achievement in knowledge use, skill acquisition, and personal development. Sometimes such assessments are criterion-referenced, comparing student achievement with goals rather than norms. Almost always the evidence of student achievement is multidimensional, supplementing standardized tests with samples of student work, teacher observations, and other such measures of growth.

DATA FOR INSTRUCTIONAL PLANNING: FACILITIES

Another area considered by most needs assessments is that of the educational facilities used by the district to accomplish its program goals. Ideally, such facilities should be designed on the basis of program concepts. An in-depth study of facilities seeks to answer the following critical questions:

- What is the overall pattern of facilities in the district?
- How adequate is each plant and site for educational use?
- How are the facilities currently being used?
- What is the net operating capacity of each facility?
- How much technology is found in the building?

Assessments of facilities and sites attempt to analyze the adequacy and capacity ratings of all plants and grounds for maximum benefit to the educational program. A basic principle of most such studies is that flexible, multiuse facilities are more beneficial than those that limit programs to a single instructional pattern. A facility (school building) is considered adequate and modern if it provides the following:

- A variety of grouping patterns
- The use of educational media
- Guidance
- Health and food services
- Adequate technology for instruction
- Special-interest instruction (music, art, home economics, science, horticulture, and so on)
- Large-group assembly
- Administrative functions

The value of such a building-by-building analysis for educational planning is that it allows school planners to see facilities in terms of the desired educational program. School plans can be compared and priorities for new building programs can be identified. If additional school sites are projected, lead-time is available for survey and acquisition. Remodeling, where needed, can be scheduled.

An important phase in the assessment of facilities is the identification and analysis of special facilities. In most school districts, special facilities are perceived as supplemental to regular instructional spaces and thus are considered a luxury. School districts must choose among a host of special rooms and spaces such as gymnasiums, art rooms, and teacher offices. Many schools have also had to plan rooms specifically for students with physical handicaps or other special needs. Decisions regarding special rooms and spaces should be based on school planning rather than convenience or familiarity.

The assessment of school facilities and sites, including special areas and use patterns, should assist school planners in developing long-range facilities planning. Such planning can eliminate an undesirable pattern of acquiring sites and building schools after needs become critical. Under the latter set of conditions, educational facilities are rarely adequate or appropriate to the needs of the instructional program.

HOW SCHOOLS IMPROVE PROGRAMS

The methodology of school reviews depends on both an understanding of curriculum development and the sophistication of the district in carrying out a review procedure. Sometimes, schools review themselves in terms of external criteria, such as when they seek professional accreditation or rely on the expert opinion of consultants who survey the district. Other districts choose to conduct an internal needs assessment, for instance, after a change of leadership when new leaders wish to have a status report. These three approaches are compared and contrasted in Table 4.1 (previous chapter).

TEACHERS IN CLASSROOMS

As previously discussed, curriculum in our schools has changed significantly during the period of 1990–2015. What has not changed, however, is more than a century of knowledge about *pedagogy,* the act of teaching and learning. Curriculum leaders responsible for ensuring that learning occurs must emphasize implementation of curriculum at the classroom level to guarantee effectiveness. Curriculum leaders must work directly with teachers to acknowledge individual differences in students and to construct meaningful strategies to accommodate uniqueness. A strictly standards-based curriculum, with its orientation toward test performance, will not suffice.

THE TRADITIONAL RELATIONSHIP

The traditional role of instruction in schools has always been perceived as a subset of curriculum planning. Curriculum development evolves through a cycle in which a situation is analyzed, a program is designed, steps are taken to implement the program, and then an assessment is made to ascertain the degree to which the program achieved its goals. Classroom instruction traditionally has followed a similar cycle; instructional planning is a cycle within a cycle. In the instructional cycle, a teacher enters the classroom with the formally planned curriculum, analyzes that plan in terms of the students being taught, and adjusts the curriculum to fit the students according to variables such as ability, interest, motivation, and/or relevance. The classroom teacher then proceeds to implement the plan (teach the lesson). In the instructional plan, the teaching concludes with some type of student assessment. This teaching act can be understood or rationalized only in terms of the purpose or objectives of the curriculum and its outcomes. In this traditional model of instruction, the teacher is like an interior decorator rather than an architect; that is, the teacher is not in charge of the purpose or design of instruction, only the delivery. A teacher who does not follow the prescribed plan is dysfunctional.

Various controls assist the teacher in ensuring that what is intended (the planned curriculum) is taught. Students are contained in a classroom space, and there is a scheduled duration for the learning. The teacher is the primary source of access to learning by the student. Curricula have both boundaries (scope) and order (sequence). The format or media (textbook, software program, video or DVD) are generally linear and predetermined. The teacher directs the student in "learning the curriculum."

Corruptions of this systematic approach can occur in this process if the teacher is unaware of, or lacks allegiance to teach, the curriculum as it is intended. In selecting content, media, grouping, pacing, and evaluation options, for example, the teacher often "colors" the curriculum. This emphasis at the classroom level either reinforces or detracts from the general plan. Because values are at the heart of all curricula, it is very important for the teacher to understand and be committed to the avowed purpose of the plan.

Adoption of the curriculum at the classroom level can be seen as a six-step cycle of instructional delivery:

1. Determine teaching tasks and student outcomes.
2. Match objectives to student abilities.
3. Design the instructional process.
4. Deliver the planned curriculum.
5. Use feedback to analyze curriculum and instruction.
6. Adjust instructional delivery.

In the first step, the teacher must arrive at an understanding of the teaching tasks, including any mandated (state standards or Common Core) student outcomes. Having extracted these critical measures of purpose, the teacher views the planning process as something of a distance–rate–time problem: Can I get students to master these objectives by the end of the semester?

The tools a teacher uses at this stage include textbooks, teacher guides, curriculum maps or outlines, and teaching standards. In some school districts, it is assumed that the teacher will conduct such an assessment. In better schools, this act of "talking through" the curriculum is a planned process in which all teachers understand their part and the role of others in meeting the student learning objectives.

A second step at the classroom level is to attempt to match these expectations with the capacity of the students being taught. Concerning the difference in academic achievement, a rough rule of thumb is that for each year in school, there is a year of range. This means that a fourth-grade teacher must accommodate a 4-year range of achievement, maturation, and native ability in planning. This rule applies until high school (a 9-year range in the ninth grade) and trails off as students drop out of school.

By questioning student ability, background, and motivation, the teacher may begin to adjust the planned curriculum in significant ways. At this point, understanding the *intent* of the curriculum (for orientation, or mastery, or application) is very important. What is the meaning of learning about the Treaty of Ghent, the periodic table, or pi? Why do we teach these things? What do we expect the student to do with these things?

In the third stage, the teacher becomes a designer of the instructional process. Here, experience and professional knowledge are essential to decision making. Most teachers learn by trial and error, and experience gives insight about what works under certain circumstances. Teachers become "professionals" when they discover that research can provide useful guidance in this process beyond their own experience. Education has a rich literature and an extensive research base that can be used by teachers who understand this designing function. For example, what does the socioeconomic composition of the class have to do with school success?

Of course, any experienced teacher knows that different students require different strategies. Individual strategies for students are a noble goal, but as long as the teacher is assigned 35 students, these strategies must be global (workbooks, reading groups) rather than individualized. For 50 years, teachers in American schools have labored to meet the needs of individual students without having the sheer physical ability to do so.

In the fourth step of this planning process, the teacher delivers the planned curriculum at the classroom level. In making minute-to-minute adjustments and confronting some of more than 3,500 classroom variables, the possibilities for distortion of the intended curriculum are numerous. The elements of time, space, materials, and media are woven together according to the perceptions of the teacher who sees the class much in the same manner as a conductor sees an orchestra. The key to success in this stage is organization. The exemplary teacher has a plan, a contingency plan, materials, equipment, and an understanding of the purpose of the lesson when she or he enters the classroom. Corrections or improvisations as conditions warrant during the school day are the elements of the art of teaching. Figure 5.10 identifies some of the options open to the teacher who understands this art.

The fifth phase of the traditional teaching act is a *feedback* phase. Here, the teacher weighs the appropriateness of both the planned curriculum and the delivered instruction and makes adjustments for future teaching episodes. Without this assessment step, teaching never changes.

---

1. *Comparative analysis.* A thought process, structured by the teacher, that employs the description, classification, and analysis of more than one system, group, or the like in order to ascertain and evaluate similarities and differences.

2. *Conference.* A one-to-one interaction between teacher and learner in which the learner's needs and problems can be dealt with. Diagnosis, evaluation, and prescription may all be involved.

3. *Demonstration.* An activity in which the teacher or another person uses examples, experiments, or other actual performance, or a combination of these, to illustrate a principle or show others how to do something.

4. *Diagnosis.* The continuous determination of the nature of learning difficulties and deficiencies, used in teaching as a basis for the selection, day by day or moment by moment, of appropriate content and methods of instruction.

5. *Direct observation.* Guided observation provided for the purpose of improving the study, understanding, and evaluation of that which is observed.

6. *Discussion.* An activity in which pupils, under teacher or pupil direction, or both, exchange points of view concerning a topic, question, or problem to arrive at a decision or conclusion.

7. *Drill.* An orderly, repetitive learning activity intended to help develop or fix a specific skill or aspect of knowledge.

8. *Experimentation.* An activity involving a planned procedure accompanied by either the control of conditions or a controlled variation of conditions, or both, together with observation of results for the purpose of discovering relationships and evaluating the reasonableness of a specific hypothesis.

9. *Field experience.* Educational work experience, sometimes fully paid, acquired by pupils in a practical service situation.

10. *Field trip.* An educational trip to places where pupils can study the content of instruction directly in its functional setting, for example, factory, newspaper office, or fire department.

FIGURE 5.10 Method Options for Instruction.

11. *Group work.* A process in which members of the class work cooperatively rather than individually to formulate and work toward common objectives under the guidance of one or more leaders.

12. *Laboratory experience.* Learning activities carried on by pupils in a laboratory designed for individual or group study of a particular subject-matter area, involving the practical application of theory through observation, experimentation, and research, or, in the case of foreign language instruction, involving learning through demonstration, drill, and practice. This applies also to the study of art and music, although such activity in this instance may be referred to as a *studio experience.*

13. *Lecture.* An activity in which the teacher gives an oral presentation of facts or principles, the class frequently being responsible for note taking. This activity usually involves little or no pupil participation by questioning or discussion.

14. *Manipulative and tactile activity.* Activity by which pupils use the movement of various muscles and the sense of touch to develop manipulative or perceptual skills, or both.

15. *Modeling and imitation.* An activity frequently used for instruction in speech, in which the pupils listen to and observe a model as a basis upon which to practice and improve their performance.

16. *Problem solving.* A thought process structured by the teacher and employed by the pupils for clearly defining a problem, forming hypothetical solutions, and possibly testing the hypothesis.

17. *Programmed instruction.* Instruction using a workbook together with either a mechanical or electronic device, or both, which has been programmed by (a) providing instruction in small steps and (b) asking one or more questions about each step in the instruction and providing instant feedback if the answer is right or wrong.

18. *Computer-assisted instruction.* An activity in which software programs provide students with practice in key skill areas or are used to search for further information about selected topics.

FIGURE 5.10   *(Continued)*

In most states, students are given standardized tests that reflect how well they have mastered predetermined skills and objectives. Content mastery from prescribed textbooks would be another possible measure of student learning. Student performance on a task is another possible measure of learning. It is important for the teacher to view teaching as a purposeful act; teaching is about students learning rather than teachers talking. The successful teacher has a way of documenting such progress, including a gradebook, portfolios, test scores on standardized tests, and other student applications. In the best districts, these "proofs" of student learning are passed on from year-to-year in a cumulative folder as the student progresses.

A final phase in instructional design is the act of redesigning the way a curriculum is delivered. A teacher's ability to reflect on and make mature adjustments in teaching behaviors depends on that teacher's intrinsic motivation. Professionalism, knowledge, and pride drive even the 20-year veteran teacher to seek new skills (staff development) and materials to be more effective. This professional assessment, of course, begins the cycle once again.

In addition to this cycle, teachers must possess a way of thinking about learning to be effective in the classroom. Teachers who have not conceptualized an approach to the

1. Is the room prepared? Is furniture arranged to promote desired learning? Is the environment conductive to what I intend to teach?
2. Do I have a plan for getting students into the room and settled in their seats?
3. Have I thought of a "motivational opener" to make the transition from the last class they attended to this one?
4. Can I give the students a preview (advanced organizers) of what we'll be doing during the period so they'll know what to expect?
5. Have I estimated the time required for each activity this period?
6. Are the major concepts for this lesson covered by my planned activities?
7. Are the essential facts I want taught in the materials to be used?
8. Have I planned for the appropriate level of affect desired?
9. Have I planned to allow each student to participate at an appropriate level of learning?
10. Are the necessary and appropriate materials present in the room?
11. Do I have a plan for discussion? Have I clarified what kind of discussion will contribute to the lesson objectives?
12. Have I planned for relevance? Do I have some real-life examples?
13. Have I considered handout procedures and steps for collecting homework?
14. How will I involve special students in this lesson?
15. What is my plan for grouping? What directions will I give?
16. Do I have a plan for possible deviant behavior today?
17. Do I want to emphasize a certain format/standards for today's homework or assignment?
18. What kind of test questions would I ask about today's material? Do I want to share these expectations with students?
19. What kind of a technique will I use for closure of today's class?
20. What is my procedure for dismissal of the class?

FIGURE 5.11 Twenty Questions Before Teaching.

teaching–learning act often present an unclear instructional pattern to their students, thereby causing students to fail in the achievement of intended outcomes. Teachers in the preparatory phase may want to ask themselves the following questions (also see Figure 5.11):

1. *What am I expected to teach?*   On arrival in any classroom, the teacher will be confronted with materials and equipment thought to be generically valuable for any occasion: texts, soft-sided instructional supplements, perhaps projection devices (overhead projectors), and (it is hoped) computers and software. Better school districts will offer detailed curriculum maps or frameworks and guides to instructional resources indicating a degree of specificity for the instructional process. Because teaching is perceived in the traditional model as the delivery of the curriculum, the absence of these items is certainly cause for alarm.

2. *To whom am I teaching this curriculum?* Because nearly all school learning is associative (learned in terms of what one already knows), it is important for the teacher to learn about the students. What are their backgrounds? What previous experience of theirs can be used as a reference point? What are their reading levels and other related skill mastery levels?

3. *What is the expected outcome or product of my teaching?* Understanding the exact expectation of these teaching episodes is vital to being successful. Many variables in the classroom are manipulated by the individual teacher (seating arrangements, use of time), and each such adjustment will change the "meaning" of the curriculum being delivered. The taxonomies (cognitive, affective, psychomotor) are helpful in targeting the desired outcome and the appropriate teaching behavior to gain such a result.

4. *How can my classroom be best organized to reach these student outcomes?* Teachers can transform their classrooms into an infinite number of learning environments by making instructional decisions prior to teaching. Generally speaking, if the planned curriculum is global (comprehension, familiarity, understanding), then a great deal of flexibility is called for so that the greatest number of students can achieve access to learning. If, on the other hand, the curriculum is specific (mastery, skill acquisition), then high degrees of structure are called for. These adoption decisions by the teacher are critical to student success. An understanding of how the curriculum and classroom instruction interfaces is an essential element in curriculum work.

5. *What can I do to get my students to learn in the intended manner?* This question may seem odd at first unless you recognize that curriculum planners predetermine both the outcome and its intended form. The testing movement, which operates under the assumption that students have learned only if they can demonstrate mastery under specific testing conditions, has reinforced this problem.

TWO LEVELS OF CLASSROOM PLANNING

Two levels of classroom planning must occur if the teaching–learning act is to be successful: preparation and delivery. In the preparation stage, the teacher makes pre-teaching decisions about classroom variables. One of the most important decisions concerns the physical environment. Will the room be formal or informal? Will chairs be arranged to allow communication or lecture? Will the wall spaces be stimulating or unfocused and bland? Will instructional materials be available to students or must they be retrieved?

The teacher must also give thought to instructional time because time is the scarcest commodity in schools. Is this teaching to be conceptual (time invested in thinking) or is it to be straightforward coverage of knowledge? Is all that is to be taught of equal value, or are there big ideas embedded within the lesson? Is there time to explore ideas that come up spontaneously (unintended learning)? Can the teacher alter the use of time in the lesson? Can the order of teaching activities be changed by the teacher?

Particularly for new teachers, planning activities and student grouping patterns are important. New teachers often over- or underestimate the time required for an activity such as a discussion. They also need to decide whether there should be small groups (dyads and triads) or ability groups (mixed or homogeneous).

Of course, the teacher must give thought to classroom management and discipline. Rules and procedures enable the teacher to be effective, and routines promote greater student focus on the lesson being presented. Record keeping is a very important part of any standards-based curriculum.

Before teaching, the teacher needs to consider resources and media. We have entered a new era in which media and technology can play a very important role in shaping lessons and giving meaning to information. Teachers must plan to utilize all the paper and electronic resources at their command to be effective. Marshall McLuhan advised more than 50 years ago that "the medium is the message" (McLuhan, 1964), and this is certainly true in teaching.

Curriculum leaders can have a major impact on the planned curriculum by helping teachers understand these planning variables and how they affect the classroom. Teaching is not a matter of unpacking a commercial package and working one by one through the bulleted items. Rather, teaching is much more like directing a play in which the teacher provides the students a script to follow. Even in a standards-based era, that script can include loops and real-life examples to enhance learning.

A second level of planning for teaching is more detailed and requires the selection of activities based on philosophy and learning theory. A point of origin would be to determine the degree to which the curriculum is to serve the student. A narrowly defined curriculum, like standards-based mastery learning, may be of a fixed, one-size-fits-all variety. Students must come to the curriculum and master it, regardless of whether it is developmentally appropriate for them. A wider definition of the curriculum might have the goal of "using" the knowledge and skills identified by the standard (realism). The widest or most adaptive approach to the curriculum would be to serve the student as a person.

CHOICES: LEARNING THEORY

The choices facing teachers in delivering the curriculum in the classroom begin with a basic learning theory. Stated simply, teachers enter the room with a set of assumptions about how *learning* occurs and, based on these assumptions, they plan and deliver instruction. Although few teachers formalize beliefs in this way on a day-to-day basis, these beliefs nonetheless undergird the process of planning and teaching. One such set of assumptions has been developed by the Committee on Behavioral, Social Sciences, and Education (1999) and is presented in Figure 5.12.

Students naturally engage in making sense out of their worlds.
Students lack experience but not reasoning ability.
Teachers understand patterns not noticed by novice learners.
Teachers demonstrate the context of knowledge application.
Technology can help students visualize and understand.
Technology can access an array of information for students.

FIGURE 5.12 Modern Instructional Theory Including the Role of Technology.
Source: Author notes from Florida Education Technology Conference, March 22, 2002.

It may also be instructive to read the words of some of this country's most revered educators when they described their assumptions about formal learning in the classroom:

John Dewey

The aim of education is to develop the power of self-control in each student. The primary source of control does not reside in the teacher, but with the student. . . . Developing experiences for students, and activities that will guide them, is the task at hand.

David Ausubel

Learning is an active process. It requires that the learner make a cognitive analysis of potentially meaningful material to determine which aspects of existing cognitive structure are most relevant.

Lev Vygotsky

Thought is born in words. . . . The origins of thought are social, coming at first from more capable others. Adults provide a context, a scaffolding, for learning, in the way they communicate with students.

Jean Piaget

Learners create new experiences and events and seek to assimilate them into existing cognitive structures. Children learn by constructing theories about their environment, struggling with disequilibrium, and thereby creating new ways of thinking.

Although there are numerous theorists, learning theories, and even more programs and strategies to promote learning, it may be simpler to present three basic "families of learning" for the reader's understanding: behavioral, developmental, and perceptual. Like the philosophies presented earlier in Chapter 2, these learning theories present the teacher with choices that lead to very different kinds of instructional delivery in the classroom.

Behavioral

The behavioral approach to teaching and learning sees the classroom from an external standpoint and assumes that learning occurs because of something that the teacher does to the student. The student is neutral until activated by the teacher. In this type of classroom, the teacher delivers specific structured and predetermined (standards-based) lessons without significant planning to accommodate student needs or differences. This type of instruction is called *direct instruction* or *mastery learning*. Teacher control in such a room is absolute. Such a lesson includes behavioral objectives, criterion-referenced expectations for student performance, a drill-and-practice methodology, and some type of summary assessment to demonstrate mastery. We refer to this as a highly structured classroom. A leading theorist for this family of learning theory was B. F. Skinner, who stated, "Changes in behavior are the result of an individual's response to events (stimuli) that occur in the environment" (as cited in Epstein, 1997).

Developmental

The developmental learning theory focuses instruction on the needs and developmental stages of growth in the student. Like the behaviorist, the developmental teacher presents a predetermined and structured curriculum but adjusts the curriculum to meet student needs. Developmentalists believe that student motivation comes from trying to fulfill certain tasks of growing up and that student performance in the classroom can be arrested when readiness levels are not achieved. The developmental learning theorist uses the stages of development, studied extensively in the 20th century, to target classroom learning.

A leading theorist for this family of learning was Jean Piaget. He observed that learning is a natural act and then identified four stages of cognitive structure development. Each successive stage allows the student more capacity to learn.

Perceptual

The perceptualist holds a much broader view of the classroom interaction, believing that the student, and not the teacher, is the key to learning. As the teacher delivers lessons, say the perceptualists, students filter the input through their previous experiences and expectations to give it meaning. When students experience success, their perceptual field widens and they become more open or responsive to more teaching. When threatened or when experiencing failure, students restrict their perceptual field and readiness to learn. For the perceptual theorist, then, factors like climate in the classroom are important. In the new technological age, the perceptualist believes that students can learn quite well without the teacher. The teacher is, for the perceptualist, a guide on the side, not the sage on the stage.

Carl Rogers (1961) would serve well as a spokesperson for this learning family. His beliefs about learning were that "significant learning takes place when the subject matter is relevant to the personal interests of the student," and "self-initiated learning is the most lasting and pervasive" (p. 328).

Of course, all of these learning families have additional legitimate advocates, and all can be supported by research on teaching and learning. Note, however, that these three teaching styles result in *different* teaching strategies and *different* learning outcomes, even when the same material is being taught in the classroom. For the curriculum developer at the classroom level, that is the teacher, a critical question is, "Why am I teaching this?"

As mentioned in Chapter 2, it is possible to use a continuum of high structure versus high flexibility to understand any school and any classroom. If the teacher believes that he or she is the source of knowledge and that the goal of schooling is to transmit predetermined curriculum efficiently to a passive student, there will be necessarily a high structure in the classroom. In such a classroom, everything will appear ordered. By contrast, in the flexible classroom, the furniture will not appear ordered, students will have visual and verbal contact, and student interests and needs will be evident. Either or both of these learning approaches can be applied to any curriculum plan.

How material is presented to the student in the classroom is also a matter of choice. The teacher can present the curriculum in a linear fashion so that students master the material the same way (in a sequential fashion). The teacher may also use a conceptual approach, providing a big picture and helping the students organize the material that follows around these larger ideas. In a third format, the teacher can integrate the curriculum so that the subjects and skills are intermingled and connected to the real world. All teachers must ask themselves, "How does a student learn?" and plan teaching from that vantage point.

TEACHING WITH A COGNITIVE FOCUS

A measurable connection exists between how the teacher instructs and how and what the student learns. For example, simple questions such as "who is the president?" receive simple answers. In planning for instruction, therefore, the teacher needs to consider the question of cognitive focus: How direct or how global do I want the student learning to be as I instruct? How well do I want the students to do to demonstrate their learning?

Strategies for teaching with a cognitive focus include linking new information to prior knowledge, restructuring student background knowledge, teaching students how to learn, establishing motivation toward a goal, and teaching students to use existing knowledge to learn more. This type of integrative learning is absent in most standards-based curriculum because the substance of the curriculum has usually been layered on from above or legislated as a package to the districts, schools, and classrooms.

In linking new information to that already held by the student, the teacher attempts to place the new information in a mental structure already known to the student. This can be done by conducting a mental review of previous understandings, by recalling something analogous to what will be learned, or by setting a specific purpose for the new learning by offering a hypothesis or posing a question to be answered. *Semantic mapping,* in which the students provide their associations to the topic to be studied, is a widely used technique.

Restructuring student background is often important because the student may hold a misconception that will distort further learning. Examples of areas where distortion can occur are religious beliefs of others, relative position and size of nations on a map, or causation for weather events. Experienced teachers often say that their students hold misconceptions or odd arrangements of common subject matter. Students studying the Gettysburg Address for the first time, without other understandings, might remember the phrase because it sounds like the word *spaghetti.* Students always learn in terms of what they know.

Teaching students how to learn, or optimizing learning, is sometimes called *metacognition* (an awareness of one's mental processes). Modeling behaviors by the teacher are one source of knowing about learning for the student. The questions a teacher asks also reveal thought patterns to the student. Having students explain their answer to a problem is yet another way to highlight thinking and learning.

Teachers can assist pupils with motivation by helping them make connections between lessons and their own tasks in the real world. Exploring new subject areas can provide satisfaction for students who "collect" information samples. Attitude development, through cooperative learning procedures, may also stimulate motivation.

Learning how to organize knowledge is a major skill for successful school learning. Students can be taught to identify the key features in specific learning episodes, and students can be assisted in integrating new information into their existing knowledge base. Use of outlines, advance organizers, and pattern guides can all contribute to this learning skill.

Beyond defining the scope of the curriculum in the classroom (by determining the cognitive focus and clarifying why the curriculum is being taught) are a whole host of strategies, methods, and media applications that can give "new form" to the structure of a curriculum. Bringing a curriculum to life through Creating Independence through Student-owned Strategies (CRISS), inquiry lessons, or even service learning can be the final filter in the classroom. The curriculum leader who works with teachers can assist in this process by conducting needs assessments, highlighting student backgrounds, studying data trends, and holding discussions among teachers about intent. Curriculum leaders can never forget that the classroom teacher is the final designer of curriculum.

INTERACTION PATTERNS IN THE CLASSROOM

Ever since the classic 1949 study by Hollingshead, it has been known that the environment has a profound influence on learning. The study by Hollingshead found that students whose homes and peer group support the values of the school achieve greater gain in academic learning than students whose home and peer group support values and expectations that conflict with those of the school. Every teacher must realize that the classroom environment influences the kind of learning that occurs in that room. Three areas define these concerns. First, the out-of-school experiences and accomplishments of students are very important to school learning because they help define the value of such school experiences. Second, students who interact with others while learning may get reinforcement for valuing school learning. Third, taking what is learned beyond the classroom (into the community) may assist learners in understanding the importance of learning.

Integrated curricula have long been used to organize and promote common learning and the life skills so important in our society. Organizing curriculum around real-life problems, issues, and skill applications provides a framework for real learning. Margaret Mead, the most famous U.S. anthropologist, stated the importance of this effort in the following way:

> Our schools have long been torn by two moralities—the morality of individual success as measured by gains in the private competitive system, and the morality of individual success as measured by socially useful work consciously directed to the welfare of the whole community. It is time that education make up its mind as to the kind of America it wants, and to educate the young on the basis of the integrated morality. (Mead, 1951, p. 116)

A deterrent to developing curriculum integration in today's schools is that most standards-based programs are set up in terms of conventional "single content" subject areas or skill areas such as reading and writing. Such curricular fragmentation makes learning difficult for even the most competent student. Recently, three professional organizations have developed more generic competencies to guide school and classroom learning, outcomes that cut across subject lines, and focus on life skills.

The proposed goals compiled by the National Study of School Evaluation (NSSE) are organized into six areas: (1) learning to learn skills, (2) expanding and integrating knowledge, (3) communication skills, (4) thinking and reasoning skills, (5) interpersonal skills, and (6) personal and social responsibility. The core standards proposed by the Center for Occupational Research and Development are a second set of global goals for schooling. These 53 core standards cut across a wide area and are coordinated with various occupational fields in business, the arts, science, and engineering (Edling & Loring, 1996). Researchers at Mid-continent Research for Education and Learning developed some general life skills that might be used to define the school curriculum. Starting with 116 standards from 14 content areas, this group focused on only four outcomes: thinking and reasoning, working with others, self-regulation, and life's work (McREL, 1999).

In 2010 the majority of states have banded together to create a common set of objectives for schooling in the areas of reading and mathematics (The Common Core). Scheduled for full implementation in 2013, the Common Core represents a unique form of cooperation among state departments of education (SDOE). The Common Core, described in detail in a later chapter, is funded by the Gates Foundation, Pearson Education, the Mott Foundation, and the U.S. government, and seeks to identify critical goals for all students at different levels of schooling.

These three lists from long-established and respected groups, and the emerging Common Core, form the basis of a new set of broad educational standards that are applicable in the classroom. The use of such generic standards allows teachers to integrate the many subjects and deliver curriculum in a manner relevant to the lives of their students, with all their differences. Teachers are ultimately responsible for achieving educational standards but should not be solely responsible for adapting them to the classroom environment. If curriculum leaders work with teachers in using an integrative approach to connect mandates from the state and district with realities in the classroom, achievement will be maintained and enhanced. One classic analyses by the National Association for Core Curriculum found that, "almost without exception, students in any type of interdisciplinary or integrative curriculum do as well as, and often better than, students in conventional departmentalized programs" (Vars, 1996).

To observe that standards-based education and high-stakes testing is controversial is to understate what is developing into a major philosophical schism in our schools. Most educators, regardless of their philosophy, would acknowledge that public schools should be compelled to present evidence that they are doing their job. Few would argue that standardized tests can help do this. Such tests can clarify achievement expectations for students and provide a solid foundation for student success.

What is at issue for curriculum specialists, however, is whether students are harmed by the emphasis on defining the curriculum so narrowly and forcing schools and districts to adhere to such a curriculum by using high-stakes testing. Audrey Amrein and David Berliner (2002) present evidence that such testing has produced negative outcomes such as reduced achievement, increased dropout rates, and reduced graduation rates, particularly among minority populations in U.S. schools.

Lorrie Shepard (2000), an assessment expert who focuses on gender and ethnic issues, states another possible problem in this manner:

> The negative effect of high-stakes testing on teaching and learning are well-known. Under intense political pressure, testing scores are likely to go up

without corresponding improvement in student learning. In fact, distortions in what and how students are taught may actually decrease students' conceptual understanding. (p. 9)

What is becoming increasingly clear to those who are professional educators and curriculum leaders is that nonprofessionals have "captured" the process of developing school programs. States in this nation have expended billions of dollars to convert the former general education curriculum, characterized by planned experiences for all, into a narrow content-based curriculum that expects all students to perform the same. Given that this is a reality in many of the schools and districts of this nation, what can be done? Within the boundaries of this most powerful curriculum reform, there is certainly opportunity to return balance to the curriculum. By managing standards-based programs more closely at the classroom level, this nation's curriculum leaders can still influence student learning.

MANAGING STANDARDS-BASED PROGRAMS

There is no question that, as long as the standards-based movement in the United States is viable and supported by state laws, educators have little choice but to manage them as mandated. Clearly, a substantial part of the curriculum has been determined by noneducators. However, your author believes that *how* the curriculum is treated determines the "meaning" of that curriculum. Therefore, designing instruction at the classroom level becomes most important for curriculum workers. To allow public schools to be routinized, like some 19th-century factory, is to abandon decades of professional knowledge about teaching and learning and ignore all of the miracles of communication technology since the Internet. Curriculum leaders must follow the standards-based curriculum into the classroom to ensure its validity and relevance for students. Concerns about managing the curriculum at the classroom level include the following:

- Ensuring proper resources
- Aligning the various instructional components
- Organizing instruction materials
- Checking for developmental appropriateness
- Helping teachers pace content
- Addressing student motivation

Ensuring that teachers have adequate resources has become a huge problem in the era of standards-based education. In some commercial programs, such as *America's Choice*, project leaders seek to replace textbooks with special paper learning packets keyed to the mastery of content and skills. When such programs terminate or fail, as they did in Jacksonville, Florida, districts can be left without libraries or texts for learning.

A more common problem is that the materials in a standards-based curriculum are not comprehensive enough to accommodate all of the learners in attendance. An old rule of thumb in education is that for each year in school, there is a year of "range." A fourth grade, for example, will have a 4-year reading range. Materials should be available to engage students at their levels, but it is common in standards-based programs to have uniform learning materials at the level of the objective.

Materials used in the classroom should integrate reference aids such as maps, pictures, glossaries, and bibliographies, but these materials are often absent; the curriculum is presented without context or references. Enrichment and remediation materials are rarely present in state-mandated curriculum materials because all children are expected to perform at a predetermined level.

Readability of the materials goes well beyond simply the level of student comprehension. The degree to which the materials are colorful, relevant, and interesting to the age group has a lot to do with student performance on a state test. In many states, resources must reflect a skill emphasis like "problem solving" or have obvious conceptual organizers.

The scale (scope) of study and the sequence of study of materials is probably a true contribution of the standards-based movement. However, tying those organized outcomes to classroom materials requires thought. The integrity of a curriculum, its structure and logical organization, is often torn apart by the testing expectations of standards-based systems. For teachers to skip over parts of the curriculum known not to be tested is to present the student with a fragmented course of study and a game-show mentality toward scholarship. Narratives and visuals are often left out of highly focused state curricula.

Working to keep the concept of developmental appropriateness in front of teachers constitutes a difficult task for curriculum leaders because such an idea is nonexistent in a standards-based curriculum. State legislation rarely addresses the capacity of children at developmental levels. Clearly, 8 year olds do not have the knowledge, or the cognitive ability, to compare and contrast Eastern and Western cultures in the Renaissance period. While your author believes, as Jerome Bruner (1962) taught, that "all concepts can be taught in some legitimate form at any age" (p. 13), the curriculum leader must help teachers translate state standards using educational logic.

Helping teachers pace their delivery of the curriculum is an important role for leaders in curriculum. Many states have started their school years earlier to get more study time in before spring testing. Helping teachers articulate the curriculum from year to year, and minimize summer losses by students, is an important task of leadership. Also, ensuring that subject matter and skills are organized around concepts or even "chunks" of knowledge is important for long-term learning and retention.

A massive task for curriculum leaders is to help teachers address learning theory and student motivation. On testing day in many states, schoolchildren experience varieties of sickness and test anxiety based on unrealistic test expectations by parents, teachers, and administrators. Such fear and anxiety suppresses test performance and begins a cycle of failure and despair for the student, the teacher, the school, and the district. The best preparation for any standardized test is confidence, understanding, and test motivation. Obviously, in many of the high-stakes testing states, dropout rates of more than 40% do not speak well for the current procedures.

REBALANCING STANDARDS-BASED CURRICULA

In the 1920s, it was observed that the best way to raise the achievement in schools was to drop out the bottom third of the students. Such a "save the best and lose the rest" mentality exists even today in some quarters. Fortunately, most persons interested in improving education see the problem more comprehensively: *All* students need to have those skills and intellectual competencies required for meaningful participation in an advanced technological society.

An achievement gap is a fact in the United States. African American, Hispanic, and Native American students are underrepresented among the high-achieving student population in our public schools. In 2003, for example, white students outscored black students by about 100 points on both the verbal and math sections of the SAT. In 2000, in the National Assessment of Educational Progress (NAEP) testing, the composite scores for white students in science, math, and reading were nearly 30 points higher than those for black and Hispanic students. Most minority students in the United States still attend school where they represent the majority of the students present. According to a 2003 study by Hoffman, 73% of black fourth graders in the United States were enrolled in a school where more than half the students were eligible to receive a free or reduced lunch (Hoffman, 2003).

It is a paradox that the high-stakes standards curricula in the United States are most developed in the southern and western parts of the country—areas which have the highest minority populations and the largest number of high school dropouts. Although a state-mandated standards curriculum can help focus basic outcomes, such a curriculum is obviously not totally effective in assisting all students. Curriculum leaders must help their districts understand this pattern and move beyond the minimum skills testing programs that characterize so many school districts. A so-called standards-plus curriculum is needed.

According to the National Task Force on Minority High Achievement (1999), all students need capabilities such as the following:

- Critical literacy and numeracy
- Mathematical and verbal reasoning
- Skills in creating and recognizing relationships
- Classification of information and stimulus material
- Problem solving from both abstract and concrete situations
- Sensitivity to multiple contexts and perspectives
- Skill in accessing and managing disparate bodies of information
- Resource recognition and utilization (seeking help)
- Self-regulation and metacognition

The task force also observed that these capabilities would be developed only through high quality teaching and learning in the classroom, trusting relationships in school, and support for pro-academic behavior in the school and community. Obviously, academic content must be integrated with an ever-changing and highly relevant social context, which results in the mental activity necessary to make sense of experiences and to solve problems.

In 2004, the North Central Regional Educational Laboratory (NCREL) identified conditions that must be promoted to serve all children in public schools. The two sets of skills are to nurture intellectual competence and to promote the transfer of knowledge to the real world (Bennett, Bridglall, Cauce, Everson, Gordon, Lee, Mendoza-Denton, Renzulli, & Stewart, 2004).

COLLABORATIVE LEADERSHIP IN CURRICULUM

During the past three decades, there have been many efforts at educational reform, and one major trend has been decentralization of school management and administration. Known as *school-based management* or *decentralized decision making,* this effort has attempted to involve teachers in instructional decision making and to make them more accountable for student achievement.

In the last decade, the school reform movement has altered teacher roles and the demands made on them. As Little and Bartlett (2002) observe, "The reform climate moved from a relatively progressive mood to a starkly conservative one, from resource flexibility to resource controls, from open-ended invitations to restructure to uniform mandates centered on state standards and high-stakes testing." The demands of these new roles, of being accountable for learning, have also had the unintended consequence of "burning out" the teaching force in our schools (Tye & O'Brien, 2002, p. 26). It is a fact that curriculum leadership needs classroom teachers to implement any curriculum reform. Two essential functions of educational leadership are to provide direction and to exercise influence. Curriculum leaders, operating in a human organization, are much more effective at distributing leadership to the classroom level.

One theorist recently hypothesized that "values" are the medium in which leadership power exists and through which it functions. From this vantage point, leadership is a function of the interaction between the follower's (teacher's) value system and that of the leader. Teachers, who are drawn into the profession by a love of children and who see themselves serving the students and their needs, cannot follow a leader who speaks exclusively of test scores (Sun, 2004).

Research has consistently shown that when teachers believe they have influence over instructional decisions they consider to be important, they express stronger belief in their ability to implement those decisions and reap positive outcomes from them (Goddard, 2001). Curriculum leaders need to understand that empowering is not synonymous with increasing the workload of teachers by adding to their out-of-classroom responsibilities. Empowerment is synonymous with autonomy (Gonzalez & Short, 1996).

Curriculum leaders need teachers who are committed to children and to the program of studies offered by the school. There are two key antecedents to such commitment: professional autonomy and workplace stressors. The former is positively associated with commitment, and the latter is negatively associated with commitment (Nir, 2002).

TEACHERS AS LEADERS

For more than 30 years, the literature on school leadership has focused on the principal as the critical player in school improvement. Identified as the gatekeeper or manager of change, the principal has served as the focal point for many curriculum initiatives in U.S. schools. However, closer examination of the social dynamics in a school, particularly concerning diffusion of an idea or program, suggests instead that the classroom teacher is the critical element in curriculum development. Despite a strong research base recognizing the "teacher as leader" (Darling-Hammond, 1999; Fullan, Bennett, & Rolheiser-Bennett, 1990; Goodlad, 1984), support for teachers as the critical curriculum players has historically been minimal. This traditional reluctance to let teachers partner in the development of curriculum is changing.

Everett Rogers (1995), long acknowledged as the expert voice in diffusion of innovation research, describes the spread of a new idea as a two-step communication process: (1) adopters gain awareness by media exposure and bureaucratic directives, and (2) opinion leaders in the organization persuade others in the organization to adopt the proposed changes. According to Rogers, these opinion leaders are always socially accessible individuals who share the group's norms yet maintain a competence that allows them to demonstrate leadership to their peers. The actual decision to adopt a curriculum change, says Rogers, is a "social exchange" in which the opinion leader and the other adopters communicate, discuss, and rationalize any changes. Seen from this perspective, any top-down curriculum change succeeds only if it is endorsed and promoted by a knowledgeable and trusted classroom teacher. Your author believes that successful curriculum improvement is always a bottom-up procedure at the school site.

TEACHERS AND THE COMMON CORE STANDARDS

Unique to current times are the additional curriculum responsibilities that teachers will have to assume during the Common Core "run-up." The reader will remember that these new standards are directed toward six global ends:

- Aligned with college and work expectations
- Are clear, understandable and consistent
- Based on rigorous content and applied higher skills
- Built on the lessons of the current state standards
- Informed by other top-performing countries
- Are evidence based

The new Common Core State Standards establish *what* a student is to learn, but not how a teacher should teach. The standards are not a curriculum, per se, but represent a shared knowledge of what students need to succeed. In the two areas, mathematics and English/language arts, they project an "approach to learning" these subjects.

Teachers will witness considerable change at the district level in order to implement CCSS. New curriculum maps and outlines in the two subject areas will be created. New teaching methods will be suggested. Professional development (training) will be prescribed for teachers in every subject. Student outcomes will be defined by new online assessments. Technological instruction will become more prevalent. And, finally, community awareness of this momentous change will be greatly expanded. In the best districts, teachers will be given a roadmap (CMP) to show the relationship of all these implementation activities. In other schools and districts, there will be considerable confusion due to the sheer scale of the change.

Your author sees several critical applications to be made by teachers as the CCSS filters into the classroom: knowing what the research says about instruction; understanding the new assessments; mastering the Common Core skills; and thinking through the multi-lingual and multi-cultural aspects of classroom expectations.

Research

The literature of the Common Core provides research seemingly based on the assumption that the purpose of the curriculum is to reach a learning outcome. While this is desirable, the problem with such a "backward design" is that there are all kinds of learning (conceptual, factual, skill-based) and each requires a different set of teaching skills. A curriculum designed to score points on a standardized test will often become skewed toward just the testing. This fact is evidenced by efforts of standardized curricula in the states for the last 30 years.

Equally important is the attempt of critics of public education to show failure in current practices. An excellent resource for all teachers is Berliner and Biddle, *The Manufactured Crisis: Myth, Fraud, and the Attacks on America's Schools* (1995). This book, and others suggested at the conclusion of this chapter, provides a more balanced picture of what works in schools. Over one hundred years of research suggests many paths to learning in schools.

New Curriculum Assessments

Standardized testing has been prominent in American schools for 30 years, and the Common Core will bring new and sophisticated tests into the classroom. The Common Core will provide more clarity about what is expected of student learning, and the assessments can be expected to be highly specific in their measure of learning.

The assessments being developed will have three formats: short and extended response items, performance-based tasks, and technology enhanced items. The curriculum will have "focus, coherence, and rigor," and it can be expected that the assessments will have the same qualities.

The assessment system will have four components. First, there will be two different "summative" assessments designed to measure student progression and provide data for accountability uses. There will also be two interim (formative) assessments for providing timely information to teachers about student progress. The interim assessments will be administered at the beginning and midway through the year. The summative assessments will be performance-based (PBA) and end of the year (EOY).

Classroom assessments will also be used to measure student progress. Among the major kinds of assessment will be traditional testing, observations, portfolios, and performance samples.

Whether using data from in-class sources or the CCSS assessments, teachers will be translating these standards into instructional practices, such as developing grade appropriate objectives and practices, planning units, and providing appropriate sequencing of activities and materials. Teachers will also be seeking to identify common points of confusion by students, error patterns, and general misconceptions about the subject matter.

Mastering the Common Core Skills

The large organizers of the math and ELA curriculum will be slightly different because of the Common Core. Organizers for grades 1–12 math will consist of number operations, pre-algebra and algebra, geometry and assessment, probability, statistics, and data analysis and problem solving. ELA will be formed from reading, phonemic awareness (blending, segmenting, oral language), phonics (orthography and spelling), fluency (sight words) vocabulary, and comprehension (textual connections, questioning, summarizing).

Teachers, according to the plan, will be provided with curriculum maps to connect or "bridge" the gulf between the standard curriculum and the new Common Core Standards. Among the tasks for the teachers in the classroom will be such things as identifying prior student knowledge, justifying methods and materials being selected, meeting student needs (corrective, developmental, enrichment), and interpretation of student learning data.

Multi-Lingual and Multi-Cultural Concerns

Issues are already present at the time of this writing that suggest a major concern for equality in the learning experience. This is most easily seen in the issue of technology and the problem of "have-nots." The plan for the curriculum and assessment of Common Core calls for computer driven systems—systems that don't exist in most school districts. The recent suggestion that students would bring their own technology to school (BYOT) begs the question of student ownership of such equipment. While the more wealthy districts in America might provide computers for all students, most districts and schools cannot. The CCSS planning teams, to date, have shown little interest in spelling out the fiscal dimensions of converting to a technological delivery of the new curriculum.

There is also a serious concern for the effect of language on performance. Teachers seeking to apply the new standards in their classrooms must be aware of the composition of their student body. In many states, ESL (English as a second language) is widespread. The dropout rate in the United States is highest among these populations due to comprehension problems.

There are numerous cultural issues that might be common including the relevancy of the curriculum materials, the values of community groups, and the fear of failure in testing procedures.

The reader should recognize that standardization of the curriculum most often means a standardized expectation for student performance. Not only are schoolchildren inherently unequal upon arrival at school, but their progress is also often defined by factors beyond their control. Students become less equal, not more equal, as they progress through school. The specialty of curriculum development has been working for half a century to "level the playing field" for students who have special disabilities, adverse social factors, or inadequate childhood experiences prior to attending school. Only at the classroom level can these realities be addressed under the new Common Core State Standards.

PROVIDING LEADERSHIP: SPECIFIC ACTIVITIES

As your author closes this chapter, the following competencies will aid you, the curriculum leader, in assisting teachers to become more effective in their classrooms:

- Produce and implement a yearlong plan focused on the problems and needs of teachers, students, and parents, including a schedule of steps toward completion and tasks that teachers can do to assist you.
- Coordinate the programming for curriculum across the various levels of schooling (articulation) in your school or district.
- Find new ways to integrate curriculum into the existing program of studies at your school.
- Seek ways to help teachers put their personal learning theories into practice.
- Develop a decision-making procedure for curriculum issues that is satisfying to all teachers at your school or in the district.
- Disseminate information on innovative practices in other schools or districts.
- Find new communication channels to encourage discussion among teachers at different levels and in different subject areas.

- Find new ways to highlight the needs of individual students and the special needs of your community to classroom teachers.
- Define, with staff assistance, the needs of teachers and a plan to meet those needs.
- Assist teachers in gaining an understanding of the new generic competencies (Common Core) that will enable the translation of state standards into integrated curriculum.
- Develop a technique to help teachers identify problems in instruction at your school or in your district.
- Find ways to demonstrate that different methods can be used to meet state standards and outcome expectations.
- Discover ways to offer staff development opportunities that meet the individual needs of classroom teachers.
- Become the primary resource person for teachers in your school or district.
- Review all budgetary expenditures for correspondence with curriculum priorities.
- Use research on human development and learning to help focus practices in your school or district.
- Involve members of the community in any re-conceptualization of standards in your district, including school-to-work initiatives.

Summary

A great deal is known about the teaching–learning act and about students who attend school. As a professional area of education, curriculum is built on the foundation of such knowledge. To be a curriculum leader and to ignore pedagogy and human development research is untenable. This is the challenge of the standards-based era now in vogue.

Curriculum development in a school setting is usually a highly routinized procedure with regular steps on a scheduled basis. Teachers can expect to be on committees and form study groups in carrying out these mechanical steps of updating.

Instruction in the classroom is a subset of curriculum. Teachers must be involved in any meaningful curriculum development. The intention of the curriculum plan rationalizes instruction. Timeworn questions about the purpose of schooling must be answered to plan teaching in the classroom. In the last decade, standards-based mandates from politicians have unbalanced the curriculum and distorted the role of the teacher.

Following their conscience, curriculum leaders may modify the standards-based curriculum at the level of classroom delivery. Working with teachers in a collegial relationship, curriculum leaders can refocus delivery around more generic goals and outcomes. Research tells us that there is no loss in student achievement in making the curriculum student-centered rather than test-centered.

Your author recommends an integrative type of curriculum design, with flexible classroom organization, to meet the instructional needs of students in the 21st century. Specific activities for the curriculum leader, in working with the teacher, have been suggested.

Activities

ACTIVITY 5.1

Your author states that many standards-based curriculum states have low achievement on standardized tests. Explain this phenomenon.

ACTIVITY 5.2

Develop a list of areas where teachers might be called upon for curriculum development. What does your list suggest for hiring practices in a school?

 Click here to take an automatically-graded self-check quiz.

Additional Reading

Coleman, D. (2012). *Revised publishers criteria for the Common Core State Standards*, Washington, DC: National Governors Association.

Cunningham, C., & Billingsley, M. (2005). *Curriculum webs: A practical guide to weaving the Web into teaching and learning* (2nd ed.). Boston, MA: Allyn & Bacon.

Lemov, D. (2012). *Practice perfect*, San Francisco, CA: Jossey Bass.

Oliva, P. (2013). *Developing the curriculum* (8th ed.). Boston, MA: Allyn & Bacon.

Ravitch, D. (2013, February 26). *Why I cannot support the Common Core Standards*. Retrieved from http://dianeravitch.net

Tomlinson, C., & Strickland, C. (2005). *Differentiation in practice: A resource guide for differentiating curriculum, grades 9–12*. Alexandria, VA: Association for Supervision and Curriculum.

Zagranski, R. (2008). *Understanding standards-based education*. Thousand Oaks, CA: Corwin.

6

Curriculum Development and the New Technologies

Learning Outcome

- To assess the role of media in curriculum development.

Time marches on, and this is particularly true where technology is concerned. New products are regularly introduced with additional capacities. At the time of this writing, smartphones and various mobile technologies dominate the commercial markets. As of 2014, 57% of all mobile phones are smartphones, capable of photographic operations, page scanning, and even purchasing products with the "phone tap" of a standard credit card. The new mobile technologies allow massive data control, multimedia downloads, and social networking. In a recent survey (*Time* magazine, 8-27-12) 84% of Americans 25–29 years of age report that they sleep with their device in the bedroom or on a table next to their bed.

In this technological environment, students possess global connections to world information at an early age. They own mini iPads and Apple 5 smartphones but are unable to bring them to school. The culture of school asks kids to check their technology at the door. It is estimated that 80% of U.S. eighth graders possess mobile devices, but more than one half of all schools prohibit the use of any mobile device. One hundred percent of U.S. schools have the Internet (up from 35% in 1994) and the number of classrooms with Internet connection is nearly universal (up from 3% in 1994). About one half of these schools are now using wireless technologies. Computers in schools, to quote Larry Cuban, are "oversold and under used."

Computers in schools are most often found in labs, prevocational and business classrooms, self-contained elementary classrooms, and English classes using the machines as word processors. The use of computers for higher level functions in secondary subjects such as science, social studies, and mathematics (academic subjects) is still not widespread. As Michele Tillier observed, "computer labs used to force standardization indicates a special kind of ignorance about the capacity of Internet-assisted instruction" (Tillier 2001). School world and the real world are not the same.

The reader may wonder why the new technologies have not captured the school curriculum. The answer is not to be found in teachers who lack knowledge. The Internet has been available since May 1995, and most teachers are full participants in email, texting, downloading movies, social networking, and doing specialized operations with various applications (or apps). These activities, of course, are out-of-school.

The new technologies have not been blocked by a lack of equipment, support, or rewards. Schools have spent billions of dollars on technology that is sparsely used in the classroom. As stated in previous editions, the real problem with the free use of technology in school-based learning is a special kind of ignorance about how it fits the curriculum. Despite wonderful software tools available to teachers, such as Thinkfinity, PBS Teachers, and Gliffy, classroom teachers seem unable to leave a paradigm where the school controls and interprets knowledge. State learning standards have narrowed the curriculum for many schools, and the Common Core Standards appear even more directive at the time of this writing. Schools must find a way out of this "box" if they are to thrive and even survive in this 21st century.

FIFTEEN YEARS INTO THE 21ST CENTURY

The 21st century is witnessing the largest period of substantial change ever experienced by humanity. Our very way of living in the world is being changed, more rapidly than can be comprehended, by forces that at times seem beyond control. The new information age that we have entered challenges all educators, the existence of schooling itself, and our way of thinking about the nature of learning. Curriculum leaders need a new paradigm in order to understand and contribute to these changes.

In 1980, futurist Alvin Toffler described the onrushing "third wave," the information age, in the following manner:

> The wave is by far the most extreme and is very difficult to grasp at a comprehensible level. The one way to think about it is to imagine change in every aspect of your life. Next, these changes must be synthesized into new schemas. This wave is marked by the benefits of massive gains in technology. These gains include things such as unlimited availability of information, energy sources, the creation of a new economic system, and the "prosumer." Socially, the third wave means more of a demand for individualism. The economic system of the third wave will reflect demassification and decentralization. The concept of work will change; workers can stay at home and work whenever they want. Large factories will succumb to technological advances which make smaller customized locations much more efficient. The national government and large corporations will be decentralized giving more economic and social power to lower level employees. This wave will be marked by the emergence of new disciplines that were nonexistent twenty-five years ago: quantum electronics, information technology, molecular biology, nucleonics, and others. In this wave the family system is unrecognizable. The nuclear family no longer serves as the standard model. (p. 384)

Fast forward 35 years and the United States is riding this third wave every day. Words like *demassification, hypermation, broadband, blog,* and *wifi* are so common they are now a part of everyday advertising. Almost 90% percent of all Americans carry cell phones. Wireless Internet service providers (ISPs) combine with cell companies to provide cordless computer access wherever cell phone service exists. Miniaturization (nanotechnology) is in full swing as wireless mobile devices (WMDs) like iPods, iPads, minis, and Apple 5's make accessing information easy. The world is dazzled by an estimated one trillion websites; untold millions of emails and blogs are used by 18% of the people on Earth on a regular basis. Many older people, the so-called nonmillennials (over the age of 15), are stunned by these changes in knowledge acquisition and exchange.

Where did these "clouds of data," these *q*-bits, digital threads, blogs, and Google algorithms come from? Why didn't we see them coming? Well, we should have! There have been portents everywhere since the last quarter of the 20th century. Little by little, our institutions in medicine, technology, transportation, military, communication, and industry have been adjusting to the new technological age. Satellites, silicon chips, computers, the Internet, outsourcing, smart bombs and drones are all part of the same information revolution. Our nation and the entire world have irreversibly changed, and we will have to deal with it. We have evolved into a new age; we have left behind the agricultural age of the 19th century, the industrial age of the early 20th century, and even the postindustrial age of the final quarter of the 20th century. This is the new age of information, and as John Naisbitt (1982) once observed, "We are drowning in information but starved for knowledge." There has been a paradigm shift.

A *paradigm* is a shared set of assumptions. Paradigms explain the world to us and help us predict the future. Paradigms are the basic or familiar way of perceiving, thinking, valuing, and doing things, and they are associated with a particular reality. Such paradigms are seldom stated explicitly; they exist as unquestioned, tacit understandings that are transmitted through culture to succeeding generations. The word *paradigm* is overworked, but as Thomas Kuhn (1962) defined it more than 50 years ago, it refers to laws, theories, and models that are the basis of coherent traditions. The paradigms we hold in curriculum are the *scaffolding* for communication, research, and practice. In the first decade of the 21st century, schools and curriculum leaders are clinging tenuously to an older set of concepts that are quickly losing all value. The core notion of these beliefs is that knowledge is education. In today's world, nothing could be further from the truth.

Since the advent of widespread Internet access in May 1995, knowledge can no longer adequately serve as an organizer for curriculum. There is no means by which new information each year can be assessed, shaped, or organized. There is no way that the instantaneous retrieval of all information can be filtered or controlled. The boundaries of our understanding, in all fields, have been overrun; there is neither scope nor sequence to the new information age. In addition, the multimedia integration of concepts, facts, images, data, and sound create meanings in ways that even Marshall McLuhan and Quentin Fiore (1967) could not have envisioned. We are awash in knowledge, and there is no end in sight to the avalanche of new information.

The technologists tell us that the speed and volume of knowledge acquisition is increasing geometrically. Computer chips in the near future will carry the volume of all organized knowledge in smaller, even molecular, sizes. Digitized information, information broken down into bits, will fly across the Earth in wireless forms. Knowledge will be accessible to anyone through tiny receivers disguised as jewelry. Voice recognition technology will eliminate keyboards, and data storage will be external ("the cloud"). A universal translator and "smart" computers are on the way. These are not dreams of the 1960s comic book character Dick Tracy. Rather, these products are already in the development stage or for sale in your neighborhood store.

UNDERSTANDING AND RESPONDING

The contrast of the new information age with the current standards-based education systems is shocking. To some degree the myopic and bit-by-bit approach to knowledge mastery currently found in our schools is simply the result of our perceptions in education. We are reminded of the saying "If you can keep your head when all of those about you are losing theirs, you probably don't understand what is happening." To understand what is happening, we must assess what we are now doing. We must differentiate between learned and learner. In the words of Peter Cochrane, "Imagine a school filled with children that can read and write, but teachers who cannot, and you have a metaphor of the information age in which we now live."

Technology has changed, forever, how we live and work and learn. Work, at least in the United States and other developed nations, will be with our heads and not with our hands. Knowledge, the traditional business of schooling, represents the true source of power in this new era. Unlike in the past, however, to know is not enough. Knowledge in the 21st century will be impermanent, for using only. Organized knowledge will double every 72 days by 2020, and in the 12 years that it takes a child to complete formal schooling, there will need to be a lot of "unlearning." An educated person in this era, to quote Carl Rogers (1961), will be "a person who has learned how to learn."

Neil Postman observed that technological change cannot be an additive change; it must be an ecological change. The control of learning will shift from teacher to student, from artificial to authentic, and from covering to discovering. If we continue to define learning as improved student performance, then technology will only be used as a vehicle to deliver the current curriculum more effectively. We will simply have old wine in new bottles!

Knowledge is going to be universally accessible in this new era, no longer contained in one place or through one medium. Most delivery will be electronic, not through print or live presentation, and there will be increasing technological fusion—from multimedia to monomedia. Marshall McLuhan observed in 1967 that "all information received is shaped by media." As we move from pencils to word processors, education will be leaving the schoolhouse. Individuals will use knowledge on a need-to-know basis. The rate and power of technology, when applied to information, will increase exponentially. People will satisfy needs and solve problems by manipulating images.

For young persons in our society, technical knowledge will be the basis of available work. By 1998, two thirds of all workers in the United States held jobs in which they had worked for less than 5 years. Children in school today may change occupations 7 to 14 times in their lives, and it is predicted that 80% of all kindergartners today in the United States will be their own employer at some point in adulthood. Like a subcontractor on a construction job, more workers will attach to and detach from work, using the existing technology to make contact. Much of this work will not have a place or even a physical product. More and more workers may not see or know their coworkers, who will be scattered around the globe (Thornburg, 2005).

Most knowledge is already digitized, broken down into parts and easily reassembled in new forms. Learning will not be linear, as in the past, but convergent. This fact alone is changing everything about learning. Learners, children and adults, will "paste together" existing knowledge for personal and impermanent reasons. There will certainly be many more Internets, each reflecting the values of those who sponsor them. Important information, such as an individual's DNA data, will be kept on gold atoms or holographic chips, 1 trillion bits per chip, and retrievable at quantum speeds, a billion times faster than in the 1980s (A. November, 2005).

How soon will all this happen the reader may ask? It already has. Distributive learning, across space, time, and media, is on your child's computer. Digitized equipment and messages are how you send email and photos using your digital subscriber line (DSL) and your digital camera. Technical convergence is taking pictures with your cell phone and emailing them to a friend. Global and interactive work is your 24-hour company sending a work product from London to Delhi to New York in an electronic format. Children learn outside of school with unknown partners around the globe on their home computers. We are already living in the new information age. The citizens of the world are, ready or not, interdependent.

And how are schools participating in all this change? Unfortunately, the school, and American education in general, is not a full and active part of this paradigm shift. Your author has stated the condition this way:

> Despite constantly accelerating social and technical change, the paradigm for education has remained essentially static. The basic format of teachers speaking, while students listen, remains intact, as it has since ancient times. Socrates, whose method of teaching by asking questions is still being reverently taught in schools of education, would feel right at home in most current secondary schools. Twentieth century America simply combined his time-honored teaching method with a factory-like setting, all the while ignoring the onslaught of changing conditions. (Wiles, 2004)

American schools are adhering to a 19th-century curriculum that equates knowing with scholarship and schooling. Using a guild mentality, we see our students learning alongside a master with a rubric that reinforces the past. Education in our schools is completely contextualized; learning counts only when done in a "school" way. In our schools, time is structured, learning is always linear, and the emphasis is on the place. We are experiencing what futurist Joel Barker (1993) called "paradigm paralysis."

Our worldview of technology seems to be based on the machines and not on their ability to contribute to learning. We can place all the technology available in this old school model without addressing the needs of modern students. Thus, we are constantly disappointed when the technology moves forward and our consumption is obsolete. Having businesspersons as our guides to technology during the past 20 years has meant a focus on product and outcome, rather than on the process of learning. Even the technology industry has been myopic in marketing new learning tools to "be integrated into the existing curriculum." We have, in the words of David Thornburg "added another car to our train."

We simply do not seem willing to abandon the old world and enter the new world of interactive technologies. Read, for example, the official position of the state of Tennessee (2000), on technology in our schools:

> Students in the 21st century must be prepared for technological advancements in life. A computer skills curriculum prepares students in the use of computers to access and apply data necessary to solve problems in a technology-based society. The computer is to extend this use within the K–12 framework of subjects. Achieving proficiency with the computer, like learning any other discipline, is based on a continuum of knowledge and skill development. The computer proficiency continuum begins with an *awareness* of what the computer is, passes through a level of *literacy,* and culminates in *mastery* in which advanced applications and sophisticated programming techniques are understood and practiced.

Even technologically savvy experts seem unable to separate the trees from the forest in describing the onrush of the new age in education. David Warlick (2004), writing about textbooks of the future, observes that "books will certainly be replaced by computers in the near future." He also acknowledges that the critical component of the electronic textbook, like Kindle, will be its digital format; allowing easy searches of content and using binary code, it will communicate text, images, sound, and animations. Warlick also sees that the electronic textbook has potential for matching learning styles and overcoming handicaps such as hearing loss and low vision. He does not see, or address, the endless possibilities of such a "learning machine" for curriculum re-design and application. The "school equals education" paradigm is still in place.

Curriculum leaders must begin to focus on the characteristics of the new technology and ask what we can do with this technology that we could not do before? In addition to digital information, we have the technical fusion of media, universal (anywhere, anytime) access, the possibilities of global connectivity, and new and strategic alliances in education such as those occurring in the business world. These changes, this paradigm shift, redefine education and learning from the ground up.

Whenever the topic of technology is discussed, the following question always surfaces: So what is new? After all, various technologies have been used in schools for over a century. This is a good question but one that reveals how large the problem is in the field of education. What is new is that better ways of accessing, processing, and applying information have come into all our lives, and these newer technologies are rapidly changing the world in which we live. Strangely, as in Plato's Allegory of the Cave, we are unable to see and accept this new and evolving reality; we seem to be focused on only the shadows. We can point to many examples of how the new technologies are changing our work, the economy, everyday living, and all learning outside school, but those realities cannot seem to penetrate our paradigm of the way education is currently structured. In our cave, education is schooling, and schooling occurs in a building where there are rooms for 30 children and a teacher, textbooks, and all the other things found in our educational institutions. Even though children and teachers can go home to retrieve and process the world's knowledge on their personal computers at any time, we cannot seem to conceptualize how these new technological gadgets should be changing our education paradigm.

Part of the problem in school, and out of school, is that the rush of technology has made us all feel powerless (anomie). Our educational role in all this massive change is essentially that of a consumer. In many of the schools in which your author has worked, in the United States and abroad, there has been a monumental commitment to acquiring technology, and an equally monumental activity to avoid using it to substantially improve learning. Only in the smallest number of schools visited has technology been fully integrated into the curriculum. In only a handful of schools has the definition of education been altered by the new technological access to knowledge. Our paradigm of schooling is so strong that we can see technology only as it is applied to the traditional knowledge-based curriculum.

This feeling of being unable to reprogram our curriculum is further hindered by the propensity of state legislators to get into the act. Passing a law to prohibit the further purchase of textbooks in 2015 (Florida), when technology to receive data from outside is lacking in many schools, leaves the educators vulnerable to unwarranted criticism. Sometimes, such absurdity is just a ploy to promote the privatization of education, or open up competing charter schools.

Educational leaders are also fearful of the legal dimensions of technological change. Forbes Magazine has estimated that 1.5% of all Internet sites are pornographic in nature, and that would mean over 100,000 sites that might be confronted by students in classroom inquiry. Few administrators and curriculum leaders wish to be responsible for such an interface. Likewise, educators fear lawsuits dealing with cyberbullying. Better to be safe than sorry, explains some leader's reluctance to integrate technology and the curriculum.

It is, however, quite amazing to see how much learning could occur, even in just the subject areas, using the Internet. In mathematics, one of the two Common Core areas to be assessed, an Internet search will yield:

- Performance objectives (www.coe.west.asu.edu)
- A complete K–12 content curriculum (www.ncpublicschools.org)
- Math lesson plans at all levels (www.mathsearch.com)
- Worksheets, puzzles, and test prep at all levels (www.edhelper.com)
- Experts and mentors, for free (www.mathforum.co/dr.helper)
- Self-scoring practice problems (www.mathmastery.com)
- A site dedicated to tutoring girls in math (www.colormathpink.com)

The reader will note that sites such as these expire automatically every six months if not renewed by their sponsors. Their replacements, however, can easily be found with the aid of a search engine such as Google or Bing.

In a nutshell, schools could create a wonderful and rich mathematics or reading curriculum from the resources already available, for free, on the Internet. The Common Core principles or standards might serve as an organizer for such a collection. The same could be said for social studies, science, and even foreign language; but that would still be employing the old paradigm, would it not? We should, and can, be doing much more.

We have the opportunity to do new things and fulfill old dreams. A century-old dream of individualizing instruction to meet human differences is attainable. Using aptitude–treatment interaction (ATI) technology and adaptive learning platforms, we could be delivering personalized learning experiences to every child in our nation as surely as we all have different telephone numbers (Tai, 1998). We could make the delivery of learning an art form simply by applying the same technologies that are now found in children's videogames. We already have the capacity to do these things; the technology is here, but we don't utilize the capacity. What is needed in curriculum is a new conceptual architecture and a core ideology for providing education for all persons. We desperately need new curriculum vision and leadership (see Knewton, 2013).

Because we are all the products of today's form of schooling, it is nearly impossible to think about an education without a school (Wiles & Lundt, 2004). But that, in fact, is what we must begin to do. After years of working in schools throughout the United States, your author has come to believe that it is the school (the building) that prevents a new conception of the curriculum. Our facilities dictate our practices; function follows form. Every innovation in the last 50 years has had to be reshaped to "fit" school. Naturally, none of these changes lasted very long because the school that we attended was not about innovation; it was about standardization. The school that we know was conceptualized in the Industrial Age in America and is no more than a factory with assembly-line organization. If the new technologies have given us an "anywhere, anytime learning delivery system," accessible without the teacher, they surely do not belong in a highly structured 19th-century school building.

But it is difficult to think of a replacement for the school or a new function for the curriculum. It is even more difficult to think "outside the box" as a passive consumer of technology, and this condition must change in the field of curriculum. Educational leaders must stop being powerless, and curriculum leaders must stop focusing on technology itself. They must question and challenge further standardization. What school personnel need to ask is what education would look like without school buildings. We must ask, What can we do with these new technologies that we could not do before? What does it mean to be literate or learned? What is learning? What do our children need to know?

A little over 125 years ago, most people went to school only through the elementary years. The family, the church, and social groups were the primary learning resources. Knowledge was not organized as we know it today. Learning had practical applications. These same conditions exist today in some private schools and in home-schooling settings. Learning and schooling, and education and schooling, are not synonymous. Today, the television, the computer, the telephone, and educated individuals in our society are all wonderful resources for learning. Self-education is attainable without the school. Schools, if we must have them, can and should take many forms. They can no longer be the sole place for acquiring knowledge.

What the new technologies can do for us that we could not do previously is personalize learning. Curriculum leaders need to articulate that children are not the same, nor should they be, and that we all live in a rapidly changing world. Allowing state legislators to mandate a standardized curriculum for all our children is the very antithesis of our modern understandings of teaching and learning. This is the professional battle looming in the near future regarding the Common Core for State Standards. A comprehensive content-based, or even skill-based, curriculum may be totally inappropriate for 21st-century living. Yes, we all need skills for college and our work life; skills that includes collaboration, problem solving, relearning, and creativity—skills needed by workers who will be global citizens and may never have a permanent job. But, where will our children get these skills if the daily curriculum is focused on scoring points on a standardized national test? Each student will need different and unique skills for life.

VISIONS FOR SCHOOLS

Recently, a number of professional organizations and agencies have projected the needs of world citizens in the future, and the lists are remarkably similar. Many of these needs appear in the literature of the new Common Core:

Association for Supervision and Curriculum Development (ASCD): Visions for Future Needs

- Healthy lifestyle
- Intellectually challenging
- Learning connected to community
- Access to caring adults
- Prepared for global environment

21st-Century Skills Group: Visions

- 21st-century content (economics, language)
- Learning skills (problem solving)
- ICT skills (using technology to learn)
- Life skills (ethics, personal responsibility)

National Technology Foundation: Visions

- Technical literacy
- Citizenship ethics
- Critical-thinking skills
- Career preparation
- Collaboration skills
- Cultural literacy
- Basic skills proficiency

International Studies in School: Visions

- Cultural awareness
- World citizen
- Collaborative
- Effective use of technology
- Literate for the 21st century

Metropolitan Learning: Visions

- Effective communications
- Problem solver
- Language proficient (two or more languages)
- Global outlook
- Core knowledge
- Social skills

Curriculum leaders must become proactive and more aggressive in proposing new directions for technology. We must focus on the uses of technology, and the application of knowledge, and resist being mesmerized by the machines themselves. We must begin to convert the curriculum into an active process in which students learn survival skills, adaptation skills, and the skills of creativity. We must tie education to work and life beyond school, but not hinder that effort with standardized learning units and a high-stakes test. Such a turnaround may or may not include facilities, schools, and the functions of the school (the curriculum) will be quite different. Curriculum leaders definitely need a new format to communicate about such matters, to dream, and to design new educational worlds. A new technological paradigm for curriculum is needed now!

For over a decade there has been a consensus among educators who project a technological future, as well as a chorus of warnings, about how we are now handling technology in schools. Michael Godet (2001), author of *Creating Futures*, warns educators that the danger of the Internet is that others will soon organize parallel education systems. Howard Rheingold (2000), in *Virtual Communities*, warns that our nation's community, democracy, education, science, and intellectual life in general are all tied to the Internet. B. F. Fogg (2002), in *Persuasive Technologies*, observes that software design can actually alter the way the brain processes information. He warns of future "charismatic computers that will offer suggestions, solicit information, simplify things, track users, and employ operant conditioning . . . in the name of learning" (p. 19). Clearly, curriculum leaders and other educators have a stake in how technology is applied to learning.

These leading authors also seem unified in their belief that the "educator as consumer" role must end. Godet likens the Internet to a computerized dumpster. Chris Dede (2005) of Harvard University states, "Computers acquired as a panacea end up as doorstops." Ted McCain and Ian Jukes (2001), in their readable *Windows on the Future*, point out repeatedly that technology is just a tool for integrating and using information. "Without the vision and understanding of an inspired educator," they warn, "little will happen (because) education is a human task."

GETTING STARTED

Stephen Covey (2004), famous for his book *The 7 Habits of Highly Effective People*, observes that to be effective in planning, we must "start with the end in mind" (p. 29). If we follow this advice, we see education (not schooling) preparing the young person for an unknown destination. It is certain that this destination will be technological and quite different from what exists today. Looking back to 1995, the first year the Internet became available to the public, it is easy for an adult to imagine the scale of change the scale of change a child might experience in the next fifty years.

We have learned that the past is no longer a prologue to the future. We know that adaptation to change will be a lifetime theme for most citizens. And we have learned that focusing on uses of technology, not equipment, is the best way to avoid feeling powerless or obsolete in this rapidly changing scene. Students will master technological fluency because they use technology every day outside school. What they need are lifetime skills such as problem solving, collaboration, technical learning, and making value judgments about knowledge. The new structures of curriculum in an age of technology must be flexible, long term, and focused on application. In the words of McCain and

Jukes (2001), "We must begin to think like a quarterback and anticipate where the receiver will be when we throw the ball" (p. 51). These "arching curves into tomorrow" must guide our thinking about the act of learning.

Carl Rogers (1961), writing about 60 years ago, provided this definition of education in an age when knowledge was first becoming unmanageable:

> The only man who is educated is the man who has learned how to learn; the man who has learned to adapt and change; the man who has realized that no knowledge is secure, and that only the process of seeking knowledge gives the basis of security. (p. 14)

Alvin Toffler (1980), renowned futurist, had this to say about a redefined curriculum in an age of technology:

> Nothing should be included in the required curriculum unless it can be strongly justified in terms of the future. If this means scrapping a substantial part of our formal curriculum, so be it. (p. 3)

With 90% of teenagers in America having access to the Web, schools must begin by connecting the curriculum to the world around them. Included in this task would be connecting home devices to school networks, providing teachers email at school that can accept attachments, increasing school bandwidth to allow more media applications, allowing student pen drives to be used on school computers, and allowing cell phone cameras and handheld devices to enter the classroom. All these items exist outside the school, and to ban them in the name of safety or curricular integrity is to further isolate the school. The threat of lawsuits in schools is real, but the risk is worth the reward.

We must view the immediate future of technology in schools as a "blend." We can't just jump to online learning for many reasons including the fact that we have little research to support such learning. Patte Barth, of the National School Boards Association, found a "paucity of research data" in reviewing practices in 2012. A 2011 study of full-time virtual charter schools by researchers at Stanford University found "in every case, students in virtual charter schools performed worse than their counterparts in the traditional school." Finally, a 2011 study of full-time online students by the Minnesota Office of Legislative Audits found such students "more likely to drop out of school than their traditional peers." Beyond these recent studies lie a decade of largely unsuccessful efforts to teach online proprietary college students.

There should be some skepticism about standards-based curriculum with high stakes testing as well. The American Legislative Exchange Council data of 2012 shows the placement of states with a significant dedication to standards and their achievement ranking among states and territories of the United States: California (30th), Kentucky (37th), Tennessee (44th), South Carolina (50th), and West Virginia (51st). Some of these states have been pushing standards and high stakes testing for over 15 years without great achievement. These are simply the facts.

Schools have a great many technologies to work with. We have old technologies like telephones and televisions. We have computers (desktops, laptops, minis, handheld); we have DVDs, cell phones (6 billion accounts worldwide), calculators, various

PDAs, digital cameras, and social outlets such as blogs, social networks, wikis, and email. There is no shortage of technologies, and the apps just keep coming. The ability to use these tools to do things we haven't been able to do is the challenge. It won't be an easy task to make the leap from the 19th to the 21st century. Wiles and Lundt, in their decade-old concept book *Leaving School, Finding Education* (2004, pp. 130–131) provide a list of tasks necessary for converting schools to the 21st century:

- Design new avenues for learning and communicating.
- Deemphasize standardization of the curriculum and testing.
- Acknowledge human differences and capabilities.
- Envision and construct new types of facilities for learning.
- Provide massive startup capital for technologies.
- Invest in and allocate resources for widespread training of teachers.
- Recruit and reward a new kind of learning leader.
- Allow students and teachers the freedom to network.
- Value knowledge for its application, rather than acquisition.

WHAT OUR SCHOOLS ARE ACTUALLY DOING

Some schools in the United States are moving forward in exciting ways to join other institutions in the new and technological 21st century. Varying studies indicate some common uses of technology in schools where the district has provided accessible equipment for students. Among the uses regularly reported are the following:

- Using email to communicate with other classes
- Using email to communicate with an expert or significant person
- Gathering data from the Internet for a class project
- Finding and using websites to enhance a subject being studied
- Monitoring an online expedition, project, or trip
- Reading works written by other students
- Reading websites for information related to current events
- Blogging and networking
- Taking a virtual field trip
- Joining an online project

Note that most of these activities are not interactive. Most resemble traditional schools, with the student as a passive recipient of some source of knowledge. The Internet, as a learning tool, is ideally suited to interactive learning such as the SchoolWorld Internet Education site (http://www.www.schoolworld.com/) in Australia. At this site, students and teachers can participate in interactive projects with students in schools throughout the world. Sample projects in 2001 included the Classroom Pet Exchange, Friends and Flags project, Great Debate project, Poets Corner, Postcard Geography, and World Weather Watch Project.

The more general condition for schools in the United States can be characterized thusly:

- A 2005 survey by *eSchool News Online* found that 89% of all student computer use in schools is in computer labs, indicating that creativity in using computers in school is not widespread ("Academic Impact of Technology," 2005).

- Approximately 10% of schools in the United States now have a computer for each child, and these are most likely to be found in the elementary schools rather than in the high schools. One-to-one programs were achieved by Maine in 2002 and Hawaii in 2012.
- In 2003, 86% of teachers surveyed by *eSchool* felt that computers increased student performance "somewhat or a great deal." By 2005, only 2 years later, that belief was held by only 61% of teachers surveyed. Only 58% of teachers surveyed in 2005 felt computers improved student performance on standardized tests. The organization concluded, "[we are still at the tip of the iceberg with respect to technology use in schools. . . . We need to do much better in helping teachers see what's possible" ("Academic Impact," 2005). Increasingly, it seems, classroom teachers do not see a role for computers in the classroom.
- Teachers report a lack of staff development opportunities to learn more about technology. A 2004 survey by *eSchool News* found that 31% of all teachers received no training during the past year. Only 11% of all teachers reported receiving 16 or more hours of training in that year ("Tracking U.S. Trends," 2004).
- A 2012 report by the Educational Testing Service, "The Status of Technology in U.S. Schools," noted that less than 20% of schools had access to satellite technology.
- According to Market Data Retrieval (MDR), technology spending for schools declined 24% from the 2001–2002 school year to the 2002–2003 school year. Hardware spending dropped a whopping 28% during this period ("Teachers' Tech Use," 2005).
- The National Center for Educational Statistics 2012 reported a 3:1 student-computer ratio when computers had Internet access.

Perhaps an even bigger problem than the number of computers is the lack of bandwidth in most schools. Bandwidth allows greater information flow such as movies and figures, as opposed to text only. Schools that "pulled wires" in the late 1980s and 1990s are now facing obsolescence in their delivery of data to computers. Promising for schools throughout the world, however, are new wireless systems (wifi), and most recently, Worldwide Interoperability for Microwave Access (WiMAX), which has a range of up to 40 miles. Such systems would allow districts to deliver curriculum from a central vantage point without wires, towers, or relay systems ("Argentine School," 2005).

Below are listed some of the curriculum issues concerning technologies in school that simply must be addressed before wide-scale implementation can be achieved.

- Access of schools to technology and the fairness of access among students
- How technology is being used in schools
- The effectiveness of educational technology
- Issues involved in connecting teachers and technology
- The quality of educational software
- The cost of deploying technology in our schools

PROJECTIONS

David Thornburg states quite clearly the challenge facing educators. A knowledge explosion has occurred, scattering the notion of curriculum development organized around subject matter. There has also been a technological fusion, and the power of that new multimedia to educate exceeds anything previously known. The implications for the near future, says Thornburg, are impermanence, a geometric progression of everything, and a need to give knowledge value. From this perspective, curriculum as a field is back to zero.

The changing nature of work begs for a new kind of education. All knowledge is now accessible, creating a new learning culture of independence rather than dependence. Learning will no longer be primarily auditory, and there will be webs of learners rather than teachers and learners.

Work will be a "head" function, and knowledge will have value in its applications rather than in mere acquisition, as in the past. Learners will need the four As: access, analyze, authenticate, and apply. Valued skills will include systems thinking, collaboration, technical learning, contracting, and technical fluency. Unlearning and relearning will be vital skills in the fast-moving 21st century.

Technology has altered both work and learning. People will spend most of their work time learning. They will need to identify problems, make connections, and think through issues. Learning will become customized (personal pathways), and teachers in some settings will be extrapolators of knowledge, learning guides, models, and co-learners. There will be no specific place or time or teacher in learning. According to McCain and Jukes, changing our schools "is absolutely essential if our children are to be properly prepared for the world that awaits them." Fifteen years into the 21st century, the future of curriculum work in the United States is slowly coming into focus. All of the hullabaloo about the new millennium and emerging technologies is quickly receding, and the trends for the next quarter century are emerging through everyday practice. In this section, we attempt to identify the major factors that might shape curriculum decision making for the next generation of workers.

This chapter began by observing that all the new technologies are raising issues about the practices of schooling and particularly about the delivery of a curriculum to children in public and private schools. Although there have been many technological bells and whistles, it is our opinion that the basic issues of curriculum remain unchanged; we are still concerned with the basic questions of defining, controlling, delivering, and assessing the curriculum.

The questions promoted by a new global age and the global economy are simply too large to be thoughtfully considered at the district level—and maybe even at the state level. In fact, there is no single agency or organization in the United States dedicated to be forward-looking in education. As James Macdonald (1971) told us years ago, the development of curriculum in America is largely a historical accident. We "layer on" new stuff over old stuff. It is probable that education will simply "bump along" over the next several decades.

No one would deny that some very strong forces have been steering schools since the late 1980s. Of all such trends, standards-based education and the new Common Core has dominated. So overwhelming has outcome-based education been that many school districts have abandoned the traditional curriculum entirely in the pursuit of test scores. But history is a great teacher when it comes to education in the United States, and the excesses of the past help us forecast the near end of this movement (Callahan, 1962).

Because of the Technology Literacy Challenge Funds and the Federal Communication Commission's E-Rate programs, 98% of all schools in the United States were connected to the Internet by 2000, but classroom use of the Internet and free use of Internet learning resources is severely limited in the world of schools 15 years after this connectivity was attained. We are not learning and communicating better, despite these new technologies.

In this stark contrast of pencils versus computers, schools have failed to adapt to the new technologies despite spending billions of valuable dollars chasing technological status. Why? In a world where telesurgery is performed across oceans in real time, where virtual courtrooms exist for international trials, and military operations are conducted electronically from thousands of miles away, why are schools still using paper textbooks and conducting business in a factory-model building? Even the factories in the United States do not do business in such buildings anymore!

The answer, of course, is a lack of vision by educators . . . the very stuff of curriculum work. Leadership in education has not completed the paradigm shift needed to view the new technologies as a means rather than as an end. The explanation for this might be that in the beginning, educators pursued technology like a consumer product; everyone wanted a computer, a lab, a T-1 line, and so forth. Also, in schools, the use of computers was seen from a business model: to use them for accounting and to keep records of progress.

We might also find the cause of our failure to make a paradigm shift in the solidity of the institution itself. Schools are the biggest and one of our most costly institutions, and they have been doing the same things for a very long time. Seeing things we could now do (like truly individualizing instruction) that we couldn't do before the advent of the new technologies is tough!

The traditional vision of school as a place where knowledge is imparted by a teacher using a text in an isolated context, with single-path progression, is simply too pervasive to overcome easily. The new visions of a distributive learning community where all have access to an overwhelming source of information, a multisensory world of linked media, a place of collaboration, exploration and inquiry-based learning is simply more than can be absorbed. Educators responded, and are still responding, with denial, myopic focus, and superficial security concerns. Curriculum leaders, historically a source of visionary statements and programs, are noticeably silent on the subject.

Perhaps the greatest perceptual roadblock to the effective use of technology in schools is the nature of the new technologies. Technology, after all, has existed in schools for over a century in the form of radio, telephones, film projectors, tape recorders, television, and VCRs, but the technology was initiated by the teacher. The new interactive technologies (Internet, cell phones, and digital cameras) create a virtual learning environment that has no boundaries. Both teachers and students are partners in a culture of learning. In the old world, transfer and assimilation of knowledge reigned. In the post-1995 (popular access to the Internet) era, the emphasis is on creation and sharing of knowledge. Knowing is a construction process based on sharing and verification. In this process, according to Harvard professor Chris Dede, both teacher and student are active participants. In a few words, preparing for active participation in our global knowledge-based society is much more important than scoring well on high-stakes testing.

Dede has been working with his students at Harvard University since 2005 to move education to the next level. He believes that small handheld devices, wireless mobile devices (WMDs), are the best bet in school settings. The world now has 6 billion cell phone subscribers; 86 for every 100 persons on Earth. He sees the new curriculum as being one of "proving concepts," where students are given an idea and then find the data with their handheld computers. Collecting samples, comparing and contrasting, accessing data, interviewing experts, and the like, combine deskwork and field studies. Students generate theories from interacting with data.

In the first decade of this century, two events seemed to promote this vision held by Dede. First, in Argentina, a new wireless technology named WiMAX was tested successfully ("Argentine School"). WiMAX provides high-throughput broadband connections over long distances in the range of 40 miles, easily the boundaries of 90% of today's school districts. Such service is now available to schools for as little as $10 per month (www.muniwireless.com, 8-1-09). Second, in the same week, the Massachusetts of Technology (MIT) announced that it had developed a $100 computer and that 15 million of the computers would be in production in 2006 (Ricciuti, 2005). Using something between a full laptop and Dede's handheld devices and receiving full Internet input from a WiMAX-type device, schoolchildren now are on the way to being investigatory learners, anywhere and anytime.

A major perceptual breakthrough for future curriculum leaders will be to see technology as something other than a product to be consumed, something other than an efficiency tool. To speak of electronic textbooks, online Scholastic Aptitude Test (SAT) preparation, or even blogging, as a literary device is to totally miss the meaning of the new technologies. The new technologies allow us to learn new things in new ways for new purposes. Rather than retrofitting all new technologies to fit the classroom and the existing standards-based curriculum, we should be moving rapidly away from that world toward a future where education and schooling are not synonymous.

If anything is clear in the many voices calling for such change it is that technology is rapidly pushing forward to that new world. Each year in the United States, there are about 122,000 new book titles, but millions of websites were introduced. The best estimate (no one knows) is that more than 550 million websites are retrievable (Google uses only 6 million sites for its search base). Technology is providing access to those information sources at an ever-faster pace while concurrently miniaturizing the transmitters/receivers. These trends change everything: the role of teacher and student, the value and utility of knowledge, the critical elements of an education.

Boggled like everyone else by the speed and scale of this change, your author projects the following trends in learning until 2020:

1. Greater learning communities inside and beyond the school
2. Totally wireless access to all knowledge sources
3. Even greater miniaturization for transport of knowledge (iPods, iPads)
4. Shift in learning emphasis to problem solving and application of knowledge
5. A major breakthrough in adaptive learning technologies allowing individualization
6. New emphasis on certification of knowledge and experience
7. An emerging global curriculum

TECHNOLOGY AND THE COMMON CORE REQUIREMENTS

The requirements of the Common Core State Standards will dominate technology in schools for the foreseeable future. Forty-six states have signed on to implement the standards of the Common Core, and deadlines have been established for such work. These deadlines will cause states, school districts, and individual schools to re-align priorities and commence massive curriculum planning immediately.

Most difficult for curriculum planners is the 2014–2015 school year deadline for assessment of the Common Core. Although the actual items for such an assessment are currently being discussed and developed, the Common Core model calls for assessments, and curriculum offerings, to be online. It is questionable if PARCC and the other agencies developing assessments can complete their work under such a deadline, but even if they are successful, schools will not be ready for online learning and testing.

The state of Florida, which is the most prepared for this conversion from textbook learning to online learning, in public schools, is worth studying. Florida has a long history of standards-based instruction and high-stakes testing. Florida has the best ratio of computers to students of all 50 states. And Florida has the state legislature and all school districts on-board for the run, including a law which states that districts can no longer buy textbooks after 2015. Staff development efforts (teacher training) are underway in all districts for the implementation of the CCSS.

Florida began securing technology for its schools in 1977 with the Florida Education Computing Project. These early legislative appropriations recognized the value of technology in the instructional process. For 35 years the state has purchased technology and collected data on the effects of these tools on instruction. By the year 2002, Florida had a student-to-instructional-computer ratio (STIC) of 3.7:1, as well as Internet access in 97% of its schools and 88% of its classrooms. Beginning in the late 1990s, other states began to lay their pencils down, but Florida had established a considerable edge in technology attainment. In 2013, the Florida STIC ratio stands at 2:1.

Other states are spread out in a wide pattern in their efforts to harness technology. Nationally, states spend 37% of the IT budgets for services, 18% for the purchase of hardware, 17% for networking and telecom options, and 15% for curriculum software. The remaining 13% of schools and district technology budgets are miscellaneous.

In terms of software currently in use in schools, security tools are the highest priority, followed by internal communication, software for instructional collaboration, software to run the school website and portals, and software that tracks student progress and instructional decision making. The reader will note that these are all administrative applications.

At the school level, 76% of American schools currently (2013) have a classroom technology standard, 67% have data display (dashboards) in place, and 65% have a digital content strategy. The remainder of schools are either working to develop such instruments or simply do not have any.

Part of the difficulty for many districts and schools is a lack of expertise in creating a technological system, Creating a network and buying broadband is a lot more difficult than ordering textbooks. Major tasks for all district superintendents is to use monies wisely to approach one-to-one computing, stronger school-to-home online connections, and online professional development opportunities for staff. Creating a design for technology in new schools, not yet built, is another constant task for district and school leadership.

School leaders at the state and district level are having difficulty in creating new virtual opportunities for students. Most states fund these schools at about two thirds of the per student cost in a "bricks and mortar" school, but the real problem is in the success of such models. The Montana Virtual Academy jumped from 2,000 to 7,000 pupils in one year. Florida Virtual, established in 1997, now services 260,000 pupils worldwide. For the many students who see such virtual schools as an opportunity to accelerate their education and graduate early, their eagerness to learn is bedeviling facility planning in secondary schools and enrollment planning in state higher education systems.

The reader can observe from this brief treatment of concerns that integrating technology into the current educational systems is complex. In every state of the world's most technological education system, leaders are preparing infrastructure for a technological future. Equipment, software, teacher training and other categories of task are proceeding as finances allow. The goal of one-to-one work stations for each of America's 46 million public school students is simply a goal at this time.

Even if the job for all school districts was to maintain technology for all students, the cost would be massive. In Florida, for example, state leaders recognized in 2001 that they could not keep up with the changes in technology itself, and they began to focus on providing a generic broadband for Internet that would accommodate most anticipated changes. Using a variety of funding sources, T-1 (integrated circuits) and T-3 lines have been added to accommodate student learning in the future. Florida continued to invest heavily in teacher training, funding hundreds of thousands of hours of professional development for teachers in 3,700 schools. The goal of such training has been to move individual teachers from simply understanding technology to becoming a self-sustaining independent learner of the constant changes.

By 2009–2013, Florida recognized that developing curriculum and assessing student progress will be the toughest part of conversion to a technological delivery of public school learning. Sharing among state chief school officers, a theme of cooperation emerged that led to the Common Core State Standards and the many efforts involved in conversion to technological delivery. Florida, California, and other states with highly developed state standards and testing programs agreed to abandon years of effort in order to create a national standard for American school students. Efforts since 2011 in Florida have focused squarely on implementation of the Common Core.

INDIVIDUAL SCHOOLS AND THE CCSS

For the 100,000 individual schools in 50 states, most curriulum work in the immediate future will center on converting CCSS in math and English/language arts into classroom curriculum. Those schools with a history of successful curriculum development will hopefully follow a pattern like the one outlined in this book. There will be a stage of analysis, followed by a design for changing, an implementation plan, and a way of evaluating success in this venture.

In the analysis of school level technology, an important factor will be the access to computers for all school members. As noted previously, there is a considerable difference in states and districts regarding what is already available. In every school and every district, students will need access to an Internet-connected computer in order to access curriculum and take the four CCSS assessments in math and English/language arts each year.

Any school-based need assessment will need to compare and contrast what is needed and what is already available as a resource. Simple questions can be used to define the existing conditions:

1. What hardware is currently available to our students for Internet usage?
2. How are these computers deployed at present (labs, classrooms)?
3. Are there restrictions on the use of Internet resources?
4. Has a budget been provided to the school by the district for CCSS?
5. Are there organized records showing student achievement in math and English/language arts?
6. To what degree do teachers now use online resources in teaching?
7. What, if any, common technology training is needed by teachers?

The answer to these and other relevant questions are then compared to the staus quo conditions to provide a quick look at discrepancies in the school. If, for instance, there is a 6:1 student-to-computer ratio, what will be needed to carry out Common Core instruction would be under review by the district.

In each major category such as equipment, training, and record-keeping, an estimate of cost must be constructed to bring the school into compliance with what will be expected. Such budget needs will have to be prioritized according to the time allocated for the implementation of the CCSS. It is probable that securing Internet-connected computers at the lowest ratio possible would precede detailed course development to conform to CCSS standards. In all cases, an emerging design will feature its parts as a kind of distance–rate–time problem. Money, always a critical variable in curriculum work, will often determine the rate of implementation of the plan.

Emerging from the needs assessment (analysis) will be a design to meet the requirements of the Common Core. A school-based plan will be constructed based on requirements (outcomes) and each subproject will be defined by steps where possible. Teacher needs for training, for example, might have major categories such as: 1) the requirements of the Common Core; 2) computer literacy; 3) developing online lessons; 4) the CC assessments; and 5) preparing the classroom for teaching with online resources. Each need will define a part of the implementation plan.The design stage of the curriculum cycle being applied in the school tells everyone what is to be accomplished.

The third stage—implementation—details how and when the parts will be addressed. For the curriculum planner to develop this plan, the priorities and the dependencies must be identified. We really can't develop a new curriculum until the CCSS standards are adopted and forwarded to the school. A schedule for converting the math and English/language arts course content must be developed with a time estimate for completion. Teacher training to field test and use the new curriculum must be scheduled. The sum of the parts and their time requirements provides a rough look at the school's implementation plan.

Finally, for each part designed there should be a product that can be evaluated and used for future planning (a re-analysis). For example, teachers in the school will be scheduled for six 2-hour workshops and their attendance will become a part of their permanent teaching file. New computers purchased to accommodate the CCSS assessments will meet a criteria adopted by planners.

When the school achieves or completes all of the activities scheduled by the implementation plan, the school will be ready to participate in the new CCSS program.

Your author would suggest that few curriculum development plans are so simple as planning and execution. There is an old adage that states "inside of every small problem is a huge problem waiting to get out." An example could be drawn from the desire of many districts to let students who have computers bring them to school, thus saving the school thousands of dollars—Bring You Own Technology (BYOT). This common sense approach to providing computers for CCSS, however, opens up the larger issues of equity and equality in education. Computer technology, since its application to schools in the 21st century, has created an unequal playing field in America among districts and schools.

There are many other problems that might derail any school's efforts to meet the requirements of the new technological curriculum called for by CCSS. For example, on a national level, 10% of all teachers retire or change schools each year. In a 4-year implementation plan, nearly one half of the teachers trained might no longer be present. Investment in remodeling of older schools for computerized instruction may delay implementation plans. Public opinion concerning the merits of online student instruction can become an issue.

Planners must see the big picture and communicate it to others who are absorbed by daily problem-solving. As a sign in one school read, "When the finger points to the problem, the educator will study the finger." One thing is certain about the curriculum development efforts this time. In 46 states, teachers will be working within their buildings to implement the Common Core Standards adopted in 2011.

Summary

Technology has provided curriculum designers with an entirely new landscape. The new communication technologies have made knowledge instantly accessible, and has led to a fusion of delivery mediums. Students possess and use such technology outside of school. In some schools, the new technologies are changing teaching and learning.

The Common Core requirements present schools with the serious challenge of providing students with 21st-century tools. These instruments are expensive, and their use for instruction is not yet fully understood. As such, these technology needs for participation and assessment in the Common Core represent the greatest challenge to success for the program.

Activities

ACTIVITY 6.1

If your school were given an allocation of one million dollars to enhance instructional technology, how would you spend these monies?

ACTIVITY 6.2

Discuss a probable scenario for any school in the United States that does not vigorously pursue technologies during the coming decade.

Click here to take an automatically-graded
self-check quiz.

Additional Reading

Adaptive learning startup Knewton takes its biggest
step yet in K-12 ... gigaom.com/2013/.../adaptive-
learning-startup-knewto.

Cuban, L. (2003). *Oversold and underused: Computers in
the classroom.* Harvard University Press.

Educational Leadership. (March 2013). *Technology
Rich Learning Issue. 70*(6).

Education Testing Service. (2012). *Computers in the
classroom: The study of technology in the United
States.* Princeton, NJ: ETS.

Levin, B. (2012). *Leading technology-rich schools.* New
York, NY: Teachers College Press.

Maloy, R. (2011). *Transforming learning with new technologies.* Boston, MA: Allyn and Bacon.

Minnesota Office of the Legislative Audit. (2011). *K–12
online learning evaluation report.* St. Paul, MN:
State of Minnesota.

National Center for Educational Statistics, 2012.

Time Magazine. (2012, August 27). The wireless issue:
10 ways your phone is changing the world.
Retreived from http://content.time.com/time/
covers/0,16641,20120827,00.html

University of California, Berkeley, CA. (2003). *How
much information.*

Webley, K. (2013, June 17). A is for adaptive. *Time Magazine.* Retreived from http://content.time.com/
time/magazine/article/0,9171,2145048,00.html

Elementary School Programs and Issues

Learning Outcome

- Understanding the special curriculum needs of younger children.

For over a century, American elementary schools have been highly innovative, and current curriculum change in each of the 67,000 separate buildings is focused on three areas: 1) changes needed to meet the needs of a new and emerging population of students; 2) changes addressing new ways of delivering classroom instruction; and 3) changes required to implement the new Common Core State Standards.

For years schools in the "Sunbelt states" have worked to accommodate students from other nations who have arrived as immigrants or illegal occupants. In Miami, Florida, for example, over forty languages are spoken in the classrooms. In the year 2000, some 18% of students in American schools spoke a language other than English in the home. By the year 2020, one in five children in our schools will be of Hispanic descent. Early programs in elementary schools, such as English for Speakers of Other Languages (ESOL) have been overwhelmed by such growth in many states. It is a simple and indisputable fact that our society and schools are now multilingual.

While our schools generally try to promote a transcultural theme in the general curriculum, the strong emphasis of testing students in English creates difficulty for those states with a high percentage nonEnglish speaking populations.

In California, for instance, 50% of all eighth graders are Hispanic, but only 14% test proficient in reading achievement. In Florida, where over a quarter of all public school students are Hispanic, only 27% are proficient in reading. In Illinois, only 27% of all students tested met eighth grade proficiency in reading. And, in New Mexico, where 45% of all students are Hispanic in origin, only 62% graduated from high school in 2010. Sixteen states in the United States have over one-half million Hispanic residents, but one-half of the total Hispanic population is found in only Texas and California.

Your author wishes to observe that the 50 million Hispanics in the United States are a racial and ethnic diverse group. While some two thirds of the Hispanic population are Mexican-American, there are large (up to 10%) populations of Cubans, Puerto Ricans,

Salvadorans, Dominicans, Colombians, and others. This observation is made because these groups bring many sublanguages and dialects to our elementary classrooms.

The economies of our states educating large numbers of English-deficient students have been hit hard by reductions in state contributions to education (26 states have made cuts to school budgets in 2012–13), and these cuts hit hardest in states with large federal supplements for programs like ESOL and special education. Worse, as achievement tests reveal poor results, the public becomes more receptive to school takeovers and charter school voucher programs. While charter schools have only about one million students at this time, they constitute a rising threat to public school education in Sunbelt states like Florida, Texas, and Arizona.

Another area of concern for curriculum planners at the elementary level is the large number of students with special needs. Approximately 14% of all U.S. students are presently categorized as having some kind of learning disability. Since 1975, when Congress first passed the Education for All Handicapped Children's Act (EHC), modified as the Individuals with Disabilities Act (IDEA), all states are required to service special students. These services must be free to students and their parents, and appropriate (FAPE), and conducted in the least restrictive learning environment (LRE). Each student with a disability, whatever their needs, must have an individualized education plan (IEP).

Elementary students with learning disabilities are placed in one of thirteen categories for receiving services. After diagnosis, students are placed in the regular classroom (Inclusion), placed periodically in the regular classroom (Mainstreamed) or placed in a special school. More than 40% of American students have some type of specific or categorical learning disability. Approximately 24% have a speech or language need, while 11% have been diagnosed as suffering a wide spectrum of autism problems. The reader might imagine the degree of planning that is necessary to accommodate so many different learning needs in a standard elementary classroom. Teachers and parents meet to develop the student's IEP, students are individually scheduled into the classroom with appropriate teachers, and special learning materials and technologies are deployed. Evaluations of student progress are individualized, for which teachers must receive special training. Record-keeping, likewise, is individualized.

Perhaps the most pressing disability for curriculum planners in the elementary school is the number of students being diagnosed with wide-spectrum autism. Worldwide, it is estimated that 70 million persons are autistic, and in the United States 1 child in 80 shows autistic symptoms. By law, school districts must provide services to such children from ages 3 to 21. At the national level, caring for these persons beyond age 21 is an issue of great discussion.

The classroom and school innovations in elementary schools focused on just instructional delivery of the curriculum are numerous. Specific themes of the last decade, such as project-based learning (PBL), and Emotional Intelligence (EI), and Integrated Studies, have given way to all kinds of technology applications and new ideas such as "flipped learning." Flipped learning makes videos and posts these episodes online, asking that the students watch these lectures at home. Class time would then be dedicated to discussions of materials viewed, thereby increasing on-task learning time. Such innovation has, of course, worked best in affluent schools with strong parental support for learning.

One of the ideas that is generating controversy in elementary schools is the idea of students bringing their own technology from home to school (BYOT). This strategy of being both innovative and thrifty brings to mind George Orwell's quotation, "All animals are created equal, but some animals are more equal than others." Unfortunately, much of what is presently innovative in our elementary schools is Internet dependent. What can be said about the many innovations found at any time in elementary schools is that they must be judged on their effectiveness to help students learn. Many innovations are marketed and "sold" by producers of materials or consultants, and it is an important task for curriculum specialists to sort and select from the many new ideas arriving each year.

Finally, elementary schools in America are under immense pressure to define and implement the many new demands of the Common Core Standards. Changes will occur in the standards applied, the curriculum taught, and assessments used. The alignment of grades 3–8 ELA and mathematics instruction with the Common Core Standards, in many states, began with the 2012–13 school year. By 2013, curriculum frameworks are to be developed, and by 2014 instructional materials will be developed. Summative assessments of student learning are scheduled to begin in the spring of 2015.

ENTER THE COMMON CORE

For local elementary schools, the Common Core movement provides an opportunity to realize systemic change and ensure that their students are held to the same high standards and expectations in math and literacy as other students worldwide. The Core will force teachers to connect learning time and student achievement in new ways.

Specifically, there are six "shifts" that must be made from the old state standards to the new Common Core Standards.

In ELA assessments:

1. Balance literary and informational texts.
2. Connect knowledge and assessment questions for grade 6 and up.
3. Increase the degree of complexity from grade to grade.
4. Provide text-based answers on assessments.
5. Write from sources.
6. Develop an academic vocabulary.

In Mathematics assessments:

1. Only priority standards will be assessed or emphasized.
2. Assessments will reflect the progression of content.
3. Students must perform without complex calculators.
4. Students will evidence a deep understanding of the subject.
5. Students will be able to provide examples of application of topic.
6. Students will evidence a dual intensity (learn and apply simultaneously).

Building principals and curriculum personnel in elementary schools will need a vision in order to transition to the Common Core. Teachers must buy in, the parents and the community must be informed, and there must be time for reflection by those who will teach to these new standards. In math, for example, the change will include a conceptual understanding, a new focus, the teaching of reasoning ability in students, and mastery of specific areas of mathematics. In ELA, students will have to master text complexity, focus on informational reading (technical), and provide evidence to support writings. Other subject areas must study how to support the ELA curriculum.

The upshot of the transition at the local school level is that students will see an increased emphasis on creative and innovative thinking, research and information fluency, communication and collaboration, problem-solving and critical thinking, and self-regulated learning. In programming the students for life and work in the 21st century, there will be an emphasis on what students can do with knowledge rather than what knowledge units they have mastered.

By 2014, local schools will be able to receive curriculum modules that will include:

1. Year-long scope and sequence documents (maps).
2. Module overview (frameworks) documents.
3. Performance tasks (outcomes) to be accomplished.
4. Sample lesson (classroom plans) plans.
5. Supporting materials (specific to the outcomes) for lesson planning.

These materials being developed under the auspices of a Pearson Education grant (24 modules total) will obviously be welcomed by local schools. The hard fact is that the average school district in the United States has only 2,500 pupils, leaving few school personnel to help local faculties in this transition. As the Superintendent of Public Instruction wrote to the Washington State School Board:

> Washington's small districts have a small number of personnel (less than .5 FTE) at the district and building levels, filling multiple leadership, administrative, and instructional roles. 93 of the 186 districts (in Washington state) report having no district staffing to support this work other than the Superintendent (of the district).

—December, 2011

Your author recommends that local elementary schools, small as well as large, focus on six tasks for implementation. First and foremost, student achievement should be evident by the mastery of core academic skills on assessment tests. Second, create a professional learning community within the school to plan and solve problems. Third, promote the realignment of instructional resources, with particular emphasis on providing a high-tech environment for learning. Fourth, encourage a school-home infrastructure made possible by remote access to digital content, software, and documents. Fifth, encourage teachers to understand the role of assessment in curriculum development and the use of data in collaborative inquiry. And, sixth, emphasize the learner-centered nature of the Common Core Standards, to help each individual student prepare for the future and meet the needs of diverse learners.

THE BASIS OF THE ELEMENTARY SCHOOL CURRICULUM

The modern elementary curriculum evolved over the past 200 years from a narrow curriculum devoted to the teaching of reading, writing, and arithmetic to a broad program encompassing not only basic skills but also a variety of learning experiences. Because schools in the United States, as in other countries, are mechanisms for social change, schools often become battlegrounds for diverse groups with conflicting interests. The history of the elementary school during the past several years has been one of continuous change. Schools in the United States, like the nation itself, are in transition. By examining the history of the elementary school, we can see that elementary schools have been responsive to the needs of our expanding and increasingly diverse society.

Elementary School History

The establishment of free elementary schools for all children by state legislation was a grand and unique experiment in this country. Free elementary schools became associated with the highest ideals of our citizens. Unlike most other countries in the world, the United States has no national system of education. Under our federal Constitution, control of schools has been delegated to the states through the principle of residual rights. Those rights not expressly granted to the federal government are the rights of the individual states.

Precedents were established early in the history of our country for the exercise of state legislative authority in educational matters. As early as 1642, the colonies enacted legislation concerning educational matters. The Colonial Assembly of Massachusetts enacted compulsory education laws in 1642 and 1647. The 1647 legislation compelled communities over a certain size to set up grammar schools. That legislation, known as the Old Deluder Satan Act, passed by the General Court of the Massachusetts Bay Colony, required towns to establish common schools and grammar schools so men could read the Scriptures and escape the clutches of Satan. The act was not only the first law in the United States requiring that schools be established but was also the first example in the history of legislation requiring that children be provided an education at the expense of the community.

By 1693, legislation was passed allowing select men authority to levy school taxes with the consent of the majority of the townspeople. Previously, each town could determine how buildings, salaries, and other matters were handled.

For more than 100 years, elementary teachers relied heavily on the *New England Primer,* a book that used Bible verses and other resources to teach reading and number skills. Disciplinary practices also followed religious lines, with flogging and other measures designed to "drive the devil out of children."

In addition to religious purposes, early elementary schools served another purpose—rallying support for the new American political system. James Madison and Thomas Jefferson both spoke out against ignorance and in favor of an educated populace. Elementary schools were established for the maintenance of society by inculcating not only religious but also political doctrine.

As the nation expanded westward and with new states admitted to the Union, the elementary school experienced reforms. Many of the reforms were influenced by European examples. Perhaps the person most responsible for building the base for the modern elementary school was the Swiss educational reformer Johann Heinrich Pestalozzi (1746–1827), who viewed child growth and development as organic (natural) rather than mechanistic. He recognized that the narrow curriculum, consisting mainly of mechanical exercises in reading, was inadequate to prepare children for intelligent citizenship. Through teacher training programs, he helped prepare elementary teachers to provide a variety of learning experiences for children. His ideas were best expressed in his book *How Gertrude Teaches Her Children.*

In the early 1800s, Prussian educators borrowed many of these European ideas to build a system of education that served their national needs. Horace Mann and other educators of the day visited Prussia and returned to the United States with glowing reports of the highly efficient Prussian system. That system, imitated in the United States for nearly 200 years, included grading students on the basis of ability, improving methods of instruction and discipline, setting up a state agency for education, and developing special teacher-training institutions.

Public education became increasingly popular in the United States in the first half of the 1800s. The first state board of education was established in Massachusetts in 1837 with Horace Mann as its initial secretary. By 1876, the principle of public elementary education had been accepted in all states. The period from 1826 to 1876, known as the *public school revival,* led to a new American consciousness regarding educating children. Legislators were pressured to provide more money for elementary schools, and the curriculum was enriched.

Expansion and Reforms in Elementary Schools

From 1876 to the mid-1930s, the United States became a great industrial nation. As the country moved from a simple agricultural society to an industrial power, schools became instruments of social change. Elementary enrollments doubled, many new subjects were added to the curriculums, and the school day was lengthened. World War I resulted in demands for new skills on the part of youth, and curriculum change in 1918 included greater literacy training and the addition of vocational programs in schools. Because new courses in psychology and methods were introduced in teacher-training institutions, the elementary curriculum began to change. By the 1930s, standardized tests were used to determine achievement in school subjects, and individual and group intelligence tests were administered. Efforts were made to differentiate instruction (individualized) for slow, average, and above-average elementary children.

During the 1920s and 1930s, educational philosophers such as John Dewey had a great influence on the elementary curriculum. Dewey and other progressive educators saw schools as agencies of society designed to improve our democratic way of life. Dewey believed that schools should be a reflection of community life, with students studying about the home, neighborhood, and community. By studying what is familiar to them, students might become more curious about the disciplines of science, geography, and mathematics. "Learning by doing" is a principle of learning that was central to Dewey's ideas about schools. Because Dewey believed that active children learn more, he argued that learning in the elementary school should not include simply rote, mechanistic learning activities but a variety of creative activities in which students are active participants in the learning process. Dewey maintained that the curricula of the elementary school should build on the interests of students and should represent real life by discussing and continuing the activities with which the child is already familiar at home.

The *progressive education* movement, led by John Dewey, George Counts, Harold Rugg, and others, heavily influenced the elementary curricula until 1957, when the launch of *Sputnik* forced a reexamination of the purpose of the elementary school. Critics such as Admiral Rickover and Arthur Bestor censured progressive education as failing to provide students with the necessary skills and knowledge to compete in a scientific world. Congressional acts establishing the National Science Foundation (NSF) and the National Defense Education Act (NDEA) pumped millions of dollars into the development of science and mathematics programs and materials. The elementary curriculum began to reflect a growing emphasis on science and mathematics in student courses such as Science: A Process Approach and inservice programs designed to improve teachers' skills in teaching science and mathematics.

The 1960s witnessed an era of innovation in the elementary curriculum. Many of the innovations dealt with organizational changes such as the absence of grades, open classrooms, and team teaching. Elementary school buildings were designed to facilitate those organizational changes. As with other innovations involving organizational changes, teachers were not necessarily prepared to cope with such new ideas. A lack of teacher inservice training, and continued turnover of elementary teachers resulted in a growing resistance to these changes. Some elementary leaders confused organizational *means* with *ends*. Although their schools were advertised as "open and nongraded," little change occurred in teaching methods or in curriculum substance.

Educators in the 1970s and 1980s, for the first time in the history of U.S. education, saw a decline in elementary enrollment. Retrenchment, funding problems, and dissatisfaction with the experimentation of the 1960s led to new forms of legislated accountability measures and increased testing programs in the elementary school. By the late 1980s, with enrollment once again growing for the first time in two decades, the elementary curriculum had expanded to include a greater variety of learning experiences, but it had narrowed its focus to the basic skills of written and oral communication and mathematics. In many schools and districts, the curriculum became "unbalanced."

ORGANIZING THE CURRICULUM

The curriculum of the elementary school is organized around the bases of knowledge, the needs of society, and human learning and development. As discussed in the previous section, early elementary schools were concerned simply with the transmission of knowledge. Later, schools were seen as an instrument of society to foster religious views and the political doctrine of early America. In the first half of the 1900s, elementary schools were seen as serving an emerging industrial society and as an instrument for the improvement of democratic institutions. Human learning and development did not influence the curriculum until the late 1920s and 1930s, when psychologists began to introduce educators to research on student learning and child growth and development. Not until the 1960s did major changes in curriculum and in training curriculum leaders result from research studies of learning and development.

From the 1960s through the 1990s, many new programs were introduced into the elementary program to accommodate young learners and those learners with special needs. Free public kindergarten programs were implemented for 5-year-old children in all states, along with a variety of other programs such as Head Start for disadvantaged young children. Special education programs for elementary students with physical and mental disabilities were greatly expanded, and programs for *gifted learners* were made available to more elementary students. Nursery school programs for 3- and 4-year-olds, extended-day centers for children before and after school, daycare centers, and even prenatal centers are now found in many elementary schools.

Individualizing Instruction

A consistent theme of elementary school learning for years has been that of *individualizing instruction* to accommodate differences among students. Because of the complexity of the concept, the term *individualization* is often misunderstood. Individualization has dimensions other than the rate of progress. Among the variables that may be manipulated in individualized instruction are the following:

- *Materials for study.*   Prescribed or individually chosen; various levels of difficulty and with varying purposes.

- *Method of study.* Prescribed or chosen methods of learning.
- *Pace of study.* Timed or untimed, structured or fluid.
- *Sequence of study.* Ordered or providing the option for personal coverage of material.
- *Learning focus.* Factual, skill-based, process, or values.
- *Place of learning.* Classroom, school, environment, or optional.
- *Evaluation of learning.* Exam-based, product-based, open-ended, or student-evaluated.
- *Purpose of learning.* Mastery, understanding, application, or experiential.

In most elementary programs, students work with similar materials at about the same pace in the same spaces, and they usually have similar, if not identical, learning criteria for evaluating their progress. Some widespread techniques are used to accommodate differences, however, including grouping, use of materials with differing levels of reading difficulty, and special programs for students at the greatest points away from group norms.

Grouping

Flexibility is the key in any grouping arrangement. The major reason for employing grouping as an instructional technique is to provide more effectively for students' individual differences. Some common groups found in the elementary school are the following:

- *A class as a whole* can function as a group. Teachers sometimes have guilt feelings about whole-class activities, but there are occasions when the teacher can address the whole class as a single group. New topic or unit introductions; unit summaries; and activities such as reports, dramatizations, and choral reading may be effectively conducted with the total class.
- *Reading level groups* formed according to reading achievement levels are commonly found in classrooms. These groups are not static and must accommodate shifts of pupils from group to group as changes in individual achievement occur.
- *Reading need groups* are formed to assist students in mastering a particular reading skill such as pronouncing a phonic element or finding the main idea in a paragraph.
- *Interest groups* help students apply reading skills to other language arts and to other content areas. Storytelling, recreational reading, writing stories and poems, and dramatization are activities that can be carried out in interest groups.
- *Practice or tutorial groups* are often used to allow students to practice oral reading skills, play skill games, and organize peer-teaching situations.
- *Research groups* allow for committee work, group projects, and other research activities. Learning centers in the classroom and research areas in the media center are often developed for research groups.
- *Individualization* allows a student to work as an individual in selecting books and references for learning projects. Developmental programs provide for individual progress through a series of lessons.

Two common terms used in grouping in the elementary school are *heterogeneous* (mixed) and *homogeneous* (like) groups. Usually, these two types of groups are used interchangeably during a school day. Teachers who organize skill groups in the classroom are using homogeneous grouping. The key is flexibility. Students are moved from group to group as they achieve required skills. Also, the skill groups are organized for only a portion of the school day. The rest of the day, students are organized into heterogeneous groups in which they can interact with students of varying abilities.

Reading Levels

Another common means of accommodating student differences is to provide books of varying degrees of difficulty. Textbook publishers regularly provide grade-specific texts (fourth-grade math, for example) with several leveled versions. Teachers use the readability of the text as a means of tailoring instruction to the student.

Programs such as Accelerated Reader and STAR Reading provide statistical data collected on students, which allow teachers to assess their students better. Those data can be put into reports for parents. *Readability* is the objective measure of the difficulty of a book or article and usually involves the use of a specific formula, with results reported in terms of grade level. Seven such formulas are listed here.

1. *Flesch Reading Ease Score*   Involves checking word length and sentence length (grades 5–12).
2. *Wheeler and Smith Index Number*   Involves determining sentence length and number of polysyllabic words (grades preK–4).
3. *Cloze Technique*   Can be used to compare the readability of two pieces of material; measures redundancy (the extent to which words are predictable), whereas standard readability formulas measure the factors of vocabulary and sentence structure; can be used to determine relative readability of material but cannot predict readability of a new sample; does not give grade-level designations.
4. *Lorge Grade Placement Score*   Uses average sentence length in words, number of difficult words per every 100 words, and number of prepositional phrases per 100 words (grades 3–12).
5. *Fry Graph*   Method is based on two factors: average number of syllables per 100 words and average number of sentences per 100 words in three randomly selected 100-word samples.
6. *SMOG Grading Plan*   Involves counting repetition of polysyllabic words (grades 4–12).
7. *Spache Grade Level Score*   Looks at average sentence length and number of words outside the Dale list of 769 words to give readability level (grades 1–3).

Armed with such assessments, the teacher can provide students with reading materials tailored to their needs and abilities.

Approaches to teaching reading vary according to how the teacher thinks children learn. Table 7.1 outlines seven approaches now found in public schools and cites their advantages and disadvantages.

Whole Language Versus Phonics

During the last decade, debate has continued about whether phonics or whole language was the better approach to teach beginning readers. *Phonics*, explicit decoding instruction, is known as basic-skills instruction. Phonics builds on a series of basic steps that introduces emergent readers to fundamental skills such as linking sounds and letters, combining sounds, and recognizing words with similar letter–sound patterns.

TABLE 7.1   Seven Basic Approaches to Teaching Reading

Advantages	Disadvantages

I. Basals

Advantages	Disadvantages
1. Is comprehensive and systematic	1. Is stereotyped and uncreative
2. Presents reading skills in order	2. Limits students to one reading book
3. Is flexible	3. Has an overabundance of material
4. Has a well-established basic vocabulary	4. Is geared to middle-class whites
5. Is equipped with diagnostic tools	5. Tends to be very expensive
6. Builds themes around familiar situations	6. Depends heavily on visual or sight-word methods
7. Gives a well-rounded reading choice	7. Leaves little time for creativity
	8. Does not facilitate much transfer from skill to functional reading

II. Language Experience

Advantages	Disadvantages
1. Integrates all listening and speaking skills	1. Has limited materials
2. Utilizes student's own language	2. Does not sequence skills
3. Develops sensitivity to the child's environment	3. Has no concrete evaluation process
4. Can be used with the culturally different	4. Limits word-attack skills
5. Encourages sharing of ideas	
6. Develops confidence in language usage	
7. Develops self-expression	

III. Individualized Approach

Advantages	Disadvantages
1. Enables the child to select appropriate books	1. Does not allow for sufficient skill development
2. Gives greater opportunity for children to interact with one another	2. Requires a large amount of record keeping
3. Fosters self-confidence as the child progresses at his or her own rate	3. Requires vast amounts of books and supplementary materials
4. Establishes one-to-one relationships through conferences with the teacher	4. Tends to allow children to limit their own selection
5. Diminishes competition and comparison	5. Makes little provision for readiness
6. Is flexible	6. Does not allow for advance preparation for words or concepts
	7. Requires teachers with a wide knowledge of books

IV. Linguistic Approach

Advantages	Disadvantages
1. Begins with familiar words that are phonetically regular	1. Has many different linguistic approaches
2. Presents words as wholes	2. Lacks extensive field testing
3. Shows letters as a function of the arrangement in the words	3. Has too controlled a vocabulary
4. Develops sentence order early	4. Encourages word-by-word reading
	5. Lacks emphasis on reading for meaning

TABLE 7.1   *(Continued)*

Advantages	Disadvantages

V. Phonics

Advantages	Disadvantages
1. Develops efficiency in word recognition	1. Tends to isolate speech sounds in an unnatural manner
2. Helps develop independence in word recognition	2. Involves too much repetition; is boring
3. Creates interest because of immediate success for the child	3. Uses the slow process of sounding out words
4. Shows association between print and sounds	4. Has too many exceptions to the rule

VI. Alphabetic Approach

Advantages	Disadvantages
1. Is simpler	1. Lacks clarification regarding techniques and materials
2. Gives opportunity for free expression	2. Makes transition from initial teaching alphabet (ITA) difficult
3. Engenders enthusiasm to read because of quick success	3. Is very expensive
4. Encourages the learning of words more rapidly	4. Confuses children because they see ITA only at school
	5. Has not been around long enough to prove its validity

VII. Programmed Instruction

Advantages	Disadvantages
1. Allows child to proceed at his or her own pace	1. Uses limited research
2. Reinforces student after each step	2. Does not consider limited attention span of student
3. Records student progress	3. Becomes repetitious
4. Is self-instructional	4. Bypasses comprehension because it is difficult to program
5. Helps teacher understand sequencing	5. Gives little room for child to develop his or her own interests or tastes in reading
	6. Is expensive

Whole language, as a teaching approach, embraces the theory that children learn to read the way they learn to talk—naturally. The whole-language teaching philosophy builds on a variety of reading and writing activities in which children choose their own books, construct meaning from their own experiences, sound out words in context, and decipher words from syntactical clues.

SELECTION OF CONTENT

Subject content in the elementary school is selected from the basic disciplines of language arts, mathematics, social studies, science, the arts, and health. Curriculum developers at the national, state, and local levels help select content. Because the United States does not have a national system of education, the work of curriculum developers and researchers must fit a variety of learning needs and expectations of students in the 14,000 school districts of this country.

Determining Appropriate Elementary School Curriculum Content

Determining appropriate content for elementary schoolchildren is not always easy. Testing programs and accountability legislation today often dictate the selection of content, especially with demands to teach more reading, writing, and mathematics. Teaching for the test has become a common practice in too many classrooms.

Language Arts

Language arts include the communication skills: reading, writing, listening, and speaking. These four modes of learning are interrelated in a developmental sequence. From listening to speaking, to reading, to writing, children begin to comprehend and use language skills. The interconnectedness of all four of the communication areas implies a need for those areas to be taught in a holistic approach.

The reading component of a total language arts program must include the development of skills in decoding and comprehension to use functional and literary written material. Although reading educators differ on their approaches to teaching reading, students who fail to master these skills will likely face a lifetime of underachievement.

Reading

Reading, perhaps the most controversial area of the elementary program, is not only an emotional issue but also a political one in many districts. Reading becomes the concern of parents long before their children enter school. Reading has also become the center of national rage and the focus of numerous research studies and a federal crusade in the past quarter century. In recent decades, millions of dollars have been poured into the development of reading programs. There are scores of reading programs that all work, yet there are still millions of nonreaders in our schools. It is debatable whether we are any closer to solving the mysteries of reading. We do know that reading has engaged the time of more teachers and received a larger share of the school dollar than any other subject in the curriculum.

What makes some students successful in reading, whereas others find only failure? Some students fail because they deem certain classroom stimuli less important and tend to ignore them; others succeed because they are in tune with the teacher and react positively to instructional stimuli.

Grouping students into high and low groups usually ensures that students will be treated differently by teachers. Students in high groups usually:

- read first, when they are more alert and eager.
- meet for a longer time-frame.
- face a warmer, more receptive teacher, one who smiles, leans toward them, and makes eye contact more frequently.
- are criticized in a softer, more respectful manner.
- are disciplined with warnings instead of actions.
- read approximately three times as much as other reading groups (of which 70% will be silent reading) and make more progress.
- are expected to self-correct reading errors but if teacher-corrected, the correction occurs at the end of the section, which does not disrupt the reader's fluency.

- are asked questions that are comprehension checks and require higher-level thinking skills.

A totally different atmosphere usually exists for students in low groups, who:

- meet for less time and later in the day, when they have already begun to tire.
- read more orally, which is slow, halting, and labored; they therefore read less and get further behind.
- have each error pointed out as it is made, allowing less time for self-correction; errors are made three to five times as often and as often as once every 10 words.
- are asked questions that tend to be literal—checking only to see whether they are listening.
- face a teacher whose body language is negative, who frowns, has pursed lips, glares, leans away, and fidgets.
- read silently only 30% of the time.
- are aware that, as "lows," they "can't read" and avoid it as much as possible.
- in large groups, are seated farthest from the teacher; these "slow" learners are given less time to respond to questions and have to think faster, thus increasing their chance of failure. (Wuthrick, 1990)

Until teachers see all students as having learning potential and provide the same stimuli to all students, low and high, reading will continue to be a problem in the elementary school.

Spelling

Two methods of teaching spelling are found in most elementary schools today. One method, *invented spelling*, has students writing how they think a word is spelled and checking it later. This method allows students to concentrate on what they are trying to communicate. It also increases the writer's freedom.

The second method, the traditional way, has students memorizing 10 to 20 words a week. Students are tested on their spelling rather than on their ability to apply rules to new words. Exercises focus on dictionary use, handwriting, and writing words several times.

New models of spelling in the elementary school suggest that spelling should not be treated as a separate subject but instead should be seen as a total language system involving writing and reading. Learning to spell should be pleasant, natural, and as easy flowing and unconscious an act as learning to speak.

Writing

Writing has again become a center of focus in today's elementary schools. Responding to demands of colleges that students know how to write better, elementary and secondary schools have devoted more time in the day to the teaching of writing skills.

Research on children's writing implies that focus on skill instruction in grammar and spelling may come at the expense of composition. Daily writing, conferences, and the focus of skills in the context of writing appear to be more effective.

Elementary schools are striving to integrate composition and literature into their language arts program and to make remedial and regular language arts programs congruent. The following are the goals of an integrated approach:

1. Place reading and composing at the center of the language arts curriculum.
2. Place skills instruction within rather than before genuine reading and writing.

3. Integrate the various components of language arts through content rather than skills.
4. Insist that all readers and writers—not just the most able learners—gain equal access to genuine reading and writing. (Armbruster, Lehr, & Osborn, 2001)

The oldest and most popular reading support program in schools is Reading Is Fundamental (RIF), founded in 1966 and heavily supported by the United States Office of Education. This program provides reading materials to children, particularly disadvantaged children, and involves parents in the process of learning to read.

Mathematics

Mathematics is more effective if it is carefully adapted to the developmental characteristics of elementary children. Early in the history of our schools, learning objectives of mathematics instruction centered on only the development of computational skills. In the 1920s and 1930s, objectives shifted to a more practical application of mathematics. Today, mathematics educators are concerned with providing a balanced program in mathematics in which students not only attain computational skills but also have an understanding of mathematics concepts and reasoning. The rapid increase in the number of microcomputers in elementary schools has resulted in the need for elementary students to perceive and understand structure in mathematics, including concepts, relationships, principles, and modes of mathematical reasoning.

Much of mathematics instruction in the elementary school involves the use of computer programs as well as textbooks. Elementary school teachers' content decisions are dictated by the standards and benchmarks they must teach. The teacher's topic selection, content emphasis, and sequence of instruction are now determined by standards and testing.

Computers, whole curricular approaches, and interdisciplinary units are giving elementary teachers new instructional options for delivery of content and skills. Practice sheets and end-of-chapter problems are giving way to these new approaches for teaching elementary mathematics.

The 1990s saw a host of efforts to reform curriculum and instruction in mathematics. *Professional Standards for Teaching Mathematics,* published in 1991 by the National Council of Teachers of Mathematics (NCTM), led the way in redefining elementary mathematics. The standards offer detailed images of the mathematics teaching promoted by many reformers in mathematics education. Approaches in teaching mathematics include cooperative learning, the use of themes and real-life problems, and the use of group grading on cooperative assignments (U.S. Department of Education, 2004).

Science

Science in the elementary school has also been influenced by the rapid advancements in technology in this country. During the 1960s, a reform movement urged a shift in science education away from an emphasis on the learning of facts toward an understanding of the processes of science. Recently, the emphasis has shifted toward the technological applications of science.

Learning scientific concepts, principles, and generalizations through an inquiry-based program allows elementary children to understand better the universe in which they live by enabling them to see orderly arrangement in the natural world and to explain the continual change in the world. Students must also develop a functional competency with the tools of science to help them live in a highly technological society ("Eight Essentials," 2006).

The *whole approach* to teaching science in the elementary school has an interdisciplinary scope. In contrast with traditional science instruction, the whole-science approach reinforces the required science curriculum with content from all subject areas in a thematic approach. The integrated approach to teaching science moves science teaching away from lectures and textbooks to a variety of materials and activities. Activities incorporate reading, writing, and mathematics while science concepts are developed. Cooperative learning and a team approach to teaching and learning science are also integral features of the whole-science approach. Figure 7.3 illustrates methods of integrating science with other subject areas.

Social Studies

Social studies instruction in the elementary school focuses on the interaction of people with one another and with their natural and human environments. Although there has been less reform in the social studies area than in the other major areas of the elementary curriculum, educators recently began to develop a more relevant program for elementary school students.

Of prime importance today is using social studies in the elementary school to teach critical thinking, develop civic responsibility, build self-concept, and improve human relationships. Children are more open to diversity in the early elementary years than in the later years. Positive self-concepts—important in positively perceiving and judging social interactions—form in the critical early years of schooling. Social studies education that moves beyond the mere acquisition of facts is being developed in many school districts. Citizenship education, in which young children are active participants in examining political feelings—social issues, as well as historical and geographic understanding—is forming the basis for social studies education in the elementary school. This approach fits with the instructional practices of cooperative learning and interdisciplinary instruction (Wineburg, 2005).

Geography

Efforts have been made in recent years to revitalize the teaching of geography in elementary schools. The National Geographic Society contributed $40 million in 1996 to a geography education foundation. The purpose of the foundation was to provide additional training for teachers and to develop classroom materials to increase geography literacy among students. Geography is thought to be particularly important as a subject in the new global economy, where students will become workers for multinational companies.

Health and Physical Education

Health and *developmental physical education* are core components of a complete elementary school curriculum. *Health education* includes learning all aspects of healthful and safe living. *Physical education* includes adaptive and developmental activities that lead to better coordination and psychomotor skills.

Because the physical being cannot be separated from the mental or social being, health and physical education programs must include activities designed to interrelate all three areas of the person—the physical, the mental, and the social. The National Association for Sports and Physical Education (NASPE) (2004) defines a physically educated person as one who:

- has the skills necessary to perform a variety of physical activities.
- participates regularly in physical activity.
- is physically fit.
- knows the implications of and the benefits from involvement in physical activities.
- values physical activity and its contributions to a healthful lifestyle. (p. 292)

Comprehensive School Health Education Program

In September 2000, the Centers for Disease Control and Prevention (CDC) published their definition of the key elements of comprehensive health education. These key elements include the following:

1. A documented, planned, and sequential program of health instruction for students in grades K–12.
2. A curriculum that addresses and integrates education about a range of categorical health problems and issues at developmentally appropriate ages.
3. Activities that help young people develop the skills they need to avoid tobacco use; dietary patterns that contribute to disease; a sedentary lifestyle; sexual behaviors that result in HIV infection, other STDs, and unintended pregnancy; alcohol and other drug use; and behaviors that result in unintentional and intentional injuries.
4. Instruction provided for a prescribed amount of time at each grade level.
5. Management and coordination by an education professional trained to implement the program.
6. Instruction from teachers who are trained to teach the subject.
7. Involvement of parents, health professionals, and other concerned community members.
8. Periodic evaluation, updating, and improvement.

The Arts

The arts in the elementary school include the visual and performing arts. Aesthetic education brings together cognitive, affective, and psychomotor areas of learning and includes experiences in music, fine arts, dance, theater, and other artistic modes of expression.

Until recently, mathematics and language were assumed to be cognitive in nature, whereas the arts were considered to deal with emotions and to be in the affective domain. Reading, writing, and arithmetic were assumed to be essential skills that made information processing possible; the ability to read or to produce in the arts was thought an end in itself, leading to nothing more than inner satisfaction. Recent research indicates that the basic distinction between intellect and emotion can no longer be rationalized. It is now more clearly understood that our mental activities always involve both intellect and feelings, that we communicate in a rich variety of modes of symbolization, and that each art medium contributes a "language" and experience that adds cognitive data to the functioning brain.

In the push for basic skills in the elementary school, the arts must not be left out of the curriculum. The arts are a necessary part of human experience. In light of recent research findings, the arts should be considered a basic part of the curriculum.

DIVERSE NEEDS OF CHILDREN

Children with Attention Deficit Disorder

Attention deficit disorder (ADD) is characterized by these symptoms: difficulty remaining seated, calling out without request, interrupting others, and talking excessively. Biochemical abnormalities in the brain are thought to be the cause of ADD. Children with this disorder are easily distracted, are disorganized, and are lacking in motor skills, and they have a limited attention span. The majority of children with ADD are found in regular classrooms rather than in special programs.

ADD affects 3% to 5% of school-age children and occurs six to nine times more frequently in boys than in girls. ADD behaviors continue to be a concern throughout a person's life. Teachers can aid the child with ADD by getting the child organized, giving effective instructions, administering consistent discipline, using nonverbal cues, developing the child's self-esteem, and communicating regularly with parents.

Attention deficit with hyperactivity disorder (ADHD), as defined by the American Psychiatric Association, is exhibited in a child with eight or more of 14 symptoms that reflect difficulties in attention, impulsivity, or motor hyperactivity with onset before age 17. Self-control strategies are very important in dealing with children with ADHD, but it is important first to determine whether a child has other behavioral or even cognitive deficits that need to be remediated before self-control strategies are implemented.

Children from Impoverished Families

Poverty remains a problem in the United States even though President Johnson declared an official War on Poverty in the mid-1960s. Figures in 2006 indicated that the younger the family is, the poorer the children are. Fifty percent of all U.S. children living in a household headed by a person 25 years of age or younger are poor. If a child lives in a family headed by a woman, chances are better than 50% that the child is poor. According to Kidcount (Casey Foundation 2012) over 20 million students, or one third of school-age children, lived with a single parent. Contrary to popular belief, the majority of poor people live in semi-isolation in towns across the country rather than in the inner cities. Two thirds of Americans who are poor are white.

Children living on the edge of homelessness are usually prevented from finding the stability that makes successful schooling possible. It was estimated in 2006 that 200,000 children were homeless each night (U.S. Department of Health Statistics, 2006).

Foster children and other displaced children often come from poor families. Drug and alcohol abuse by parents have contributed to the large numbers of children in juvenile detention centers.

One fourth of mothers receive no prenatal care. Teachers are seeing more learning disabilities as a result of poor healthcare and drug abuse by mothers. Children who were cocaine babies continue to enter school in large numbers, and their care is adding huge costs to already overburdened school budgets.

Children from Different Cultures

America's newest students speak many languages, practice many religions, come from many different backgrounds, and carry both hopes and frustrations into their new life. The 2000 census figures showed large increases in students who speak Spanish as a first language. In Florida, for example, Hispanics were the largest minority group in 2010. The number of Asian students continues to grow in American schools as well. Schools, as the melting pots, are helping non-English-speaking students by creating a safe and warm learning environment for them. English as a second language (ESL) programs have been revised to allow students to learn English while retaining their cultures. Students are encouraged to express themselves and relate their experiences. Working with parents by giving them make-and-take materials and showing them techniques for playing with their children are also important elements of bilingual education programs (see Figure 7.1).

In some states, there are specific standards for English Language Learners (ELL). These benchmarks seek to ensure that children who are of limited English proficiency, including immigrant children, achieve at high levels in core academic subjects. In some states, such as Tennessee, these children are held to the same state academic content and achievement standards as other students.

Finding teachers and aides who speak the language of students remains a challenge. Finding qualified instructors who speak Cambodian or Creole (for Haitian students) often frustrates district educators who have large concentrations of those non-English-speaking students. Several school districts are experimenting with peer-tutoring programs in which older students who speak the same language as the ELL student tutor younger students. Buddy systems are also used to pair non-English-speaking students with English-speaking students.

Children with Various Disabilities

The period from 1975 to 2010 represented an era of significant progress for students with special needs or disabilities. Public concern resulted in laws guaranteeing access to the curriculum and public dollars to ensure implementation of special programs for these children.

Although 195 federal laws specific to those with disabilities were enacted between 1927 and 1975, the National Advisory Committee on the Handicapped reported in 1975

Qualification for ESL Designation:

1. A language other than English is spoken in the home of the student.
2. Another language is the student's first language and English needs to be practiced.
3. Student was not born in the United States, and English is not his/her native language.
4. The student is an Alaskan native or Native American.
5. Student is struggling to perform academically in curriculum that uses English.
6. Student needs to develop cognitive learning skills in English.

FIGURE 7.1   Who Is an ESL Student?

This Part of ECIA	**Replaces These Programs**

Chapter 1—Financial Assistance to Meet Special Educational Needs of Disadvantaged Children	ESEA Title I
	    Basic Grants to Local Districts
	    Special Grants
	State-Administered Programs for
	    Migratory Children, Handicapped
	    Children, and Neglected and
	    Delinquent Children
	State Administration

Chapter 2—Consolidation of Federal Programs for Elementary and Secondary Education	

Subchapter A—Basic Skills Development	ESEA Title II—Basic Skills
	    Development (except Part C, Sec.
	    231), Inexpensive Book Distribution
	    Program

Subchapter B—Educational Improvement and Support Services	ESEA Title IV
	Part B—Instructional Materials and
	    School Library Resources
	Part C—Improvement in Local
	    Educational Practices
	Part D—Guidance, Counseling, and
	    Testing
	ESEA Title V—State Leadership
	ESEA Title VI—Emergency School Aid
	Precollege Science Teacher Training*
	    (Sec. 3(a)(1), NSF Act of 1950)
	Teacher Corps (Part A, HEA)
	Teacher Centers (Sec. 532, HEA)

FIGURE 7.2   The Education Consolidation Improvement Act: How Merged Programs Fit into ECIA.

*Separate, fiscal year (FY) 1982; consolidated, FY 1983.

that only 55% of children and youths with disabilities were being served appropriately. Of the 195 acts passed, 61 were passed between March 1970 and November 1975. Public Law 93-380, the Education Consolidation Improvement Act (ECIA), passed in 1974, was the most important of the laws passed; it extended and amended the Elementary and Secondary Education Act (ESEA) of 1965 and established a national policy on equal educational opportunity. Figure 7.2 notes the changes in ESEA.

The most far-reaching and significant federal act affecting those with disabilities was Public Law 94-142, the Education of All Handicapped Children Act of 1975, which was an amendment to Public Law 93-380. PL 94-142 has been described by many educators as "a bill of rights for those with disabilities." This law sets forth specific procedures that school districts must carry out to establish due process for students with disabilities. The most important feature of the law is that all such students between ages

3 and 21 must have available to them a free and appropriate public education. The law includes an emphasis on the regular class as the preferred legal decisions and legislation have made it clear that the rights of all children must be respected in our schools. Unfortunately, legal decisions and legislation do not ensure the development of adequate or appropriate programs. Inservice education is necessary to provide teachers with more specialized skills to deal with specific behavioral and academic problems. Mainstreaming can succeed only with a strong partnership of curriculum specialists, teachers, and supervisory personnel working cooperatively to provide the most appropriate education for all children.

EDUCATING DISABLED CHILDREN IN THE REGULAR CLASSROOM

Although the Education of All Handicapped Children Act requires school districts to identify and label children with special needs, it never mandated separate programs. Both federal and state laws have been amended since 1975 to insist on placing special needs students in the least restrictive environment—usually in the regular classroom unless their disabilities are severe.

Labeling also lowers student self-esteem, and moving students out of the regular classroom often limits students' expectation of success. Mainstreaming students with disabilities, even those with severe disabilities, seems to be a better approach. The team approach with regular classroom teachers allows the special needs teacher to work in a more integrated instructional environment.

Two new areas in the education of students with disabilities are (1) the emphasis on preschool identification and services, and (2) the transition from school to the world of work. At the preschool level, federal and state mandates require services for very young children. At present, the mandate is age 3, but it is expected that such service will soon begin at birth. The idea is that early intervention is best when dealing with disabling conditions.

INCLUSION: WHAT DOES IT MEAN?

Inclusion is a term for which few authors can agree on a definition. Some teachers lump inclusion with mainstreaming. Others believe it means keeping all special needs children in the regular classroom while retraining the special staff. Still others believe inclusion means *some* children, and full inclusion means *all* children. The term is also used to include teachers of students with disabilities who accompany their students into regular classrooms. The most common definition of inclusion states that inclusion involves keeping special education students in regular education classrooms and taking support services to the child rather than bringing the child to support services.

A major question on inclusion has been whether placing severely dysfunctional children in a regular classroom without providing adequate training or support for the teacher puts the other students at risk. Without such training and support, teachers take up much instructional time dealing with distractions, disruptions, and sometimes violence.

Much progress has been made in the first decade of the 21st century in building successful inclusion programs. When elementary schools have a clear philosophy of inclusion, mission statements that include goals for *all* students, and a curriculum that balances the needs of general and special education students, inclusion can be successful (Holloway, 2001).

Gifted Students

It has been estimated that over 2.5 million, or about 6%, of all young Americans are endowed with academic, artistic, or social talents far beyond those of their peers. These gifted children come from all levels of society, all races, and both sexes.

All 50 states have programs for gifted children, but there are still problems with identifying and providing for talented young students. For instance, many gifted children cannot be identified by IQ tests alone. New yardsticks for identifying gifted children have to be used, including measures of creativity; advanced social skills; and even exceptional physical aptitude such as the type that marks fine surgeons, watch repairers, and engineers.

As a group, talented and gifted children tend to learn faster and retain more than their peers. A gifted child is also a divergent thinker. All these characteristics can be unsettling in a class, and sometimes, gifted and talented children are seen as troublemakers. Other gifted children are bored by their classes and become alienated from school.

The Office of Elementary and Secondary Education of the U.S. Department of Education has adopted the following national definition for giftedness:

> Gifted and talented children are those identified by professionally qualified persons who, by virtue of outstanding abilities, are capable of high performance. These are children who require differentiated educational programs in order to realize their contribution to self and society.

The office has also identified the following six specific ability areas included in giftedness:

1. General intellectual ability
2. Specific academic aptitude
3. Creative or productive thinking
4. Leadership ability
5. Ability in the visual or performing arts
6. Psychomotor ability

The debate over how to educate gifted children often centers on the equity-versus-excellence issue. Some question whether it is fair to give special treatment to some children and not to others. Some educators have also seen cooperative learning as a threat to gifted children because it holds such students back. Others say cooperative learning works just as well in a homogeneously grouped gifted class because its real strength is bringing out the potential of each child in class. Tracking, often associated with gifted programs, has come under fire by many educators who see it as discriminating against poor children, who are most often found in low groups.

The gifted and talented remain a group of students who need special attention, whether in separate programs or differentiated instruction in a heterogeneous grouping. The models and research on gifted and talented children help provide a sound basis for differentiating instruction and evaluating programs for them.

Differentiating instruction, fostering creativity, allowing for independent study, and encouraging peer learning are all-important tasks of teaching. They are especially important for nurturing the diverse aptitudes and abilities of gifted and talented children. Organizational procedures such as cluster grouping, mainstreaming, and part-day grouping are all used with gifted and talented children.

Other Students with Needs

Between the special education student, who is categorically identified, and the gifted student, who is provided for by a special program, are all other students. Most of these "normal" students have needs, too, particularly during the elementary years. Figure 7.3

1. Gross motor and motor flexibility
   _____ Is uncoordinated and has poor balance
   _____ Has difficulty with jumping/skipping/hopping (below age 9)
   _____ Is confused in games requiring imitation of movements
   _____ Has poor sense of directionality
   _____ Is inept at drawing and writing at chalkboard
   _____ Is inaccurate when copying at chalkboard
   _____ Eyes do not work together
   _____ Eyes lose or overshoot target

2. Physical fitness
   _____ Tires easily
   _____ Lacks strength

3. Auditory acuity, perception, memory/speech
   _____ Confuses similar phonetic and phonic elements
   _____ Inconsistently pronounces words usually pronounced correctly by peers
   _____ Repeats, but does not comprehend
   _____ Forgets oral directions, if more than one or two

4. Visual acuity, perception, memory
   _____ Complains that he or she cannot see blackboard
   _____ Says that words move or jump
   _____ Has strained facial expression
   _____ Holds head to one side while reading

5. Hand–eye coordination
   _____ Has difficulty in tracing/copying/cutting/folding/pasting/coloring at desk
   _____ Lacks success with puzzles/yo-yos/toys involving targets, etc.

6. Language
   _____ Has difficulty understanding others

FIGURE 7.3   Checklist for Identifying Students Who May Need Educational Therapy.

provides a checklist of needs for students who are not served by special programs but who may need assistance.

Early Intervention

Prekindergarten programs are designed to smooth the transition from home to school and also from kindergarten to the upper grades. Prekindergarten programs stress *cooperative* or *shared learning* experiences. The focus of the curriculum for preschool programs is on developmentally appropriate activities, which include equal emphasis on physical, cognitive, social, emotional, and creative development. Often, prekindergarten programs

---

_____ Has difficulty associating and remembering

_____ Has difficulty expressing him or herself

7. Intellectual functioning

_____ Intellectual development is uneven

_____ Learns markedly better through one combination of sensory avenues than another

8. Personality

_____ Overreacts to school failures

_____ Does not seem to know he or she has a problem

_____ Will not admit he or she has a problem

9. Academic problems

_____ Cannot tolerate having routine disturbed

_____ Knows it one time and doesn't the next

_____ Writing is neat but slow

_____ Writing is fast but sloppy

_____ Passes the spelling test but cannot spell functionally

_____ Math is accurate but slow

_____ Math is fast but inaccurate

_____ Reads well orally but has poor comprehension

_____ Does poor oral reading but comprehends better than would be expected

_____ Lacks word-attack skills

_____ Has conceptual/study skill/organizational problems in content areas

10. Parents

_____ Are seemingly uninformed about nature of learning problem

_____ Are seemingly unrealistic about student's problems

FIGURE 7.3 *(Continued)*

use other students as models. Retired teachers, grandparents, and other older citizens also become involved in such programs.

In many districts, kindergarten is no longer a part-time, play-oriented introduction to school. It is "real" school where children go for the whole day and spend a great deal of their time in academic pursuits. For that reason, many children are failing kindergarten, and educators are concerned that a skill-based academic program is inappropriate for those students. Kindergarten teachers and elementary principals who are holding firm to a developmental approach are under increasing pressure to step up formal instruction.

With a focus on early childhood, one cannot forget the term *developmentally appropriate*. The National Association for the Education of Young Children (NAEYC) (1977), the nation's largest professional organization of early childhood educators, believes one index of the quality of primary education is the extent to which the curriculum and instructional methods are developmentally appropriate for children 5 through 8 years of age.

Other writers point out that cognitive psychology has generally reaffirmed the beliefs of Dewey, Piaget, and Elkind about the construction of meaning and the *constructivist* view of learning. In the constructivist view, students are more active agents in their own education. The constructivist approach would also work well with the use of information technology, according to other writers.

ELEMENTARY SCHOOL PRACTICES

Cooperative Learning

In *cooperative learning*, a technique that gained great favor in the late 1980s and 1990s, children are trained to use one another as resources for learning. Each child plays a specific role in a group such as facilitator, checker, or reporter. Teachers learn to delegate authority to a group of students and to encourage students to engage in a process of *discovery learning*. Cooperative learning requires assignments and curriculum materials different from those used in traditional classroom instruction. Tasks and materials that encourage student interaction are most needed in cooperative learning situations. Teachers who are not skilled in the organization and monitoring of small groups need inservice training in cooperative learning.

Grade-Level Retention

Two position papers in 1993—*Grade Level Retention: A Failed Procedure,* by the California State Department of Education, and *Grade Level Retention,* from the Florida Department of Education—summarized studies on grade-level retention (the practice of requiring an underperforming student to repeat an entire grade in school). Research studies showed that grade-level retention is not an effective remedy for students who are not achieving their potential. It is ironic that the state of Florida passed legislation in 2003 mandating retention in grade 3 for students not reading at grade level.

When students are held back, they fall behind the students entering the grade in which they are retained. Also, retained students are more likely to drop out of school. Finally, their self-esteem is lowered so much that most such students become disenchanted with school.

Unfortunately, many teachers and the general public still believe that grade-level retention works. Alternatives to grade-level retention, such as using a continuous-progress model, intensifying efforts to involve parents in school, and earlier intervention efforts, have been proposed in place of the practice of failing and retaining students.

Organization and Grouping of Students

Organizational patterns in elementary schools may include self-contained classrooms, grade-level teams, cross-grade teams, a total ungraded structure, or a combination of these patterns. For instance, the primary grades may be ungraded while the upper elementary grades retain the traditional grade levels. Also, teams may operate at certain grade levels, and other grade levels may be self-contained. Classes may also be self-contained or departmentalized.

Vertical and Horizontal Organization of Students

The two basic types of organization groups for instruction are *vertical* and *horizontal*. Vertical organization refers to the movement of students from grade to grade or level to level. Horizontal organization refers to the grouping of students within a grade or level and the assignment of teachers to a grade or level. Self-contained classes and departmentalized classes, with a separate teacher for each discipline, fall within a horizontal organization. Vertical organization may include both graded and nongraded plans.

Two or more teachers may engage in team teaching, in which each teacher contributes his or her special competencies, and the team is jointly responsible for providing instruction for a group of students. *Interdisciplinary teams* may teach all the disciplines, or they may have lead teachers in each discipline who take the major responsibility for the teaching of a subject area. Teams may be organized within a grade level or across grade levels. Teams may employ self-contained departmentalized and interdisciplinary instruction during a school year.

Organization and grouping, however, should be flexible; schools should be counseled against using a single pattern of organization or grouping arrangement. A sound approach is to organize and group according to the needs of students, the abilities of teachers, and the availability of facilities and resources. No single pattern can fit all situations.

Figure 7.4 illustrates an elementary scheduling pattern that includes both a graded and a nongraded grouping arrangement. The school is organized into two schools within a school. School A includes grades K–3; School B includes grades 4–6. In a block schedule, a unit of time is allowed for both graded and nongraded courses, thus allowing for timeframes for instruction in the discipline to be used. Enrichment classes are taught by all faculty members and are nongraded within both Schools A and B.

The governance of the school illustrated in Figure 7.4 includes the principal; the curriculum assistant, who also chairs the curriculum committee; and the chairperson of the steering committee. The steering committee consists of the chairperson of School A,

School A (K–3)	School B (4–6)	Time
Homeroom _(Nongraded/Reading Level)_	_Homeroom_ _(Nongraded/Reading Level)_	
		9:15–9:30
		9:30–9:45
Language arts (nongraded)	Language arts (nongraded)	9:45–10:00
		10:00–10:15
		10:15–10:30
Mathematics (nongraded)		10:30–10:45
	Mathematics (nongraded)	10:45–11:00
		11:00–11:15
Lunch (nongraded)		11:15–11:30
	Physical ed. (nongraded)	11:30–11:45
		11:45–12:00
		12:00–12:15
	Social studies (graded)	12:15–12:30
		12:30–12:45
		12:45–1:00
Social studies (graded)	Lunch (graded)	1:00–1:15
		1:15–1:30
Science (graded)		1:30–1:45
	Science (graded)	1:45–2:00
Physical ed. (graded)		2:00–2:15
		2:15–2:30
Enrichment program	Enrichment program	2:30–2:45
		2:45–3:00
		3:00–3:15

FIGURE 7.4   Schedule with Graded and Nongraded Grouping.

the chairperson of School B, a representative from the specialists' group (physical education, art, special education, media, music), and one other teacher from School A and another from School B (a total of five members). The chairperson of each school is selected yearly by staff members of that school. The chairperson of the steering committee is also selected annually by that group.

Summary

The elementary school in the United States has been arranged in many configurations during its nearly 300 years of existence. The grades 1–8 pattern of the 19th century was replaced by grades 1–6 and K–5 in the 20th century. Currently, the trend is to return to a seamless grades K–8 school that appears best suited for implementing a standardized curriculum. The program of the new K–8 school will be defined by practice over the next decade.

The most common format for elementary schools in the United States is still the grades K–5 model. This model houses two developmental stages, early childhood and later childhood, and is traditionally a broad and balanced program for students. Maintaining a developmentally appropriate curriculum in an age of standards and testing has proven challenging to elementary school leaders.

The diversity of the elementary student population has also proven a challenge to leaders. In urban areas and rural farming communities, language barriers are significant, and the various cultures of the subgroups are sometimes at odds with the general education design of the school. New special education requirements also present elementary school leaders with additional organizational requirements.

Activities

ACTIVITY 7.1

Identify what distinguishes the elementary school as a distinct level of educating.

ACTIVITY 7.2

Most American elementary schools have a "human development" rationale. How will practices based on this philosophy (grouping, grading, promoting) conflict with a standards-based rationale as found in the new Common Core?

 Click here to take an automatically-graded self-check quiz.

Additional Reading

Applebaum, M. (2008). *One-stop guide to implementing RTI*. Thousand Oaks, CA: Corwin Press.

Calkins, L. (2012). *Pathways to the Common Core:Accelerating achievement*. London, England: Heinneman.

Downy, C., et al. (2007). *50 ways to close the achievement gap*. Thousand Oaks, CA: Corwin Press.

Elkind, D. A. (1974). *Sympathetic understanding of the child: Birth to sixteen*. Boston, MA: Allyn & Bacon.

Gelineau, P. (2011). *Integrating the arts across the curriculum*. London, England: Cengage.

Lemlech, J. (2009). *Curriculum and instructional methods for the elementary and middle school* (7th ed.). Upper Saddle River, NJ: Merrill/Prentice Hall.

Xue, R., & Prissle, J. (2008). *Educating immigrant students in the 21st century*. Thousand Oaks, CA: Corwin Press.

Middle School Programs and Issues

Learning Outcome

■ To understand special curriculum concerns for older children and preadolescents.

There are presently three forms of intermediate school in the United States: the Junior high school (3,000), the middle school (13,200) and the new K–8 school (5,000). The grades 6–8 middle school is still the most common intermediate school configuration and is found in all 50 states. It can be expected that middle schools will continue to be a regular part of the American education landscape for a long while, and as such the middle school represents the curriculum model for preadolescents.

The K–8 school has a favorable track record in public and private education for student performance. Because there is no break during the first nine years of schooling, student achievement is superior in K–8 schools, and parents like their smallness and community atmosphere. The shortcomings of the K–8 model are its inability to fully service the preadolescents in the school and, often, a rather shallow or narrow academic offering.

THE MIDDLE SCHOOL: A HISTORICAL PERSPECTIVE

The junior high school that originated in 1910–1914 was intended to move the secondary program into the elementary grades. The familiar bulletin, Seven Cardinal Principles of Secondary Education, recommended that a school system be organized into two parts, a 6-year elementary school for children and a 6-year high school designed to serve pupils 12 to 18 years of age (U.S. Department of the Interior, 1918). The bulletin also suggested that secondary education be divided into two distinct periods, the junior period and the senior period. Thus, junior high schools were thought to be a part of the high school, and for nearly 50 years the curriculum of the junior high school tended to parallel that of the high school. Activities such as varsity athletics, marching bands, and even cap-and-gown graduation exercises tended to exert considerable pressure on junior high students. Teacher-training institutions also prepared "secondary" teachers for positions in the junior high schools. Most junior high schools were organized with grades 7 through 9.

By 1960, a number of factors led to the emergence of a new school known as the middle school. According to documents by the Association for Supervision and Curriculum Development (ASCD), critics of the junior high school were trying to reform the junior high school in the 1940s and 1950s, but they could not break the junior high away from the high school mold (ASCD, 1961).

Four factors led to the emergence of the middle school. First, the late 1950s and early 1960s were filled with criticisms of American schools, classroom and teacher shortages, double and triple sessions, and soaring tax rates. Books such as *Why Johnny Can't Read* (Flesch, 1986) triggered new concerns about the quality of schooling in the United States. The successful launching of *Sputnik* in 1957 led to a new wave of criticism about the curricula of elementary and secondary schools. *Sputnik* created an obsession with academic achievement, especially in the areas of science, foreign languages, and mathematics. A renewed interest in college preparation led to a call for a 4-year high school in which specialized courses could remain under the direction of the college preparatory school—that is, the high school. Likewise, the inclusion of grades 5 and 6 in the intermediate school could strengthen instruction by allowing subject-area specialists to work with younger students. Many of the first middle schools were organized with grades 5 through 8.

A second factor leading to the emergence of the middle school was the elimination of racial segregation. *The Schoolhouse in the City* (Education Facilities Laboratories, 1966, p. 10) stated that the real force behind the middle school movement in the larger cities (New York City, for example) was the desire to eliminate de facto segregation.

A third factor leading to the emergence of the middle school was the increased enrollment of school-age children in the 1950s and 1960s. The shortage of buildings resulted in double and even triple school sessions in some districts. Because older children in high schools were able to cope with overcrowding better than younger students, the ninth grade was moved to the high school to relieve the overcrowded junior high school. The same rationale was used to relieve the elementary school by moving the fifth or sixth grade to the junior high school.

A fourth and final factor was the bandwagon effect. Because many middle schools received favorable exposure in education journals and periodicals, administrators determined that the middle school was the thing to do; they "hopped on the wagon." All these factors may not have provided a valid reason for middle school organization, but they did provide the right opportunity for reform of the American intermediate school.

The reader will note that none of these reasons addressed the curriculum of the middle school. Throughout the 1970s and 1980s, junior high schools were converted to a middle school design in record numbers, with the same four factors at play. In the 1990s, a new increase in the school-age population caused even more conversions to middle schools. By the end of the 1990s, about 90% of intermediate schools in the United States were classified as middle schools.

Your author believes that the following reasons, related to providing a more relevant and appropriate program and learning environment for *transescent* (the period between childhood and adolescence) learners, are easier to justify:

- To provide a program especially designed for the 10- to 14-year-old child going through the unique transescent period of growth and development. Students in this age range constitute a distinct grouping—physically, socially, emotionally, and intellectually.

- To build on the changing elementary school. Historically, the post-*Sputnik* clamor to upgrade schools prepared the way for elementary school personnel to accept the middle school concept. The introduction of the "new" science, the "new" social studies, the "new" mathematics, and the "new" linguistics in elementary schools eroded the sanctity of the self-contained classroom. As part of the reorganization of curriculum that followed *Sputnik*, elementary teachers tended to cultivate a specific content area in the curriculum. This led to a departure from the self-contained classroom toward more sharing of students among teachers.
- To counter a growing dissatisfaction with the standard junior high school. The junior high school, in most cases, did not become a transitional school between the elementary and senior high school. Unfortunately, it became a miniature high school with all the sophisticated activities of the high school. Instruction was often formal and discipline centered, with insufficient attention given to the student as a person.
- To provide a catalyst for much-needed innovations in curriculum and instruction. By creating a new school—the middle school—rather than remodeling the outmoded junior high school, educators provided an atmosphere for implementing those practices long talked about but seldom implemented.

FUNCTIONS OF THE MIDDLE SCHOOL

Both in format and in numbers, middle schools have become a separate, intermediate institution in the United States. Cumulative experience and research, and middle school success, have resulted in widespread acceptance of the middle school design by children, teachers, administrators, and parents. Your author defines the middle school as a transitional school concerned with the most appropriate program to cope with the personal and educational needs of emerging adolescent learners. The middle school is an institution that has the following characteristics:

1. A unique program adapted to the needs of the pre- and *early adolescent* (transescent) student.
2. The widest possible range of intellectual, social, and physical experiences.
3. Opportunities for exploration and the development of the fundamental skills needed by all, with allowances for individual learning patterns and an atmosphere of basic respect for individual differences.
4. A climate that enables students to develop abilities, find facts, weigh evidence, draw conclusions, and determine values, and that keeps their minds open to new facts.
5. Staff members who recognize and understand the students' needs, interests, backgrounds, motivations, and goals, as well as stresses, strains, frustrations, and fears.
6. A smooth educational transition between the elementary school and the high school that allows for the physical and emotional changes of preadolescence.
7. An environment in which the child, rather than the program, is most important and one in which all students are ensured the opportunity to succeed.
8. Guidance in the development of the mental processes and attitudes needed for constructive citizenship and the development of lifelong competencies and an appreciation for the effective use of leisure.
9. Competent instructional personnel who will strive to understand the students they serve and who will develop professional competencies that are both unique and applicable to the transescent student.

	Elementary	Middle	High
Teacher–student relationship	Parental	Adviser	Random
Teacher organization	Self-contained	Interdisciplinary team	Department
Curriculum	Skills	Exploration	Depth
Schedule	Self-contained	Block	Periods
Instruction	Teacher-directed	Balance	Student-directed
Student grouping	Chronological	Multiage development	Subject
Building plan	Classroom areas	Team areas	Department areas
Physical education	Skills and games	Skills and intramurals	Skills and interscholastics
Media center	Classroom groups	Balance	Individual study
Guidance	Diagnostic/development	Teacher helper	Career–vocational
Teacher preparation	Child-oriented generalist	Flexible resource	Disciplines specialist

FIGURE 8.1   Schools in the Middle.

10. Facilities and time to allow students and teachers an opportunity to achieve the goals of the program to their fullest capabilities.

Figure 8.1 illustrates the unique and transitory nature of the middle school.

The middle school, then, presents a renewed effort to design and implement a program of education that can accommodate the needs of the preadolescent population. It is a broadly focused program of education, drawing its philosophy and rationale from the evolving body of knowledge concerned with human growth and development. The middle school represents a systematic effort to organize the schooling experience in a way that facilitates the maximum growth and development of all learners.

The middle school program consists of arrangements and activities that attempt to tie formal learning directly to the developmental needs of the students. To date, identified developmental tasks represent the most promising criteria for curriculum development that will intersect school activity with learner growth and development.

ESTABLISHING AN IDENTITY FOR THE MIDDLE SCHOOL

Education for emerging adolescents has been intensively reexamined over the past 5 decades. One result has been the verification of a need for a school with a differentiated function for early adolescents—those aged 10 to 14. The need for a distinct school, unlike the elementary school, high school, or even the junior high school, is more defensible than ever in light of recent information about the growth and development of emerging adolescents. Changing social conditions have also helped establish the need for a school in the middle with an identity of its own. As middle schools have grown in number and quality, some of the following common elements have contributed to their special identity:

- The absence of the "little high school" approach.
- The absence of the "star" system, in which a few special students dominate everything, in favor of an attempt to provide the experience of success for greater numbers of students.

- An attempt to use instructional methods more appropriate to this age group: individualized instruction, variable group sizes, multimedia approaches, beginning independent study programs, and inquiry-oriented instruction.
- Increased opportunities for teacher–student guidance; may include a home base or advisory group program.
- Increased flexibility in scheduling and student grouping.
- Some cooperative planning and team teaching.
- Some interdisciplinary studies, in which teachers from a variety of academic areas provide opportunities for students to see how the areas of knowledge fit together.
- A wide range of exploratory opportunities, academic and otherwise.
- Increased opportunity for physical activity and movement and more frequent physical education.
- Earlier introduction to the areas of organized academic knowledge.
- Attention to the skills of continued learning, those skills that will permit students to learn better on their own or at higher levels.
- An emphasis on increasing the student's ability to be independent, responsible, and self-disciplined.
- Flexible physical plant facilities.
- Attention to the personal development of the student: values clarification, group process skills, health and family life education when appropriate, and career education.
- Teachers trained especially for, and committed to, the education of emerging adolescents.

THE MIDDLE SCHOOL STUDENT

The middle school espouses the same goals as did the junior high: to provide a transition between the elementary school and the high school and to help students bridge the gap in their development between childhood and adolescence. Emerging adolescent learners in the middle school represent the most diverse group of students at any organizational level of schooling. As ninth-graders moved to the high school and sixth-graders came into the middle school, the middle school became a real transitional school, with students at all levels of physical, social, and intellectual maturity. Unlike junior high schools, which tend to treat all students as adolescents, middle schools have attempted to develop programs to help students bridge the gap in development between childhood and adolescence.

Pre- and early adolescents experience dramatic physical, social, emotional, and intellectual changes resulting from maturational changes. More biological changes occur in the bodies and minds of youngsters between the ages of 10 and 14 than at any other period in their lives except the first 9 months of their development. Because the transitional years between childhood and adolescence are marked by distinct changes in the bodies and minds of boys and girls, the success of the middle school depends on teachers and administrators who understand each learner and his or her unique developmental pattern. Figure 8.2 describes in detail the characteristics of emerging adolescents and the implications of those characteristics for the middle school.

Characteristics of Emerging Adolescents	Implications for the Middle School
Physical Development	
Accelerated physical development begins in transescence, marked by increase in weight, height, heart size, lung capacity, and muscular strength. Boys and girls are growing at varying rates. Girls tend to be taller for the first two years and tend to be more physically advanced. Bone growth is faster than muscle development, and the uneven muscle/bone development results in lack of coordination and awkwardness. Bones may lack protection of covering muscles and supporting tendons.	Provide a health and science curriculum that emphasizes self-understanding about body changes. Guidance counselors and community resource persons (e.g., pediatricians) can help students understand what is happening to their bodies. Schedule adaptive physical education classes to build physical coordination. Equipment design should help students develop small and large muscles.
In pubescent girls, secondary sex characteristics continue to develop, with breasts enlarging and menstruation beginning.	Intense sports competition; avoid contact sports. Schedule sex education classes; health and hygiene seminars.
A wide range of individual differences among students begin to appear. Although the sequential order of development is relatively consistent in each sex, boys tend to lag a year or two behind girls. There are marked individual differences in physical development for boys and girls. The age of greatest variability in physiological development and physical size is about age 13.	Provide opportunities for interaction among students of different ages, but avoid situations where physical development can be compared (e.g., communal showers). Emphasize intramural programs rather than interscholastic athletics so that each student may participate regardless of physical development. Where interscholastic sports programs exist, the number of games should be limited, with games played in the afternoon rather than the evening.
Glandular imbalances occur, resulting in acne, allergies, dental and eye defects—some health disturbances are real and some are imaginary.	Provide regular physical examinations for all middle school students.
Boys and girls display changes in body contour—large nose, protruding ears, long arms—have posture problems, and are self-conscious about their bodies.	Health classes should emphasize exercises for good posture. Students should understand through self-analysis that growth is an individual process and occurs unevenly.
A girdle of fat often appears around the hips and thighs of boys in early puberty. Slight development of tissue under the skin around the nipples occurs briefly, causing anxiety in boys who fear they are developing "the wrong way."	Films and talks by doctors and counselors can help students understand the changes the body goes through during this period. A carefully planned program of sex education developed in collaboration with parents, medical doctors, and community agencies should be developed.
Students are likely to be disturbed by body changes. Girls especially are likely to be disturbed by the physical changes that accompany sexual maturation.	
Receding chins, cowlicks, dimples, and changes in voice result in possible embarrassment to boys.	Teacher and parental reassurance and understanding are necessary to help students understand that many body changes are temporary in nature.

FIGURE 8.2 Development of Emerging Adolescents and Implications for the Middle School.

Source: From Jon Wiles and Joseph Bondi, *The New American Middle School*, 3rd ed., pp. 33–36. Copyright © 2001 by Prentice Hall. Reprinted by permission.

Characteristics of Emerging Adolescents	Implications for the Middle School
Physical Development (Continued)	
Boys and girls tend to tire easily but will not admit it.	Advise parents to insist that students get proper rest; overexertion should be discouraged.
Fluctuations in basal metabolism may cause students to be extremely restless at times and listless at others.	Provide an opportunity for daily exercise and a place where students can be children by playing and being noisy for short periods. Encourage activities such as special-interest classes and hands-on exercises. Students should be allowed to move around physically in classes and avoid long periods of passive work.
Boys and girls show ravenous appetites and peculiar tastes; they may overtax digestive system with large quantities of improper foods.	Provide snacks to satisfy between-meal hunger as well as nutritional guidance specific to this age group.
Social Development	
Affiliation base broadens from family to peer group. Conflict sometimes results because of splitting of allegiance between peer group and family.	Teachers should work closely with the family to help adults realize that peer pressure is a normal part of the maturation process. Parents should be encouraged to continue to provide love and comfort even though they may feel rejected. Teachers should be counselors. Homebase teacher-adviser, house plan arrangements should be encouraged.
Peers become sources for standards and models of behavior. Child's occasional rebellion does not diminish importance of parents for developing values. Emerging adolescents want to make their own choices, but authority still remains primarily with the family.	Sponsor school activities that permit students to interact socially with many school personnel. Family studies can help ease parental conflicts. Parental involvement at school should be encouraged, but parents should not be too conspicuous a presence. Encourage co-curricular activities. For example, an active student government can help students develop guidelines for interpersonal relations and standards of behavior.
Society's mobility has broken ties to peer groups and created anxieties in emerging adolescents.	Promote familylike groupings of students and teachers to provide stability for new students. Interdisciplinary units can be structured to provide interaction among various groups of students. Clubs and special-interest classes should be an integral part of the school day.
Students are confused and frightened by new school settings.	Orientation programs and buddy systems can reduce the trauma of moving from an elementary school to a middle school. Family teams can encourage a sense of belonging.
Students show unusual or drastic behavior at times—aggressive, daring, boisterous, argumentative.	Schedule debates, plays, play days, and other activities to allow students to show off in a productive way.
"Puppy love" years emerge, with a show of extreme devotion to a particular boy or girl; however, allegiance may be transferred to a new friend overnight.	Role-play and guidance exercises can provide the opportunity to act out feelings. Provide opportunities for social interaction between the sexes–parties and games, but not dances, in the early grades of the middle school.

FIGURE 8.2 *(Continued)*

Characteristics of Emerging Adolescents	Implications for the Middle School
Social Development (Continued)	
Youths feel that the will of the group must prevail and sometimes can be cruel to those not in their group. They copy and display fads of extremes in clothes, speech, mannerisms, and handwriting; they are very susceptible to media advertising.	Set up an active student government so students can develop their own guidelines for dress and behavior. Adults should be encouraged not to react with outrage when extreme dress or mannerisms are displayed.
Boys and girls show strong concern for what is "right" and for social justice; they also show concern for those less fortunate.	Foster plans that allow students to engage in service activities, for example, peer teaching, which allow students to help other students. Community projects (e.g., assisting in a senior citizens' club or helping in a childcare center) can be planned by students and teachers.
They are influenced by adults and attempt to identify with adults other than their parents.	Flexible teaching patterns should prevail so students can interact with a variety of adults with whom they can identify.
Despite a trend toward heterosexual interests, same-sex affiliation tends to dominate.	Plan large-group activities rather than boy-girl events. Intramurals can be scheduled so students can interact with friends of the same or opposite sex.
Students desire direction and regulation but reserve the right to question or reject the suggestions of adults.	Provide opportunities for students to accept more responsibility in setting standards for behavior. Students should be helped to establish realistic goals and be assisted in helping realize those goals.
Emotional Development	
Erratic and inconsistent behavior is prevalent. Anxiety and fear contrast with reassuring bravado. Feelings tend to shift between superiority and inferiority. Coping with physical changes, striving for independence from family, becoming a person in his or her own right, and learning a new mode of intellectual functioning are all emotion-laden problems for the emerging adolescent. Students have many fears, real and imagined. At no other time in development are they likely to encounter such a diverse number of problems simultaneously.	Encourage self-evaluation among students. Design activities that help students play out their emotions. Activity programs should provide opportunities for shy students to be drawn out and loud students to engage in calming activities. Counseling must operate as part of, rather than an adjunct to, the learning program. Students should be helped to interpret superiority and inferiority feelings. Mature value systems should be encouraged by allowing students to examine options of behavior and to study consequences of various actions.
	Encourage students to assume leadership in group discussions and experience frequent success and recognition for personal efforts and achievements. A general atmosphere of friendliness, relaxation, concern, and group cohesiveness should guide the program.
Chemical and hormone imbalances often trigger emotions that are little understood by the transescent. Students sometimes regress to childlike behavior.	Adults in the middle school should not pressure students to explain their emotions (e.g., crying for no apparent reason). Occasional childlike behavior should not be ridiculed. Provide numerous possibilities for releasing emotional stress.

FIGURE 8.2   *(Continued)*

Characteristics of Emerging Adolescents	Implications for the Middle School
Emotional Development (Continued)	
Too-rapid or too-slow physical development is often a source of irritation and concern. Development of secondary sex characteristics may create additional tensions about rate of development.	Provide appropriate sex education and encourage participation of parents and community agencies. Pediatricians, psychologists, and counselors should be called on to assist students in understanding developmental changes.
This age group is easily offended and sensitive to criticism of personal shortcomings.	Sarcasm by adults should be avoided. Students should be helped to develop values when solving their problems.
Students tend to exaggerate simple occurrences and believe their problems are unique.	Use sociodrama to enable students to see themselves as others see them. Readings dealing with problems similar to their own can help them see that many problems are not unique.
Intellectual Development	
Students display a wide range of skills and abilities unique to their developmental patterns.	Use a variety of approaches and materials in the teaching—learning process.
Students range in development from the concrete-manipulatory stage to the ability to deal with abstract concepts. The transescent is intensely curious and growing in mental ability.	Treat students at their own intellectual levels, providing immediate rather than remote goals. All subjects should be individualized. Skill grouping should be flexible.
Middle school learners prefer active over passive learning activities and prefer interaction with peers during learning activities.	Encourage physical movement, with small-group discussions, learning centers, and creative dramatics suggested as good activity projects. Provide a program of learning that is exciting and meaningful.
Students are usually very curious and exhibit a strong willingness to learn things they consider useful. They enjoy using skills to solve real-life problems.	Organize curricula around real-life concepts (e.g., conflict, competition, peer-group influence). Provide activities in formal and informal situations to improve reasoning powers. Studies of the community and the environment are particularly relevant to the age group.
Students often display heightened egocentrism and will argue to convince others or to clarify their own thinking. Independent, critical thinking emerges.	Organized discussions of ideas and feelings in peer groups can facilitate self-understanding. Provide experiences for individuals to express themselves by writing and participating in dramatic productions.
Studies show that brain growth in transescents slows between the ages of 12 and 14.	Learners' cognitive skills should be refined; continued cognitive growth during ages 12 to 14 may not be expected. Provide opportunities for enjoyable studies in the arts. Encourage self-expression in all subjects.

FIGURE 8.2   *(Continued)*

THE MIDDLE SCHOOL TEACHER

The middle school teacher, more than any other factor, holds the key to the realization of the type of effective middle school required for emerging adolescents. The middle school teacher must have all those characteristics that research indicates are necessary for teachers of all age groups; however, because of the ages encompassed in the middle school, the middle school teacher is responsible for children who are striking in their diversity. A teacher in the middle school is confronted with a rapidly changing group of children in different stages of development. A number of key competencies have been identified for teachers in the middle school; see Figure 8.3 for a list.

---

1. Possesses knowledge of preadolescent and early adolescent physical development, including knowledge of physical activity needs and the diversity and variety of physical growth rates.
2. Understands the socioemotional development, including the need to adjust to a changing body.
3. Possesses the necessary skills to allow interaction between individual students as well as the opportunity to work in groups of varying sizes.
4. Understands the cultural forces and community relationships that affect the total school curriculum.
5. Can organize the curriculum to facilitate the developmental tasks of preadolescence and early adolescence.
6. Understands the transitional nature of grades 5 through 8 as they bridge the gap between the children of the lower elementary grades and late adolescents and early adults of the upper grades.
7. Possesses the skills needed to work with other teachers and school professionals in team teaching.
8. Can plan multidisciplinary lessons and/or units and teach them personally or with other professionals.
9. Commands a broad academic background, with specialization in at least two allied areas of the curriculum.
10. Possesses the skill to integrate appropriate media and concrete demonstrations into presentations.
11. Can develop and conduct learning situations that promote independent learning and maximize student choice and responsibility for follow-through.
12. Possesses the knowledge and skills that allow students to sort information, set priorities, and budget time and energy.
13. Can teach problem-solving skills and develop lessons that are inquiry-oriented.
14. Has the ability to teach students how to discover knowledge and use both inductive and deductive methods in the discovery of knowledge.
15. Possesses the knowledge and skills necessary to use role playing, simulation, instructional games, and creative dramatics in teaching the content as well as the affective domain in a middle-grade classroom.
16. Commands the knowledge and skill needed to organize and manage a classroom, which allows individuals to learn at a rate commensurate with their ability.
17. Possesses verbal behaviors that promote student input in a variety of group settings.
18. Has the knowledge and skills needed to diagnose strengths and weaknesses, to determine learning levels of individuals, to prescribe courses of action, and to evaluate the outcomes.
19. Has experience in innovation and possesses the skill to experiment with teaching techniques to find the ones that are most effective in given situations.
20. Can teach the communication skills of reading, writing, and speaking in all subject areas.
21. Commands knowledge of reading techniques that enable students to progress and improve their reading in the subject areas.
22. Has knowledge of the techniques necessary to promote positive self-concepts and self-reliance.

FIGURE 8.3   Key Competencies for Teachers in the Middle School.

Source: Wiles & Bondi, *The New American Middle School*, "Key Competencies for Teachers in the Middle School," pp. 55–58, © 2001. Reproduced by permission of Wiles, Bondi and Associates.

23. Possesses a knowledge of group dynamics and the ability to organize groups that will make decisions and provide their own leadership.
24. Has knowledge of careers and the ability to help students explore career options.
25. Possesses the skills necessary to effectively manage groups of students in activity settings.
26. Possesses the ability to recognize difficulties that may be emotional and/or physically based.
27. Works with extracurricular activities in the school.
28. Gathers appropriate personal information on students using questionnaires, interviews, and observation.
29. Provides frequent feedback to students on learning progress.
30. Functions calmly in a high-activity environment.
31. Handles disruptive behavior positively and consistently.
32. Builds learning experiences for students based on learning skills (reading, math) obtained in elementary grades.
33. Works cooperatively with peers, consultants, resource persons, and paraprofessionals.
34. Exhibits concern for students by listening and/or empathizing with them.
35. Selects evaluation techniques appropriate to curricular objectives in the affective domain.
36. Utilizes values clarification and other affective teaching techniques to help students develop personal value systems.
37. Provides an informal, flexible classroom environment.
38. Cooperates in curricular planning and revision.
39. Evaluates the teaching situation and selects the grouping techniques most appropriate for the situation: large-group instruction (100+ students), small-group instruction (15–25 students), or independent study.

FIGURE 8.3 *(Continued)*

MANAGING MIDDLE SCHOOL PROGRAMS

A well-designed middle school features a balanced program focusing on personal development, basic skills for continuous learners, and use of knowledge to foster competence. Thus, the curriculum of a middle school closely follows the developmental stages represented in the students that it serves.

There has been much progress in recent years in developing new and exciting programs for emerging adolescent learners, yet much still needs to be done. New pressures brought on by the call for a return to basics have narrowed the curriculum of the middle school to the teaching of rote skills and the transmission of knowledge. Exploratory programs, guidance services, and health and physical education programs have been cut back in many schools. Thus, the curriculum area of personal development has been changed in many middle schools. This development has forced an imbalance in the middle school program and a return to the more content-centered junior high or imitation high school model in many middle schools. With sixth graders being housed in many middle schools, the result has been the thrusting down of a high school program to an even younger group of students. Combined with a six- or seven-period departmentalized organizational model, the lack of emphasis on personal development has signaled a return to a secondary emphasis in the middle grades.

The gains in program development won in the 1960s, 1970s, and 1980s by middle school educators were swept away in the 1990s in many places by a return to the high school or secondary model, which was believed to be more academic and was easier to schedule and administer. The lessons learned by the failure of the junior high school were lost in the face of doing what was easier and less costly.

A period of great activity in the middle school movement occurred during the 1980s. Organizations such as the Association for Supervision and Curriculum Development (ASCD), local and state leagues of middle schools, the National Middle School Association, the National Education Association, the National Association of Secondary School Principals, the National Association of Elementary School Principals, and the National School Boards Association all began presenting conferences, publications, and position papers advocating the original purposes of the middle school as proposed in the national position document *The Middle School We Need* (Bondi, 1960). Legislation encouraging middle school development and teacher training was passed in Florida, California, Ohio, and other states that were active in the early middle school movement. The Carnegie Corporation report *Turning Points* (1989) was the culmination of an active decade of middle school support.

A milestone in the middle school movement occurred with the publication of the best-selling ASCD publication *Making Middle Schools Work* (Wiles & Bondi, 1986). That publication addressed the major difficulty in getting middle schools to remain middle schools in program and organization as initially developed. The "shining light" syndrome with middle schools reflected the often-repeated situation in which a new middle school would be developed that would draw hundreds of visitors. That school would be a model for a year or two until the principal left or the staff changed. It would then revert to a junior high school type of program while a new shining light popped up somewhere else.

Seeing the frustration, and recognizing that there was an Achilles heel in the middle school success story (evaluation) throughout the United States, Wiles and Bondi introduced the curriculum management plan (CMP) model for development of middle schools.[1] The CMP model recognized that at the very heart of implementing true middle schools is solid, traditional curriculum development. The Wiles–Bondi CMP model drew from the previous work of Ralph Tyler and Hilda Taba and superimposed management techniques on a widely used accreditation format. Put simply, the CMP introduced regularity into the change process (by managing it). Without such logic, a complex design such as the middle school faced multiple pitfalls. Both then and now, the key to successful implementation of middle school programs remains successful planning.

THE MIDDLE SCHOOL PROGRAM: OVERVIEW

Successful middle schools using the CMP model conduct an analysis and then develop a design document that outlines program objectives and standards in detail.[2] Each design, or blueprint, is based on an extensive needs assessment outlining the academic, social, and physical needs of middle school students.

---

[1] The CMP model has been used successfully in the transition to true middle schools in districts such as St. Louis (MO), Denver (CO), Dallas (TX), Orange County (Orlando, FL), Dade County (Miami, FL), Duval County (Jacksonville, FL), Baton Rouge (LA), Long Beach (CA), and hundreds of large and small school districts in the United States. The process has also been used by the Kellogg Foundation in developing a national model middle school program in Michigan.

[2] Design documents found in Dade County, FL; Duval County, FL; St. Louis, MO; San Bernardino, CA; and other school districts. See also Wiles and Bondi, *Making Middle Schools Work* for Orange County, FL, model.

In curriculum planning, leaders must not lose sight of the purpose of the middle school. The middle school is a transitional school and must not be a replica of the high school or elementary school. The need for balance in the program and organizational flexibility has never been greater. In addition to the normal developmental changes that middle school students are experiencing, social changes have a major impact on the lives of emerging adolescents. Consider the following:

- The American family is breaking down. For more than half of marriages today, there is a divorce. In 2010, 27% of children in the middle grades where living in a single-parent home.
- More adults moonlight now than at any other time in the history of our country.
- Only 8% of American homes today have the family pattern of a mother at home and a father working.
- By the end of the ninth grade, 20% of adolescents will suffer a serious drinking problem.
- Forty-three percent of all persons arrested for serious crimes in the United States (rape, murder, robbery) are juveniles, yet juveniles make up only 20% of the population.
- One in two Americans moved during the past 5 years.
- More than one half of all U.S. births in 2011 were to unwed mothers. One of 10 girls will be pregnant before age 18. An estimated 18 million teenage boys and girls are sexually active.
- The third leading cause of death among teenagers 10–14 is suicide.
- It is estimated that pre- and early adolescents spend one third of their waking hours watching television and/or texting.
- Psychologists regard the lack of a stable home as the biggest contributor to delinquency.

Dealing with emerging adolescents has become a national priority. In funding the National Institute of Education (NIE) during the 1990s, Congress mandated that the number one priority of NIE be research on emerging adolescent learners. The Carnegie report on adolescent development in 1989 pointed out the serious deterioration of healthcare and the myriad social problems facing preadolescents and emerging adolescents. Consider the following:

- The middle-grade years represent the last chance for students to master basic skills.
- The middle grades represent the last time for formal schooling for many of our youth. Low achievers drop out after the middle grades.
- The final attitude toward self and others, as well as a lasting attitude toward learning, is established in the middle grades.
- The future school success and work success—indeed, future life success—can be predicted for most students in the middle grades.

Curriculum leaders must take a strong stance to prevent the middle school from becoming an imitation high school again. There are still many good models of middle schools and reformed junior high schools that offer promise for curriculum developers desiring to improve middle grade education. Figure 8.4 illustrates the three major program elements needed in the middle school.

I. Personal Development

Guidance—Physical education—Intramurals—Lifetime sports—Sex education—Health studies—Law education—Social services—Drug education—Special interest—Clubs—Student government—Development groupings—Programs for students with special needs—Mainstreaming—Alternative programs—Advisory programs—Intramurals.

II. Education for Social Competence	III. Skills for Continuous Learning
Basic studies	Communication
Science	Reading
Social studies	Writing
Mathematics	Listening
Language arts	Speaking
Exploratory studies	Mathematics
Practical arts	Computation
Home economics	Comprehension
Industrial arts	Usage
Business-distributive	
education	Observing and comparing
Fine arts	
Music	Analyzing
Art	
Foreign language	Generalizing
Humanities	
Environmental studies	Organizing
Outdoor education	
Career exploration	Evaluating
Consumer education	
Media study	

FIGURE 8.4   Program Design for the Essential Middle School.

Source: From J. Wiles and J. Bondi, *The Essential Middle School*, p. 84. Copyright © 1986 by Bondi and Associates, Tampa, FL. Reprinted by permission.

Balance in the Middle School Program

A balanced program to serve the diverse group of students found in the middle grades should include the following:

- Learning experiences for transescents at their own intellectual levels, relating to immediate rather than remote academic goals.
- A wide variety of cognitive learning experiences to account for the full range of students who are at many different levels of concrete and *formal operations*. Learning objectives should be sequenced to allow for the transition from concrete to formal operations.
- A diversified curriculum in exploratory and fundamental activities resulting in daily successful experiences that will stimulate and nurture intellectual development.

- In-school opportunities for the development of problem-solving skills, reflective-thinking processes, and awareness of the student's environment.
- *Cognitive learning* experiences so structured that students can progress in an individualized manner; however, within the structure of an individualized learning program, students can interact with one another. Social interaction is not an enemy of individual learning.
- A curriculum in which all areas are taught to reveal opportunities for further study, to help students learn how to study, and to help them appraise their own interests and talents. In addition, the middle school should continue the developmental program of basic skills instruction started in the elementary school, with emphasis on both developmental and remedial reading.
- A planned *sequence* of concepts in the general education areas, major emphasis on the interests and skills for continued learning, a balanced program of exploratory experiences and other activities and services for personal development, and appropriate attention to the development of values.
- A common program in which areas of learning are combined and integrated to break down artificial and irrelevant divisions of curriculum content.
- Encouragement of personal curiosity, with one learning experience inspiring subsequent activities.
- Methods of instruction involving open and individually directed learning experiences. The role of the teacher should be more that of a personal guide and facilitator of learning than that of a purveyor of knowledge. Traditional lecture–recitation methods should be minimized.
- Grouping criteria that accommodate not only cognitive, but also physical, social, and emotional criteria.
- Consideration for who the student is and becomes, his or her self-concept, self-responsibility, and attitudes toward school and personal happiness as for how much and what he or she knows.
- Experiences in the arts for all transescents to foster aesthetic appreciations and to stimulate creative expression.
- Teaching methods that reflect cultural, ethnic, and socioeconomic subgroups within the middle school student population.

Advisory Programs

The advisory program helps bridge the gap between the close, one-to-one relationship of the self-contained elementary school to the less directed, more independent world of the high school. It offers middle school students the best of both worlds. It provides every student with an adviser, a teacher who has a special concern for the student as an individual. The program also provides instruction that encourages the independence and personal growth needed at the high school level.

Finally, an adviser–advisee (A/A) program is designed to help students feel good about themselves and the contributions that they can make to their school, community, and society. An A/A program can serve as a prescriptive antidote for unmotivated, reluctant learners and at-risk students who face such societal influences as sexual promiscuity, suicide, substance abuse, unsupervised leisure time, and criminal activities.

Such an awareness is certainly worthy of commitment, consistency, and effort on the part of middle-level educators to help young adolescents become happy, fully functioning citizens of our society. This is the role as advisers and the purpose of an advisory program. The characteristics of an effective advisory program include the following:

- Advisory should be at a time and place where students feel comfortable and at home.
- Advisory should be in a place where students can foster peer relationships.
- Advisory student numbers should be as low as possible. An *optimum* number of students in one class is 20.
- Ideally, a student should begin the day with his or her advisory teacher.
- All information concerning an advisee should be communicated to the advisory teacher.
- The advisory program should have a name decided on by the teachers, students, administration, and parents of a particular school, district, or county.
- A formal program consisting of a philosophy statement, operating guidelines, and activities should exist and should be formulated by the teachers, administration, parents, and students of a particular school, district, or county.

Physical Education Programs

The physical education program should address both the needs of the individual student and the diversity of the group. Each student should have the opportunity to grow physically, intellectually, socially, and emotionally. Through a broad range of experiences, students should have the opportunity to explore, to develop physical competence, and to view themselves in a positive light.

Traditionally, the physical education curriculum for grades 6–8 has been activity centered. It has been organized around games, sports, gymnastics, and dance activities identified as the content of physical education. Units in basketball, volleyball, tumbling, and dance are examples of these activities. Specific skills are taught as they relate to a specific activity. They are means to developing the ability to perform in the activity. The activity has been viewed as the end.

A skill-theme curriculum reverses the means–ends relationship. The curriculum is organized around specific skills or groups of skills, and the focus is on student outcomes. Activities become means through which the student can practice, refine, and develop competence in the skills. The end is the development of students who are able to use skills in a variety of contexts and situations.

Intramural Programs

Intramurals are activities that provide for the participation of students in an organized and supervised program. This participation takes place among all students within one school. The program is structured so that all students take part, regardless of their athletic ability or gender. Intramurals strive to offer success for everyone, with a great deal of emphasis on fun.

The *intramural program* serves as an extension of the skills and activities previously learned in physical education. Middle school students are offered the opportunity to further develop these skills; intramural programs promote recreational activities, physical fitness, mental and emotional health, social contact, group loyalty, success, and a permanent interest in leisure-time activities. The following are objectives found in most intramural programs:

- To offer a program within the school day to provide fun and enjoyment for all students.
- To provide skilled professional leadership through the physical education department for a varied number of activities.
- To offer activities that are adapted to the age and skill development of the students and to promote activities that afford wholesome use of leisure time.
- To provide opportunities for experience in human relationships, such as cooperation, development of friendships, and acceptance of group responsibility.
- To provide the opportunity for the development of desirable personality traits, such as perseverance, self-confidence, self-discipline, self-direction, good sportsmanship, courage, and ethical conduct.
- To provide recognition to develop group pride and loyalty, and to serve as a means of motivation.
- To provide separation of grade levels on intramural days, with the intramural program as the only activity at that time.
- To provide for the participation and cooperation of all teachers and instructional support staff.
- To provide an intramural advisory council, who will advise and counsel an intramural director.
- To provide funding for adequate staff, facilities, and equipment for a safe environment.

Exploratory Programs

The exploratory program offers students in the middle school a chance to explore many areas of interest. Courses taught by specialists include industrial technology, music, art, business, foreign language, agriculture, computer technology, and others. Special interest courses and clubs, taught by all staff members, allow further exploration for middle school students. Media persons and counselors also contribute to exploratory activities.

Programs for Students with Special Needs

A full range of programs for special needs students, including those for students with physical and mental disabilities, non-English-speaking students, gifted students, and disruptive students are part of middle school curricula. Through processes such as inclusion, mainstreaming, and teaming, students are included in team activities and other school programs.

Inclusion is a philosophy or belief that educational services to students with disabilities should be provided in general education settings, with the same peers, and in neighborhood schools to the extent appropriate for each school. There are many advantages of an inclusion component in the middle school, the most important of which is that labeling is deemphasized.

The middle school offers a balanced, comprehensive, and success-oriented curriculum. The middle school is a sensitive, caring, supportive learning environment that will provide those experiences that will assist in making the transition from late childhood to adolescence, thereby helping each individual to bridge the gap between the self-contained structure of the elementary school and the departmental structure of the high school.

Middle school curriculums are more exploratory in nature than those of the elementary school and less specialized than those of the high school. Realizing that the uniqueness of individual subject disciplines must be recognized, an emphasis on interdisciplinary curriculum development will be stressed. Curriculum programs should emphasize the natural relationship among academic disciplines that facilitate cohesive learning experiences for middle school students through integrative themes, topics, and units. Interdisciplinary goals should overlap subject area goals and provide for interconnections such as reasoning, logical and critical thought, coping capacities, self-management, positive personal development, and career awareness.

The academic program of a middle school emphasizes skills development through science, social studies, reading, mathematics, and language arts courses. A well-defined skills continuum is used as the basic guide in all schools in each area including physical education, health, guidance, and other educational activities. Exploratory opportunities are provided through well-defined and structured club programs, activity programs, and special-interest courses, thereby creating opportunities for students to interact socially, to experience democratic living, to explore areas not in the required curriculum, to do independent study and research, to develop and practice responsible behavior, and to experience working with varying age groups.

The middle school curriculum will be a program of planned learning experiences for our students. The three major components for our middle school curriculum are (1) subject content (2) personal development, and (3) essential skills.

FIGURE 8.5   A Sample Philosophy/Goal Statement.

Guidance

Guidance is an integral part of the total middle school program. All instructional and special service personnel should be involved in guidance programs. Guidance counselors serve as leaders of advisory programs and provide instructional guidance to students while also dealing with the specific needs of individual students.

Despite much progress in the past 20 years in developing new programs for emerging adolescent learners, much remains to be done. Whether programs for students in the middle grades are housed in organizational structures called middle schools or in upper elementary schools, junior high schools, "elemiddle" schools, or secondary schools, the focus of such programs should be the developmental characteristics of the emerging adolescent learner group itself. Figure 8.5 summarizes the middle school program in a sample philosophy/goal statement.

ORGANIZING FOR INSTRUCTION IN THE MIDDLE SCHOOL

Middle school educators, building on a philosophy and knowledge of the emerging adolescent learner, have structured a broad and relevant program for the varied needs of students found in the middle grades. To facilitate that program, the middle school

Teams Should	**Teams Should Not**
Provide a constructive climate	Promote rivalry
Focus goals for students	Challenge school policy
Encourage self-esteem	Be fund raisers
Set discipline standards	Share negative feelings
Coordinate activities	Overburden one member
Help all students succeed	Isolate one member
Build school spirit	Take away one's teaching style
Be the parent contact	Handle severe student problems
Raise academic performance	
Share work burdens	
Set examples for students	
Make school fun	

Goals for the School Year

Get closer to elective teachers	Get team bulletin boards
Meet more often with administrators	Get more teacher input into team
Develop interdisciplinary instruction	formation
patterns	Make team leader councils really work
Involve counselors in team activities	

Indicators of a Successful Team

Attendance	Improved discipline
Academic achievement	School/team pride
Validating team goals	Funds allocated to team activities
Getting team bulletin boards	Family atmosphere
Establishing team-to-team communication	

FIGURE 8.6   Tasks of Teams in Middle Schools.

Source: Dade County, Florida, workshop by Jon Wiles and Joseph Bondi, August 30, 1990. This list is the product of brainstorming by approximately 200 team leaders in Dade County schools, August 30, 1990.

must be organized to accommodate a flexible approach to instruction. Block schedules; teams of teachers with common planning periods teaching common groups of students; and special activity periods for advisory programs, intramurals, and other activities are essential elements of true middle schools. Inflexible, departmentalized high school organizational structures do not facilitate the broad program needed by middle-grade students.

The interdisciplinary team approach to planning and implementing instruction has distinct advantages over a self-contained or departmentalized teaching pattern (see Figure 8.6). Some of these advantages are the following:

- More than one teacher with the knowledge of scheduling, use of instructional materials, grouping, and instructional methods benefits individual student learning.
- Curricula among subject areas can be coordinated so that the students can relate one subject to another; this leads to greater breadth of understanding.

- Teachers can better understand individual differences in students when more than one person is making observations and evaluations. This enables teachers to cope with differences more effectively and handle discipline problems more easily. Guidance for students is discussed among the team.
- The team approach enables teachers to contrast a student's behavior and ability from class to class, thereby helping them develop a systematic and consistent approach to helping the child.
- Closer work with guidance counselors and other specialists is possible.
- *Block scheduling* allows the teacher greater flexibility in grouping to accommodate large- and small-group instruction, remedial work, and independent study.
- Flexible time schedules are more conducive to children's developmental needs at this age level than are rigid departmentalized schedules.
- A number of instructors can lend their individual expertise to a given topic simultaneously.
- Large blocks of time are available for educational field trips, guest speakers, and so on; at the same time, scheduling is not disrupted. Less teaching time is lost to repetitious film showing.
- Teachers can be more aware of what their students are learning in other classes—what assignments, tests, and projects are making demands on their time.
- *Common planning time* can lead to more creativity in teaching approaches and consistency in teaching strategies.
- Interdisciplinary teaching leads to economy of learning time and transfer among students.
- Student leadership is distributed among all the teams because each team's students are typical of the total school community.
- Students are able to identify themselves with a smaller school within a school; with team representation on student council, they are more closely related to student government.
- Correlated planning of content and project work is more easily carried out.
- Parent conferences can be arranged by the guidance counselor for times when all of a student's academic teachers are available.
- Individual teams may rearrange time and period schedules without interfering with the overall school program. For example, each team may individually manipulate its block of time to provide periods of various lengths. All students do not move in the hallways at the end of 55 minutes.
- Field trips can be planned by teams, and built-in chaperoning is thus provided. Longer times for such trips are available without disrupting a multiple number of classes.
- One of the greatest advantages of team teaching is the assistance provided to the beginning teacher.
- Building use is improved; large- and small-group space is used as well as regular classrooms.
- An interdisciplinary team scheduling arrangement promotes the professional growth of the teachers by encouraging the exchange of ideas among the members of the teaching team.

An example of block scheduling to facilitate interdisciplinary teaming is found in Figure 8.7.

6th Grade	7th Grade	8th Grade	8:30
Advisory	Advisory	Advisory	← 1 8:50 ← 2

Basics
 	
90
	Exploratory/
	Physical education
	90
		Basics
		  English
		  Math
		  Reading
		  Science
		  Social studies
		
		210	

Exploratory/ Physical education 90	Basics 60		
	Lunch 30		
Lunch 30	Basics 150		
Basics 120		Lunch 30	12:20 3 ← 12:50
		Exploratory/ Physical education 90	← 4 2:20
Enrichment and remediation 40	Enrichment and remediation 40	Enrichment and remediation 40	← 5 3:00

FIGURE 8.7 Parts of a Block Schedule.

Source: From *The Essential Middle School*, p. 231, by J. Wiles and J. Bondi. Copyright © 1986 by Wiles, Bondi and Associates, Tampa, FL. Reprinted by permission.

Alternative Scheduling Models

Following the high school lead, some middle schools have implemented long blocks of time for classes—from 75 to 90 minutes. Longer periods provide teachers with fewer students to teach during the school day, cut down on the number of class changes for students (thus reducing potential discipline problems), and allow time for more depth of instruction.

The longer block schedule takes many forms. In the four-by-four block, students spend 90 minutes in four courses every other day, which creates eight subject loads in a school year. In the 75-75-30 plan, students follow a fairly typical middle school schedule for the first 150 days. Courses end after 75-day terms, and students enroll in specialized courses during the last 6 weeks. The specialized courses can be academically enriching programs or remedial courses to help students master grade-level courses.

Two problems are created for middle school teachers with the longer teaching block—the need to carry out instructional activities and the difficulty in coordinating a common planning time for teachers teaching the same students, a major element of the middle school concept.

Inservice Programs

Because inservice programs for middle school teachers have not been sustained in many schools, and preservice training has not changed from the old model of training secondary teachers, many teachers prefer the secondary program model and organizational pattern. To counter that preference, a much more systematic approach has to be implemented so that veteran teachers can become accustomed and so that new teachers are prepared for the modern middle school (see Figure 8.8).

COMPREHENSIVE PLANNING FOR MIDDLE SCHOOLS

The curriculum of the middle school, with its concern for the special needs of pre- and early adolescents, its comprehensive definition of education, and its promotion of continuity in learning and development, is more than a series of catchphrases and education innovations. The middle school is, in fact, a highly complex plan for educating a special learner. Because of the complexity of the educational design, successful implementation of the program calls for a significant degree of planning.

The curriculum planning model suggested earlier is necessary if middle schools are to succeed. In assisting in the development of middle schools across the United States, your author has noted that planning often determines the fine line between success and failure. Such planning is necessary at the district, school, and classroom levels. The following district-level planning steps, in sequence, are recommended for the establishment of middle schools.

Analysis

The middle school should arise from need. Ideally, school systems and communities will proceed through value-clarification processes that reveal the logic of the middle school design, and programs will be initiated on what is known about their students. Overcrowding, integration, or building availability are all poor reasons for choosing the concept.

An important point in making such an analysis is not to allow the search to be focused only on problems. The analysis should also be projective: What type of an educational experience do we want for students during this period of development?

Involvement

Preliminary investigations of the middle school concept should involve all parties with vested interests in intermediate education. A step often taken in planning the middle school is to explore the concept without involving those who will be most directly affected by its activation: students, teachers, parents, and the community. At a superficial level,

Certification Component   (Middle Level Education—Orange County Public Schools Component #20561)

This component will focus on the following topics of study:

1. The middle grades
2. Understanding the middle-grades student
3. Organizing Interdisciplinary Instruction
4. Curriculum development
5. Developing critical and creative thinking in students
6. Counseling functions of the teacher
7. Developing creative-learning materials
8. Planning and evaluating programs

To meet the requirements of the component, each participant will attend 10 two-hour workshops. The program will consist of 30 hours of instruction in a workshop setting and 30 hours of supervised in-school follow-up activities.

It is anticipated that successful completion of this component plus 1 year of successful teaching in a middle school will lead to middle school certification for the participants.

Leadership for Team Leaders and Grade Coordinators

This training will focus on group process and communication skills that will enhance the ability of team leaders and grade coordinators to carry out their assigned responsibilities. The participants will receive 6 hours of skills-based training. All participants will be expected to have successfully completed the Middle Level Education component prior to attending this training.

Overview of the Middle School

An audiovisual presentation giving an overview of middle-level education in Orange County public schools. It addresses the planned structure and curriculum of the middle school.

This will be a 1-hour activity.

Program of Instruction

An overview of the instructional program of the middle school covering the subject content, areas of personal development, and essential skills. This activity will be 1 hour of information with opportunity for participants to ask questions.

Middle Level Education for School-Based Administration

The presentation will be modeled on the certification component (OCPS Component #20561—Middle Level Education) with emphasis in those areas of special interest to the school-level administrator. It will consist of 20 hours of instruction with specified activities to be carried out at the school site.

Selected Topics

The training will include topics from the certification that meet special needs of those personnel who deal with the middle school child in other than classroom settings—for example, "Understanding the Middle Grades Student" for school secretaries, custodians, and other classified personnel. This will be a 1-hour activity.

FIGURE 8.8 Middle School Training Components.

Source: From *The Essential Middle School*, p. 35, by J. Wiles and J. Bondi. Copyright © 1986 by Wiles, Bondi and Associates, Tampa, FL. Reprinted by permission.

the elimination of this stage will probably lead to future confrontations over both programs and policy (interscholastic athletics, social events, grading policies, community-based learning). More important from the planning standpoint, however, is the dedication and support that will be needed to put such a program in practice in the first place. The middle school cannot be implemented and maintained unless those involved believe in it.

Of the constituencies mentioned in the paragraph above, particular attention must be given to the community in which the middle school will reside. Unaccustomed to educational jargon and unfamiliar with national trends in educational programs, many citizens may resist the middle school idea because of misunderstandings about the academic nature of the program and the necessary organizational arrangements. Without a clear understanding of the rationale of the program and the reason for these arrangements, community resistance will be high. By involving community members representing all segments of the population in the initial analysis of student needs, in the investigation of the middle school concept, in the drafting of documents, and in the planning of implementation stages, educators build in a means of communicating with the community at later times.

Commitment

Philosophical commitments to the middle school definition of education should be secured prior to activating the program. This text has repeatedly underscored the necessity of understanding and accepting the philosophical concept of the middle school as a prerequisite for successful implementation of such a program. A lack of understanding of the middle school concept represents the largest potential stumbling block to successful implementation. Without such understanding and a basic philosophical acceptance of the middle school concept, there can be no substantial rationale for practices and programs found in the middle school.

It is important to note that this understanding and acceptance must go beyond school board approval and superintendent acquiescence, although both are important. Such an understanding, and commitment, must be demonstrated by the building principal, the involved teachers, and the parents of involved students.

Funding

Appropriate monies must be earmarked for activation of the plan. An observable phenomenon in education in the United States is that finance is the "fuel" of progress. Few major innovations of the past 20 years (middle schools being a notable exception) have succeeded without substantial financial support.

Although it is not impossible for a building faculty to implement the middle school concept with sheer dedication, two simple facts about middle schools are worth noting: (1) Middle schools are a much more complex form of education than traditional programs, and (2) because of this complexity, they require more energy and money to operate.

Every deviation from standardized patterns of education, such as uniform textbooks, the classroom-confined learning experience, and single-dimension instruction, requires effort and expense. School districts that commit to the middle school concept must also commit to financing building conversion, materials acquisition, staff development, and so forth.

Resources

Resources commensurate with the task must be allocated. One of the common pitfalls in establishing middle schools is to assume that they can operate on the same resource base as traditional intermediate schools. To rely on teacher-made materials exclusively, overlook a consumable materials budget, fail to allocate materials to build up the instructional resource center, or make no provision for off-campus experiences, is to doom in advance the programs of the middle school. Middle schools, if properly operated, require substantial resources for instruction.

Personnel

Middle schools must be staffed with dedicated and enthusiastic teachers. The middle school will be only as effective as its personnel in succeeding at new roles. With only a few colleges in the nation training teachers and staff members exclusively for middle school positions, most teachers and support personnel will enter the middle school from other, more traditional educational designs. Such persons, regardless of their belief in and allegiance to the middle school philosophy of education, will need special assistance in adjusting to their new roles. Predictably, the middle school staff will need extensive assistance in assuming new roles.

A problem witnessed in many school districts is that middle school teachers are prone to return to traditional patterns if sufficient support is not maintained. Many middle schools open under the so-called Hawthorne effect (a term that originated with the Hawthorne studies, in which workers were found to be more productive, regardless of work conditions, if they first received sufficient attention as being special). Teacher enthusiasm and energy are understandably high in the beginning; however, as program development slows or resource bases erode with the gradual lessening of attention, it is not unusual for old patterns of teacher–pupil interaction and learning to creep in. Therefore, instead of offering only one short summer training session for the middle school staff, your author suggests long-term, systematic training opportunities.

Detailed Planning

From an administrative/organizational perspective, it is crucial that schools conduct detailed planning to implement the middle school concept smoothly. The past experience of many middle schools suggests that a "broken front" approach to this concept does not work. Prior to the development of a middle school, the district must have an understanding of objectives, a commitment to this definition of educating, the involvement of those who support the school, money and resources to implement its components, and capable personnel willing to assume the required roles. The timeframe for opening a middle school must allow for the magnitude of the process proposed.

Although the amount of preparation time required to open a fully functioning middle school depends on environmental conditions in the community, a minimum period appears to be 18 to 24 months. This estimate is based on several definable steps of planning:

1. Awareness and study phases
2. Educating the community and gaining commitments
3. Budgeting for development

4. Selection of staff
5. Construction of a detailed implementation plan
6. Intensive training of staff
7. Development of curriculum
8. Construction or conversion of the site
9. Opening of the middle school

In some communities and school districts, it is possible to accomplish these steps in six months or less because of central office organization and support from the community leaders. The experience of many middle schools, however, suggests that to hasten through steps 2, 6, and 7, or to proceed with step 8 prior to step 7, can lead to significant problems later on. Eroding community support, an ill-prepared staff, a superficially constructed curriculum, and a poorly functioning site are all causes of middle school failure.

ASSESSING THE MIDDLE SCHOOL

Traditional Patterns

Often missing in the development of middle schools is an evaluation plan that will measure the success of program and organization changes. The following middle school hypotheses, on which middle school evaluations in most school districts today are based, provide areas from which data can be compiled:

- The middle school will provide a rich program of exploratory courses.
- Social and psychological problems will be fewer and less intense.
- Students will develop more adequate self-concepts.
- Students will become more self-directed learners.
- Graduates will succeed better in high school.
- Teacher turnover will be lower.
- Teacher morale will be higher.
- The organization will facilitate better use of individual teacher competencies and skills.
- Attendance of students will increase.
- Teachers will use a greater variety of media to meet the diverse needs of preadolescent learners.
- Patrons (parents, students, teachers) will hold more positive attitudes toward the objectives and procedures.
- Student achievement on standardized tests will equal or exceed that of students in conventional schools.

Sample measures of evaluation appropriate for the middle school are offered in Figure 8.9.

The Newer Assessment Pattern

Whereas traditional criteria for existing middle schools suggest a comprehensive and flexible approach, the new technological middle schools of the 21st century will need highly individualized assessment designs. In these new middle schools, teachers will

Measures of Evaluation	Measures of Growth
Academic aptitude tests	Aspects of thinking
Reading tests (comprehension and vocabulary)	Work habits and skills
Achievement tests in subjects	Reading
Emotional and social adjustment measures	Development of social attitudes
Health assessments	Development of wider interests
Home conditions	Development of appreciations
Pupil questionnaires	Development of social sensitivity
Behavior ratings	Ability to make social adjustments
Interest indexes	Creativity
Writing sample inventories	Development of personal philosophy
Work habit measures	Physical health
Teacher classroom behavior assessments	Mental health

FIGURE 8.9 Measures of Evaluation.

create instructional materials, and the degree of individualization for each student will be much greater. Districts will need to anticipate these changes to help teachers prepare for this coming era.

As stated earlier, curriculum frameworks and learning objectives will guide teachers in their selection of learning experiences for students. The new Common Core will be the master guide for student work in math/ELA. All learning objectives should be specific about the following points:

1. Learning is defined in terms of global outcomes using measures such as the cognitive and affective taxonomies of Bloom and Krathwohl to target the desired results of instruction.
2. All learning should include thinking and problem-solving skills to emphasize that middle school learning is about life in the future.
3. Affect (emotion) should be employed as a criterion for selecting learning opportunities for middle school students. The higher the affect (feeling) present in the learning episode, the more lasting or impressionable the learning episode will be.
4. Learning objectives should be sequential and within the *scope* of the curriculum. This is especially important when using the Internet because of the many enticing and interesting topics available.
5. Objectives should imply a level of attainment or a range of attainment, but not standardized growth. Underestimating, as well as overestimating, student capacity is a regular problem in many middle school classrooms.
6. All objectives should suggest evidence of participation or attainment, with the majority not being of the paper-and-pencil test variety.

As teachers begin to develop curricula (units, triptiks, exploratories), they should consider the following evaluative criteria:

1. Concepts should guide any content selection. Middle schools feature big-picture learning, and detail is often forgotten.
2. Content is usually sampling-oriented rather than mastery-oriented. A piece of literature is selected as representative of a type of literature rather than as good in itself.

3. Information should be developmentally appropriate for middle school students.
4. Information should be current and accurate. When using the Internet, the teacher must remember that there is no quality-control agent.
5. The scope of the learning is defined. With Internet learning, the information horizon is limitless. The student must have guidance in selecting experience.
6. Content on the Internet is always connected to more content, especially using search engines. Teachers should draw information webs or maps for the student, with search guide words provided.

In terms of instructional design, teachers must understand that learning changes behavior. When we program a learning episode, we expect something to happen. The accidental curriculum is dangerous because it trivializes formal learning and suggests that all information is equally important. The following guidelines might aid in evaluating instructional plans:

1. All teaching strategies recognize and acknowledge that students have individual learning styles and preferences.
2. Lessons for self-directed learning should be defined by time and anticipated attention span.
3. All groups of lessons should be ordered and logical, and this order should reflect an overall curriculum plan for the subject or year.
4. Until individual student work habits are known, an instructional pace should be suggested for each student (expectations for learning materials).
5. Teachers should be able to build in optional learning activities and suggest peripheral learning paths for better students.
6. Middle school learning designs can be for groups of students (local area networks [LANs]) and should always show applications of the principles, concepts, or skills learned.

Selection of instructional materials is a very important part of any evaluation component. As we enter the age of Internet learning, we must be cognizant of the fact that Internet materials are extensive, dynamic, and easily accessible (see Chapter 7). The ultimate use of such materials will be found in the meaning attached to them, not in the access to the materials. Use of computers allows the processing of information: deleting, adding, connecting, and constructing knowledge. Without guidance, students can easily become overwhelmed. The teacher's role in the new middle school will be greatly enhanced.

Many teachers are anxious about students in their classrooms taking unguided learning trips on the Internet. Providing the students with the appropriate addresses, bookmarking menu items on the browser, and even using existing projection devices to see what students are viewing will make early use of Internet materials less stressful for the teacher. The following guidelines are also suggested for evaluating criteria:

1. Select materials thought to be motivators for individual students.
2. Do not get trapped in using only the computer. Use books, films, and other media to engage students. Like television watching, computer viewing is hard on the eyes and has been shown by research to irritate some students.
3. Make sure the student understands the connection between suggested materials.
4. Use the Internet to supplement teacher lessons, not vice versa.

5. Try to ascertain the appropriate print size and reading difficulty for any assigned materials.
6. Take advantage of materials and plans recommended by state and national agencies. Most of these subject-area plans are on the Internet.
7. Look out for inaccurate, false, or enticing information on the Internet. Remember that there is no filter beyond the classroom teacher for the new technological curriculum materials.

In addition to following these suggestions, the new middle school teacher needs to see him- or herself as in charge of learning. Over the past 20 years, publishing companies have taken away much of the control of learning in America's classrooms by producing so-called teacher-proof learning systems. The advent of Internet technology has changed all that—the teacher is once again in charge!

Teachers in the new middle school must become experts in philosophy and instructional criteria if they are to design learning once again. Middle school students are unique, and instruction in middle school is not like that at the elementary or secondary school.

Finally, teachers need to see evaluation of instruction as an assisting venture that makes learning more and more purposeful. The questions suggested in the preceding section are designed to sharpen the instructional focus of classroom teachers.

NEW STANDARDS FOR THE MIDDLE SCHOOL

A century-old promise of intermediate educators to build an instructional program for a unique learner, the preadolescent, can now be fulfilled. The middle school can declare itself once and for all and be consistently progressive in its philosophy and its programs. The network of emerging technological middle schools can only become more powerful through synergy.

Given these changes, new middle schools must clarify their mission and update their standards for evaluation. Your author offers the following list for the consideration of middle school leaders.

The Middle School Will Do The Following:

A. Use communicative technologies to redefine school learning.
  1. Provide each student with developmentally appropriate materials.
  2. Individualize learning for each student.
  3. Deliver learning experiences at the level of student readiness.
B. Develop a new and exciting exploratory curriculum.
  1. Expand on the natural growth of each student.
  2. Teach skills of access, assessment, and application.
  3. Stress an action learning format.
  4. Be future-oriented, focused on learning to solve problems.
  5. Be high growth in design, allowing for student expression.
C. Feature teachers who have transitioned to 21st-century learning.
  1. Teachers will be guides to and designers of learning.
  2. Teachers will be the chief developers of curriculum.

     3. Teachers will be at the center of a world learning community.

     4. Teachers will train and be trained by other teachers.

     5. Teachers will be lifelong learners.

D. Possess evaluation measures that are relevant.

     1. Evaluation will be a joint venture among teachers, parents, and students.

     2. Evaluation will reflect the comprehensive nature of middle school education.

     3. Evaluation will assess students as individuals.

THE MIDDLE SCHOOL AS PART OF THE TOTAL CURRICULUM

As is true of the elementary and high school, the middle school does not stand alone. It must build on the curriculum of the elementary school and, in turn, form a solid educational base for students entering the high school. Early in the middle school movement, educational leaders fought for a separate identity for the middle school to prevent it from following the path of the junior high school, but leaders are increasingly emphasizing an articulated (coordinated) K–12 curriculum rather than building separate programs for elementary, middle, and high school students. The move toward developing a unified K–12 curriculum is a welcome one. Regardless of housing patterns or grade-level organization, students should be viewed as individuals progressing through definite stages of development. An articulated curriculum that accommodates the developmental needs of youngsters is more important than grade organizations of schools. The middle school, however, must be a strong bridge that holds together the total K–12 curriculum.

In concluding this section on middle-grade education, here is a list of some common and recurrent problems, with questions worth discussing, in middle schools:

1. Absentee rates for students in the intermediate grades are generally higher than those at the elementary and secondary levels. What may be some of the factors causing this condition? How can curriculum leaders address this problem?

2. Because many educators view the high school as a distinctive level of specialized academic preparation, many students are retained at the eighth-grade level. What price do we pay for such retention? What is a reasonable retention rate? What can curriculum personnel do about this problem?

3. Students in the intermediate grades have many interpersonal concerns related to growing up. Yet the average counselor-to-student ratio for this age group is 1 to 450. What can be done in the curriculum to address this problem?

4. Declining achievement scores on national tests are a common phenomenon in the intermediate grades. What is the cause? What can curriculum teachers do about it?

Summary

After nearly 50 years of existence, the American middle school stands as the dominant form of intermediate education in the United States. As a unique curriculum design, the middle school has provided an option to the curriculum planner that is quite distinct from the content-based curricula of the past. The newer K–8 intermediate model will continue strong in our major cities.

Middle schools find their rationale in human development and serve a special stage of human development—preadolescence. The preadolescent student experiences the most change of any student in school, and flexibility is called for in working with this group.

The middle school curriculum consists of a balanced set of experiences including content, learning skills, and personal growth. Regular organizational features found in the middle school include team teaching, block schedules, advisory guidance, exploratory wheels (short-term electives), and interdisciplinary units.

Teachers in the middle school must fulfill many roles and embrace change. Teachers in middle schools must be able to work with other adults, know several subject areas, enjoy working with students, and understand the issues of human development during the preadolescent period.

The new Common Core presents a challenge for middle schools since their philosophy and instructional rationale is based on the growth and development of the students. Your author does not see a conflict in developing the Common Core curriculum if extensive work is done with classroom teachers in translating the principles into learning experiences.

Activities

ACTIVITY 8.1

A citizens group in your community is advocating the removal of art and music from the curriculum in order to provide more time for Common Core study in math and English. How would you respond to this community request?

ACTIVITY 8.2

If your school district were to combine the elementary and middle schools into a new K–8 school, what issues might you anticipate from the two faculties?

 Click here to take an automatically-graded self-check quiz.

Additional Reading

Brown, D., & Knowles, T. (2007). *What every middle school teacher should know* (2nd ed.). New York, NY: Heineman.

Common Core. (2011). *Curriculum maps*. Hoboken, NJ: Jossey-Bass of Wiley and Sons.

Elkind, D. A. (1974). *Sympathetic understanding of the child: Birth to sixteen*. Boston, MA: Allyn & Bacon.

Hough, D. (2010). *Research supporting middle grade practices*. Charlotte, NC: IAP.

Marzano, R. (2013). *Using common core standards*. Bloomington, IN: Marzano Laboratories.

National Middle School Association and Association for Middle Level Education. (2010, January 1). This we believe: Keys to educating young adolescents (4th ed.).

Schwols, A., Dempsey, K., & Kendall, J. (2013). *Common core standards for middle school mathematics*. Alexandria, VA: ASCD.

Wiles, J. (2009). *The new K–8 school*. Thousand Oaks, CA: Corwin Press.

Wiles, J., & Bondi, J. (2006). *The essential middle school* (4th ed.). Upper Saddle River, NJ: Prentice Hall.

9

Secondary School Programs and Issues

Learning Outcome

- To understand special concerns of educating adolescent learners.

At a time when the world economy is realigning itself, and national interdependence is growing, the secondary schools of countries throughout the world are racing to link learning and working. Those nations that match the curriculum studied to the economic needs of the future will be at an advantage. In those nations where schools at the secondary level fail to make such an adjustment, there may be dysfunction and economic turmoil.

Schools in most nations are controlled by the national government, making the implementation of curriculum decisions seamless from top to bottom. The United States, by contrast, has a constitutional provision (the residual rights clause) that places responsibility for schooling at the state level. In many states, there is loose control of public and private education, and many of the important decisions are made by the 14,000 local school boards. This pattern has not produced satisfactory results during the 21st century.

Consider the following facts:

- Only 68% of ninth graders in the United States graduate on time.
- Of the 68% graduating, only 40% will enter some kind of college.
- Of the 40%, only 18% will earn an associate's or bachelor's degree within 6 years of high school graduation.
- Of the 27 members of the Organization for Economic Co-operation and Development (OECD), the United States ranks 21st in student achievement. This is true despite the fact that the United States spends more on education, as a percentage of the gross national product (GNP), than all but two nations (Israel and Iceland). Despite spending an estimated 7.4% of our national wealth on education ($10,615 per student in 2013), we have a very low high school completion rate and very low achievement as measured by international tests.

The picture looks even worse when we consider that only 23% of 12th graders in the United States are "proficient" on an international mathematics assessment. The percentage of those who demonstrate competency over challenging subject matter falls to only 15.6% when dropouts are considered in the calculation. Such sad statistics are further magnified by the poor performance of secondary schools in our major cities and areas of large immigrant populations, where the dropout rates are highest and the achievement levels are the lowest.

Should the United States nationalize its curriculum and control decision making from Washington, DC? Three recent U.S. presidents have moved the country in that direction by favoring standards, national testing, and legislation such as No Child Left Behind (NCLB), Race to the Top (RTTT), and the Common Core. While dodging the constitutional issue of state control of education, the Common Core represents an effort to put our schools on a "more level playing field" with other nations. Such a move, supported by state school boards in 43+ states, is risky. The Common Core represents the largest single change in our schools—ever!

HISTORICAL DEVELOPMENT OF THE SECONDARY SCHOOL

Although elementary schools were developed for students at public expense from the mid-1600s, the public secondary school did not become a reality for a majority of American youth until late in the 19th century. From the middle of the 18th century until the Civil War period, the principal instrument of secondary education in the United States was the academy. Benjamin Franklin is credited with the establishment of the first academy, the Philadelphia Academy and Charitable School, which opened in 1751. The academy achieved great popularity in New England and the mid-Atlantic states. The academy was neither wholly private nor wholly public (unlike the Latin Grammar School, which was both highly selective and private); it did not open the door to all youth in need of a secondary education.

In the mid-1800s, leaders in Massachusetts, led by Horace Mann, were successful in obtaining strong support for public schools. The first high school in the United States was founded in Boston in 1821. Known as the English Classical School, the school provided a 3-year sequence of English, mathematics, history, and science.

Secondary education in the United States was extended by state legislation and later by court cases. Again taking the lead, the Commonwealth of Massachusetts enacted laws that required towns with 500 or more families to establish high schools with 10-month programs. Earlier, Massachusetts had required the establishment of elementary schools in towns of 50 families or more and had reorganized the state's responsibility for the preparation of teachers by establishing, under Horace Mann's leadership, the first state *normal school*. Massachusetts also passed the first compulsory attendance law in 1852. Today, all states compel students to attend school until a certain age, usually 16.

As secondary schools emerged in more and more states from the mid-1850s to the 1870s, there was great debate about whether high schools should be provided at public expense. The high school coexisted for a long time with the academy. Not until the famous *Kalamazoo (MI)* case in 1874 was the concept of a free high school education for all youths firmly established.

In that case, a taxpayer in Kalamazoo, Michigan, challenged the right of the school board to establish a high school with public funds and to hire a superintendent. In 1874, the Michigan Supreme Court ruled that a school district was not limited to the support of elementary schools but could establish whatever level of schools it wished as long as the voters were willing to pay the taxes. This historic decision affirmed the idea that secondary education was a legitimate part of the program of public schools. The decision has never been challenged in higher courts.

After the *Kalamazoo* decision, public secondary schools grew in number. Student population rose from 200,000 in 1890 to nearly five million by 1920. The most popular grade-level organization of schools was the eight–four pattern (8 years of elementary school and 4 of high school). Later, other patterns emerged, including the popular six–six pattern (6 years of elementary school and 6 years of high school or secondary school). Not until 1910 was the junior high school established, and a three-level organizational system emerged. The popular organizational pattern then became the grades 1–6 elementary school, grades 7–9 junior high school, and grades 10–12 high school. For almost 50 years, the elementary/junior high/high school pattern dominated American schools. In the 1960s, a new school emerged—the middle school—which was to force a realignment of grade levels in American schools (see Chapter 8).

REFORM MOVEMENTS IN SECONDARY EDUCATION

Many commissions and reports have called for high school reform in the last three decades, and those working in American high schools have never lacked for advice on how to improve their school programs. The tradition of secondary school reform began in the 1890s with a number of committees and commissions organized to examine the high school curriculum, especially its effectiveness in preparing students for college. The Committee of Ten on Secondary Schools, the Committee of Fifteen on Elementary Education, and the Committee on College Entrance Requirements organized in 1893–1894 endorsed the idea of moving high school subjects into the upper elementary grades (grades 7, 8, and 9).

In 1913, the National Education Association (NEA) appointed the Commission on the Reorganization of Secondary Education, whose report took 5 years. In 1918, the report resulted in the famous Seven Cardinal Principles of Secondary Education. The report recommended that every subject be reorganized to contribute to the goals expressed in the cardinal principles. Most important, the commission endorsed the division of secondary education into junior and senior periods. The commission recommended that vocational courses be introduced into the curriculum and that a comprehensive program be offered to both junior and senior high school students. The moving down of the high school program into the upper elementary grades continued to be an issue even as district after district reorganized to include the junior high school

The high school was strongly criticized in the late 1950s and early 1960s following the launch of the Soviet satellite *Sputnik*. Although weaknesses in science and mathematics programs were attacked, other areas of the secondary school, such as foreign language instruction, also came under assault. The problem of "why Johnny can't read" was perceived primarily to be a problem of the elementary school. Secondary educators joined in placing blame for low high school achievement on the lower grade levels.

James Conant, president of Harvard, led a movement in the 1950s to expand the high school curriculum to include both vocational and academic courses for students in a unitary, multipurpose school—the comprehensive high school. Conant and others were finally developing the kind of unitary high school recommended in the 1918 report of the NEA commission. Such a comprehensive school would serve as a prototype of a democracy in which various groups could be federated into a larger whole through the recognition of common interests and ideals. The establishment of cooperative federal-state programs for vocational education in 1917 had resulted in separate specialized vocational schools (modeled after the European system), a pattern that prevailed until the late 1950s.

The 1970s proved to be a decade in which serious reforms of the American high school were recommended and, in some cases, attempted. Throughout the land, prestigious commissions met to assess the needs of secondary education and to make suggestions for reform. Among those best-known commissions were the following:

- The National Association of Secondary School Principals, whose report *American Youth in the Mid-Seventies* (1972) recommended increased "action learning" programs in the community.
- The President's Science Advisory Committee, whose report *Youth Transition to Adulthood* (1973) advocated the creation of alternative high schools and occupational high schools.
- The Institute for the Development of Education Activities (IDEA), whose report *The Greening of the High School* (1973) called for a new type of institution for modern students, with an emphasis on individual needs and student choice.
- The U.S. Department of Health, Education and Welfare (HEW), whose report *National Panel on High Schools and Adolescent Education* (1975) recommended decentralization of the comprehensive high school and reduction of the secondary school day by 2 to 4 hours.

These observations and recommendations were reflected in a number of innovative secondary schools that emerged and then receded when primary leadership was withdrawn, including the following:

- Nova High School (Fort Lauderdale, Florida), an experiment with the application of technology to instructional processes.
- Parkway Schools (Philadelphia, Pennsylvania), an attempt to move learning out into the community—the school without walls.
- McGavok High School (Nashville, Tennessee), a truly comprehensive school with a broad range of occupational tracks under one roof and tied closely to business interests in the community.
- Melbourne High School (Cocoa Beach, Florida), an academic high school with five tracks, including Quest, an advanced placement program in which students could progress to their limits.
- Berkeley High School (Berkeley, California), employing the "public school of choice" concept (premagnet) in which parents and students selected their high school by philosophy and purpose.
- Adams High School (Portland, Oregon), an experimental school in which students participated in the governance of the program, thereby learning basic democratic procedures for citizenship.

Typical of the broad goals for education during this period were those advocated by Harold Spears, a longtime advocate of the comprehensive high school (see Figure 9.1). In addition to many special programs, the actual course offerings of high schools grew extensively, as suggested by the English offerings of one high school shown in Figure 9.2.

1. Learn how to be a good citizen.
2. Learn how to respect and get along with people who think, dress, and act differently.
3. Learn about and try to understand the changes that take place in the world.
4. Develop skills in reading, writing, speaking, and listening.
5. Understand skills and practice democratic ideas and ideals.
6. Learn how to examine and use information.
7. Understand and practice the skills of family living.
8. Learn to respect and get along with people with whom we work and live.
9. Develop skills to enter a specific field of work.
10. Learn how to be a good manager of money, property, and resources.
11. Develop a desire for learning now and in the future.
12. Learn how to use leisure time.
13. Practice and understand the ideas of health and safety.
14. Appreciate culture and beauty in the world.
15. Gain information needed to make job selections.
16. Develop pride in work and a feeling of self-worth.
17. Develop good character and self-respect.
18. Gain a general education.

FIGURE 9.1   The Goals of Education.

Source: From a lecture by Harold Spears given at George Peabody College, Vanderbilt University, Nashville, TN, 1972.

English IX	Practical Communication	Films—Communications
English X	Science Fiction (Depth)	Creative Writing I
English X (AP)	Science Fiction (Survey)	Creative Writing II
English XI (AP)	Speech	Film Making
English XII (AP)	Sports Literature (Depth)	Folklore
Secretarial English I	Sports Literature (Survey)	American Literature
Secretarial English II	Techniques of Research	(Focus)
Humanities	Women in Literature	American Literature
American Dream	Themes: Modern Life	(Images)
Your America	Eng. as a Second Lang.	Contemporary Literature
American Novel	Reading–Grade 9	English Literature (Past)
Basic English Skills	Advanced Reading–Grade 9	English Literature
Directed Reading	Acting I	(Modern)
	Acting II	Journalism

FIGURE 9.2   The English Curriculum in One Comprehensive High School.

As early as the mid-1960s, American educators began to anticipate a new age and the need for a new secondary school in the United States. One such visionary, Kimball Wiles, offered the following scenario:

> In the home and in the elementary school, children will learn to read, spell, and compute at their own rate of learning by the use of teaching machines. In the school for adolescents, mathematics, foreign languages, and many scientific processes and formula will be taught by machines supervised by librarians and a staff of technicians. Machines will teach basic skills as efficiently and as effectively as a teacher. Wiles saw the real function of the future secondary school as advisory, Students in small groups will discuss problems of ethics, social concerns, and applications of knowledge with a skilled teacher-counselor. (Alexander, 1968, pp. 5–9)

Around 1974, secondary education in the United States began to change dramatically, and proposals for the expansion of the role of the American high school were no longer heard. Among the major factors causing this reversal were the following:

- *Declining enrollment.*   Between 1970 and 1980, secondary enrollment declined naturally by a full 25%. This decline, which was projected to last until 1992, meant falling teacher–pupil ratios and an increased cost per pupil in many districts.
- *Inflation.*   By 1974, the inflationary effects of the Vietnam War were in full bloom, and taxpayers became painfully aware of the soaring cost of education in a time when the purchasing power of the dollar was shrinking and being wasted in overseas adventures.
- *Unionization of teaching staffs.*   Between 1966 and 1977, the number of states recognizing the right of teachers to enter into collective bargaining rose from 11 to 30. By 1977, 80% of all teachers were members of either the National Education Association (NEA) or the American Federation of Teachers (AFT). Because high school teachers tended to be older, with more years of experience, and more expensive to the taxpayer, they were often identified with the union movement.
- *Declining achievement.*   Throughout the 1970s and continuing to the end of the 20th century, the media regularly reported declining achievement as measured by nationally normed standardized tests such as the Scholastic Aptitude Test (SAT) and various international examinations. The public interpreted this decline to mean that schools were failing.

Between 1980 and 1985, two well-known projects were aimed largely at improving test scores and academic achievement rather than addressing larger social problems in the society: *The Paideia Proposal* (Adler, 1982), which proposed a 12-year, single-track academic program with no electives, and the National Commission on Excellence in Education, which produced the report *A Nation At Risk* in 1983. Other reform efforts after 1983 were aimed at specific problems such as the dropout rate and mathematics and science achievement rather than overall school reform. Curriculum work in our secondary schools ceased to be futuristic and progressive.

In 1984, a well-known national curriculum leader, John Goodlad, published a very significant and influential book, *A Place Called School,* Goodlad shared the findings of a research project affecting thousands of teachers and pupils, and his report was not glowing. Writing about the secondary school, Goodlad observed:

> Usually we saw desks or tables arranged in rows oriented toward the teacher at the front of the room. Instructional amenities, occasionally present in elementary classrooms, were rarely observed in the secondary classes. (p. 94)

Regarding the organization of the standard secondary school, Goodlad observed:

> What begins to emerge is a picture not of two kinds of instructional activities in each class appealing to alternative modes of learning, but two curricular divisions in the secondary school. On one side are the more prestigious academic subjects, largely shunning manual activity as a mode of learning. On the other side are the non-academics, generally characterized by the trappings of academic teaching but providing more opportunities to cultivate handedness and often featuring aesthetic qualities. (p. 143)

The power of reputation and the reinforcement of observation by researchers made *A Place Called School* the "important book" of the 1980s and encouraged further inquiry into secondary school programs.

In another book, *Horace's Compromise,* a 1984 study of public education, author Ted Sizer encouraged the push for a higher mission of secondary schools. Sizer led a partnership of Brown University and more than 700 schools, called the Coalition of Essential Schools, to help students use their minds. Restructured schools in the coalition made a commitment based on Sizer's nine principles not only to get students to use their minds well but also to apply school goals to every student, to allow students to have the opportunity to discover and construct meaning from their own experiences, and to make teaching and learning personalized. Diplomas would be awarded on successful demonstration of mastery and exhibition, not simply passing courses.

The school reform movement that began in the 1980s continued into the 1990s. The secondary school reform movement was closely tied to the nation's quest for greater economic competitiveness fueled by a new global economy and a technology-fed revolution in the American workplace. The industrial age of the first half of the 20th century was being replaced by the technological age; then the high-technology age; and finally, by the end of the century, the new information age. New high-tech jobs stressed brains over brawn. The lunch bucket of the Industrial Age was replaced by the personal computer, and pencils were replaced by the handheld device. Rather than exit skills of basic reading, writing, and arithmetic, high school graduates in the new century were expected to exit with "thinking skills" and the ability to master any new knowledge on the job.

In 1991, in a widely circulated report, the Secretary's Commission on Achieving Necessary Skills (SCANS) took a hard look at six of the National Education Goals of *America 2000,* which was produced while George H. W. Bush was president and was implemented by President Bill Clinton. In addition to these goals, the commission also identified five SCANS competencies. National Education Goals 3 and 6 stated:

> By the year 2000, all students will leave grades 4, 8, and 12 having demonstrated competency over challenging subject matter including English, mathematics, science . . . and every school in America will ensure that

all students learn to use their minds well, so they may be prepared for responsible citizenship, . . . and productive employment in our Nation's modern economy (Goal 3). By the year 2000, every adult American will be literate and will possess the knowledge and skills necessary to compete in a global economy . . . (Goal 6).

Although SCANS originated in the U.S. Department of Labor, the implications of the educational observations were paramount for American secondary schools. Two conditions were identified as changing what young people needed before entering the world of work:

1. The globalization of commerce and industry
2. The explosive growth of technology on the job

Those developments meant that schools had to do a better job of preparing graduates. The five competencies of SCANS are outlined in Figure 9.3.

The late 1990s brought many changes to secondary schools, including new national and state standards, more rigorous academic programs, large blocks of time for instruction, benchmark tests, academic skills placement tests, tech-prep programs that replaced traditional vocational programs, and an increasing number of students in advanced placement and international baccalaureate programs. Alternative schooling and alternative schools, including magnet schools and later charter schools, became commonplace in many school districts. The information superhighway ran right into many high schools, linking even the most remote and smallest schools with new and high-tech information sources, courses never before offered, and a rich variety of learning opportunities. For the first time in 100 years, the high school had truly begun to change.

RECENT CHANGES IN THE SECONDARY SCHOOL

In the first 15 years of the 21st century, there has been an acceleration of innovation in our secondary schools. Throughout the nation, high schools have become more integrated with postsecondary institutions, adopted new interactive technologies, focused on life outside school and in the world of work, and attempted to redefine "the basics." In many cases, schools are making irreversible decisions that affect funding, curriculum, and teaching roles (such as the Common Core).

Reflecting the thinking of this reform was Intel's fourth annual Education Visionary Conference, held in Washington, DC, on May 24, 2005, and attended by representatives from most major technological companies. Attendees were confronted with the shocking statistic that high school graduation in America had fallen to 68%. It was observed that technology companies had been focused on integrating their products into the current curriculum (integrated curriculum) when what was needed was a transformation (transformational curriculum) to a 21st-century model. The challenge, stated a representative of the U.S. Department of Education, was to build a curriculum for personalized and customized use by each student. The American high school was characterized by speaker Ken Ender as "totally disconnected [and] unable to meet the expectations of the 21st-century workforce and the basic 21st-century literacy skills necessary for colleges."

Resources: Identifies, organizes, plans, and allocates resources
    A. *Time*—Selects goal-relevant activities, ranks them, allocates time, and prepares and follows schedules
    B. *Money*—Uses or prepares budgets, makes forecasts, keeps records, and makes adjustments to meet objectives
    C. *Material and facilities*—Acquires, stores, allocates, and uses materials or space efficiently
    D. *Human resources*—Assesses skills and distributes work accordingly, evaluates performance and provides feedback

Interpersonal: Works with others
    A. *Participates as member of a team*—Contributes to group effort
    B. *Teaches others new skills*
    C. *Serves clients/customers*—Works to satisfy customers' expectations
    D. *Exercises leadership*—Communicates ideas to justify position, persuades and convinces others, responsibly challenges existing procedures and policies
    E. *Negotiates*—Works toward agreements involving exchange of resources, resolves divergent interests
    F. *Works with diversity*—Works well with men and women from diverse backgrounds

Information: Acquires and uses information
    A. *Acquires and evaluates information*
    B. *Organizes and maintains information*
    C. *Interprets and communicates information*
    D. *Uses computers to process information*

Systems: Understands complex interrelationships
    A. *Understands systems*—Knows how social, organizational, and technological systems work and operates effectively with them
    B. *Monitors and corrects performance*—Distinguishes trends, predicts impacts on system operations, diagnoses deviations in system's performance and corrects malfunctions
    C. *Improves or designs systems*—Suggests modifications to existing systems and develops new or alternative systems to improve performance

Technology: Works with a variety of technologies
    A. *Selects technology*—Chooses procedures, tools, or equipment including computers and related technologies
    B. *Applies technology to task*—Understands overall intent and proper procedures for setup and operation of equipment
    C. *Maintains and troubleshoots equipment*—Prevents, identifies, or solves problems with equipment, including computers and other technologies

FIGURE 9.3 Five Competencies of SCANS.
Source: U.S. Department of Education, 1993.

Reform addressing such needs can be identified throughout the United States, but because there is no comprehensive cataloguing of these efforts, we can provide only the following examples:

- In Oregon, where only two thirds of students graduate from high school and fewer than half the students pass state reading and math tests, schools are implementing smaller schools or schools within schools (Portland's Madison High School), reading in every class taken by high school students (Scappose High), service learning and a capstone project for seniors (Colton High School). In many high schools, such as Scio High in Salem, seniors are taking classes that provide both graduation and full college credit.

- Award-winning Houston County High School, in Warner Robins, Georgia, is using a ninth-grade academy concept for smoother transition to high school. Time management, decision-making skills, and study skills are major parts of the general curriculum.
- The Bergen Catholic High School in Oradell, New Jersey, is using technology to develop a worldview for their 800 male students. Among the advantages gained by this massive infusion of technology are a global view in the classroom and adjustment to student learning styles. It also provides for differentiated curriculum in classrooms, enhances faculty–student–parent communication, creates a community of learners, and strongly promotes learning as a lifetime endeavor.
- The Clark Advanced Learning Center, opened in Stuart, Florida, as a joint project of the Martin County Schools and the Indian River Community College. Its goal: to prepare students to learn, live, and work in an information-rich, technologically advanced society. Students attending the center can earn up to 24 college credits while in high school.
- MacArthur High School in Irving, Texas, is one of many schools trying to achieve a one-to-one laptop program at the high school level. This ethnically diverse school boasts a 92% graduation rate, and teachers are active as "guides on the side" in the classroom. Because of these new communication devices, school–community partnerships are growing and are a primary feature of the curriculum.
- The New Technology High School (NTHS) in Napa, California, features a personal computer for each student and a classroom environment that models the industries in nearby Silicon Valley. Everyday learning is project-based, and the school recorded no suspensions for the 2000 school year. Students are provided choice in their studies and have personal responsibility to meet distant deadlines for projects. Workstations are clustered, and "rows of chairs" are not seen at NTHS.
- At Empire High School in Vail, Arizona, students are learning without textbooks! The school has issued iBooks made by Apple Computer to students, who access their materials over the school's wireless Internet network. Assigned readings, news items, online discussions, and even movies are now accessible by students in a variety of patterns. Some 5,000 school districts across the United States had provided similar 21st-century learning instruments to their high school students as of 2010.
- South St. Paul Senior High School in Saint Paul, Minnesota, is a high school where students are enrolled in an exemplary international baccalaureate program. Cutting back on administration costs, among other cost-saving measures, the district has found ways to fund the international baccalaureate program.
- Annandale High School in Fairfax County, Virginia, is a high school with 2,500 students that come from 92 countries and speak more than 45 native languages. Many students live close to the poverty line, yet with an international baccalaureate program and significantly high numbers of students taking rigorous courses, the school continues to be a model for success.

- Salem County Vocational Technical School in Woodstown, New Jersey, exemplifies how much the world of career and technical education has changed from 2000 to 2010. Instead of a vocational course for misfits and troublemakers, this career and technical education program is about computer-aided drafting and premed bioethics. Students in career and technical programs are expected to take advanced academic classes, thus undoing high school tracking and blurring the lines between college and career prep.

It is obvious from the examples listed above that some secondary schools in America are moving toward reform; only the names of the latest models change from year-to-year. These schools are easily identified from a host of awards given annually for innovation in school. Unique to American education, this reform is an open and broken-front approach to change. With help from corporations such as Microsoft and Pearson Education, environments are being altered, and curriculum is being retooled (Common Core). Most important, the roles of student and teachers are changing, and the purpose of education is shifting from "going to college" to the dual mission of college and the needs of a worker in a technological society. The boundaries of secondary education, postsecondary education, and technical training for the world of work are blurring even as this edition was being written.

THE CHANGING CURRICULUM OF THE SECONDARY SCHOOL

During the 20th century, the high school curriculum remained basically the same. The high school consisted of a number of courses that a student had to complete to graduate. Credits were given for successful completion of required courses. When a student earned a certain number of credits, he or she would graduate. To ensure that each student received a basic education during the high school years, certain courses and credit hours were required. The number of credit hours required by states varied, but most of the course titles and content were the same. Some states added a proficiency test that students needed to pass to graduate. Today, many schools are requiring competency tests for graduation.

Trends in International Mathematics and Science Study (TIMSS)

American business and educational leaders have been concerned about basic skill development in students. In 2007, the Trends in International Mathematics and Science Study (TIMSS) was the largest and most ambitious study of comparative educational achievement ever undertaken. In total, TIMSS achievement testing in mathematics and science involved the following:

- More than 40 countries
- Five grade levels (3rd, 4th, 7th, 8th, and 12th)
- More than half a million students
- Millions of written responses to open-ended questions
- Performance assessment
- Student, teacher, and school questionnaires about the tests for schooling

TIMSS was conducted with attention to quality at every step of the way. Rigorous procedures were designed to translate the tests, and numerous regional training sessions were held in data-collection and scoring procedures. Quality-control observers monitored testing sessions. The procedures for sampling the students tested in each country were scrutinized according to rigorous standards designed to maximize inclusion, prevent bias, and ensure comparability.

The 2007 TMISS was the fourth comparison of mathematics and science achievement carried out since 1995 by the International Association for the Evaluation of Educational Achievement (IEA), an international organization of national research institutions and governmental research agencies. In 2007, 36 countries participated at grade 4 and 48 countries participated at grade 8.

Based on these results, pressures were brought on schools to embark on a long-awaited curriculum reform movement. Rather than advocating more courses or credits and more tests, reforms reflected a concern about what was taught, how it was delivered, and how the curriculum could prepare students for the demands of a high-tech workplace and global economy. Leading the way were groups of educators building national standards in the major school disciplines of mathematics, English, science, and social studies. Other discipline groups followed with standards.

The term *world class* began to be used to describe new standards. In other words, what would students in the United States need to know to compete with the best and brightest graduates from around the world? The "race" was on.

Although many countries have national examinations, the United States does not. Because our system of education is legislated at the state level, only if states agree to impose tests, or standards for that matter, will any national standards or tests be implemented. This is exactly what occurred when the NGA (National Governor's Association) and the CSSO (chief state school officers or state superintendents) came together with educators to advocate for a common core of national standards.

With states jealously guarding their rights to determine what is taught in their jurisdictions, it appeared that only a national crisis, such as the global economic slow-down, would precipitate any national approach to education in the United States. The economic collapse of 2008–2009 brought on new awareness and discussions of how to use education as part of a national economic policy.

A major shift in curriculum for the content areas that had taken place in the last 10 years of the 20th century was revisited. New common standards encouraged a move away from the mastery of low-level, isolated facts to a more comprehensive curriculum emphasizing problem solving, integrated tasks, real-life problems, and higher-order thinking processes and using *portfolios* and exhibitions. Assessments of students' work became more authentic. The National Council of Teachers of English (NCTE) Standards for Assessment of Reading and Writing reflect these approaches in their goals:

1. Students must constantly be encouraged about their work in terms of what they can do versus what they cannot do.
2. The primary purpose of assessment of writing is to improve teaching and learning.
3. Students need to realize that they have other audiences besides a teacher for which they can write.
4. Educators need to take into account the outside influences on a student's work when assessing it.
5. Assessment must be fair and equitable, taking into account the diverse ethnic and social groups in the country.

6. The consequences of assessment procedures are important, and each paper that a student writes should have a specific set of criteria to be used in grading it. (Schauweker, 1995)

Social studies instruction has undergone extensive changes, too. Students now have fewer lectures and more collaborative learning activities and technology-driven interactive writing activities. Thematic teaching that integrates social studies with other disciplines has also made social studies instruction more relevant and more interesting.

Mathematics saw a host of inventive curriculum projects in the first decade of the new century. Reformers invested much time and energy creating new mathematics and state curriculum frameworks. Mathematics content moved from an almost exclusive focus on computation skills and measurement to a wide variety of activities requiring students to understand the processes and systems of mathematics and apply them to problem-solving situations. The Interactive Mathematics Program funded by the NSF resulted in programs that integrate traditional mathematics materials with additional topics recommended by the National Council of Teachers of Mathematics (NCTM), such as probability and statistics. The programs also use graphing calculator technology to enhance student understanding.

Science received much attention in the first decade of the 21st century, too. New science programs using unifying concepts such as systems and change and the application of science concepts rather than the accumulation of unrelated facts replaced traditional programs. Themes demonstrating the relation of science to other disciplines and its contributions to solving world problems have also been an exciting focus of the new science curriculum of the secondary school.

Other content areas, including the arts, physical education, and the extracurricular curriculum, have been the focus of national groups because the need for well-rounded youth has never been greater. Vocational education and the practical arts have faced demands for reassessment of their mission since 1990. The Carl D. Perkins Vocational Applied Technology Act of 1990 began an approach to using vocational courses to prepare all students for the world of work by integrating academic and vocational education. With the advent of technology in the workplace, "tech prep" became the focus of most secondary schools, forcing production types of vocational courses out of the curriculum. Even in agriculture, new technology and the decline of the family farm forced a new approach.

During the previous decade, the demands of a global economy forced even more drastic changes in vocational education. A high-tech workplace, the need for smarter workers, and the decline of traditional jobs blurred the traditional distinction between the academic and vocational curriculum.

Magnet, Charter, and Alternative Schools and Programs

The first 15 years of this century has seen a rapid increase in the number of choices of school programs for students at the high school level. Magnet schools and *magnet programs,* often used as a means of desegregation, were established to offer specialized programs in areas such as the arts, science, business and technology. Alternative schools and programs offering new approaches to learning and discipline also served to break the mold of traditional high school offerings. Charter schools, an option to escape failing secondary schools, have grown dramatically in the 21st century.

Alternative education schools, around since the 1970s, usually offer smaller classes and work-at-your-own-pace incentives for students. Many of the students enrolled in these programs have had trouble conforming to traditional programs and classrooms. Computer software and curriculum packaging have made it possible for students to complete courses more quickly and reduce the time spent in high school. Alternative programs usually provide smaller classes, individualized learning, an emphasis on improving life skills, and close ties to the community. Alternative education takes the form of separate schools or separate school programs within traditional schools.

Charter school growth in some states has been quite phenomenal and appears as a political alternative to standard secondary public schools. As much as 15% of all secondary schools in some states are now public and privatized charter schools.

Advanced Placement/International Baccalaureate Programs

Advanced placement (AP) allows high school students to attain college credit by passing a national examination in a content area. Many high schools offer such opportunities by providing AP courses to prepare students to pass such exams. More than 15,000 U.S. public and private schools offered AP exams in 2010, a number that is almost the equivalent of the number of high schools offering an AP class according to the New York City–based College Board, which sponsors the AP program. In 2012, one third of all high school students in the United States took at least one AP test.

Since 1967, the international baccalaureate (IB) program has prepared students for further study in colleges and universities both in the United States and around the world. As the United States attempts to raise the standards of secondary education, the growth of the international baccalaureate diploma program, which originated in Europe, offers great hope to those who want the United States to have a world-class secondary program.

Amid heightened concern about preparing students for the global economy, the academically demanding international baccalaureate program is booming in American high schools. International baccalaureate began operating in 1968 largely as a way for the children of European diplomats, business executives, and other professionals to keep up with their college prep studies while they were abroad. Although IB offers programs in elementary, middle, and high schools in the United States, the high school or diploma program is the largest and most common of these.

Offerings may vary from school to school, but each school must offer one course in each of the IB's six content areas and fulfill uniform curriculum and course guidelines. Students enrolled in the 2-year IB diploma program must take a sequence of subject classes, plus write a 4,000-word research paper on an approved subject. A student must also participate in 150 hours of creativity, activities, and service such as extracurricular arts, sports, and community service. Other requirements include passing exams in the six content areas and mastery of a second language.

This *global education* program is an integrated form of study that offers a broad, liberal arts approach complemented by the opportunity to study a subject in depth. The IB founders' goal was to help students learn how to learn; how to analyze; and how to reach considered conclusions about people, their languages and literature, ways of society, and the scientific forces of their environment. The birth of the International Baccalaureate Office (IBO) in 1967 started from a concern for students who had attended many schools in the course of their educational experiences. The IBO was created to foster an examination system that could be used and recognized worldwide. After several years of preparation, the first diplomas were issued in 1971.

The IBO operates on four continents, including North America, and meets annually in Geneva, Switzerland. The founders of the IB desired a world-class curriculum that would emphasize internal coherence and would maintain rigorous integrity. The 2-year preparation stresses subjects that cover the many fields of human experience as well as academic pursuits. Almost all the subjects offered have syllabi for two levels of achievement. The material included on the higher level requires 2 years of preparation for the examination, assuming 5 class hours per week, or a minimum of 240 teaching hours. The subsidiary level requires half as much time, which may extend over 1 or 2 years. During the last 2 years of secondary school, an IB candidate studies six subjects, three of which must be studied on the higher level and three on the subsidiary level. From the courses being offered, the candidate selects one from each of the following areas:

1. *Language A*   Study in the native language includes world literature in translation from at least two other language areas.
2. *Language B*   A second language at a level similar to that of Language A but distinguished by not requiring the same depth and breadth of understanding of cultural and historical contexts.
3. *People*   A choice of one of the following courses, using a thematic, comparative, and intellectual approach: history, geography, economics, philosophy, psychology, social anthropology, or business studies.
4. *Experimental sciences*   A choice of one of the following options: biology, chemistry, physics, physical science, or scientific studies.
5. *Mathematics*
6. *Electives*   A choice of one of the following: art; music; a classical language; a second language B; an additional option under 3, 4, or 5; computer studies; or special syllabi developed by the IB schools, including theater arts.

In addition to these six courses, the candidate takes a course developed for the IB on the philosophy of learning, known as the Theory of Knowledge. This course ensures that the students critically reflect on the knowledge and experience acquired. The student also prepares a 4,000- to 5,000-word research paper based on one of the subjects of the IB curriculum. The student must also engage in 150 hours of extracurricular activities in the Creativity, Action, Service (CAS) Program.

Assessment procedures include written examinations and oral examinations in languages. Grades awarded by the IB examiner are based on a scale of 1 through 7. A minimum of 24 grade points is necessary to be awarded a diploma.

Awareness of the IB program as an educational tool around the world and as a placement device in U.S. colleges and universities is increasing. The comprehensive nature of the program is commendable; its international approach to education is formidable. In this era of expanding global networks and a growing need for international understanding, the steady growth of an innovative contribution to world education is an inspiration and is invaluable to American secondary education.

Acceleration Options

A significant trend in the last decade has been the growth of graduation options for students. In some state, such as Texas (Bill 3, 81st Legislature), universities can partner with school districts to offer alternative routes to a high school diploma. Another popular route is for students to take dual-credit courses in high school, often at the university campus, to earn up to 60 credits of college work before graduating from high school. Finally, the traditional GED (trademark of ACE) tests in science, mathematics, social studies, reading, and writing are being taken by many students wanting to enter college early. Upon demonstration of proficiency, the students are awarded a Certificate of High School Equivalency, which allows passage into some universities.

Comprehensive School Designs

A number of comprehensive school designs have affected K–12 schooling, including Accelerated Schools, the Comer School Development Model, the Coalition of Essential Schools, the Modern Red School House, Co-NECT, the Community for Learning (from Temple University, PA) (Odden, 2000), and the New Century High School Initiative. The cost of training in the various designs varies. Some designs have no technology requirements, whereas others require substantial technology. Some of the designs require additional personnel such as educational facilitators. All require substantial change and commitment on the part of the school staff to make the programs work. Whether these designs will result in better schools and better achievement on the part of students to justify the often high cost continues to be a source of debate in U.S. education.

ORGANIZATIONAL PRACTICES IN THE SECONDARY SCHOOL

The organizational structure of a secondary school is designed to carry out the instructional program. The dominant pattern of organization in most secondary schools is *departmentalization,* which operates under the assumption that the disciplinary construct is the purest form of organizing knowledge. The curriculum is organized around separate disciplines that are taught by teachers in a department, such as the mathematics or social studies departments. Scheduling is fairly simple in a departmentalized school. Courses are taught in uniform lengths of time, for example, 55-minute periods.
   For years, most secondary schools operated under the following assumptions:

1. The appropriate amount of time for learning a subject is the same uniform period of time, 50 to 60 minutes in length, six or seven periods a day, for 36 weeks out of the year.
2. A classroom group size of 30 to 35 students is the most appropriate for a wide variety of learning experiences.
3. All learners are capable of mastering the same subject matter in the same length of time. For example, everyone takes the same test on Chapter 5 on Friday. Everyone from level 1 of algebra passes to level 2 in June.
4. Once a group is formed, the same group composition is equally appropriate for a wide variety of learning activities.
5. The same classroom is equally appropriate for a wide variety of learning activities. Conference rooms are not provided for teacher–student conferences. Large-group facilities are not provided for mass dissemination of materials. Small-group rooms are unavailable for discussion activities.

6. All students require the same kind of supervision.
7. The same teacher is qualified to teach all aspects of his or her subject for one year.

Operating on these assumptions, students are locked into an educational egg crate with 30 other students to a compartment from 8 a.m. to 3 p.m., 5 days a week. In short, schools operating under these assumptions exist more for the convenience of teaching than for the facilitation of learning.

Secondary schools today are attempting to break this lockstep approach to instruction. Rigid class sizes, facilities, and fixed schedules are being challenged. Subject matter is being organized in terms of more than a single disciplinary instruction. *Core* or correlation of subjects, interdisciplinary instruction, and *fused* curriculum (which provides for the merging of related subjects into a new subject) represent alternative patterns of curriculum organization.

The organizational structure in a secondary school must be flexible enough to allow for groups of different sizes to serve different functions. Scheduling in a secondary school should come after determining what kind of instruction is desired. For example, if departmentalization and interdisciplinary teaming are desired, a flexible schedule should be developed to accommodate those goals. Arrangements should be made to accommodate individual teaching, small groups, large groups, and laboratory study groups.

Teaming and variable grouping can be used to better serve student needs and draw on teacher talents. Interdisciplinary teaming can facilitate the correlation of subject matter. Common groups of students, shared by common groups of teachers, with common planning times are necessary for interdisciplinary teaching to succeed.

Year-Round Schooling

To help with the increasing numbers of students entering public schools each year and to make better use of school facilities, many school boards are adopting operating policies that provide for a year-round schedule. Using a year-round calendar, students attend the same types of classes and receive the same amount of instruction as those attending schools with traditional 9-month calendars. From a national perspective, year-round education has proved to be more widely used than other reforms because each district must design its schedule to meet the needs of the community. Year-round education calendars include the following:

- *Block 45/15.*   All students are placed on a single track and attend the same 9-week instructional blocks and 3-week vacation blocks.
- *Flexible 45/15.*   Individualized instruction is used so that students may jump tracks for special reasons in four 9-week learning blocks and 3-week vacation blocks.
- *Staggered, block, flexible 60/20.*   Students rotate through three 60-day and three 20-day learning periods, with one of the four groups always on vacation.
- *Concept 8.*   Eight 6-week terms with students selecting or being assigned six of the eight terms.
- *Concept 16.*   Sixteen 3-week terms (students select 12 of the 16 terms).
- *Multiple access.*   A partially individualized 45/15 plan in which students can enter or leave at any 3-week interval, with the curriculum in 3- or 9-week units.
- *Quarter plan.*   Four 12-week terms with students selecting or being assigned three of the four terms.

- *Quinmester.*   Five 9-week quinmesters with students selecting or being assigned four of the five quins.
- *Extended school year.*   A calendar of more than 180 days with staggered blocks.
- *Summer term.*   A conventional 9-month calendar but with full summer terms that offer continuous learning integrated with the 9-month curriculum rather than short, 6-week, discontinuous summer school courses.
- *Flexible all year.*   School is open 240 days, of which students select 180 days. The curriculum consists of small, self-paced packages to allow for interrupted learning blocks and differentiated vacation periods of 1 day to several weeks at any time.

Advantages of year-round schooling include the following:

- Students retain more and perform as well or better because of shorter vacations.
- Time needed for post-vacation review is reduced.
- There are timely opportunities for intersession tutoring and special-interest courses.
- Students exhibit better attitudes and less boredom.
- There is better morale among teachers.
- It can reduce overcrowding.
- The dropout rate decreases.

Disadvantages of year-round schooling include the following:

- Disrupts friendships because friends are often scheduled for vacations at different times.
- Causes conflicts with summertime activities.
- Disrupts family vacations.
- Increases difficulty for students who are not time-efficient.
- Causes frequent breaks in learning.
- Poses childcare problems.

Block Scheduling

The previous decade saw a major scheduling innovation implemented in secondary schools—the block schedule. As part of the restructuring movement, this scheduling innovation allowed secondary schools to make significant departures from conventional school organization and practice.

Different schools have had different reasons for considering block scheduling. Common reasons given are (1) to create larger blocks of time for instruction; (2) to permit students to enroll in one or more additional classes during the year; (3) to increase the time available for professional development; and (4) to allow teachers to teach fewer students for longer periods of time, thus getting to know them better (Hackman, 1995). The bottom line, though, in all considerations should be the answer to the following question, What is best for students?

If "stand and deliver" did not work in a traditional schedule, it certainly cannot work in a longer block of time. Reorganizing instruction to include a variety of learning activities, using technology, and encouraging greater participation in students' own learning appear to be the greatest challenges of block scheduling.

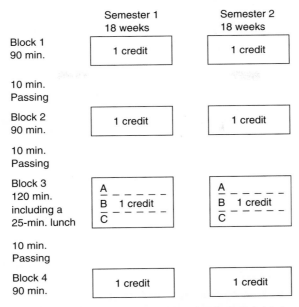

FIGURE 9.4   Straight Four-by-Four Block Schedule.

Figures 9.4 through 9.8 illustrate commonly used block scheduling models. Figure 9.4 allows 8 credits over the school year and 32 possible credits during a 4-year high school experience. Figure 9.5 allows classes to meet every other day for the school year, with Fridays split as A week or B week. Figure 9.6 is a college-type schedule that

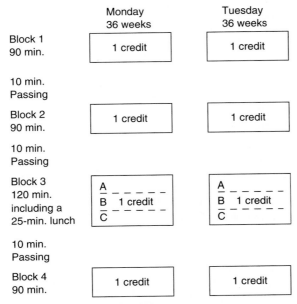

FIGURE 9.5   Rotating A/B Block Schedule.

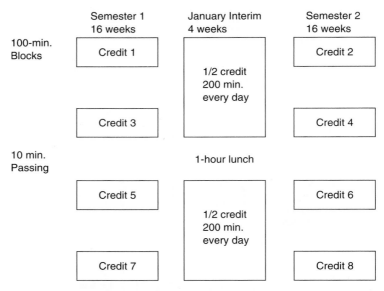

FIGURE 9.6 Four-by-One-by-Four Model.

features an interim 4-week session, thus allowing 9 credit hours a year instead of 8. Figure 9.7 works better with smaller schools. The "skinny" block (reference to small blocks of time) can be placed anywhere in the school day, and more than one block can be divided. This schedule does reduce the benefit of having just four classes in a day.

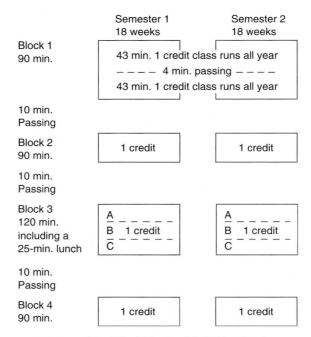

FIGURE 9.7 Modified Block with "Skinnies."

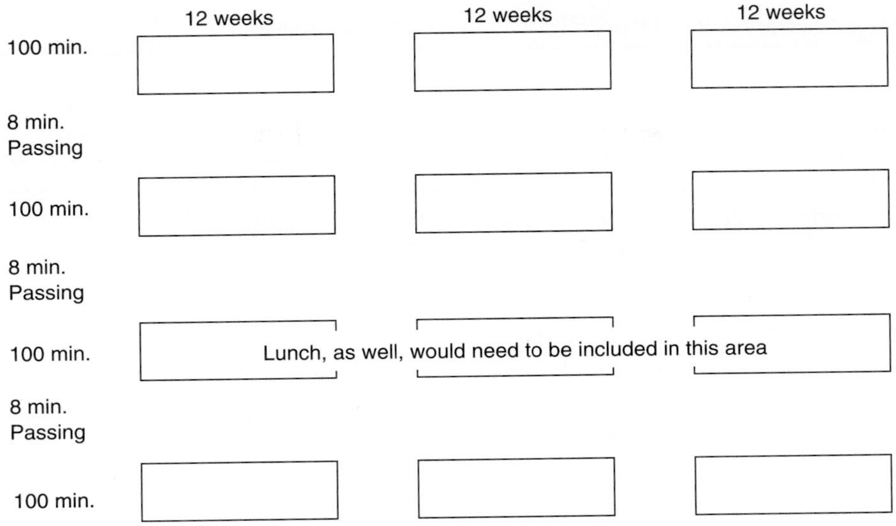

	12 weeks	12 weeks	12 weeks
100 min.			

8 min.
Passing

| 100 min. | | | |

8 min.
Passing

| 100 min. | Lunch, as well, would need to be included in this area | | |

8 min.
Passing

| 100 min. | | | |

FIGURE 9.8   Trimester Model.

Figure 9.8 is a trimester model that adds about 45 minutes to the school day and increases each class by about 10 minutes. This model allows for 12 credit opportunities during a year and 48 credits over 4 years (Canady & Rettig, 1995).

PROFESSIONAL VISIONS FOR THE SECONDARY SCHOOL

In nations throughout the world, educators and government leaders are seeking to align school programs with social needs. The curriculum of each nation's system, particularly at the secondary level, represents a vision of what that nation wishes to be. In a time of economic turmoil, most nations are attempting to adjust to rapid changes in technology and the new global economy. The wisdom of these education and government leaders in planning curriculum will determine the options available to their citizens.

In the United States, there is a general understanding of the change that is upon us. As citizens have experienced the power of consumable technologies, they have seen their lives change. Communication, work, the use of leisure, and the production of goods and services are different than they were only a decade ago. Work, the tapestry of all lives, has been altered to significant levels by these forces, as evidenced by the list in Table 9.1 of the fastest growing occupations in the near future.

Because education is the traditional means by which we prepare for our lives as citizens, family members, and workers, there must be an understanding of what is happening in both the present and the apparent future. If curriculum designers fail to get the vision correct, our educational institutions will program youth for failure. In the United States, there is considerable effort underway to understand the near future and its implications for education.

TABLE 9.1   Fastest Growing Occupations, 2006–2016 (Numbers in Thousands)

2006 National Employment Matrix Code and Title Title	Code	Employment Number 2006	Employment Number 2016	Change Percent	Change Numeric	Quartile Rank by 2006 Median Annual Earnings[1]	Most Significant Source of Postsecondary Education or Earnings
Network systems and data communications analysts	15-1081	262	402	53.4	140	VH	Bachelor's degree
Personal and home care aides	39-9021	767	1,156	50.6	389	VL	Short-term, on-the-job training
Home health aides	31-1011	787	1,171	48.7	384	VL	Short-term, on-the-job training
Computer software engineers, applications	15-1031	507	733	44.6	226	VH	Bachelor's degree
Veterinary technologists and technicians	29-2056	71	100	41.0	39	L	Associate degree
Personal financial advisers	13-2052	176	248	41.0	72	VH	Bachelor's degree
Makeup artists, theatrical and performance	39-5091	2	3	39.8	1	H	Postsecondary vocational award
Medical assistants	31-9092	417	565	35.4	148	L	Moderate-term, on-the-job training
Veterinarians	29-1131	62	84	35.0	22	VH	First professional degree
Substance abuse and behavioral disorder counselors	21-1011	83	112	34.3	29	H	Bachelor's degree

[1]Fastest growing occupations, 2006–16. Monthly Labor Review, November 2007, p 95.

What is known to planners is that new technologies have altered the way we learn, in significant ways, and that traditional schooling practices must change. Because the Internet has the potential to individualize the learning experience for any child or adult, we must begin to use this instrument of education more effectively. Among the benchmarks for the 21st century are the following:

- Technology should be the access vehicle for most information retrieval.
- Learning does not need to be so place-bound.
- The student, not the teacher, will be the focus of learning.
- All learning will have an increased vocational relevance in school.
- Students will employ constructivist techniques in learning.
- The curriculum will emphasize skills of learning and use of knowledge.

The curriculum of the near future will be specific to living in the new and interactive world of the 21st century. This substance of learning will be thematic:

- Learning connected to the community.
- Preparing for citizenship in the global environment.
- Mastering core knowledge, languages, and life skills.
- Technical literacy and career preparation.
- Becoming aware of and developing acceptance of cultures.
- Using new technologies to collaborate.

Certainly, if there are school buildings as we have known them in the United States for 150 years, they will be characterized by features such as the following:

- Considerable community interface.
- Multipurpose studios.
- Spaces for creation of new applications and products of learning.
- Flexibility of learning spaces.
- Places of solitude to encourage thinking.

More difficult to envision are the learning instruments that will mediate between the student and the world of knowing, such as the following:

- Internet-assisted curriculums.
- Portable, handheld, learning instruments.
- Digital classes using blogs, wikis, and iPods or their newer forms.
- School/home/community learning blends.
- Nonstandard learning certifications.
- ATI-driven, adaptive software formats.
- Incentives based on work destinations.

All such ideas are being discussed in writings, conferences, and discussions among educators even as you read this textbook. Your author believes the application of these notions will occur first at the secondary level of schooling, where failure and opportunity are most prominent in American education. Breaking away from the past, in the United States and throughout the world, will demand that educators and government leaders hold new curriculum paradigms.

Perhaps the greatest challenge facing the secondary school today is to establish its real role of education in our society. In the early years, the secondary school was viewed as an academic school designed to prepare students for college. Later, the high school assumed a greater function—that of preparing students for the immediate workforce. Fed by legislation after World War I, vocational programs were organized in school districts to train students who were not going on to higher education. By the 1950s, high schools had assumed yet another function: to provide a comprehensive curriculum of academic and vocational courses for students.

In the United States, in 2020 and beyond, the very survival of the society and its values may rest on how well the curriculum is defined by education and government leaders. As the economic issues of 2008–2015 have illustrated, every nation needs functional and contributing citizens who possess the ability to accept change on short notice.

A CHANGING COUNTRY IN A CHANGING WORLD

To understand the growing interdependence of the world that the secondary education graduate will enter, consider the number of multinational products produced and the military and economic partnerships within and outside the Northern Hemisphere. If our world were a village of 1,000 people, it would have:

- 564 Asians
- 210 Europeans
- 86 Africans
- 80 South Americans
- 60 North Americans

The religious breakdown would be:

- 300 Christians (183 Catholics, 84 Protestants, 33 Eastern Orthodox Christians)
- 175 Muslims
- 128 Hindus
- 55 Buddhists
- 47 animists
- 85 people following other religions
- 210 atheists or persons without religion

The demographics of our nation and the world are changing. In the United States, and many other nations, minority students are increasing in numbers, while the percentage of the nation's population under age 18 is declining. Of the estimated 62 million school-age students in the United States in 2010, over one-half (32 million) live in the nine largest states. Of those 32 million school-age students, 16 million are minority. Over half of the students in 13 states plus Washington, DC, are from minority backgrounds. In 2013, the fastest growing minority groups in our nation were Asians and Pacific Islanders and Hispanics.

The aging of the United States population continues. More than 13% of Americans were identified in 2011 as over 65 years of age. This is also a problem in Europe, Japan, and other wealthy industrialized countries.

The economic collapse of 2008–2009 also signaled the final end of the industrial age in the United States. The political clout of the American blue-collar worker in industries such as automobiles was gone. What was stable employment that delivered decent wages and good benefits over generations became a thing of the past for millions of workers. Except for high-tech industries such as airplane and automobile manufacturing, there were few industries where people would go to work each day making something one could touch or hold. About 5.8 million manufacturing jobs were lost in the period 2000–2009. The service industry drives 80% of the American economy today. Table 9.1 illustrates vividly the changes in the employment matrix.

Employers say that schools should no longer prepare students to hold one job for the rest of their lives. The future of the United States seems to be in the area of high-value services and products, and thus better-educated workers are required. The years of mass-production jobs requiring low skills and eighth-grade reading comprehension are gone. The Perkins Vocational and Technical Education Act, reauthorized in 1998, was visionary because it included for the first time a requirement that technical–vocational education students meet the same academic standards as other high school students.

The full-service school, offering healthcare and social programs along with academic programs, may well be the typical school of the future. Subsidized housing and free or reduced transportation for the poor to go to work, along with health and social services centered at school sites, may need to be increased to avoid a permanent underclass.

IMPROVING TEACHER QUALITY

For the first time, the United States now has national standards of excellence for master teachers who demonstrate exceptional performance. The National Board for Professional Teaching Standards (NBPTS), an independent, nonpartisan group of teaching professionals, has developed standards for highly accomplished teachers; however, quality concerns exist about teachers teaching out of their field and teachers not being given the training and time to acquire new skills to teach to high standards of excellence. The U.S. Department of Education, through its Partnerships in Education Program, offers the following checklist for helping schools improve teaching:

- Initiate programs that actively recruit talented young people and midcareer professionals to become teachers.
- Work with colleges to reinvent teacher preparation for beginning teachers, including an induction period for their beginning years of teaching.
- Participate in efforts underway in many states to develop performance-based assessments for new teachers, such as those of the Interstate New Teacher Assessment and Support Consortium (INTASC).
- Redesign professional development for the most experienced teachers so they get the training they need to help students master the basics and reach high standards in the core academic areas.
- Encourage master teachers to be nationally board certified.
- Identify and provide peer-assistance programs to improve the performance of burned-out or low-performing teachers.
- Expand efforts to help teachers become more technologically literate, and use technology to improve training available to teachers.
- Find ways to get current information to teachers, thus addressing the isolation that is all too common in teaching.

A CLOSING NOTE

As a curriculum developer, your author is concerned about the trends in the first decade of the 21st century as they relate to the American high school. In the rush to return to the basics, raise achievement scores, and legislate quality control, we seem to have forgotten a purpose for secondary education that underpinned most planning prior to 1975: to foster a strong democracy. This thought cannot be lost as we struggle to redefine our nation's curriculum using Common Core Standards.

Democracy is a word that was used frequently by early curriculum writers such as Dewey, Bode, Kilpatrick, and Rugg. These leaders spoke of democracy not as a system of government in which supreme power is vested in the people—although they understood this concept—but rather as a way of life in which no single group can dominate others on the basis of class distinction, heredity, or privilege. These cherished educators perceived a danger in our way of life that pitted social equality against economic competition. If capitalism and competition became dominant, they reasoned, basic human rights might be trampled. Schools, according to Dewey (1916), "were the institution best organized to serve Democracy's cause." Horace Mann, cited earlier as the "father of American education," observed, " Education, beyond all other devices of human origin, is the great equalizer of the condition of men, the balance-wheel of social machinery."

Throughout the past century, education has been the key response to repressive social relations. The education system, perhaps more than any other contemporary social institution, is the laboratory in which competing solutions to the problems of personal liberation and social equality were tested and the arena in which social struggles were fought. In short, democracy is *the* historical value or social ideal that has given direction to our educational aims. If education in public schools is our nation's primary instrument for shaping our destiny as a society, then should not our curriculum be planned with essentials first and refinements second?

Summary

Because high school is the exit school for many American youth, the secondary school is expected to find solutions for many of the problems of society. The secondary school has experienced its share of reform movements during the past century. Over the course of the history of secondary education, numerous committees and commissions have been established to improve the curriculum. Now, however, a new global future poses challenges for educators and government leaders to reconstruct the high school once more. The Common Core State Standards will be the generic instrument. Leaders in the United States and in other nations of the world must revisit the basic questions of curriculum and once again redefine education in terms of national priorities and the basic needs of citizens.

Activities

ACTIVITY 9.1

What is the basic difference between the high school of 1900 and the high school of today? What is common to both forms of the secondary school?

ACTIVITY 9.2

With a national dropout rate approaching 40%, many think the American secondary school should be left behind or totally re-designed. On what basis would you justify continuing this American institution?

 Click here to take an automatically-graded self-check quiz.

Additional Reading

Alexander, W. (1969). *The high school of the future: A memorial to Kimball Wiles.* Columbus, Ohio: Charles Merrill.

Boyington, B. Top 10 Public High Schools 2013, *U.S. News and World Report.* Retrieved from http://

www.usnews.com/education/high-schools/ slideshows/best-high-schools-2013

Gordon, E. (2008, December 28). The 2010 meltdown: Solving the impending jobs crisis. *USA Today*.

Kellough, R., & Carjuzara, J. (2009). *Teaching in the middle and secondary schools* (9th ed.). Boston: Allyn and Bacon.

Miller, M. (2012). *Measurement and assessment in teaching*. Upper Saddle River, NJ: Pearson Education.

Nelson, K. (2008). *Teaching in the digital age* (2nd ed.). Thousand Oaks, CA: Corwin.

Ornstein, A. (2011). Contemporary issues on curriculum. Upper Saddle River, NJ: Pearson Education.

Tomlinson, C. A., Kaplan, S. N., Renzulli, J. S., Purcell, J. H., Leppien, J. H., & Burns, D. E. (2009). *The parallel curriculum* (2nd ed.). Thousand Oaks, CA: Corwin, The Parallel Curriculum (Paperback).

10

Global Perspectives of the Curriculum Process

Learning Outcome

■ To compare and contrast curriculum strategies of other nations.

This book edition began with the observation that the field of curriculum development is a vital educational function in every nation. Leaders in all countries share the task of preparing future citizens with the knowledge and skills needed for survival and growth. All cultures, even the most primitive ones, have something akin to a school, a mechanism for preparing the young for the future. Through rituals, rites of passage, stories, and the passing down of vital information, the culture is preserved and enhanced.

After just fifteen years of the 21st century, it is obvious that the arrival of new communication technologies and the resulting new global economy challenge many of the basic assumptions of the modern world. Each nation, in its own manner, seeks to adjust to global interdependence and a brand new set of premises about how things work. Nowhere is this need greater than in education because education is the process for renewal in all societies. To confront the pressing problems of the world economy, security, resource allocation, and national development, education stands at the center of decision making in all nations. As Singapore has stated so eloquently in its Education Vision Statement, "Thinking School; Thinking Nation."

In educational systems throughout the world, the curriculum development function is the critical piece of an emerging puzzle. How can nations design and develop educational programs that promote their preferred values and aspirations? How can leaders of any nation clarify these values; understand capacity, limitations, and governance issues; and still restructure schooling for the desired effect? The paradigms presently held in curriculum are the scaffolding for communication, research, and practice. And, as Bruce Joyce observed, "educational procedures are generated from general views about human nature."

It is interesting to note that the process of education is not defined the same way in all countries. Education in China (Jiao Yu) means to give birth. In Japan, Education (Kyolka) is nurturing. In the United States, Education (the curriculum) is defined as

271

"the race." In cultures where religious influence is strongest, Education is defined as "awakening (Buddhism), "sacred knowledge" (Hinduism) or "the path" (Taoism). In the vast majority of Muslim nations, Education is equated with acquiring religious knowledge.

In the second decade of the 21st century, curriculum leaders in western nations have been clinging tenuously to an older set of concepts that are rapidly losing value. At the core of these notions is the idea that education is about knowledge acquisition. In today's world, this premise no longer holds up. Communication technologies are presenting the world with many new options to retrieve, process, assess, store, and apply knowledge. Digitized information bits fly around the Earth, accessible to all, even non-readers. Education can no longer be just about acquiring such knowledge because a knowing person is no longer distinguished. Governments are trying to distinguish the difference between learning and being *learned*, and it is in the interest of all nations to do so quickly. Specifically, the primary problem for all nations is to connect the education process with globalization and the new world order. The new communication technologies that are so admired are a means to an education, not the end.

NATIONS AT WORK

In his important study of British education, *Fifteen Thousand Hours* (1979), John Rutter concluded that special features and functions of a school can have a direct impact on student achievement. Your author believes his insightful longitudinal study also establishes a more general working premise about curriculum work:

> The manner in which education is organized will determine the kind of learning that can take place.

Take Rutter's finding to the next level and beyond, and it is probable that how nations organize and deliver education for their citizens will largely determine that nation's future. In the second decade of the 21st century, citizens have only just begun to recognize the importance of education, and especially the curriculum design function, in national development. Schools "program" students for some anticipated future. If a national education program is accurate in its perceptions of the future, it will arrive at that future with functional citizens and a positive national destiny. If that nation has misjudged or misunderstood the trends leading to that future, and has programmed its future citizens for obsolescence or behavioral dysfunction, that nation will fail to develop properly and may even perish. Decisions about education being made in the United States and throughout the world are of vital importance in this new age. As one African adage states, "as the crab walks, so walks its children."

In the United States, as in other nations, political leaders, business interests, and educators are working to identify and bring about a preferred future. The Common Core movement, currently being pursued in the United States, represents a somewhat dramatic departure from over a century of professional knowledge about teaching and learning. As one of a very few nations with a de-centralized education system (states' rights), leaders are attempting to "cobble together" a set of guiding standards that will make citizens more competitive in the 21st century. The curriculum being projected is a highly structured affair and will use computer-delivered tests to monitor student progress. That progress will be defined by pre-determined learning standards and nothing else will matter. There will be very little room for error in this transition as the vast majority of state educational systems break down their education standards to implement the new national design for learning in math and English/language arts.

Without question, the stakes are very high for the United States. Getting a new system in place that will prepare young persons for the future will determine the standard of living and even national security. For this reason, leaders of the Common Core movement must keep the goal of "international competitiveness" in view. It has been said that innovations in schools have a "half-life" of two years. It will take that long to get the pieces in place!

Under the influence of the many new technologies and an ever-interdependent global economy, basic truths and old paradigms are breaking down throughout the world, and the lines between nation-states are blurring. Every country is struggling to answer four traditional curriculum questions:

1. What is our curriculum?
2. Who controls our curriculum?
3. How will our curriculum be delivered?
4. What will be the outcome of our curriculum?

These four questions form a relevant structure for understanding all education in the 21st century. Using these traditional questions, students of the education process can group, compare, contrast, and assess the work of nations, states, districts, and even individual schools. Whether a curriculum is exclusive or mandatory, for example, will explain the kind of human resources (human capital) available to a country 15 years into the future. Whether the curriculum is state-controlled, controlled by religion, commercial/proprietary, or self-directed will make a huge difference in the product or outcome. Whether delivery is found in a school setting, on a jobsite, systematically delivered by computer, or self-accessed by the learner is of importance. Whether the vision of education is general or highly specific reveals a great deal about the curriculum experience. All curriculum work begins with a vision. The vision shapes the process and determines the outcome.

In the section that follows, a number of nations will be described in terms of their needs, focus, organization, and projects in education. Like the United States, they are working to re-design their education system. Your author has been privileged to have worked as a curriculum planning consultant in most of these countries in Africa, Asia, Europe, and North America. In witnessing the work of these nations in defining their educational systems, it is noteworthy that the curriculum tasks are similar in each nation. The outcome of such work in each nation, however, is very different depending on their respective visions and the instruments used to make things happen.

GLOBAL PERSPECTIVES

As you, the reader, might imagine, the vision and programs of education around the world are quite disparate. One can easily extrapolate from these assessments and see the same phenomenon when comparing advantaged districts and the poorer school districts in their own country. The range of such curriculum planning activity and concern, worldwide, is from very basic to futuristic. Some nations, like Singapore, can articulate their visions clearly, while so many others nations cannot. It is true, as the African educator Mantengu Katululu observed, that "an old field is easier to cultivate." The majority of nations do what they have always done.

The majority of the world's 195 nations are underdeveloped and dreadfully poor. Like Cambodia, discussed in Chapter 1, they lack strong, educational organization structures, or they suffer recurring wars (equatorial Africa) or cyclical national disasters (Bangladesh). Most underdeveloped nations lack a substantial education infrastructure of any kind, and advanced planning by leadership for a preferred future is nonexistent. Progress has been scanty in many of these countries since they received their freedom in the 1960s from colonialism.

The wealthiest nations on Earth, by contrast, are engaged in a process to adjust to new world forces and keep or improve what they have. Since the early 1980s, the world economy has been directly affected by new technologies, communication, and work patterns. Those nations that correctly navigate their way to a preferred future will survive and flourish.

The efforts of poor counties such as Sudan, El Salvador, or Afghanistan are constantly overturned by unanticipated events (systems breaks). Governments change regularly, civil wars erupt, forces of nature intervene, and budgets are always thin or dependent on outside sources. Teachers in such nations are often the last student to reach the tenth grade. Classes can be huge. And, if there is a vision of education and its role in the future of that nation, it is borrowed from the successful 19th century French or English models.

Pakistan

In the case of some underdeveloped nations, social values creep into the planning process and influence the distribution of scanty resources. Pakistan is one such nation where visioning is not active. Your author's Pakistani colleague, Dr. Zakia Sarwar, writes this about her nation, "the lessons of a growing knowledge base, the developments in technology, and the increasingly globalized perspective have not yet been appreciated." Dr. Sarwar describes Pakistan as an educational system of rote learning and students regurgitating from worn textbooks, in classes that sometimes approach 150 students. In a nation that "has not seen education as a critical need, much questionable content has crept into classroom materials . . . to the extent that racial hatred is often nurtured by the curriculum." "Our system," she writes, "has been captured by religious fervor. It is like a terminally ill patient."

Pakistan is a 65-year-old nation with a traditional but largely dysfunctional education system. Religion and poverty combine to retard growth of even a general literacy program in this 6th most populous nation on Earth. An out-of-control birthrate promotes a population that increased by 27 million in the 4-year period from 2007–2011. Wars, conflict, political unrest, and a high rate of illiteracy combine to make long-range planning for the improvement of education unlikely in the near future. The nation is unstable and so is its process for preparing the young for the future.

Like many other poor and fundamental Muslim nations, Pakistan has a vastly different definition of education than any western nation. Article 31 of the Constitution of Islamic Republic of Pakistan mandates that the education system ensures "the preservation, practice, and promotion of Islamic ideology in accordance with the Holy Qur'an and the teachings of the Holy Prophet."

Pakistan's last National Education Policy, 1998–2010, aimed at the attainment of universal primary education and a literacy rate of 70% by 2010. Under the plan 45,000 new primary schools and 30,000 secondary schools were to be built. The plan projected raising the allocation for education from 2.2% to 4% of the GNP. Under this plan there was to be a major shift toward scientific and technical education by encouraging communication technologies in all public sector institutions. Partnerships between the public and private sectors were to be encouraged.

Unfortunately, the war in neighboring Afghanistan, a change of leadership in the national government, and an unreliable source of financial support from western nations (the United States), contributed to the downgrade of these planning aspirations. All of these events, these "breaks," couldn't have come at a worse time for a nation where 60% of the citizens are under 18 years of age.

South Africa

South Africa began to reconstruct its educational system in 1994 following the end of Apartheid. Apartheid, or the separation of persons by race, mandated separate and unequal school systems for whites and non-whites. Throughout the 1980s, young persons in South Africa physically attacked the schools as a symbol of the apartheid government, and by the 1990s there was a great shortage of buildings and teachers in the reborn nation. Some young black students had never attended school until the end of apartheid.

As apartheid laws were lifted in the 1990s, the South African government addressed the task of creating a nonracial school system from the two previously separate and unequal systems. Religion, language, and community values were all issues in South Africa, as was the whopping 23.5% of the national budget needed for the reconstruction of the education system. Some 26,000 individual schools in the new South Africa began the task of creating a reformed system and a new curriculum that would enroll 12 million students. Twenty years later, the task of rebuilding that education system is still being addressed.

In South Africa, the national Department of Education provides a framework for school policy, but administrative responsibility lies with the provinces and with locally elected school boards. Education is compulsory from age 7 to 15, and there are three levels of education including college. From the mid-1990s to 2005, the passing rate for all students rose from 40% to over 68%. Still, with a national illiteracy rate of about 24% in the general population, much is still to be done.

The largest challenge for educational planners in South Africa, as in so many other developing nations, is in the poorer population areas of the country. South African schools in the KwaZulu-Natal region account for 40% of all the educational facilities in the nation. Fee-free programs, a National Schools Nutrition Programme, local school gardens, and HIV-Aids awareness programs are conducted in these most underprivileged schools. For its part, the national Department of Education has emphasized the use of new technologies in these formerly disadvantaged schools, and it is implementing FOCUS schools (a kind of magnet program) to address work-related issues in the country.

As can be seen from these two examples, very different purposes are being promoted in many underdeveloped countries. Your author believes that a study of such nations would reveal a kind of hierarchy of purpose in these nations. Most basic in these poorer nations is an effort to pull together the resources needed for learning. Unfortunately in most poor nations, education is not perceived as the most essential social service, and help from outside sources is unreliable.

At a second level, if adequacy of material has been met, a literacy curriculum is established and enhanced to the highest degree possible. Such systems are usually traditional in every sense of the word, and they may provide the nation with the leaders and public officials capable of operating the governmental apparatus. In such nations, however, the schools are not connected in a meaningful way to the national prosperity or destiny but rather to a class of citizens.

At a third level, in underdeveloped nations, there is an effort to make education work for the nation. In the following examples, Vietnam and Brazil begin to take control of education and make it work for their people.

Vietnam

Many nations, like Vietnam and Brazil, are attempting to move beyond a marginal education system and make schools an engine for national economic development. Vietnam represents a very interesting case of development in education systems. Following four exhausting wars with France, the United States, Cambodia, and China, the nation found itself financially depressed and in need of restructuring almost all basic institutions. During the past two decades, Vietnam managed to establish a substantial educational structure and is poised to explore the use of new technologies to effectively educate its youth.

The Vietnam Educational Act of 2005 established the definition of education in this way:

> To train the Vietnamese people who develop fully, and who can obtain moral conduct, knowledge, health, aesthetic sense, and work, be faithful to the ideal of independence of the nation and socialism, develop and foster personality, virtue, and competence of citizens meet the requirements to build and defend the nation.

Traditionally, the Vietnamese operated a Chinese-Confucian system of educating that existed until freedom was obtained from the French colonial government. At this time a broader "United States model" was employed in the south part of the country and a communistic (Marxist-Leninist) model was employed in the north. After war and reunification in 1975, the Communist system was applied throughout the country. Literacy, under the new system, is now reported to be 94% for all persons over 15 years of age.

Geography challenges educators in Vietnam since secondary schools are not found in many of the mountainous tribal regions. Unlike neighboring Cambodia, however, nearly 24% of Vietnamese (20 million) have Internet access, and educational and government leaders are exploring how this tool might be used to make secondary education universal in the country. This possibility of applying 21st century technology to a 19th century problem may result in the nation being able to "jump over the 20th century" by eliminating the need to provide the very expensive infrastructure (school buildings, teacher training institutions, books, and so forth.) This effort is moving forward at a slow pace.

Education in Vietnam is organized into five distinct levels: pre-primary, primary, intermediate, secondary, and higher education. Children may enter level one as early as 18 months of age, and primary education begins at age 6. Secondary education is only grades 10–12. In order to graduate from secondary schools, an examination is held in each of six subjects: Vietnamese literature, foreign languages, mathematics, and three other subjects chosen each year by an Educational Board.

Because of the Confucian heritage, education in Vietnam is very exam-oriented and teaching methods very traditional. Because the Vietnamese schools have a practice of keeping students together throughout their education, strong group bonds are formed among students but few personality characteristics are developed or expanded. Many graduates are unable to find appropriate employment or transfer credits to overseas universities as a result of poor accreditation at the university level. Only around 5% of all college-age students in the nation attend higher education in Vietnam.

While now unified, the north and south ends of Vietnam seem on different courses for the near future. In the south, commerce flourishes and technology has become a tool for education and outreach to the world. In the north, by contrast, leaders from the past still impose a kind of paternal leadership on the people and their educational programs. To the credit of these leaders in Hanoi, where the Minister of Education and Training (MOET) is located, more than 7,000 schools have been built and a unified curriculum has been established in the nation. Twenty-two million children now attend school at the primary level, and literacy has risen to 94% among adults.

Curriculum leaders in Vietnam address issues such as establishing quality assurance, using technology in schools, securing accreditation for higher education, introducing modern teaching methods in schools, increasing the number of qualified teachers in the nation, and securing a reliable resource base for education. Despite so many challenges, leaders now seem confident that education will lead this nation into the global age with greater participation among Asian nations.

Brazil

Brazil represents another largely underdeveloped and inefficient educational system. In a society with 9% illiteracy (14.6 million), the focus of schooling has remained basic. School attendance is around 91%, but like South Africa and Vietnam, remote populations are not being fully served. Approximately four million potential students, mostly in the northern parts (Amazon basin) of the country, do not attend school. Achievement in the schools is generally low with only 26% of ninth graders attaining the expected level in language and only 14% attaining grade level expectations in mathematics. Brazil is a vey large nation, physically speaking, and sponsors some 200,000 individual schools.

The government of Brazil is concerned with the effectiveness of the schools because the nation has the world's 6th largest economy but a less-than-adequate workforce. The nation spends about 5% of its GNP on education, about the same as the United States and Great Britain. It is the belief of the Ministry of Education that technology can help the nation overcome its education deficiencies and physical remoteness. Recently, broadband Internet was placed in 52,000 schools, and the government distributed some 600,000 computer tablets produced by Intel in Brazil. The model technology center in the nation is located in Portal Brazil, a suburb of Rio de Janeiro.

LARGER DEVELOPING NATIONS

Another stage of curriculum development work can be observed in the larger nations of Russia, India, and China. In these three examples, the governments have begun to actively use their schools to foster preferred national development. Each nation employs complex multi-year educational plans to attain desired goals for their country.

Russia (Soviet Union)

During the Cold War years between 1960–1990, the Soviets used Five Year Plans to move from point-to-point in their national development. These highly detailed plans produced scientists, engineers, artists, athletes, and made the Union of Soviet Socialist Republics (USSR) a world leader in space exploration, medicine, and military ventures. In particular, Russia employed an unusual tool for promoting academic development—the academic village—and the Novosibrisk center demonstrated the power of focusing efforts.

In the 1950s, the Soviet Union sought to encourage development in the region of Siberia. Entire collectives of scientists were moved from Moscow and Leningrad to Novosibrisk, and a new Town of Science was located 20 kilometers to the south and named Akademgorodok. The new town soon became the educational and scientific center of the region. Ultimately, 35 research institutes, 16 institutions of higher education, a state university, a medical academy, and a large science library were constructed along with apartments, hospitals, and hotels. At its peak of influence, 65,000 scientists and their families lived in "Academy Town."

While the Soviets produced many mathematicians and scientists under their regular Five Year Plans, the effort at Akademgorodok paid major dividends in promoting the national economy. Since the work conducted was pure and fundamental, not simply for military purposes, the area soon was chosen as sites for the USSR Academy of Agriculture and the USSR Academy of Medicine as well. Currently, the city population stands at around 100,000 persons. As such, the Russian effort demonstrates the power of focus in educational planning.

India

In addition to Russia, India and China are nations that are rapidly developing by using schools to promote their preferred futures. India is a country of over one billion persons, a third of whom are functionally illiterate. While government-supported tertiary education promotes an exaggerated image of technical accomplishment to the world, the overall condition of the public Indian education system is dim. Plagued by poverty, overcrowding, poor healthcare, and low income, government support of schooling in India is low even among under-developed countries.

Government schools in India educate about three fourths of all students in primary schools, and some Indian children are privately educated at the secondary level. Article 45 of the Constitution of India guarantees all students a full 10 years of education but, in reality, few pupils achieve that goal since 48% of all Primary students drop out of school and only 28% of public school students make it to the 11th and 12th grades.

Literacy in India, defined as reading and writing in any language, is around 74%, although that rate is much higher for males than females. Around 304 million Indians are illiterate, with the highest rate found in rural areas and among females. A hard core of Dalit (oppressed underclass) never attend school.

Government funding for education, aided by international programs like the World Bank and UNICEF, has been directed toward the primary level and has shown success in opening 160,000 new schools since 1994. Targeted in legislation to equal a 6% share of the GNP, the contribution to education has been in steady decline since the year 2000 and is now below 4%. A full 30% of these government funds are earmarked for higher education institutions. Even so, according to UNESCO, India has the lowest public expenditure on higher education per student in the world.

Education is delivered at three levels: primary, secondary, and tertiary. Around one tenth of the students in India have a higher education experience of some type. Despite this systemic attrition, India has the third largest higher education system in the world after the United States and China.

The issues for Primary and Secondary schools are predictable and numerous. Overall, facilities in the nation are substandard with many lacking even roofs and drinking water. Accreditation of schools is focused on facilities rather than academic achievement. Teachers, for the most part, are untrained and recent surveys have documented enormous absenteeism among teachers and a general "shirking" of traditional responsibilities in the classroom. Materials are in short supply and record keeping of all kinds is, at best, irregular.

The private school sector is only slightly improved and much of that advantaged condition can be attributed to urban locations where facilities and teachers are more plentiful. Private education has mushroomed wherever the government control is lacking. The curriculum, in the public and private schools, is dominated by rote learning and newer technology is severely limited in most schools.

Higher education in India is overseen by the University Grants Commission, a body that enforces standards and accredits institutions. Some 20 central universities, 215 state universities, 16,000 colleges, and 100 "deemed" colleges make up the higher education system of 10.5 million students. Three universities, the Indian Institutes of Technology, have been recognized as being among the top 200 universities in the world by the Times Higher Education List.

There is some good news in India as far as curriculum planning is concerned. As a Soviet satellite in the 1950s, India began to use Five Year Plans to push their economy forward. In 1951, Prime Minister Jawaharial Nehru inaugurated the Indian Institute of Technology. The Minister envisioned "India's City of the Future," a place where scientists could get away and produce ideas and programs that would lead the nation's development (much like the Soviet city of Akademgorodok). The city of Bangalore in the state of Karnataka (today called Bangalulu) was selected as the location for this vision.

Among the achievements of this heavily funded center over the past 60 years have been a science center, an Indian space program, and a nuclear weapons program. Bangalore is best known to the rest of the world as a center for technology housing 15 major education and research centers including the Indian Institutes of Technology. Five of these institutes, located throughout the nation, have been rated in the top 10 science and technology universities in Asia. In 2011, India passed legislation to add five more Institutes throughout the country. Americans know of Bangalore, of course, because of its influence on computer services.

Three steps are credited for India's economic "miracle." First, the Indian Ministry of Information and Technology formed an umbrella group of agencies to deal with IT comprised of university, business, and government personnel. Second, a software technology park was developed where business, government, and academia could meet and work together. Finally, the government reached out to the global Indian diaspora to keep contact with those working on IT projects abroad. Communication with this group has been excellent.

If the public and private schools of India contributed to this "bunching of resources approach," it would be found in 1) 30% of the educational budget going to higher education, 2) a disproportional number of college students from traditional high status groups (Brahmans) in India, and 3) the consolidation of private education, universities, and the new IT industry in just the four-state area along the coast. In a word, a new state-within-a-state was created by both circumstance and planning. A final factor, perhaps most important, was the creation of premier educational facilities (Indian Institutes of Technology) focused on STEM (science, technology, engineering, medicine) themes. Credit can be given to active participation of professional societies in engineering and other areas for these valuable institutions.

In 2005, the Prime Minister of India (Manmohan Singh) constituted a new National Knowledge Commission to serve as a "think-tank" for national development. Specifically, the NKC is charged with advising the Prime Minister on policy issues and reforms needed to make India even more competitive in the knowledge industry. In the education sector, reform ideas were solicited in areas of research and intellectual property legislation. The idea of institutionalizing a sort of "sensor" for national development promises to pay dividends as India competes in the new global economy.

China

While China has become a 21st-century economic power, it is still nevertheless a developing nation, using education in a systematic fashion to design and promote its visions of the future. As the world's largest Communist nation, China has made dramatic changes in its national institutions since the repudiation of the Cultural Revolution (1966–1976). By tying the advancement of education to the goal of economic modernization, China has demonstrated competence in social engineering using curriculum planning. The Chinese government has understood, from its earliest days, the power of education.

As a nation, China houses one fifth of the world's population in a country 17 times larger than France. Since 1950, literacy among the young and middle aged population has risen from 20% to nearly 95%. The country now offers nine years of compulsory education to all youth, with elementary and junior high school enrollment at nearly 95% of those eligible.

China's education system is dedicated to five purposes:

1. Developing good moral character
2. Developing love of the motherland
3. Literacy and intellectual development
4. Healthy bodies
5. Interest in aesthetics

China began the modernization of its educational system following the death of leader Mao Zedong. In 1978, leader Deng Xioping outlined the four modernizations that included agriculture, industry, technology, and defense. These four areas were projected to make China a great economic power by the early 21st century. This planning commitment would require great advances in science and technology that, in turn, required a revamped education system. Because higher education in China had been "shut down" during the Cultural Revolution, education at most levels had to be redesigned. Creating a system to serve 69 million students, representing 56 ethnic groups, with most living in rural areas was a challenge; a vast and varied school system was called for. Over 800,000 primary schools have been established or reestablished in the nation since 1978.

Over a period of two decades, the curriculum in the People's Republic of China was made universal, attendance for nine years of schooling compulsory, and an examination system to insure quality was installed. Vocational and technical schools were also established as part of the "two-legs" policy.

Governance of education in China rests with the national authorities, but management of local programs has always been a role for the local Communist Party in each community. In terms of curriculum work, these local members oversee expenditures, hire teachers, establish rules, develop curricula plans, and organize activities in the community. Moral training may also be conducted under the supervision of Party members.

Children may begin pre-primary school in China at age 3½ years. They enter primary school at age 7 and attend 5 days a week, 9.5 months per year. The Primary curriculum includes Chinese, mathematics, physical education, music, art, and instruction in nature, morals, and society. Students are expected to do work around the school grounds. Teamwork, love of the country, selflessness, love of the Party, and respect are stressed. A foreign language, usually English, is introduced in the third grade.

Chinese and mathematics, the "Big 2," account for 60% of class learning time. Morality and ethics are subjects mandated by the Minister of Education.

If China has had a secret approach to such a rapid development of its high quality education programs, it would be found in the exams, key schools, and study abroad policies. Exams are used to sift the vast population and establish quality controls in desired areas such as math and technology. The reestablishment of "key schools" means that some schools receive superior resources and may recruit superior students. Finally, because the school population is so large, China has effectively used overseas institutions of higher education to train many of their leaders. Nearly 20,000 students, for example, study in the United States each year for advanced and specialized academic training. When finished, they return home to China.

In 2010, China unveiled a new 10-year plan to promote what is being called a "learning society." The plan promises universal pre-school education and a modern system that will make China rich in terms of human resources. The plan also promises to rid the nation of illiteracy among the young and middle age groups by 2020.

Implementation of the educational reform plan will follow the already-established Five Year Plans (FYP), and will be under the direct supervision of the Central Committee of the Communist Party of China (CPC). Already, the Central Committee has ordered local parties to engineer desired changes.

DEVELOPED NATIONS

In the developed industrial world, a number of nations have moved beyond simply tying education to national destiny and are, in addition, attempting to fully adjust to the forces of the 21st century. The question for these nations is "where do we go from here?" Singapore, France, Japan, Scotland, and the United States are sample nations at this level of development.

Singapore

Singapore, an island nation located just south of Malaysia, is best known in education for its world-class test scores. Granted independence in 1965, Singapore has become the leader in mathematics achievement following implementation of a four-step plan for development.

In the beginning, like other developing nations, this small nation struggled to survive and to create a unitary education system. Once established, the nation's education system improved efficiency, implemented tracks so that technically trained persons would provide for further national development, and established close ties to industry.

Using these connections and planning avenues, Singapore focused on communication technologies and the upgrading of teaching capacity. Finally, in recent years, Singapore has made education a collaborative effort between business and education.

Singapore schools are conducted in English—thought to be the world language for commerce. Control of schools is under the direction of the Ministry of Education which allocates funding from a national budget that dedicates approximately 20% to education.

France

The French trace the roots of their education system to the time of Charlemagne (742–814 A.D.), and the modern form of *lécole republicane* (Republican School) to the 1880s when mandatory attendance to age 15 was enacted by the Minister of Public Education. The French education system today serves 15 million students and the nation boasts a literacy of 99 % throughout the country. The dropout rate in France is less than 20% of those who attend secondary education. Higher education is free.

The three-tier French system (primary, secondary, tertiary) is a national system, free to all, and all teachers are civil servants of the nation. Thirty-five "academies" (like states) administered the education programs. All schools follow a common calendar, and secondary school (lycée) is dominated by passing exams to earn the "baccalaureat." The exam, covering mastery of eight or nine areas, is required for graduation and is used also for college entrance.

In a word, France has a highly traditional system of education, based on knowing and examinations, which is both stable and copied by developing countries throughout the world. French education produces quality scholars and has high educational attainment. But in France, there is unease because this system that has served the nation so well for centuries is failing to prepare the nation for a technological future and a global economy. Unemployment and underemployment are problems, and the large number of recent immigrants to France also seem outside of the process, in terms of successful school performance. Many citizens of the nation wonder if their schools are still doing a good job.

Japan

Education was an essential tool for Japan following World War II. Superimposing an American model of educating on the traditional Japanese society produced a highly efficient hybrid educational system for nearly 40 years. Today, Japan educates more than 90% of the school age population through high school and enrolls about 2.5 million students in colleges and universities. International tests scores in Japan are among the highest in the world.

Traditional Japanese education employed Buddhist and Confucian teachings adopted from China in the 6th century. Scholars were developed through a rigorous examination system (merit), but the system was sometimes "compromised" by various power groups. During the late 19th century, foreign scholars were imported to add academic emphasis at the university level and in military academies. Soon after, such scholars were sent away, and the Japanese system became closed. Following the defeat of Japan in World War II, reforms were made in education to "democratize" the system.

Japan maintains a three-tier system of elementary, middle, and high school. Schools run year-round on a trimester system with a minimum of 210 days. Oddly, despite extensive examinations, students are not grouped by ability, and the curriculum is balanced (broad) rather than narrow.

Japan has always sought to instill respect for the society and an orderly life. Schools stress diligence, organized study habits, and self-criticism. Correct attitudes and moral development (character development) are standard in all schools. Critical thinking is not a concept that is highly valued in Japan.

The curriculum, until recently, has been textbook-dominated and test directed. Students start serious study in pre-school, attend "cram schools" on their own, and compete under highly competitive conditions for success. Such competitive conditions have led to problems such as bullying (Ijime), general violence in schools, and the need for increased disciplinary activity. Many reports of declining respect for teachers in Japan are found in the literature of Japanese education.

As a developed nation with a powerful economy, Japan seeks to transition from a model of education such as that found in the 1980s that "fed" talent to corporations to a newer model of education that taps into the skills and talents of all people. A very flat economy in the 1990s, however, left many citizens believing that the education was failing the nation. Economic conditions in the early 21st century have placed further pressure on educational leaders in that nation. How to tie the schools to the new global economy and to absorb the relentless pressures of the many new communication technologies are immediate concerns for Japanese educators. Relevance of the curriculum and the governance role of the Ministry of Education are also constant educational issues.

Scotland

Scotland has a long history of providing universal public education to its citizens. The Scottish Education Act of 1696 established the first national system of education in the world. Education became compulsory for all children between ages 5 and 13 in 1872. Literacy among men and women in Scotland is 99%. Today, children in Scotland may attend nursery school at age 3, start primary school between ages 4 and 5, remain in primary school for seven years, and then spend 4–6 years in secondary school.

The curriculum of the secondary school is rigorous but distinctively broad compared to other developed nations. Religious education, for example, is mandatory for all public school students. Practical subjects such as computer usage, technical studies, and drama are woven into the total offering. The purpose of the curriculum for students between ages 3–18 is "to enable all children and young people to become successful learners, confident individuals, responsible citizens, and effective contributors to society and at work." Schools in Scotland are owned and operated by local authorities.

Upon completion of secondary school, students in Scotland take examinations to qualify for higher education. Higher education in Scotland has been established for centuries, and it is characterized as being more broad than English, Welsh, and Irish systems. Early entry into college is possible for "advanced highers."

Scotland, like other developed nations, is struggling to adjust to a post-industrial world economy, and has suffered high unemployment for years. In 2002, the Scottish Executive (national offices) opened a "national debate on education" to further define the curriculum. Defining values, establishing principles for curriculum design, and defining curriculum levels more closely have structured this on-going national discussion. Each year a national "Learning Festival" is held in Glasgow, attended by every teacher and educational leader, to stimulate new thinking about schooling.

Much of the discussion about education in Scotland has been concerned with how education matches up with the national economy and the new global economy. One primary initiative resulting from these talks has been a decision to develop a closer relationship with the People's Republic of China. A new language emphasis in school and an increased exchange program is laying a foundation between the nations. In the mind of Scottish officials, some European nations will become "favored" trade partners with the emerging economy of China, and Scotland would like to be in such a role in the future.

The United States

The United States of America possesses an educational system envied by much of the world. Without question, it has been the dominant education system during the whole of the 20th century. Now, however, Americans are struggling to confront unflattering test scores and a disconnect between school and work. The country has not embraced technological delivery of the curriculum. Like other nations, the United States is attempting to reform its system.

From this nation's earliest days, Americans have been providing educational services as a right of citizenship. Public education operates from the primary through graduate school with taxpayer support and a budget approaching 1.5 trillion dollars. Each year, each student in the United States public school system is funded at over 10,000 U.S. dollars. American educators operate with one of the world's most wealthy support systems.

During the 19th century, American educators built a significant infrastructure for free and universal education through grade 12. Additionally, a massive public system of higher education was established and developed, complementing a private university system. In the 20th century, most work in curriculum was concerned with adapting a traditional content curriculum to a diverse student population. Despite numerous challenges, American schools have adjusted to change and provided all students with a high quality educational experience.

American education is quite unique in the world in its general design of decentralized control. Education, according to the American Constitution, is a residual right reserved for the individual states. There is no "national" curriculum, and most operational resources are provided from state and local sources. While similar, each state has the right to define education as they wish as long as the curriculum does not violate the rights of all citizens as defined by the U.S Constitution (primarily the First and Fourteenth Amendments).

America's planning for education has always been futuristic and, beginning in the 1960s, the literature on education in the United States began to project dramatic social changes to come by the 21st century. In the subsequent 50-year period, the United States has changed immensely because of wars, the onset of new technologies, immigration patterns, and the new global economy. By 1980, many serious calls for the reform of schools in the United States began (see Chapter 8).

Over a 15-year-period from 1980–1995, numerous public and private commissions met and wrote reports calling for a more direct and responsive education system. Schools were generally perceived as obsolete, expensive, inefficient, divisive, irrelevant, racist, and a host of other unpleasant things. The early call by the business community in America for reform encouraged state legislatures to develop new curricula, standards of achievement, and tests measuring outcomes. These changes were instituted, and school learning became more highly focused.

Unfortunately, the issues of excellence and equity are not so easily compatible. An odd pattern emerged placing academic rigor side-by-side with compensatory programs. Budgets were oddly skewed by special pleading from various pressure groups and legal mandates from the courts. Legislators hopped in and out with demands for political-ticket items like charter schools and teaching religious beliefs in the classroom.

Just at a time when true reform seemed within the reach of American educators, the Internet became a public instrument (May 1995) and began to challenge most basic assumptions about how education is conducted. As the world economy became global, defining the curriculum in schools became much more difficult. The cost of implementing a transition to new technologies in schools was difficult, even for the largest economy on Earth. Local schools, under state supervision, simply did not have the "vision" to absorb the many changes confronting them. As early as 2005, technology use in the United States schools began to decline, and the thrust to connect American students to the outside world diminished.

As in all of the other developed nations on Earth, the decisions that the United States is making about education today will define its immediate economic future. We are living tomorrow's past. While America has achieved the world's highest computer penetration in schools, there has been a total institutional failure to see the Internet as an innovative curriculum delivery device. An instrument that can individualize learning for each and every student continues to be utilized, in most schools, like a substitute teacher. Any effort to activate learning, and apply it to work in the new global economy, will necessitate a complete redesign of the curriculum and its delivery system in the United States. Ironically, 80% of all educational expenses in American school systems fund facilities and teachers salaries. New technologies in schools could free up significant national resources for other pressing needs.

In addition to becoming "modern," schools in the United States must continue to be responsive to one of the world's most diverse cultures. Each subgroup in the United

States has its own set of aspirations for schools, and curriculum leaders must find ways to re-define the schooling experience to satisfy all clients. Failure to do so will certainly lead to additional lawful challenges to tax support for schools, and an increase in the trend to fund private education, homeschooling, charter schools, and proprietary education outlets. The schools operate in an "open system," and decisions must be both thoughtful and backed by logic.

The current effort to implement a Common Core of standards is America's response to national planning found in the schools of other countries. Positive results of centralized planning in places like Singapore and India are observable. Whether this Common Core effort in the United States can maintain momentum is in question as of this writing, due to the high costs associated with securing appropriate technologies. Only 43 states are on board, as of this writing. It is likely others will disconnect before 2015.

There can be no doubt that the Common Core initiative is extremely important to the United States, its economy, and to the quality of life for its citizens. It is unfortunate that so much of the decision making that has led up to this initiative has been based on commerce rather than education.

Finally, your author believes it may be necessary to amend the United States Constitution in order to redefine the role of the national government in reforming education. While there is some safety in a broken-front approach to change in education, whether it is led by state government or selected businesses, the stakes are entirely too high to leave educational design to chance. The very destiny of the nation rests on a solution for tying the educational process—the curriculum—to the world of work. Without greater control, the federal government can only observe and support schools with earmarked monies.

IN REVIEW

In reviewing how underdeveloped, developing, and developed nation are using education to create their preferred future, it appears that there may be at least three distinct stages of design and decision making. In underdeveloped nations, most effort goes into creating a basic structure for promoting literacy in the population. In this majority of all nations, planners are simply trying to find resources to build schools, train teachers, and secure learning resources. Such efforts are often disrupted by famine, war, or general instability in the governance structure of the nation-at-large. Without intervention, such nations will first establish an elite path in education and then struggle to do what can be done for the general population. Literacy is the first general goal, whether it is designed to foster religion, civic behavior, or political ends.

The developing nations, such as South Africa, India, Vietnam, and China, often have to restructure education following turmoil. It is noteworthy that all of these countries are young in comparison to the most developed nations. In the case of these four examples, there are major success stories as the "lift and take-off" (Rostow, 1960; Boulding, 1966) occurs. Buildings are built, teachers are trained, literacy rises, and the general structure of an educational "system" emerges as resources are applied. In the case of China (Key Schools), South Africa (Focus Schools), and India (technology sectors), there is obvious excellence in spots as the "bathtub is slowly filling up." These nations are bunching resources for specific goal attainment, and they are moving forward.

Developing nations are often handicapped in structuring their systems by variables such as especially poor regions (South Africa), traditions of class and caste (India), sheer scale (China and India), religious or political beliefs (Vietnam), or governance issues (Pakistan). The great advantage for these nations who are still in the process of developing their educational programs is their flexibility; they can adapt as they go forward. They are not so invested in comparison to developed nations. Efforts can be "bunched" for greater effect in dealing with special populations or needs. In these nations, there is time and opportunity to think "outside of the box" (Vietnam and Brazil technological delivery).

The developed nations of the world, small in numbers and large in influence, face a totally different problem in re-programming education for a preferred future. These nations invested heavily in infrastructure and processes that cannot be easily reversed. Education in the United States, for instance, is an institution about 15 times larger than the military. Things that are being done today have often been done in the same manner for generations. The logistics of any large-scale change are burdensome. In addition, social commitments to human rights and Constitutional guarantees tie the hands of policy makers, particularly in democracies. The systems are fixed, committed, and inflexible.

Ironically, a special kind of problem for developed nations today is that their education systems have served them so well in the past. Japan, for instance, has recorded some of the highest student achievement in the world with its "hybrid" system of organization and procedure. The decline in whatever efficiency exists in the Japanese system is, ultimately, a result of its success. Being able to connect learners with the new world economy, instill traditional values, and solve governance issues will require more than tinkering for all such developed nations.

France presents a stunning case-study of a nation at the pinnacle of knowledge-based education at a time when knowledge is too abundant. Like many of the world's developed systems, France is running a system developed in another age, for a different future. The superior academics that the schools produce find that employment is elusive beyond the world of school. The graduates will have to unlearn, in the words of Carl Rogers, in order to participate in a rapidly changing and technological environment.

The United States has many of these same problems. While operating the most expensive system of education in the world, American schools suffer lower-than-expected achievement and are grossly inefficient. Efforts to foster academic excellence are in competition with equality issues in the public schools. Currently, there really is no substantive connection in the United States between the schooling process and working in the new global economy. There is no answer, at present, for the issue dealing with the new and large immigrant populations. And, there is very little understanding of how the sea of new technology in the United States can be used to curb costs and tailor learning to special purposes. In short, there is no national vision, the starting place for a nation's development.

In smaller but nonetheless developed nations, like Scotland and the Cayman Islands, one can see the opportunity to make significant adjustments in shorter periods of time and at less cost to the systems. Scotland can call together every teacher and educational leader each year at a Learning Festival in Glasgow (SETT) to discuss policy and priorities in that nation. The simple application of resources to a priority program (linking to China) can be done without great effort. Similarly, the Cayman Islands can use its size and wealth to an advantage by adopting technological delivery of its curriculum;

there is no longer a penalty for being geographically isolated in today's new interactive education world.

The emerging hierarchy of curriculum tasks for educators throughout the world is tied directly to the purposes of the educational systems they serve. In the beginning, precious resources must be collected to build a foundation of buildings and teachers and materials. Such a beginning program strives to promote literacy of its population. Further development of this literacy might be defined by political, civic, or religious purposes.

Following achievement of a foundational literacy, however, the nation will tend to direct learning to the traditional patterns of scholarship, following models provided by historic 19th century systems such as that of France or England. The more pragmatic systems such as those found in the United States, Japan, or the former Soviet Union can also guide development. These models present the developing nation with a tested way of proceeding. Unfortunately, the paths offered from the most established countries are costly and possibly obsolete.

Finally, both the developing and the developed nations face the task of defining their country's values and tailoring the basic programs to those ends. When a country's citizens begin to understand that education is the tool to create the preferred future, they begin to organize their education systems for action (see Figure 10.1).

Their vision of the changes being experienced in the 21st century will determine their success in moving toward a future.

---

1. Borrow resources and secure grants to meet change (underdeveloped nations).
2. Export graduate students and import foreign scholars.
3. Form multi-nation partnerships.
4. Provide for heavy expenditures (GNP share) on education.
5. Upgrade teaching capacity.
6. Incorporate extensive applications of technology in schools.
7. Create a standards commissions.
8. Create a national education "think tank."
9. Emphasize examinations to discover/develop talent.
10. Create technical support systems for education.
11. Establish principles and specifications for curriculum design.
12. Involve professional societies in planning education.
13. Encourage business and education partnerships.
14. Form umbrella groups of participating agencies.
15. Focus on STEM subjects.
16. Create multi-year education development plans.
17. Legislate education development policies.
18. Encourage diaspora (world networks of nationals).
19. Bunch resources for special purposes.
20. Cluster academics and create academic "parks."
21. Create special schools (Key schools, Focus schools).
22. Encourage local control of curriculum development.
23. Support and fund compensatory efforts.
24. Redefine national education standards.
25. Employ a "broken-front" development strategy.

FIGURE 10.1 Twenty-Five Strategies for Educational Reform in the Global Era

EXTRAPOLATION TO LOCAL CONDITIONS

The reader will note that as your author speaks of nations (macro level) and their efforts to use education to shape their destiny, the same explanations could be used to describe the efforts of community schools and state education programs at home (micro level). It is obvious that in most of the world's nations, it is often a struggle to just simply construct and maintain a universal education system regardless of the curriculum. This is also true in most of the school districts of the United States. The number of school systems with the time and resources to plan for the future is small.

As schools and districts develop beyond an infrastructure, their values and priorities will determine which programs, from many possibilities, are given the most support. Many districts in the United States have "show schools" or "model programs" while maintaining an otherwise average curriculum in other schools. Such curriculum preferences can trigger issues of local governance and control, leading to general instability and frequent changes in leadership. Like the underdeveloped and developing and developed nations described in this chapter, school districts are regularly interrupted in their work by events and crises. Only leadership can keep them on their path to improvement.

But in the study of the great curriculum programs, whether at the school, community, state, or national level, those educational agencies with a vision emerge and are universally superior. Clarity of values, or philosophy if you prefer, is the critical element to an otherwise mechanical and deductive process of curriculum development. Clarification of purpose is the most important task in curriculum work.

If nations, like India and China and South Africa, can "bunch" their resources for special effects, so can local schools, districts, and states. The price of such a development strategy must always be weighed against the critical values promoted by the schools. Egalitarian values within democratic nations like the United States make favored programs or uneven strategies much more difficult. Gaining balance in this area, that is, promoting purposeful change while safeguarding fairness, is the immediate task for the United States.

Once schools become established with a full array of resources and programs, leaders must look ahead to assess the effect (not efficiency) of their efforts. The premise of this chapter—that the organization of education determines its ability to promote specific kinds of learning—poses a challenge to all educational leaders. We must design our curriculum carefully, so that it serves our students fully. We must have a shared vision of the preferred future. We must follow a timeworn path to reach our goals.

Summary

Education is a critical function in local, state, and national development. When the curriculum is visionary and accurate, the community, state, or nation is well served. By contrast, a faulty or dysfunctional educational program can threaten the well-being of any educational agency or nation. The manner in which education is organized, based on its vision or purpose, will determine the kind of learning that can take place within a country. And, this learning will determine the kind of citizens a country will have in the future.

This chapter has used national education reform (the macro level) to illustrate the sequential process of improving education. In this new global age, all nations are acting to adjust to novel conditions, and can be compared by how they answer four traditional curriculum questions. The same is true of local schools in your communities.

Activities

ACTIVITY 10.1

Discuss the probable scenario for the Common Core reform in the United States if funding of technology is a dominant issue.

ACTIVITY 10.2

Describe the relationship of culture and vision to the curriculum development process in the nations of the world.

 Click here to take an automatically-graded self-check quiz.

Additional Reading

Association for Supervision and Curriculum Development. (2012). "International Models of Excellence & Innovation," in World Class Education. Alexandria, Virginia: ASCD.

Boulding, K. (1956, April). General systems theory, management science, 2, 3. *General Systems, Yearbook of the Society for General Systems Research (1)*, 197–208.

Boulding, K. (1964). The stages of economic growth. In *The meaning of the twentieth century: The great transition*. New York, NY: Harper & Row.

Countries discussed within the chapter:
* Cayman Islands: see www.brighterfutures.gov.ky
* India—National Knowledge Commission: see http://knowledgecommission.gov.in
* Scotland—Scotland Learning Festival: see http://www.educationscotland.gov.uk, http://www.Itscotland.org.uk/curriculumforexcellence/whatisscfe/values.asp
* Vietnam: see Jamieson, N. (1995). *Understanding Vietnam*. Berkeley, CA: University of California Press.

Evans, Richard. (1995). *Deng Xiaoping and the making of modern China*. London, England: Penguin Books.

Hsu, Immanual. (2000). *The rise of modern China* (6th ed.). New York, NY: Oxford University Press.

Kem, V. (2004, September). *Wireless technology for bridging the digital divide in developing countries*. Cambodia: Ministry of Posts and Telecommunications.

Ministry of Education and Training. *Education development strategy 2001–2010*. 49 Dai Co Viet Street, Hanoi.

Rostow, W. (1960). *Economics analysis: Microeconomics*. New York, NY: Harper & Row.

Sarwar, Zakia. *Still terminally ill*. Retrieved from http://www.himalmag.com

Xinhau News Agency. (2010, May 6). China's cabinet approves education reform plan. *China Daily*.

RESOURCES

RESOURCE A

Key Organizations Affecting Curriculum Development

CITIZENS' ORGANIZATIONS

National Coalition for Children and Families
800 Compton Road, Suite 9224
Cincinnati, OH 45231
513-521-6227
www.nsvrc.org

National Congress of Parents and Teachers
541 North Fairbanks Court, Suite 1300
Chicago, IL 60611-3396
800-307-4782
www.pta.org

CONTENT STANDARDS ORGANIZATIONS

Arts

Music Educators National Conference
1806 Robert Fulton Drive, Suite 1
Reston, VA 20191
703-860-4000
www.menc.org

Civics and Government

Center for Civic Education
5145 Douglas Fir Road
Calabasas, CA 91302-1467
800-350-4223
www.civiced.org

Economics

National Council on Economic Education
1140 Avenue of the Americas
New York, NY 10036
212-730-7007
www.nationalcouncil.org

English Language Arts

National Council of Teachers of English
1111 West Kenyon Road
Urbana, IL 61801
877-369-6283
www.ncte.org

International Reading Association
800 Barksdale Road
P.O. Box 8139
Newark, DE 19714-8139
800-336-7323, ext. 266
www.reading.org

Foreign Languages

American Council on the Teaching of Foreign Languages
6 Executive Plaza
Yonkers, NY 10701-6801
914-963-8830
www.actfl.org

Geography

National Council for Geographic Education
Jacksonville State University
206A Martin Hall
Jacksonville, AL 36265-1602
256-782-5293
www.ncge.org

Mathematics

National Council of Teachers of Mathematics
1906 Association Drive
Reston, VA 20191
703-620-9840
www.nctm.org

Physical Education

National Association for Sport and Physical Education
1900 Association Drive
Reston, VA 20191
703-476-3410
www.aahperd.org

Science

National Science Education Standards
National Academies Press
500 Fifth Street NW
Washington, DC 20055
800-624-6242
www.nap.edu

Benchmarks for Science Literacy
American Association for the Advancement of Science
NW 1200 New York Avenue
Washington, DC 20005
202-326-6400
www.aaas.org

Skill Standards

U.S. Department of Labor
Office of Policy and Research
200 Constitution Avenue NW
Washington, DC 20210
866-487-2365
www.dol.gov

U.S. Department of Education
Office of Vocational and Adult Education
APR 400 Maryland Avenue SW
Washington, DC 20202-7100
202-245-7700
www.ed.gov/ovae

Social Studies

National Council for the Social Studies
8555 16th Street, Suite 500
Silver Spring, MD 20910
301-588-1800
www.socialstudies.org

EDUCATIONALLY RELATED ORGANIZATIONS AND ASSOCIATIONS

American Association for Higher Education
1 Dupont Circle NW, Suite 360
Washington, DC 20036
202-293-6440
www.aahe.org

American Association of School Administrators
801 North Quincy Street, Suite 700
Arlington, VA 22203-1730
703-528-0700
www.aasa.org

American Council on Education
1 Dupont Circle NW
Washington, DC 20036
202-939-9300
www.acenet.edu

American Educational Research Association
1230 17th Street NW
Washington, DC 20036
202-223-9485
www.area.net

American Association for Vocational Instructional Materials
220 Smithonia Road
Winterville, GA 30683
1-800-228-4689
www.aavim.com

Association for Supervision and Curriculum Development (ASCD)
1703 North Beauregard Street
Alexandria, VA 22311-1714
703-578-9600
www.ascd.org

Children's Television Workshop
1 Lincoln Plaza, Floor 2
New York, NY 10023
212-595-3456
www.ctw.org

College Entrance Examination Board
45 Columbus Avenue
New York, NY 10023
212-713-7700
www.collegeboard.org

Council for American Private Education
13017 Wisteria Drive, #457
Germantown, MD 20874
301-916-8460
www.capenet.org

Council of Chief State School Officers
1 Massachusetts Avenue NW, Suite 700
Washington, DC 20001-1431
202-336-7000
www.ccsso.org

National Art Education Association
1916 Association Drive
Reston, VA 20191-1590
703-860-8000
www.naea-reston.org

National Association for the Education of Young Children
1509 16th Street NW
Washington, DC 20036
202-232-8777
www.naeyc.org

National Association of Elementary School Principals
1615 Duke Street
Alexandria, VA 22314
800-386-2377
www.naesp.org

American Association for Adult and Continuing Education
10111 Martin Luther King, Jr. Highway
Suite 200 C
Bowie, MD 20720
301-459-6261
www.aaace.org

National Association of Secondary School Principals
1904 Association Drive
Reston, VA 20191-1537
703-860-0200
www.nassp.org

National Council of Teachers of English
1111 West Kenyon Road
Urbana, IL 61801-1096
877-369-6283 or 217-328-3870
www.ncte.org

National Council of Teachers of Mathematics
1906 Association Drive
Reston, VA 20191-1502
703-620-9840
www.nctm.org

National Education Association
1201 16th Street NW
Washington, DC 20036-3290
202-833-4000
www.nea.org

National Middle School Association
4151 Executive Parkway, Suite 300
Westerville, OH 43081
800-528-6672
www.nmsa.org

National School Boards Association
1680 Duke Street
Alexandria, VA 22314
703-838-6722
www.nsba.org

National Science Teachers Association
1840 Wilson Boulevard
Arlington, VA 22201-3000
703-243-7100
www.nsta.org

Ethnic and Minority Organizations

National Council of Negro Women, Inc.
633 Pennsylvania Avenue NW
Washington, DC 20004
202-737-0120
www.ncnw.com

National Indian Education Association
110 Maryland Avenue NE, Suite 104
Washington, DC 20002
202-544-7290
www.niea.org

National Organization for Women (NOW)
1100 H Street NW
Washington, DC 20001
202-628-8669
www.now.org

FEDERAL BODIES

House of Representatives
Washington, DC 20515
202-224-3121
www.house.gov

National Institute of Science Education
NIH Office of Science Education
6100 Executive Blvd., Suite 3E01
MSC 7520
Bethesda, MD 20892-7520
301-402-2469
http://science.education.nih.gov

National Science Foundation
4201 Wilson Boulevard
Arlington, VA 22230
703-292-5111
www.nsf.gov

U.S. Department of Education
400 Maryland Avenue SW
Washington, DC 20202-7100
1-800-USA-LEARN (1-800-872-5327)
www.ed.gov

U.S. Senate
Washington, DC 20510
202-224-3121
www.senate.gov

GENERAL ASSOCIATIONS

Committee for Economic Development
2000 L Street NW
Washington, DC 20036
800-676-7353
www.ced.org

National Association of Manufacturers
Economic Development Department
1331 Pennsylvania Avenue NW
Washington, DC 20004-1790
202-637-3000
www.nam.org

National Urban League
120 Wall Street
New York, NY 10005
212-558-5300
www.nul.org

LABOR ORGANIZATIONS

American Federation of Teachers
555 New Jersey Avenue NW
Washington, DC 20001
202-879-4400
www.aft.org

PUBLISHERS

Association of American Publishers
71 Fifth Avenue, 2nd Floor
New York, NY 10003-3004
212-255-0200
www.publishers.org

RESOURCE B

Additional Practice Applications

In this appendix, you get to test your understanding of the material found in the various chapters. Each of the chapter summaries is followed by practice applications used by your author in his curriculum classes.

CHAPTER 1: CURRICULUM DEVELOPMENT IN A GLOBAL AGE

This chapter reviews the past in terms of history, procedures, and definitions of curriculum. History is reviewed in terms of an evolutionary era, a modern era, and a postmodern era. Five foundations for curriculum planning are presented. The new age of curriculum is presented in terms of issues and impediments.

ACTIVITY 1.1

React to the following statement regarding the use of knowledge as the basis of curriculum:

> There is no way that the instantaneous retrieval of all information can be filtered or controlled. The boundaries of our understanding, in all fields, have been overrun; there is neither scope nor sequence to the new information age. In addition, the multimedia integration of concepts, facts, images, data, and sound create meanings in ways that even Marshall McLuhan and Quentin Fiore (1967) could not have envisioned. We are awash in knowledge, and there is no end in sight to the avalanche of new information.
>
> The technologists tell us that the speed and volume of knowledge acquisition is going to increase geometrically. Computer chips will carry the volume of all organized knowledge in smaller, even molecular, sizes. Digitized information, information broken down into bits, will fly across the earth in wireless forms. Knowledge will be accessible to anyone through receivers disguised as jewelry. Voice recognition technology will eliminate keyboards, and data storage will be external. These are not dreams or Dick Tracy–like fantasies. Rather, these products are already in the development stage.

ACTIVITY 1.2

In closing Chapter 1, the author identified old curriculum issues that are still relevant to the new technological age. Are there also new issues, never before seen, that result from the entry of the new technologies into American life? *Identify these new curriculum issues.*

CHAPTER 2: PHILOSOPHY AND CURRICULUM DESIGN

Curriculum work begins with a set of beliefs about purpose. When formalized, we refer to such beliefs as *philosophies*. The field of curriculum always addresses value-laden philosophical questions before initiating the development process. Five common families of philosophy were presented in Chapter 2, and 15 observable variables are described for identifying philosophies in school practice.

ACTIVITY 2.1

Using the 15-point School Assessment Worksheet (Figure 2.23) found in your text on page 69, *visit a real school and "type" the philosophy* using the measures of structure–flexibility found in Chapter 2 in Figures 2.1 to 2.22. With your classmates, compare the different "designs" that you find. In your school, which items seem inconsistent with the others?

ACTIVITY 2.2

Attempt to *connect educational philosophy with some of the issues and practices found in schools today.* For example, which philosophies might support ability grouping? Cooperative learning? Whole-language reading? High-stakes testing? The Common Core State Standards? How would you summarize these relationships?

ACTIVITY 2.3

Curriculum designs can be thought of as patterns of activity in a school. How would an "open education" school differ from a standards-based school according to the 15 dimensions of structure–flexibility? *Identify the principle to be applied.*

CHAPTER 3: FOUNDATIONS OF CURRICULUM PLANNING

Curriculum development is a deductive process that occurs after the philosophy (purpose) has been determined. The deductive logic of curriculum development progresses from the philosophy to goals, then to objectives, and finally ends with focused lesson plans in the classroom. This process can be envisioned according to the curriculum cycle: analyze, design, implement, and evaluate.

ACTIVITY 3.1

Write a behavioral objective that places the student's learning at Level 3 cognitive domain and Level 3 affective domain. What does this objective suggest about the role of the teacher and the role of the student in the classroom for this activity?

ACTIVITY 3.2

Respond to the author's observation that the Internet challenges the traditional and sequential logic of curriculum development. If this is true, then what is the curriculum development process in the information age?

CHAPTER 4: LARGE SCALE CURRICULUM DEVELOPMENT

Standards are pervasive in today's schools and contribute to focusing the curriculum. Mandated standards create "curriculum systems" that constrain all teaching toward mastery of the standards. If the curriculum becomes unbalanced by top-down standards and high-stakes testing, the curriculum can be rebalanced at the classroom level by emphasizing methods that address larger outcome goals. The curriculum development process and public input to what is taught in schools are threatened by special-interest standards that are formed in a highly politicized atmosphere.

ACTIVITY 4.1

Review online the 1983 report A Nation at Risk http://www2.ed.gov/pubs/NatAtRisk to determine what evidence was provided to support the assertion that our schools were a "rising tide of mediocrity."

ACTIVITY 4.2

E. D. Hirsch, in his book *Cultural Literacy,* has developed a list of things that all American students should know to be "culturally literate." *Review Hirsch's book to determine the criteria for inclusion and exclusion on this list* (www.goodreads.com/book/show/76884). What person(s) or group(s) should have the authority to create such a mandate?

CHAPTER 5: CURRICULUM DEVELOPMENT IN SCHOOLS

The traditional classroom relationship between teacher and student has been altered by the new interactive technologies. Your author suggests that the traditional behavioral learning theory found in schools may soon give way to constructivist approaches. Teachers are the key to any new curriculum development efforts at the classroom level, and curriculum leaders must begin to see teachers as leaders in any such process. Specific acts that would lead to such a transformation were suggested.

ACTIVITY 5.1

Develop a job description for a teacher who will teach in schools using new technologies. Of these attributes, which do you think are the most important for successful classroom teaching?

ACTIVITY 5.2

Teachers as leaders means that classroom teaching bridges the gap between school knowledge and Internet resources. Visit two of the following websites and try to *determine the unique features of the "electronic frontier"*:

Blueweb'n   http://www.kn.pacbell.com/wired/blueweb'n

Gateway   http://www.thegateway.org

Kathy Schrock	http://schooldiscovery.com/schrockguide/
PBS Teachersource	http://www.pbs.org/teachersource
Tappedin	http://www.tappedin.org
21st Century	http://1p.21ct.org

ACTIVITY 5.3

Nathan Shedroff's (2001) model of understanding includes noise, data, information, knowledge, and wisdom. In this conception, *data* are simply dispersed elements, *information* is data in patterns, *knowledge* is validated information, and *wisdom* is knowledge integrated into daily life. Develop a theory explaining how technology can help teachers move up this scale.

CHAPTER 6: CURRICULUM DEVELOPMENT AND THE NEW TECHNOLOGIES

Technology is altering our society as we discover new ways to live, learn, and work. Schools have been slow to adopt (i.e., not purchase) technology, and there are signs of decline, defection, and even attacks on our schools. Curriculum leaders must understand the paradigm shift that has occurred and work with teachers to transform our schools. Traditional and nontraditional views of the education process were presented.

ACTIVITY 6.1

Your school district has just created a new position, Director of Instructional Technology, and is advertising for a nontechnical curriculum person to lead the integration of new technologies in the classroom. You have been invited to apply, and you have been given the following structuring questions. *Prepare your answers for the interview session.*

1. How do you define *education,* and what is the role of technology in teaching and learning?
2. Which technologies do you prefer using to enhance learning in the school district?
3. If you had a budget of $5 million for technology, how would you allocate such resources?
4. How would you approach the problem of getting teachers to use technology in the classroom?
5. What issues would you anticipate in incorporating technology into the instructional process in the district?
6. How long do you anticipate it will take to implement technology-driven instruction in the district?
7. How would you evaluate your efforts to implement technology in the schools?
8. What questions would you wish to ask the board about this new initiative?

ACTIVITY 6.2

Policy has been defined as "a matter of the authoritative allocation of values" (Easton, 1990). *What policies would you pursue* if you were in charge of implementing the new technologies in schools?

ACTIVITY 6.3

In moving schools toward the future, *write a curriculum development* plan that includes the following components:

1. A scenario describing the context of the planned curriculum change
2. A description of the culture (mores, values, ways of working) in schools and how you anticipate it will affect your planned change
3. A list of the operational assumptions you are making about the change prior to activating your plan
4. General strategies (the approach) you will use in promoting your plan
5. Goals (program standards) that will be accomplished by this plan, including benchmark indicators that can be observed or assessed
6. A short description of events that will contribute to the accomplishment of each goal; these may be "clusters" of activities.
7. A timeline showing the relationship of these goals, events, and activities
8. A one-page executive summary of this effort, complete with visuals
9. References used to complete this plan

CHAPTER 7: ELEMENTARY SCHOOL PROGRAMS AND ISSUES

A new trend in intermediate education, found primarily in the large city systems of the United States, is to replace middle schools with K–8 elementary/middle or "elemiddle" schools. Although research supporting this change is scanty, it is believed that such a change will reduce discipline problems and boost achievement test scores. As a longtime leader in middle school education, your author acknowledges this change and seek to determine how these programs might be connected. A key component will be new learning standards for middle schools such as those that exist at the elementary level.

ACTIVITY 7.1

State your professional position on a community movement to replace K–5 elementary schools with a new K–8 curriculum model?

ACTIVITY 7.2

Many elementary schools are experiencing an "unbalanced curriculum" as they move toward high stakes testing. *Discuss* how you could encourage greater balance among the typical subjects in the American elementary school?

CHAPTER 8: MIDDLE SCHOOL PROGRAMS AND ISSUES

The middle school, a unique American curriculum design, has dominated intermediate education for nearly 50 years. The design has exhibited strengths and weaknesses. Many school districts, particularly in urban areas, are moving away from this design and returning to an even more historic K–8 configuration. Only time will tell whether the middle school will survive or disappear like the junior high school model.

ACTIVITY 8.1

What do you feel should be taught in the first eight grades of school? *Review the standards for kindergarten to grade 8 in your* state by visiting the state department of education webpage. Is there subject matter that could be eliminated from the curriculum? Are there topics not being taught that should be added to the curriculum?

ACTIVITY 8.2

What is the meaning of the statement that "middle schools are a human development design?"
Name 5 elements in the middle school design addressing human growth and development.

CHAPTER 9: SECONDARY SCHOOL PROGRAMS AND ISSUES

Historically, the secondary school has been a stable level of education with a traditional curriculum focused on content mastery. In the 1920s, 1940s, 1960s, and 1970s, however, there were serious efforts to reform secondary education. In the 21st century, high school and postsecondary education are being targeted for change. Technology, schools of choice, and even homeschooling are providing options for secondary students. High school courses and postsecondary education are becoming seamless as students master the curriculum and move on.

ACTIVITY 9.1

In the late 1980s and early 1990s, secondary educators were concerned with the school-to-work connection. The Department of Labor developed a list of desired skills for workers (Secretary's Commission on Achieving Necessary Skills [SCANS]). In your opinion, how well have schools made this connection between school and work in the last two decades? *Document your conclusion.*

ACTIVITY 9.2

Many secondary schools in the United States are instituting service learning to make the secondary school curriculum more relevant. Using the Internet, find examples of exemplary programs that feature service-learning requirements.

CHAPTER 10: GLOBAL PERSPECTIVES OF THE CURRICULUM PROCESS

The field of curriculum has been altered by advances in technology and the global interdependence of nations during the first decade of the 21st century. In all nations, education will be the primary response to such change, and the field of curriculum will lead their nations in designing responses to these novel conditions.

In this chapter your author provided a model of development in education that can help leaders focus resources and see the connection between schooling and national destiny. While there are many universal tasks in curriculum development, not all nations have a similar focus in designing schools.

ACTIVITY 10.1

What are the common tasks of any society in creating and operating schools? *Identify some examples* of unique tasks faced by curriculum developers in their own countries?

ACTIVITY 10.2

This chapter suggests that the most economically advanced nations must redefine the act of schooling and the definition of education. Identify the premises undergirding this observation, and what information must planners possess to be successful in redesigning the relationship between the school and their nation's needs?

ACTIVITY 10.3

Your author suggested in this chapter that it may be possible for some developing nations to skip the stage of amassing buildings, books, and teachers through the use of new technologies. In your class, *debate this premise, pro and con.*

GLOSSARY

ability grouping. Organizing pupils into homogeneous groups according to intellectual ability for instruction.

academic freedom. The right of instructors to decide the materials, methods, and content of instruction within legal and ethical parameters.

accountability. Holding schools and teachers responsible for what students learn.

accreditation. Recognition given to an educational institution that has met accepted standards applied to it by an outside agency.

achievement test. Standardized test designed to measure how much has been learned from a particular subject.

affective domain. Attitudinal and emotional areas of learning, such as values and feelings.

aligned. Term used to indicate that a school curriculum is matched with state and national standards as well as with state and national tests.

alternative education. Instructional programs that modify traditional approaches in one or more of the following areas: setting, structure, scheduling, instructional materials, curriculum development, and assessment.

alternative school. A school—public or private—that provides alternatives to the regular public school.

attribution training. Training that deals with the role of the individual's explanation for his or her own successes or failures.

balanced curriculum. A curriculum that incorporates all three areas: essential learning skills, subject content, and personal development.

behavioral approach. An approach that focuses on observable behaviors instead of on internal events such as thinking and emotions.

behavioral objective. Precise statement of what the learner must do to demonstrate mastery at the end of a prescribed learning task.

bilingual education. Educational programs in which both English-speaking and non-English-speaking students participate in a bicultural curriculum using both languages.

block scheduling. The reorganization of the daily or annual school schedule to allow students and teachers to have larger, more concentrated segments of time each day, week, or grading period on each subject. *See also* modular scheduling.

career education. Instructional activities designed to provide students with the knowledge and skill necessary for selecting a vocation as well as for making decisions regarding educational and training options.

categorical aid. Financial aid to local school districts from state or federal agencies for specific, limited purposes only.

certification. The licensure of personnel through prescribed programs of training and education.

cognition. The process of logical thinking.

cognitive domain. In Bloom's taxonomy, memory and reasoning objectives.

cognitive learning. Academic learning of subject matter.

common planning time. A scheduling procedure that allows teachers to share the same period for instructional planning. The provision of common planning times facilitates collaborative efforts among teachers.

competency. The demonstrated ability to perform specified acts at a particular level of skill or accuracy.

competency-based instruction. Instructional programming that measures learning through the demonstration of predetermined outcomes. Mastery is assessed through an evaluation of the process as well as the product.

conditioning. The reinforcement of learning through repetitive response.

continued learning. Refers to skills used in all disciplines, for example, reading, writing, research skills.

cooperative learning. Two or more students working together on a learning task.

core (fused) curriculum. Integration of two or more subjects, for example, English and social studies. Problem and theme orientations often serve as the integrating design. *See also* interdisciplinary program.

criterion-referenced evaluation. Evaluation that measures success by the attainment of established levels of performance. Individual success is based wholly on the performance of the individual without regard to the performance of others.

criterion-referenced test. Evaluation that measures performance compared with predetermined standards or objectives.

cultural diversity. The existence of several different cultures within a group; encouraging each group to keep its individual qualities within the larger society.

cultural pluralism. Cultural diversity; the existence of many different cultures within a group; encouraging different cultures to maintain their distinctive qualities within the larger society.

curriculum. The total experiences planned for a school or students.

curriculum alignment. The matching of learning activities with desired outcomes, or matching what is taught to what is tested.

curriculum compacting. Content development and delivery models that abbreviate the amount of time to cover a topic without compromising the depth and breadth of material taught.

curriculum guide. A written statement of objectives, content, and activities to be used with a particular subject at specified grade levels; usually produced by state departments of education or local education agencies.

Curriculum Management Plan (CMP). A systematic method of planning for change (for example, Wiles–Bondi Curriculum Management Plan Model).

deductive learning. A type of learning in which instructional materials and activities allow students to discover the specific attributes of a concept through an exploration that moves from the general to the particular.

departmentalization. The division of instructional staff, resources, and classes by academic disciplines; service delivery models such as separate general and special education programming; or some other arbitrary structure for compartmentalization.

developmental physical education. Instruction based on the physical development of the individual preadolescent learner as opposed to a team sports approach.

developmental tasks. Social, physical, maturational tasks regularly encountered by all individuals in our society as they progress from childhood to adolescence.

discovery learning. A type of inquiry, emphasized especially in individualized instruction, in which a student moves through his or her own activities toward new learning, usually expressed in generalizations and principles; typically involves inductive approaches. *See also* inductive learning.

early adolescence. The stage of human development generally between ages 10 and 14 when individuals begin to reach puberty.

educational goals. A statement of expectations for students or a school program.

environmental approach. An approach to learning that is concerned with the restructuring of the learning environment or the students' perceptions so they may be free to develop.

epistemology. A branch of philosophy that examines (a) how knowledge is gained, (b) how much can be known, and (c) what justification there is for what is known.

essentialism. A philosophy rooted in idealism and realism that began in the 1930s as a reaction to progressivism. Reading, writing, and arithmetic are the focus in elementary schools. English, mathematics, science, history, and foreign language make up the secondary curriculum. Essentialism is subject-centered, like perennialism, but maintains a contemporary orientation. The arts and vocational education are rejected.

essential learning skills. Basic skills, such as reading, listening, and speaking that are introduced in the elementary school and reinforced in the middle school and high school.

exploration. Regularly scheduled curriculum experiences designed to help students discover and/or examine learning related to their changing needs, aptitudes, and interests. Also known as *the wheel* or *miniclasses*. *See also* minicourses.

extinction. The conditioning of learning by withdrawing reinforcement.

feedback. Evidence from student responses and reactions that indicates the degree of success being encountered in lesson objectives. Teachers seek feedback by way of discussion, student questions, written exercises, and test returns.

flexible scheduling. Provisions in scheduling allowing for variance in length of time, order, or rotation of classes.

formal operations. The last stage in Piaget's theory of cognitive development, characterized by an ability to manipulate concepts abstractly and apply logical methods in the solution of complex problems. Children are not generally expected to exhibit these abilities before 11 to 15 years of age.

formative evaluation. A method of assessment that occurs before or during instruction to (a) guide teacher planning or (b) identify students' needs.

gifted learner. The term most frequently applied to those with exceptional intellectual ability, but may also refer to learners with outstanding ability in athletics, leadership, music, creativity, and so on.

global education. Instructional strategies and curriculum frameworks that include multiple, diverse, and international resources through the use of technology.

goals, Educational. Desired learning outcomes stated for a group of students and requiring from several weeks to several years to attain.

graded school system. A division of schools into groups of students according to the curriculum or the ages of pupils, as in the six elementary grades.

heterogeneous grouping. Student grouping that does not divide learners on the basis of ability or academic achievement.

homogeneous grouping. Student grouping that divides learners on the basis of specific levels of ability, achievement, or interest. Also known as *tracking*.

house plan. Type of organization in which the school is divided into units ("houses"), with each having an identity and containing the various grades and, in large part, its own faculty. The purpose of a house plan is to achieve decentralization (closer student–faculty relationships) and easier and more flexible team-teaching arrangements.

identification. A defense mechanism in which a person identifies part of him- or herself with another person.

imitation. A process in which students learn by modeling the behavior of others.

independent study. Work performed by students to develop self-study skills and to expand and deepen interests, without the direct supervision of the teacher.

Individualized Education Program (IEP). The mechanism through which a child's special needs are identified; goals, objectives, and services are outlined; and methods for evaluating progress are delineated.

individualized instruction. Instruction that focuses on the interests, needs, and achievements of individual learners.

inductive learning. A type of learning in which instructional materials and activities are designed to assist students in the acquisition of knowledge through the mastery of specific subskills that lead to more general concepts and processes.

innovations. New instructional strategies, organizational designs, building arrangements, equipment utilizations, or materials from which improved learning results are anticipated.

inservice education. Continuing education for teachers who are actually teaching, or who are "in service."

integration of disciplines. The organization of objectives under an interdisciplinary topic that allows students to use skills and knowledge from more than one content area within a given instructional activity or unit of study.

interdisciplinary program. Instruction that integrates and combines subject matter ordinarily taught separately into a single organizational structure.

interdisciplinary team. Combination of teachers from different subject areas who plan and conduct coordinated lessons in those areas for particular groups of pupils. Common planning time, flexible scheduling, and cooperation and communication among team teachers are essential to the interdisciplinary team.

interscholastic program. Athletic activities or events whose primary purpose is to foster competition among schools and school districts. Participation usually is limited to students with exceptional athletic ability.

intramural (intrascholastic) program. Athletic activities or events held during the school day, or shortly thereafter, and whose primary purpose is to encourage all students to participate regardless of athletic ability.

learning. A change of behavior as a result of experience.

learning center. Usually, a large multimedia area designed to influence learning and teaching styles and to foster independent study. Also known as a *learning station.*

least restrictive environment. The program best suited to meet the special needs of a child with a disability while keeping the child as close as possible to the regular educational program.

magnet program. A specialized school program usually designed to draw minority students to schools that historically have been racially segregated. School-based programs are developed around a common theme, discipline, theory, or philosophy. Performing arts, mathematics, and medical fields are representative of the curriculum and instructional components on which magnet programs have been built.

mainstreaming. A plan by which exceptional children receive special education in the regular classroom as much of the time as possible.

metacognition. The process by which individuals examine their own thinking processes.

middle school. A school between elementary and high school, housed separately (ideally in a building designed for its purpose), and covering usually three of the middle school years, beginning with grade 5 or 6.

minicourses.   Special-interest (enrichment) activities of short duration that provide learning opportunities based on student interest, faculty expertise, and community involvement. Also called *exploratory courses, short-interest-centered courses,* or *electives.*

minimum competency testing.   Exit-level tests designed to ascertain whether students have achieved basic levels of performance in areas such as reading, writing, and computation.

mission statement.   A statement of the goals or intent of a school.

model.   A written or drawn description used to improve understanding.

modeling.   Demonstrating a behavior, lesson, or teaching style.

modular scheduling.   The division of the school day into modules, typically 15 or 20 minutes long, with the number of modules used for various activities and experiences arranged flexibly.

multicultural education.   Educational goals and methods that teach students the value of cultural diversity.

need-structured approach.   A learning theory concerned with the needs and drives of students that seeks to use their natural motivational energy to promote learning.

nongraded school.   A type of school organization in which grade lines are eliminated for a sequence of two or more years.

nonverbal communication.   The act of transmitting and/or receiving messages through any means not having to do with oral or written language, such as eye contact, facial expressions, or body language.

normal learning curve.   The expected progress of the average student in a class.

normal school.   Historically, the first U.S. institution devoted exclusively to teacher training.

norm-referenced grading.   Evaluation that measures a student's performance by comparing it with the performance of others.

paraprofessional.   A person employed by a school, program, or district to assist a certified professional and extend the services provided to the students. The paraprofessional may have entry-level training but is not a fully licensed educator or therapist.

performance objective.   Targeted outcome measures for evaluating the learning of particular process-based skills and knowledge.

personal development.   The intellectual, social, emotional, and moral growth of students fostered through programs such as adviser/advisee, developmental physical education, and minicourses.

portfolio, learner's.   A diversified combination of samples of a student's quantitative and qualitative work.

process-pattern learning.   A learning design that focuses on each student's experience rather than on a predetermined body of information.

progressive education.   An educational philosophy emphasizing democracy, the importance of creative and meaningful activity, the real needs of students, and the relationship between school and community.

readiness.   The point at which a student is intellectually, physically, or socially able to learn a concept or exhibit a particular behavior.

reinforcement.   The strengthening of behavior through supportive action.

restructuring.   The change of a school's entire program and procedure as opposed to the change of only one part of the curriculum.

scaffolding.   A context for student learning such as an outline or question stem. The term was first used by Vygotsky in relation to education.

scope.   The parameters of learning; for example, a subject-matter discipline sets its own scope, often by grade level.

self-contained classroom.   A form of classroom organization in which the same teacher conducts all or nearly all the instruction in all or most subjects in the same classroom for all or most of the school day.

semantic mapping.   The organization of meaning in language.

sequence.   The organization of an area of study. Frequently, the organization is chronological, moving from simple to complex. Some sequences are spiral, using structure, themes, or concept development as guidelines. A few schools use persistent life situations to shape sequence.

social competence.   The ability to interact positively with persons and groups.

special learning center.   A designated area of a classroom, media center, or some other setting on the school campus with materials and activities designed to (a) enrich the existing educational program or (b) provide students with additional drill and practice in a targeted skill.

staff development.   A body of activities designed to improve the proficiencies of the educator–practitioner.

subject content.   A type of curriculum that stresses the mastery of subject matter, with all other outcomes considered subsidiary. Also known as *subject-matter curriculum. See also* homogeneous grouping.

support personnel.   Ancillary personnel such as guidance, media, custodial, clerical, and social services persons who help facilitate the instructional program.

teacher empowerment.   Policies and procedures that enlarge the scope of decisions educators are allowed to make individually as well as in collaboratively. Curriculum, instructional materials, budget, scheduling, and pupil assignments in particular classes are a few of the areas that practitioners are increasingly called on to address.

Teachers Training Teachers (TTT).   An inservice process by which teachers receive instruction from peers, usually at the school level.

team teaching.   A plan by which several teachers, organized into a team with a leader, provide the instruction for a larger group of children than would usually be found in a self-contained classroom.

tracking.   The method of grouping students according to their ability level in homogeneous classes or learning experiences.

transfer.   In learning, shaping the student to a predetermined form by connecting behavior with response.

unified arts.   All nonacademic subjects such as the fine arts, vocational education, and physical education.

unified studies.   The combination of subjects around themes or problems. Also known as *integrated* or *interdisciplinary studies.*

unstructured time.   Periods of time during the school day that have not been designated for a specific purpose and that present students with less supervision. The time between finishing lunch and the ringing of the bell to return to the classroom is an example of unstructured time.

voucher plan.   Governmental funding program that allows students and their parents to select among options for schooling by providing predetermined tuition allotments that can be applied to private or public institutions.

work-study program.   Collaborative efforts between the schools and community-based employers that allow students to earn course credit for time spent working. Students attend school for a designated number of periods per day and work a predetermined number of hours per week. Grades for work in the community are assigned based on the number of hours worked and the evaluation of the employer.

REFERENCES

Adler, M. (1982). *The Paideia proposal*. New York, NY: Macmillan.

Alexander, W. (Ed.). (1968). *The high school of the future: A memorial to Kimball Wiles*. Columbus, OH: Charles E. Merrill Publishing.

Alexander, W. M. (October 29, 1974). *Curriculum planning as it should be*. Address to Association for Supervision and Curriculum Development Conference, Chicago, IL.

Altbach, P. G. (1991). *Textbooks in American society*. Albany, NY: State University of New York Press.

Amrein, A., & Berliner, D. (2002). High stakes testing, uncertainty, and student learning. *Education Policy, 10*(18).

Apple, M. (1990). *Ideology and curriculum*. New York, NY: Routledge.

Argentine school tests WiMax technology. (2005, September 20). *eSchool News Online*.

Armbruster, B., Lehr, F. & Osborn, J. (2011). *Put reading first: The research building blocks for teaching children to read: Kindergarten through grade 3*. Center for the Improvement of Early Reading Achievement, National Institute for Literacy. This booklet is part of the Partnership for Reading, a collaborative effort by the National Institute for Literacy, the U.S. Department of Education, and Amazon Digital Services, Inc.

Aronowitz, S., & Giroux, H. (1991). *Postmodern education*. Westport, CT: Greenwood.

ASCD Commission on Secondary Education. (1961). *The junior high we need*. Alexandria, VA: Association for Supervision and Curriculum Development.

ASCD Working Group on the Emerging Adolescent. (1960). In J. Bondi (Ed.), *The middle school we need*. Alexandria, VA: Association for Supervision and Curriculum Development.

Ball, D. L. (1996). Teacher learning and the mathematics reforms: What we think we know and what we need to learn. *Phi Delta Kappan, 77*(7), 500–508.

Barker, J. (1993). *Paradigms: The business of discovering the future*. New York, NY: Harper Collins.

Bellack, A. A. (1966). Conceptions of knowledge: Their significance for curriculum. In W. Jenkins (Ed.), *The nature of knowledge: Implications for the education of teachers*. Milwaukee, WI: University of Wisconsin.

Bennett, A. L., Bridglall, B. L., Ana Mari Cauce, A. M., Everson, H. T., Gordon, E. W., Lee, C. D., Mendoza-Denton, R., Renzulli, J. S., & Stewart, J. (2004). *All students reaching the top: Strategies for closing academic achievement gaps*. Report of the National Study Group for the Affirmative Development of Academic Ability, pp. 9–21. Naperville, IL: North Central Regional Educational Laboratory.

Berliner, D., & Biddle, B. (1996). *The manufactured crisis: Myths, fraud, and the attack on American public schools*. Reading, MA: Addison-Wesley.

Bestor, A. (1956). *The restoration of learning*. New York, NY: Knopf.

Bigge, M. L. (1971). *Learning theories for teachers*. New York, NY: Harper & Row.

Billing, S. (2000). Impacts of service-learning on youth, schools, and communities: Research on K–12 school-based service-learning, 1990–1999. Retrieved March 15, 2000, from http:// learningindeed.org/research/slresearch/ slrsrchsy.html

Blakemore, B. (Reporter). (1991, September 3). *ABC Evening News; American agenda: Education reform*. [Television broadcast]. New York, NY: ABC News.

Bobbitt, F. (1918). *The curriculum*. New York, NY: Houghton Mifflin.

Bobbitt, F. (1924). *How to make a curriculum*. New York, NY: Houghton Mifflin.

Bode, B. H. (1931). Education at the crossroads. *Progressive Education, 8*, 543–544.

Bondi, J. (1960). *The middle school we need*. Alexandria, Virginia: ASCD.

Boulding, K. (1964). *The meaning of the twentieth century*. New York, NY: Harper and Row.

Boulding, K. (1966). *The impact of the social sciences*. Newark, NJ: Rutgers University Press.

Bowles, S., & Gintis, H. (1976). *Schooling in capitalist America*. New York, NY: Bantam.

Bracy, G. (2004). *Setting the record straight: Responding to misconceptions about American education* (2nd ed.). Portsmouth, NH: Heinemann.

Briggs, T. H. (1926). *Curriculum problems*. New York, NY: Macmillan.

Brookover, W. B. (1981). *Effective secondary schools.* Washington DC: ERIC Clearinghouse.

Bruner, J. (1962). *The process of education.* Cambridge, MA: Harvard University Press.

Bruner, J. (1963, March). Structures in learning. *NEA Journal, 52,* 26.

Bureau of Employment Security. (1991). *A dictionary of occupational titles* (4th ed.). Washington, DC: U.S. Department of Labor.

Burke, L. (2001, February 18). *State costs in adopting and implementing Common Core Standards.* Washington, DC: The Heritage Foundation.

Calkins, L. (2012). *Pathways to the Common Core-Accelerating student achievement.* Portsmouth, NH: Heinemann.

Callahan, R. (1962). *Education and the cult of efficiency.* Chicago, IL: University of Chicago Press.

Canady, R., & Rettig, M. (1995, November). The power of innovative scheduling. *Educational Leadership, 53*(3), 4–10.

Carnegie Council of Adolescent Development. (1989). *Turning points: Preparing American youth for the 21st century.* New York, NY: Carnegie Corporation.

Caswell, H. L., & Campbell, D. S. (1935). *Curriculum development.* New York, NY: American Book.

Charner, I., Fraser, B., Hubbard, S., Rogers, A., & Horne, R. (1995). Reforms of the school-to-work transition: Findings, implications, and challenges. *Phi Delta Kappan, 77*(1), 40, 58–60.

Chayefsky, P. (Writer). (1977). *Network* [Motion picture]. United States: United Artists.

Cherniss, C. (2000, April 13–16). *Emotional intelligence: What it is and why it matters.* Paper presented at the Annual Conference of the Society for Industrial and Organizational Psychology, New Orleans, LA.

Claxton, C.S., & Murrell, P.H. (1987). *Learning styles: Implications for improving educational practice.* ASHE-ERIC Higher Education Report No. 4. Washington, DC: George Washington University.

Cochrane, P. (2004). *Uncommon sense: Out of the box thinking for an in the box world.* North Mankato, MN: Capstone Press.

Coleman, D. (2011). *Publishers criteria for Common Core State Standards English and language arts.* Storrs, CT: Connecticut Department of Education.

Combs, A. (2006). *Being and becoming: A field approach to psychology.* New York: Springer Publishing Company.

Commission on the Reorganization of Secondary Education. (1918). *Cardinal principles of secondary education.* Department of the Interior Bureau of Education. Bulletin No. 35 (pp. 12–13). Washington, DC: U.S. Government Printing Office.

Counts, G. (1932). *Dare the schools create a new social order?* New York, NY: Day.

Covey, S. R. (2004). *The 7 habits of highly effective people.* New York, NY: Simon & Schuster.

Covey, S. (2012). *The 4 disciplines of execution: The secret to getting things done, on time, with excellence.* New York, NY: Simon & Schuster.

Darling-Hammond, L. (1999). Educating teachers of the next century. In G. Griffin (Ed.), *The education of teachers.* Chicago, IL: University of Chicago Press.

Dede, C. (2004, September). Enabling distributive learning communities via emerging technologies: Part One. *T.H.E. Journal.* Retrieved from http://www.thejournal.com/articles/16909

Dede, C. (2005, April 2–4). Address to General Session, National Conference of Association for Supervision and Curriculum Development, Orlando, FL.

Dewey, J. (1902). *The child and the curriculum.* Chicago, IL: University of Chicago Press.

Dewey, J. (1916). *Democracy and education.* New York, NY: Macmillan.

Dewey, J. (1938). *Experience and education.* New York, NY: Macmillan.

Dillon, S. (2011, May 22). Behind grass-school advocacy, Bill Gates. *The New York Times.* Retrieved from http://www.nytimes.com/2011/05/22/ AM

Doll, R. (1995). *Curriculum improvement* (7th ed.). Boston, MA: Allyn & Bacon.

Doll, W., Jr., (1993). *A post-modern perspective on curriculum.* New York, NY: Teachers College Press.

Eastin, D. (1998). *A message from the state board of education and the state superintendent of public education.* Sacramento, CA: California State Board of Education.

Easton, D. (1990). *The political system: An inquiry into the state of political science.* New York, NY: Alfred A. Knopf.

Edling, W., & Loring, R. (1996). *Education and work: Designing integrated curricula.* Waco, TX: Center for Occupational Research and Development.

Edutopia News. (2005, May 12). *Eight essentials of inquiry-based science (K–8).* San Francisco, CA: George Lucas Foundation.

Epstein, R. (1997). Skinner as a self-manager. *Journal of Applied Behavioral Analysis, 30*, 545–569.

Feller, B. (2005, July 27). Business wants more attention for math and science. *Deseret Morning News*. Salt Lake City, UT: Deseret Morning News.

Feng, L. (2013, February 26). How online learning companies bought America's schools. *The Nation*, 1–9.

Fein, S., & Spencer, S. J. (1997, July). Prejudice as self-image maintenance: Affirming the self through derogating others. *Journal of Personality and Social Psychology, 73*(1), 31–44.

Feyereisen, K., Fiorino, A. J., & Nowak, A. T. (1970). *Supervision and curriculum renewal: A systems approach*. New York, NY: Appleton-Century-Crofts.

Flesch, R. (1955). *Why Johnny can't read and what you can do about it*. New York, NY: Harper and Row, Publishers.

Fitzpatrick, K. (1997). *Indicators of schools of quality. Vol. 1: Schoolwide indicators of quality*. Schaumburg, IL: National Study for School Evaluation.

Flanagan, J. C. (1964). *Project talent*. United States Office of Education (H.E.W.). Pittsburgh, PA: University of Pittsburgh.

Freire, P. (1973). *Education for a critical consciousness*. New York, NY: Seabury Press.

Freire, P. (1985). *The politics of education*. South Hadley, MA: Bergin & Garvey.

Friedman, T. L. (2005). *The world is flat: A brief history of the twenty-first century*. New York, NY: Farrar, Straus and Giroux.

Fullan, M., Bennett, B., & Rolheiser-Bennett, C. (1990). Linking classroom and school improvement. *Educational Leadership, 47*(8), 13–91.

Gates, W., III. (2005, February 26). Keynote address at National Education Summit on High Schools. Washington, DC. Retrieved January 30, 2006, from http://www.gatesfoundation.org/MediaCenter/Speeches/BillgSpeeches/BGSpeechNGA-0502226.htm

Gatto, J. T. (2003, September). Against school: How public education cripples our kids, and why. *Harpers' Magazine*, 33–38.

Goals 2000: A world-class education for every child. (1994). Washington, DC: U.S. Department of Education.

Goddard, R. (2001). Collective efficacy: A neglected construct in the study of schools and student achievement. *Journal of Educational Psychology, 93*(3), 467–476.

Gonzalez, E., & Short, P. (1996). The relationship of teacher empowerment and principal power bases [Electronic version]. *Journal of International Psychology, 23*(3), 210.

Goodlad, J. (1984). *A place called school*. New York, NY: McGraw-Hill.

Graziano, C. (2005, February/March). School's out. *Edutopia Magazine*, 40–45.

Grolund, N. (2009). *Assessment and student achievement* (9th ed.). Upper Saddle, New Jersey, Pearson Education.

Hackman, D. (1995). Ten guidelines for implementing block scheduling. *Educational Leadership, 53*(3), 24–27.

Hall, E. (1959). *The silent language*. New York, NY: Doubleday.

Hammerman, E. (2006). *Eight essentials of inquiry-based science, K-8*. Thousand Oaks, CA: Corwin Press.

Hattie, J. (2008). *Visible learning: A synthesis of over 800 meta-analyses relating to achievement*. New York, NY: Routledge.

Hauenstein, S., & Bachmeyer, A.D. (1974). *The world of communications: visual media*. Bloomington, Illinois: McKnight.

Havighurst, R. J., Bowman, P., Liddle, G., Mattens, C., & Perce, J. (1962). *Growing up in River City*. New York, NY: Wiley.

Hayes, H. (2008). *American digital schools: Six trends to watch*. Encinitas, CA: The Greaves Group.

Hirsch, E. D., Jr. (1986). *Cultural literacy: What every American needs to know*. New York, NY: Random House.

Hollingshead, A. B. (1949). *Elmstown youth*. New York, NY: Wiley.

Holloway, J. (2001). Research link/inclusion and students with learning disabilities. *Educational Leadership, 58*(6), 86–88.

Huff Post Tech. (2013, April 9). World has about 6 billion cell phone subscribers, according to U.N. telecom agency report. *The Huffington Post*. Retrieved from http://www.huffingtonpost.com/2012/10/11/cell-phones-world-subscribers-six-billion_n_1957173.html

Hutchins, R. M. (1936). *The higher learning in America*. New Haven, CT: Yale University Press.

Hutchins, R. M. (1963). *On education*. Santa Barbara, CA: Center for the Study of Democratic Institutions.

Illich, I. (1971). *Deschooling society*. New York, NY: Harper.

Jacobs, H. (Ed.). (2010). *Curriculum 21: Essential education for a changing world.* Alexandria, VA: ASCD.

Johnson, M. (1970/Winter 1971). *Appropriate research directions in curriculum and instruction.* Curriculum Theory Network, 6, 25. Ontario Institute for Studies in Education/University of Toronto. Toronto, ON: John Wiley & Sons, Inc.

Joyce, B. (Ed.). (1990). *Changing school culture through staff development, 1990 Yearbook.* Alexandria, VA: Association for Supervision and Curriculum Development.

Kaufman, B. (1965). *Up the down staircase.* Upper Saddle River, NJ: Prentice Hall.

Keating, M. (2001). *Learningwebs: Curriculum journeys across the Internet.* Upper Saddle River, NJ: Prentice Hall.

Kelley, E. C. (1947). *Education for what is real.* New York, NY: Harper.

Kem, V. (2004). *Wireless phones for bridging the digital divide in developing countries.* Ministry of Posts and Telecommunincations of Cambodia.

Kilpatrick J. (2003). *State proficiency testing in mathematics.* Retrieved August 24, 2005, from http://www.ericdigests.org/2003-2/math.html

Kohlberg, L., & Mayer, R. (1972, November). Development as an aim of education. *Harvard Educational Review, 42,* 452–453.

Kohn, A. (2004, April). Test today, privatize tomorrow: Using accountability to reform public schools to death. *Phi Delta Kappan, 85*(8), 569–577.

Kramer, E. (2004, November/December). From the hands of babes. *Psychology Today, 23*(8) 16–22.

Kuhn, T. (1962). *The structure of scientific revolutions.* Chicago, IL: University of Chicago Press.

Kulik, J. A., (2003). *Effects of using instructional technology in elementary and secondary schools: What controlled evaluation studies say.* Arlington, VA: SRI International

Little, J. W., & Bartlett, L. (2002). Career and commitment in the context of comprehensive school reform. *Teachers and Teaching: Theory and Practice, 8*(3), 345–354.

Macdonald, J. (1971). Curriculum development in relation to social and intellectual systems. In H. G. Richey & R. M. McClure (Eds.), *The curriculum: Retrospect and prospect. Yearbook of the National Society for the Study of Education.* Chicago, IL: University of Chicago Press.

Mager, R. F. (1972). *Goal analysis.* Belmont, CA: Fearon.

Marsh, C., & Willis, G. (1995). *Curriculum alternative approaches: Ongoing issues.* Upper Saddle River, NJ: Prentice Hall.

Maley, R. (2011). *Transforming learning with new technologies.* Boston, MA: Allyn and Bacon.

McCain, T., & Jukes, I. (2001). *Windows on the future.* Thousand Oaks, CA: Corwin.

McCarthy, T. (2005, September 5). On the frontiers of search. *Time Magazine,* 52–54.

McClure, R. M. (1971). The reforms of the fifties and sixties: A historical look at the near past. In H. G. Richey & R. M. McClure (Eds.), *The curriculum: Retrospect and prospect. Yearbook of the National Society for the Study of Education.* Chicago, IL: University of Chicago Press.

McCullen, C. (1995). World Wide Web in the classroom: The quintessential collaboration. *Learning and Leading with Technology, 23*(3), 7–10.

McLuhan, M. (1964). *Understanding media: The extensions of man.* New York, NY: McGraw-Hill.

McLuhan, M., & Fiore, Q. (1967). *The medium is the massage: An inventory of effects.* New York, NY: Bantam.

McNeil, J. D. (2005). *Contemporary curriculum. In thought and action.* Hoboken, NJ: John Wiley & Sons.

McREL: Mid-continent Research for Education and Learning. (1999). www2.**mcrel**.org/compendium/docs/factsheet.asp?

Mead, M. (1951). *The school in American culture.* Cambridge, MA: Harvard University Press.

Miniwatts Marketing Group, Internet World Stats, Top 20 Internet Users, June 30, 2012

Mitchell, N. (2005, August 31). Florida SAT scores tumble close to the bottom. *Jacksonville Times Union,* p. B5.

Mosteller, F., & Moynihan, D. (1972). *On equality of educational opportunity.* New York, NY: Random House.

Naisbitt, J. (1982). *Megatrends: Ten new directions transforming our lives.* New York, NY: Warner.

National Association for Sports and Physical Education. (2004). *National standards for beginning physical education teachers* (2nd ed.). Reston, VA: Author.

National Commission on Excellence in Education. (1983, April). *A nation at risk.* Washington, DC: U.S. Department of Education.

National Council of Teachers of Mathematics. (1991). *Professional standards for teaching mathematics.* Reston, VA: Author.

National Education Association. (2000, May 3). *Modernizing our schools: What will it cost?* Washington, DC: NEA Press Center.

National Standards & Grade-Level Outcomes for K-12 Physical Education. (2004). Retrieved from http://www.aahperd.org

Neill, A. S. (1960). *Summerhill.* New York, NY: Hart.

Nir, A. E. (2002). School-based management and its effect on teacher commitment. *International Journal of Leadership in Education, 5*(4), 323–341.

November, A. (2005, January 26–28). Address to the Florida Education Technology Conference, Orlando, FL.

Odden, A. (2000). The costs of sustaining educational change through comprehensive school reform. *Phi Delta Kappan, 81*(6), 433–438.

Oliva, P. F. (2012). *Developing the curriculum, 8th.* New York, NY: Longman.

$100 laptops for kids of the world ready to launch. (2005, September 29). *Jacksonville Times-Union,* p. 1.

Parker, F. (2003). *Talks on pedagogics.* Whitefish, MT: Kessinger. (Original work published 1894).

Pestalozzi, J. (1977). *How Gertrude teaches her children: An attempt to help mothers to teach their own children and an account of the method (1894).* In D. Robinson (Ed.). Frederick, MD: University Publications of America.

Phenix, P. H. (1962). The disciplines as curriculum content. In A. Harry Passow (Ed.), *Curriculum crossroads* (p. 64). New York, NY: Teachers College Press.

Piaget, J. (1959). *The language and thought of a child.* New York, NY: Doubleday.

Pitts, L. (2012, July 25). Dumbing down America one child at a time. *Miami Herald.*

Pool, C. (1997). Up with emotional health. *Educational Leadership, 54*(8), 12–14.

Popham, J. (2010). *Classroom assessment: What teachers need to know.* (6th ed.). Upper Saddle River, NJ: Pearson Education, 2010.

Postman, N. (2011). *Technopoly: The surrender of culture to technology.* New York, NY: Vintage.

President's Advisory Commission on Science. (1973). *Youth: Transition to adulthood.* Washington, DC: U.S. Government Printing Office.

Ravitch, D. (2013, February 26). Why I can't support the Common Core Standards. Retrieved from http//:dianeravitch.net, 1-14

Reese, C. (2000, September 12). Scrap public education altogether. *Orlando Sentinel,* p. A10.

Reich, C. (1970, September 26). The greening of America. *New Yorker,* 43–44.

Ricciuti, M. (2005, September 28). The $100 laptop moves closer to reality. *CNET News.com.* Retrieved from http://news.com.com/The+100+laptop+moves+closer+to+reality/2100-1044_3-5884683.html

Rogers, C. (1961). *On becoming a person: A therapist's view of psychotherapy.* New York, NY: Houghton Mifflin.

Rogers, E. (1965). *Diffusion of innovations.* New York, NY: Free Press.

Rostow, W. (1960). *Economics analysis: Microeconomics.* New York, NY: Harper & Row.

Rothman, R. (2012, Dec./Jan.). Common Core: Putting the pieces in place. *Educational Leadership, 70*(4), 18–22.

Rugg, H. (Ed.). (1926). Curriculum-making: Points of emphasis. *Yearbook of the National Society for the Study of Education, 26*(1). Chicago, IL: University of Chicago Press.

Rugg, H. (Ed.). (1926). The foundations and technique of curriculum construction; Curriculum-making: Past and present. *Yearbook of the National Society for the Study of Education, 26*(1). Chicago, IL: University of Chicago Press.

Rugg, H. (Ed.). (1927). The foundations of curriculum-making. *Yearbook of the National Society for the Study of Education, 26*(1). Chicago, IL: University of Chicago Press.

Rutter, M., (1982). *Fifteen thousand hours: Secondary schools and their effects on children.* Cambridge, MA: Harvard University Press.

Saylor, J. G., & Alexander, W. M. (1974). *Curriculum planning for schools.* New York, NY: Holt, Rinehart & Winston.

Schaefer, R. J. (1972). Retrospect and prospect. In H. G. Richey & R. M. McClure (Eds.), *Yearbook of the National Society for the Study of Education.* Chicago, IL: University of Chicago Press.

Schauweker, M. (1995, March). A review of standards for the assessment of reading and writing. *The Clearing House,* 233–234.

Secretary's Commission on Necessary Skills. (1991, June). *What work requires of schools: A SCANS report for America 2000.* Washington, DC: U.S. Department of Labor.

Shedroff, N. (2001). *Experience design 1.* Indianapolis, IN: New Riders.

Shepard, L. (2000, October). The role of assessment in the learning culture. *Educational Researcher, 29*(7), 1–14.

Silberman, C. (1970). *Crisis in the classroom*. New York, NY: Random House.

Sizer, T. (1984). *Horace's compromise: The dilemma of the American high school*. Boston, MA: Houghton-Mifflin.

Skinner, B. F. (1972). *Beyond freedom and dignity*. New York, NY: Bantam/Vintage Books.

Slavin, R. (1991, February). Synthesis of research on cooperative learning. *Educational Leadership, 48,* 71–82.

Smith, B. O., Stanley, W. O., & Shores, J. H. (1957). *Fundamentals of curriculum development*. New York, NY: Harcourt Brace Jovanovich.

Solomon, P. (2009). *The curriculum bridge: From standards to actual classroom practice*. Thousand Oaks, CA: Corwin.

State of Tennessee, Department of Education. (2000). *Computer technology K–12: Rationale*. Nashville, TN: Author.

State of Virginia. (2004). *The standards of quality* (Rev. ed.).

Stewart, V. (2012). *A world class education: Learning from international models of excellence and innovation*. Alexandria, VA: ASCD.

Sternberg, R. J. (1997). The concept of intelligence and its role in lifelong learning and success. *American Psychologist, 52,* 1030–1037.

Stiggins, R. (2004, September). New assessment beliefs for a new school mission. *Phi Delta Kappan, 86*(1), 22–27.

Streyer, J. (2003). *The other parent: The inside story of the media effect on our children*. New York, NY: Atria Publishers.

Stufflebeam, D. (1994). *CIPP evaluation model checklist*. Kalamazoo, MI: The Evaluation Center, Western Michigan University.

Sun, J. (2004). Understanding the impact of perceived principal leadership style on teacher commitment. *International Studies in Educational Administration, 32*(2), 18–31.

Taba, H. (1945). General techniques of curriculum planning. In N. B. Henry & R. W. Tyler (Eds.), *American education in the postwar period: Current reconstruction. Yearbook of the National Society for the Study of Education, 44*(1), 58. Chicago, IL: University of Chicago Press.

Taba, H. (1962). *Curriculum development: Theory and practice*. New York, NY: Harcourt Brace Jovanovich.

Tai, D. (1998). Dissertation Proposal. University of South Florida.

Tanner, D., & Tanner, L. (2006). *Curriculum development: Theory into practice*. Upper Saddle River, NJ: Pearson Education.

Teachers' tech use on the rise. (2005, August 29). *eSchool News Online*.

Tennessee State Board of Education. (2001, August 31). *Curriculum standards*. Retrieved from http://www.state.TN.US/education/ci/standards

Tennessee State Board of Education. (2001, August 31). *Mathematics curriculum standards*. Retrieved from http://www.state.tn.us/education/ci/standards/math

Thornburg, D. (2002). *The new basics: Education and the future of work in the telematic age*. Alexandria, VA: Association for Supervision and Curriculum Development.

Thornburg, D. (2005, January 26–28). *The meaning of technology*. Address to Florida Educational Technology Conference, Orlando, FL.

Thorndike, E. L. (1920). Intelligence and its uses. *Harper's Magazine, 140,* 227–235.

Tillier, M. (2001). *Learningwebs: Journeys on the internet*. Prentice Hall.

Time Magazine. (2012, August 27). The wireless issue. Retrieved from http://content.time.com/time/covers/0,16641,20120827,00.html

Toffler, A. (1968). *The schoolhouse in the city*, as reported in Education Facilities Laboratory. Washington DC: EFL.

Toffler, A. (1970). *Future shock*. New York, NY: Random House.

Toffler, A. (1980). *The third wave*. New York, NY: Bantam Books.

Tomlinson, C. (1999, October). *The challenge with mixed-ability groups*. Arlington, VA: American Association of School Administrators. Retrieved from http://www.aasa.org

Tracking U.S. trends. (2004, May 19). *Education Week*.

Tucker, T. L. (2000). Training tomorrow's leaders: Enhancing the emotional intelligence of business leaders. *Journal of Education for Business, 75*(6), 331–337.

Tye, B., & O'Brien, L. (2002, September). Why are experienced teachers leaving the profession? *Phi Delta Kappan, 84*(1), 4–32.

Tyler, R. W. (1949). *Basic principles of curriculum and instruction*. Chicago, IL: University of Chicago Press.

Tyler, R. W. (1957). The curriculum then and now. In *Proceedings of the 1956 conference on testing problems* (p. 79). Princeton, NJ: Educational Testing Service.

U.S. Department of Education. (2004). *Helping your child learn mathematics*. Washington, DC: Author.

U.S. Department of Education. (2006). *Elementary and secondary education; Subpart 6: Gifted and talented students*. Retrieved from http://www.ed.gov/policy/elsec/leg/esea02/pg72.html

U.S. Department of Health Statistics. (2006). *Report on the homeless*. Washington, DC: Author.

Vars, G. (1996). Effects of interdisciplinary curriculum and instruction. In P. S. Hlebowitsh & W. G. Wraga (Eds.), *Annual Review of Research for School Leaders* (pp. 147–164). Reston, VA: National Association of Secondary School Principals and Scholastic Publishing.

Warlick, D. (2004, May 15). Textbooks of the future. *Technology and Learning Magazine*. Retrieved from http://www.tltgroup.org/

Webley, K. (June 6, 2013). *The adaptive learning revolution*. Retrieved from http://nation.time.com/2013/06/06/the-adaptive-learning-revolution/

White, B. L. (1973). *Experience and environment: Major influences on the development of the young*. Upper Saddle River, NJ: Prentice Hall.

Wiggins, G., & McTighe, J. (2005). *Understanding by design, expanded* (2nd ed.). Upper Saddle River, NJ: Pearson Education.

Will, G. F. (2005, April 10). New educational solutions shift focus to teachers and students. *Washington Post*.

Wiles, J. (2008). *Leading curriculum development*. Thousand Oaks, CA: Corwin.

Wiles, J., & Bondi, J. (1981, August/September). The care and cultivation of creativity. *Early Years, 12*(1), 34–37, 46, 108.

Wiles, J., & Bondi, J. (1985). *A guide and plan for conducting ten workshops with the NEA Middle School Training Program*. Washington, DC: National Education Association.

Wiles, J., & Bondi, J. (1986). *Making middle schools work*. Alexandria, VA: Association for Supervision and Curriculum Development.

Wiles, J., Bondi, J., & Stodghill, R. (1982, November). *Miracle on Main Street: The St. Louis story*. Alexandria, VA: Association for Supervision and Curriculum Development.

Wiles, J., & Lundt, J. (2004). *Leaving school: Finding education*. St. Augustine, FL: Matanzas Press.

Wiles, J., & Reed, J. (1975). *Quest: Education for a technocratic existence*. Unpublished manuscript.

Williams, J. B., & Williams, J. C. (2004). Leaving school. *Educational Technology and Society, 7*(4), 221–223.

Wineburg, S. (n.d.). *Sam Wineburg dares to ask if the teaching American history program is a boondoggle*. Retrieved from http://hnn.us/article/76806#sthash.5CJ9HJSQ.dpuf

Xinhau News Agency. (2010, May 6). China's cabinet approves education reform plan. *China Daily*.

NAME INDEX

SUBJECT INDEX

Page numbers followed by "f" indicate figure; and those followed by "t" indicate table.